Local Government since

Making Contemporary Britain Series

General Editor: Anthony Seldon
Consultant Editor: Peter Hennessy

Published

Northern Ireland since 1968
Paul Arthur and Keith Jeffery

The Prime Minister since 1945
James Barber

British General Elections since 1945
David Butler

The British Economy since 1945
Alec Cairncross

Britain and the Suez Crisis*
David Carlton

Town Planning in Britain since 1900
Gordon Cherry

The End of the British Empire
John Darwin

Religion in Britain since 1945
Grace Davie

British Defence since 1945
Michael Dockrill

British Politics since 1945
Peter Dorey

Britain and the Falklands War*
Lawrence Freedman

Britain and European Integration since 1945
Stephen George

British Social Policy since 1945
Howard Glennerster

Judicial Politics since 1920: A Chronicle*
John Griffith

Consensus Politics from Attlee to Major
Dennis Kavanagh and Peter Morris

The Politics of Immigration
Zig Layton-Henry

Women in Britain since 1945*
Jane Lewis

Britain and the Korean War*
Callum Macdonald

Culture in Britain since 1945
Arthur Marwick

Crime and Criminal Justice since 1945*
Terence Morris

Electoral Change since 1945
Pippa Norris

The British Press and Broadcasting since 1945
Colin Seymour-Ure

The Labour Party since 1945
Eric Shaw

Third Party Politics since 1945
John Stevenson

The Trade Union Question in British Politics
Robert Taylor

The Civil Service since 1945
Kevin Theakston

British Science and Politics since 1945*
Thomas Wilkie

British Public Opinion
Robert M. Worcester

Local Government since 1945
Ken Young and Nirmala Rao

Forthcoming

British Industry since 1945
Margaret Ackrill

British Foreign Policy since 1945
Anthony Adamthwaite

The Conservative Party since 1945
John Barnes

Education in Britain since 1945
David Crook

Sport in Britain since 1945
Richard Holt and Tony Mason

Class and Inequality in Britain since 1945
Paul Keating

Parliament since 1945
Philip Norton

British Youth Cultures since 1945
William Osgerby

* Indicates title now out of print.

The series *Making Contemporary Britain* is essential reading for students, as well as providing masterly overviews for the general reader. Each book in the series puts the central themes and problems of the specific topic into clear focus. The studies are written by leading authorities in their field, who integrate the latest research into the text but at the same time present the material in a clear, ordered fashion which can be read with value by those with no prior knowledge of the subject.

THE INSTITUTE OF CONTEMPORARY
BRITISH HISTORY

Senate House
Malet Street
London WC1H 7HU

Local Government since 1945

Ken Young and Nirmala Rao

Copyright © Ken Young and Nirmala Rao, 1997

The right of Ken Young and Nirmala Rao to be identified as authors of this work has been asserted in accordance with the Copyright, Designs and Patents Act 1988.

First published 1997

2 4 6 8 10 9 7 5 3 1

Blackwell Publishers Ltd
108 Cowley Road
Oxford OX4 1JF
UK

Blackwell Publishers Inc.
350 Main Street
Malden, Massachusetts 02148
USA

All rights reserved. Except for the quotation of short passages for the purposes of criticism and review, no part of this publication may be reproduced, stored in a retrieval system, or transmitted, in any form or by any means, electronic, mechanical, photocopying, recording or otherwise, without the prior permission of the publisher.

Except in the United States of America, this book is sold subject to the condition that it shall not, by way of trade or otherwise, be lent, resold, hired out, or otherwise circulated without the publisher's prior consent in any form of binding or cover other than that in which it is published and without a similar condition including this condition being imposed on the subsequent purchaser.

British Library Cataloguing in Publication Data

A CIP catalogue record for this book is available from the British Library.

Library of Congress Cataloging-in-Publication Data

Young, Ken.
Local government since 1945 / Ken Young and Nirmala Rao.
  p. cm. — (making contemporary Britain)
Includes bibliographical references and index.
ISBN 0–631–19581–5. – ISBN 0–631–19582–3 (pbk.)
1. Local government—Great Britain. 2.Great Britain—Politics and government—1945–
    I. Rao, Nirmala, 1959– . II. Title. III. Series.
JS3095.Y68   1997   97–10418
352.14'0941—dc21   CIP

Typeset in 10 on 12pt Ehrhardt
by Grahame & Grahame Editorial, Brighton
Printed and bound in Great Britain by MPG Books Ltd, Bodmin, Cornwall

This book is printed on acid-free paper

Contents

	General Editor's Preface	viii
	Acknowledgements	x
	Abbreviations	xii
1	Introduction	1
2	The Spirit of Reconstruction, 1941–1945	9
3	Building Jerusalem, 1945–1964	51
4	A Structure in Tension, 1945–1964	87
5	Paying for Growth, 1945–1964	117
6	The Consensus Crumbles, 1964–1979	148
7	Into the Melting Pot, 1964–1995	194
8	The New Accountabilities, 1964–1995	233
9	Into the Twilight, 1979–1995	265
10	Conclusion	300
	Bibliography	307
	Index	320

General Editor's Preface

The Institute of Contemporary British History's series *Making Contemporary Britain* is aimed directly at students and at others interested in learning more about topics in post-war British history. In the series, authors are less attempting to break new ground than presenting clear and balanced overviews of the state of knowledge on each of the topics.

The ICBH was founded in October 1986 with the objective of promoting the study of British history since 1945 at every level. To that end, it publishes books and a quarterly journal, *Contemporary Record*; it organizes seminars and conferences for school students, undergraduates, researchers and teachers of post-war history; and it runs a number of research programmes and other activities.

A central theme of the ICBH's work is that post-war history is too often neglected in British schools, institutes of higher education and beyond. The ICBH acknowledges the validity of the arguments against the study of recent history, notably the problems of bias, of overly subjective teaching and writing and the difficulties of perspective. But it believes that the values of studying post-war history outweigh the drawbacks, and that the health and future of a liberal democracy require that its citizens know more about the recent past of their country than the limited knowledge possessed by British citizens, young and old, today. Indeed, the ICBH believes that the dangers of political indoctrination are higher where the young are *not* informed of the recent past.

This is the first book in the series to focus on local government. It is an important addition, not least because the subject has changed more rapidly than most areas of British politics and administration, and the nature and extent of this change needs to be more widely appreciated.

The authors provide a picture of local government which in 1945 was a vital partner to central government in the delivery of public services. They focus in this book on education and housing. By 1995, local government had shrunk to a pale image of its former self. During the 1960s and 1970s, it changed from being seen as part of the solution for making Britain a better country to being part of the problem. The Conservative government after 1979 continued the attack on local government autonomy, systematically took away its functions and independence, and rendered it by 1995 a minor agent of central government, tolerated but unloved.

The authors combine the historical and analytical approaches in their text. They examine the three great themes of local government – function, finance and structure – together, and in so doing show their interdependence. As functions and independent finance were gradually reduced, the structure of local government, that had existed since the late nineteenth century, was altered by the reforms of the early 1970s, ushering in a period of uncertainty that has continued to the present day.

This is in some ways a nostalgic book. The authors write as passionate believers in the importance of autonomous, or semi-autonomous, local government to the health of the Body Politic. With political change again in the air at the end of the twentieth century, it may be that the trends that they describe, and to some extent deplore, may be reversed.

Anthony Seldon

Acknowledgements

This book has been a long time in the making, and our first thanks must be to Anthony Seldon, the series editor, and Tessa Harvey at Blackwells for their patient acceptance of our every excuse for late delivery. We are also deeply grateful to Dr Martin Maw for his diligent and unsparing help during our research at the Bodleian, as well as to the staff of the Public Record Office at Kew for their cheerful assistance.

We owe a long-standing debt of gratitude to our mentor, Sir Charles Carter. Both of us have, at different periods in our careers, personally profited from his encouragement and guidance. Moreover, his leadership of the Joseph Rowntree Foundation's local and central government research initiative over a period of more than a decade did so much to promote the study of central–local government relations in Britain. This programme represented more than just the mining of a neglected seam in recent political history: it brought a neglected subject to life again. Throughout the whole enterprise ran Sir Charles' passion for fairness and rationality in government, which so inspired those around him. It shaped our own work profoundly. This book, which we dedicate to him, is our small tribute to his matchless contribution to this field.

Our other debts are to Lord Silsoe, for access to his father's papers, and to Mr Alistair Cooke, for permission to use and to quote from the papers deposited in the Conservative Party Archives.

We conclude with a word of explanation to the reader about our citation conventions. Our two principal sources are the public records at Kew and the Conservative Party Archives at the Bodleian Library, Oxford. The former are readily identifiable. Cabinet papers are listed by the appropriate volume number in the CAB 129 series; Cabinet discussions are cited simply as 'Cabinet minutes' for the relevant date. Departmental papers are listed by departmental class: mainly HLG (Health, later Housing and Local Government) and ED (Education). Conservative party papers are listed as catalogued at the Bodleian, with the prefix CPA (Conservative Party Archives).

Ken Young and Nirmala Rao

Abbreviations

AEC	Association of Education Committees
ALA	Association of London Authorities
AMA	Association of Metropolitan Authorities
AMC	Association of Municipal Corporations
CCA	County Councils Association
CCT	Compulsory Competitive Tendering
CUTA	Conservative and Unionist Teachers' Association
DES	Department for Education and Science
DfE	Department for Education
DLO	Direct Labour Organisation
DoE	Department of the Environment
DSO	Direct Service Organisation
EEG	Exchequer Equalisation Grants
ERA	Education Reform Act 1988
GIA	General Improvement Area
GLC	Greater London Council
GMS	Grant Maintained Status
GNI	General Needs Index
GRE	Grant-Related Expenditure
HAT	Housing Action Trust
HRA	Housing Revenue Account
LBA	London Boroughs' Association
LMS	Local Management of Schools
MHLG	Ministry of Housing and Local Government
MoH	Ministry of Health
NCC	National Curriculum Council
NFER	National Foundation for Educational Research

NNDR	National Non-Domestic Rate
NUT	National Union of Teachers
PWLB	Public Works Loans Board
RDG	Rate Deficiency Grant
RSG	Rate Support Grant
SCAA	School Curriculum and Assessment Authority
SEAC	Secondary Examinations Assessment Council
SRA	Special Review Area
SSA	Standard Spending Assessment
TEC	Training and Enterprise Council
TUPE	Transfer of Undertakings (Protection of Employment) Regulations
UDC	Urban Development Corporation
UDCA	Urban District Councils Association

For Sir Charles Carter,
Who made a dull subject fun

1 Introduction

To write a book about local government in Britain during the period 1945–95 may seem a great act of presumption. The scope of local government – what local authorities do, and how they work – is wide enough to justify a series of its own, or at least a multi-volume history. We could, then, only attempt this book by being highly selective. Many readers might wish us to have selected differently, and may feel this or that aspect of the sprawling subject of modern local government to have received less than its due. To them, our only defence can lie in the reasoning that led us to write the book in the way that we did. And that means explaining, at the outset, what this book is, and what it is not.

There are two ways of looking at the subject of local government (although the best studies will always seek to combine them). The first is to look at local government as it operates on the ground, drawing together the experiences of a wide range of different places. Providing a series of snapshots, this approach serves well to capture the variety and the texture of local government. Yet it is ill-suited to portraying change over time. The alternative is to examine how local government has been perceived and shaped by the ministers and civil servants who control the national system of government. That approach can more readily encompass change, albeit at the expense of any picture of what has happened on the ground. We have chosen this second course, to focus the book on the 'high politics' of local government since 1945.

From Attlee to Major

Two post-war Prime Ministers only – Clement Attlee and John Major – have had the experience of serving on a local authority. Their premierships mark our starting point and our finishing point. If they were to be transposed, how recognizable would the Lambeth of the 1970s be to Attlee, and the Stepney of the 1920s to Major? Probably they would find much that was familiar, especially in the ways in which councillors and their officers conducted the business of local government. But beyond that their experiences would seem worlds apart. Moreover, when Attlee took power in 1945 local government would not have differed greatly from his early experiences of the East End of London. By the time John Major entered Downing Street, the position of local government had been so transformed that Attlee would scarcely have recognized it. To show how, why and when those changes came about is our aim in this book.

Under Attlee, local government was the most important single agent of social reconstruction, playing a crucial role in the development of social policy within the overall framework of the Welfare State. Under Major, the picture was to be very different. Local authorities have lost their pre-eminence in the delivery of local services. Equally importantly, they no longer receive the political deference – the respect of ministers and that of ordinary people – that sustained their former position in the machinery of the state. In this book we show how local government entered the post-war world as the partner of central ministries in the reshaping of modern Britain. We identify the moments at which that partnership became problematic, when ministers and civil servants sensed the danger of local authorities sliding into the status of mere agents of the centre, but saw no reason to avert it. The result has been a continuing decline in the standing of local government, from Attlee's partner to Major's agent.

The decline of local government is inextricably linked to the collapse of the post-war consensus. Local authorities were destined to be the first casualties of that collapse, as new and highly contested policy initiatives led to central intervention to promote party policy at the expense of local responsibility. In time, the status of local government itself was to become an issue. From being part of the solution to the making of post-war Britain, local government became part of the problem.

To focus the book on this process requires us to exclude a great deal. We do not concern ourselves with – nor even mention in passing – the wide range of local authority services that do not speak directly to our theme. Even many of those that do – for example, the police and social services – have to be excluded for reasons of space. Our intention is not to provide a descriptive catalogue of what local government does; and still less of what it did once and does no more.

Nor is this in any balanced sense a book about Britain. It will be immediately apparent that we have taken an Anglocentric standpoint, with Scottish and Welsh local government remaining on the horizons of the story. Here the justification follows from our concern with the high politics of local government. British politics is Anglocentric, and nowhere more so than in the governance of territory itself – the view from above rarely extends beyond the English borders. British governments since 1945 have treated Wales as an adjunct or an afterthought, and Scotland as a proving ground for essentially English experiments.

If the logic of our approach excludes much, then by the same token it must also include much else. The three principal components of any system of local government are well known: structure, functions and finance. Successive governments, and the various enquiries they set in train, have been rightly criticized for contriving to ensure that the three were never considered together. We could have no justification for doing the same. We have tried to show how the three components work together to articulate the relationship between central and local government, and our chapters are organized so as to deal in turn with these three themes.

First, structure. The reconstruction period from 1941 to 1945 laid the ground for the post-war debates and legislative struggles to achieve a 'modern' structure of local authorities. The need to resolve the internal conflicts of local government structure ran through the incremental reforms of the 1950s and the more fundamental changes of the 1970s. It continues today, and shows no sign of reaching a new settlement. Our structural theme is, then, that of recurrence, for each successive episode that we examine plays out the same issues that preoccupied the Churchill coalition.

Secondly, functions. Whereas the story of structure is one of continuity and recurrence, that of functions is one of growth and decline. To tell this story we have focused on the two key areas of housing and education, the services that represent the larger part of local authorities' capital and current expenditure. Closer to people's lives than other services, they have accordingly attracted the most political attention within central and local government, and among the population at large. For our purpose in this book, housing and education also express the themes of expansion and decline more vividly than any other sphere of local authority service provision.

Thirdly, finance. No single topic points up more sharply the unstable tension of 'partnership' and the impetus towards 'agency' than the ways in which local authorities are funded by the central government. All post-war governments have been concerned about the control of public expenditure, and have sought, with increasing success, to tighten their control upon local financial decision-making. The development of the grant system was the first preoccupation. Later, as local expenditure continued to rise, and services expanded, it became clear that the grant regime could not deliver sufficient control over local expenditure decisions. Attention shifted to the rating system itself, as national leaders sought to find new ways of limiting local expenditure.

All three issues had implications for the autonomy and freedom of action that local government enjoyed. Taken together, they proved potent, not just in their own right, but because they forced national politicians to think about the position – the 'constitutional position' would be to put it too grandly, if accurately enough – of local government within the national system of government. This was hardly a revival of the Victorian enthusiasm for 'the local government question'. But it did challenge the cosy assumptions about 'partnership', bring the issues to the surface and, eventually, ensure they were settled on central government's own terms.

The Structure of this Book

We begin not with 1945, but with the war years, during which the foundations of the post-war debates were laid down. Chapter 2, 'The Spirit of Reconstruction' shows how the experience of war itself – the disruption of the blitz, and government by regional commissioners – raised the question of local government reform and its relationship to the emerging plans for Britain's Welfare State. Local government would play a major role in the delivery of welfare, but for the first time its capabilities began to be seriously questioned. A prolonged struggle to get radical reform on to the agenda was deferred, rather than resolved, by the coalition government's modest proposals for post-war adjustment. The plans made for social housing and public education were tailored to fit the existing system of local government, its defects notwithstanding.

Chapter 3, 'Building Jerusalem', shows how those plans were pursued. The first part of the chapter deals with the development of housing policies and programmes in the first two decades of the period, from the election of the Attlee government to that of Harold Wilson in 1964. Housing policy was dominated by numbers and targets, from the first wildly optimistic plans of the new Labour government, through the achievement, and later relaxation, of Harold Macmillan's 300,000 homes programme. The number of homes built was taken as an index of electoral advantage, until housing policy began to take a new direction, in which municipal housing lost its central place to building for owner-occupation. The second part of the chapter traces the steady progress in implementing the education reforms of the Butler Act of 1944, beginning with the establishment of a new structure of education administration. As Butler's children began to work their way through the primary schools, the issue of how local authorities should provide secondary education – on a selective or a 'comprehensive' basis – began to emerge.

Chapter 4 returns to the wartime issue of the framework of local authorities, which is presented here as 'A Structure in Tension'. When the coalition decided against radical change, they bequeathed to the Attlee government a mechanism for reviewing areas and bringing needed changes into effect: the Local Government Boundary Commission. Another minister might have made it work, but the fiery Aneurin Bevan had little liking for the coalition's half-hearted measures. He led the Commission into a trap, engineered a confrontation and persuaded his Cabinet colleagues to abolish it. That cleared the path to more fundamental reform, plans for which Bevan now pressed forward, only to be stopped in his tracks by Whitehall warfare. The Conservatives picked up the pieces, and found themselves led once again down the path of gradual reform. By 1958 they had new review machinery in place. By the time they left office in 1964, it was already bogged down.

Chapter 5, 'Paying for Growth', introduces the third component of the story, that of local finance. Labour again inherited work done by the coalition, and soon moved to nationalize valuation for rating, the mechanism of assessment that determined each local area's own financial resources. The other changes that they carried through, and their willingness to drive local services by means of central grants in aid, raised a constitutional question: Were local authorities truly the partners of the central ministries, or their mere agents? The Conservatives had a clear answer, and worked over a period of three years to bring about reforms of the grant system that were intended to bolster the independence of local government. Unhappily for town and county hall, these changes coincided with two other developments. The first was a lurch towards stricter control of public expenditure, which bore heavily on local authorities' commitments and eradicated their room for financial manoeuvre. The second was the growing discontent over the rating system itself, as the financial burdens of post-war service expansion at last began to press upon the ratepayers. The desire to assuage their discontent drove governments towards palliative measures that did little to sustain the independence of local government.

Labour's return in 1964 marked the end of 'Butskellism'. Chapter 6, 'The Consensus Crumbles', explores the years in which ageing Labour ministers sought to relive the Attlee era, while the political initiative was actually passing to a younger, technocratic Conservative party. The failure of the 1964–70 Labour governments to achieve their aims in public housing opened the door to new Conservative policies that sought to squeeze local authority housing. The Conservative ultras were, as yet, only in the foothills of politics, and their policies on rents and the sale of council houses did not progress far before Labour returned in 1974. While Labour had few new ideas in housing, the period 1964–79 saw the abandonment of the 'partnership' in education policy in favour of central direction. The issue was comprehensive education, where Labour suddenly showed that they meant business. The Conservatives fought back, partly on a platform of autonomy for local authorities, but there was little they could do in the 1970–74 interlude to resist a rising tide. The Labour government that followed had soon isolated the few die-hard local authorities, and the battle was all but over. Meanwhile, the new issues of educational standards threatened to put Labour on the defensive again, and the scene was set for another major shift of power towards the centre.

In the 1940s and 1950s, ministers of both parties had been reluctant to cast local government 'Into the Melting Pot'. Chapter 7 shows that to have been its fate from the 1960s, when the Labour government moved decisively to reject gradualism in favour of a clean sweep. Time was against them, and it fell to an unprepared Conservative party to push the restructuring of local government through Parliament. But once the nineteenth-century structure had been undone, instability was the only persisting result. The 1972 reforms began to collapse almost as soon as they were implemented, as it was realized that local government structure was not immutable after all, but could be formed and reformed by governments according to their interests. Less malleable was the internal structure of local government, the system of political management by which decisions came to be taken, and resources committed. It soon became clear that the political consensus on the ways in which local authorities were led and managed was under strain. A search began for new conventions to meet these new realities, as if conventions could be conjured into existence independently of the tacit understandings of those who had to operate them.

Chapter 8, 'The New Accountabilities', deals with the continuation of the relentless search for better functioning in the areas of finance and service management during the period 1964–95. The more the government sought to change the rating system, the further they were drawn into the search for an alternative to rates. Finding a sustainable balance of power between central and local government came a poor third to these more powerful impulses. Almost every government intervention in this period shifted power to the centre, at some points in ways so fundamental as to count as real constitutional change. After the rise and the fall of the poll tax, the introduction of the new hybrid council tax and its associated grant regime drove home the point that central government now both paid the piper and called the tune. Nowhere was its power to do so more amply demonstrated than in the introduction of compulsory competitive tendering into the provision of local authority services. What began as a challenge to entrenched practices gradually gained momentum, forcing local authorities to come to terms with the disciplines of the marketplace. By 1990 enforced competition was beginning to cut deep into local authorities' management styles, as ministers began to see the possibility of consigning old-style municipal bureaucracies to history, putting in their place a new mode of public management.

Changing structures and changing financial regimes brought about fundamental change in local government over this fifty-year period, but with the introduction of new policies in education and housing, local government passed 'Into the Twilight'. Chapter 9 examines first the housing policies of the Thatcher and Major governments, devoted as they were to the goal of reducing the scope of municipal provision. Most of the special initiatives aimed at securing this end achieved very little; some were quietly buried by Mrs Thatcher's successor. But the general thrust of policy, to privatize municipal housing, and relegate local authorities' role as housing providers to the margins, continued to bite. The Conservative policies for education had similar effect. The transformation of local education authorities was achieved by shifting power downwards and outwards, from the local education authority to schools and to parents themselves, as well as upwards to the central department. Education had been the quintessential local authority service, by far the most significant financially, and the one most explicitly based upon the notion of partnership between central and local government. The conscious abandonment of that notion after half a century wrote the last sad epitaph for local government in modern Britain.

With a structure that combines the chronological and the thematic, there is more than one way in which this book can be read. The reader interested in the reform of structure of local government (including its internal structure) will begin with the wartime debates in chapter 2, pick up their continuation during 1945–65 in chapter 4, and return to the topic in chapter 7, which brings the story up to the present day. Those concerned with finance can confine themselves to chapters 5 and 8. The theme of the rise of local authorities as providers of both public housing and education is established in chapter 2, and continued for the period 1945–64 in chapter 3. Chapter 6 shows the beginning of decline in the period 1964–79, and the story is again brought up to the mid-1990s in chapter 9. The final chapter takes stock of the entire post-war period and provides an overview of these four linked themes.

2 The Spirit of Reconstruction, 1941–1945

During the Second World War, Britain was governed for almost the entire period of hostilities by a coalition of the major parties. Churchill's government dominated the House of Commons, mobilizing the support of people of all classes, and of almost all opinions. The effect of jointly governing the country drew the parties close together. Many Conservatives were as keen for reconstruction and social reform as any Labour MP, and the post-war disputes over social policy, when they came, 'were not much more than synthetic sound and fury'.[1] The coalition's lasting achievement was the making of the post-war consensus.

As in the Great War of 1914–18, the business of thinking about reconstruction was hived off to a separate set of administrative arrangements. A Committee on Reconstruction Problems was established in January 1941, mainly in response to confusion over Britain's war aims, and as the extent of the physical damage to be repaired at the end of hostilities began to become apparent. Some lessons were learned from the previous exercise, which had been overweighted with civilian intelligentsia, and prone to dream up grand and impracticable schemes. The official history of reconstruction noted that 'the old Ministry of Reconstruction dug its own grave by being too ambitious and by arousing opposition amongst the long-established departments...'. As a result,

> It was determined on all sides not to repeat that experience, and from the beginning the minister in charge of reconstruction was not expected to do

more than collate and co-ordinate, and in exceptional cases to inspire departments to produce official proposals.[2]

The second attempt at planning reconstruction would thereby avoid many of the problems of its prototype. Yet forward thinking remained handicapped in the way that any forward-thinking group at the centre of government must be handicapped: it was isolated from the ongoing decisions in other departments of state, and not privy to their thinking.

The minister in charge was initially Arthur Greenwood, Minister Without Portfolio in the War Cabinet, who was asked by Churchill to look to the end of the war, and imagine a continuing coalition which would want to act in 'four or five great spheres of action' in the first three years. In the eyes of Churchill, the reconstruction team 'was to a large extent a safety valve for the release of some of the pressure on the cabinet as a whole'.[3] At a political level, the reconstruction committee was to suffer due to its uncertain status *vis-à-vis* the powerful Lord President's Committee of the Cabinet, chaired first by Sir John Anderson, and later by Attlee. Greenwood, popular on the Labour benches, was no longer a man of real influence. Indeed, his appointment was read as signalling the backwater status of the reconstruction committee.[4]

Operating from the Cabinet Office, the reconstruction secretariat (formerly the war aims secretariat) could set their own agenda for discussions, and their importance derived less from executive power than from the extent to which they symbolized the object of the struggle against fascism. Greenwood had served in the Ministry of Reconstruction set up in 1917, and was well aware of the limits of his position. 'I am not a Minister of Reconstruction', he wrote to an old friend from those days,

> but the chairman of a cabinet committee composed of ministers whose departments will have to discharge the business of reconstruction when the time comes . . . We solemnly abjure, and in practice most rigidly avoid, any assumption of executive functions or responsibilities . . . Of course we have a very long way to go yet and, as the work develops, it may become desirable to recast our present committee organisation into the actual form of a Ministry of Reconstruction. The Prime Minister has foreshadowed the possibility of some such development. If, however, this does come to pass and I am still responsible for the work you may be sure that we shall remain a policy-forming and not an executive department.[5]

Uncluttered by executive responsibilities, the reconstruction team could afford to look to the long-term future and open up matters for examination that others with day-to-day responsibilities found it more convenient to keep closed. In February 1941 the post of Minister of Works and Planning was established for Sir John Reith, to 'guide the formulation by local authorities of town and country planning schemes which will adequately reflect the national policy for urban and regional development'.[6] It was a landmark decision, and while the hoped-for national planning body was shelved for the duration, there flowed from it a handful of master-plans which, in the case of that prepared for London by Abercrombie and Forshaw, continued to influence physical development half a century later. But reconstruction was more than a matter of town and country planning. It would involve the investigation of the entire framework of sub-national government, as Reith made clear:

> Some services will require treatment on a national basis, some regionally, and some locally. Here there are issues of devolution of central responsibilities and co-ordination of local ones. The importance of maintaining the character and independence of local authorities is recognised, but it will probably be found necessary to re-adjust their present functions to enable certain of their powers to be exercised on a wider basis. We must consider impartially the whole administrative machinery.[7]

Part of that consideration would be a review of the structure and working of local government.

Because all parties looked forward to a period of intense reconstruction effort once the war was won, solving the problem of local government acquired an urgency it had not enjoyed before, as local authorities would be the principal vehicles of social policy in the post-war period.[8] Meanwhile, the country had to be administered effectively through the crisis, during which civilian defence had to be maintained through an unprecedented period of bombardment. That was to put local authorities on their mettle, for their fate in time of peace would rest on their ability to hold their ground during a period when power was centralized as never before in the interests of total war.

Local Government under Fire

The period from 1941 to 1944 saw the first skirmishes over the problem of local government structure. Many in government circles believed there to be too many local authorities, many of them too small. Often their areas made little sense, while the structure laid down in the nineteenth century entirely failed to provide for the problems of urban growth. In the absence of any workable method of securing continuous adaptation to changes in the distribution of people and industry, some sought to take the opportunity of the wartime emergency to advance proposals for sweeping change. But the entrenched interests of the local authorities, the internal rifts, and the role of the Ministry of Health (MoH) in maintaining its own 'secret garden' of local administration combined to see off these attempts, thus providing a dress rehearsal for the struggles of the peace.

Structure in stalemate

The structure of local government at the outbreak of war in 1939 was essentially that laid down fifty years before. Its principal characteristic was the fissure between countryside and town which had been built into the nineteenth-century settlement. From 1899, local government was mostly based on two levels or 'tiers' of primary authorities, with a third village-level parish council in many of the rural districts. Outside London and the older and larger cities, county councils operated the majority of functions, with lesser responsibilities in the hands of the urban and rural district councils, and the longer-established municipal boroughs. London government was dominated by the all-powerful London County Council, a unique 'urban county', under which the metropolitan borough councils exercised little more than residual powers.

The main problems of local government lay in the major provincial towns, as it had been clear from the outset that the large boroughs would not submit to being placed under the jurisdiction of the new county councils. The local government bill as introduced in 1887 proposed that nineteen of these should become counties-of-boroughs, or 'county boroughs', all-purpose authorities in the areas of which the writ of the surrounding county council would not run. The House of Lords succumbed to local pressures and, as a result, when the bill became law sixty-one boroughs were granted county borough status. A continuing difficulty thereafter was that the rapidly growing second rank of municipal boroughs aspired to win county borough status and the autonomy that it brought with it, while the present county boroughs sought to extend their areas and take in greater slices of the surrounding county.

After the initial designation of the county boroughs in 1888, it remained open for a municipal borough that subsequently grew to a population of 50,000 or so to seek promotion to county borough status and thus 'escape' from the jurisdiction of its county. The means of doing so was by application to the Local Government Board, which had taken powers under the 1888 Act to confer county borough status by Provisional Order. Equally, county councils could apply to the Board for a boundary alteration, or for alterations and mergers of any districts within them, including the merger of a county borough with the county – in effect, to bring about the extinction of the county borough. Additionally, the county councils could themselves make Orders, subject to the confirmation of the Board, for the alteration of their urban and rural districts or of any parish.

The manoeuvres that took place over boundary disputes were not mere matters of municipal pride. As the system of local finance was based on the rates, or property tax, a loss or gain of area brought with it a loss or gain of rateable resource, with direct consequences for the demands that would be made on future local ratepayers.[9] Here, then, lay a continuing tension and conflict of interest. Nor was it a static picture. The patterns of urban growth in the early twentieth century, and especially in the years of rapid growth following the 1931 depression, created a group of booming towns and expanding suburbs, the existing limits of which were overrun by housing and industrial growth. While this growth stoked up future conflict over boundaries, the mutual antagonism of town and county also worked to prevent any voluntary co-operation over larger areas than those of the immediate authorities. The London problem, although constitutionally different, was no more than the same issue writ large, as the growth of the metropolis had begun to overwhelm the innermost parts of the Home Counties from the early years of the century.[10]

The county boroughs were the gainers, and counties the losers, in this battle for territory. The counties ceded more than a fifth of their population and rateable value to new and existing county boroughs in a series of acrimonious local disputes. Between 1889 and 1929, twenty-one new county boroughs were created on application to the Board. A total population of around 1.3 million and an area of around 100,000 acres were lost in this way to the counties, with a significant corresponding loss of rateable resources. Existing county boroughs were equally successful in adding to their territories by boundary extension, taking in a further total of 1.7 million people and another 250,000 acres from their surrounding counties. Twenty-seven counties had been affected by these changes, losing on average 23 per cent of their population and 21 per cent of their rateable value.[11] Not a single county borough was dissolved into its surrounding county.

Civil servants and the more detached of their ministers took a lofty view of this process, seeing the conflicts between counties and their actual or potential county boroughs as a fruitless diversion from larger problems. But given the fact of the county boroughs, with their total exemption from county government, change and adjustment was bound to cause conflict. From one point of view, the mechanism established by the 1888 Act, and subsequently refined in 1926 and 1929, was effective and successful, in that it enabled the growing cities to achieve a high rate of boundary extension and thereby create more sensible administrative areas, while county initiatives also brought about a limited rationalization of district councils into fewer, stronger units. Problems of co-ordination over a larger area did remain, most particularly in London and the South-East. But local government could not reasonably be expected to solve problems on a regional scale alone, and Ministers of Health from Neville Chamberlain onward cajoled the local authorities into acting together under central government guidance.

It cannot be denied, however, that the procedures were politically awkward. First, county councils tended to avoid the disputes that would inevitably follow any attempt to change local district boundaries, and many chose not to make use of the power to undertake their own reviews. Secondly, the processes of county borough creation and extension necessarily involved the Local Government Board (and the Ministry of Health, which succeeded it in 1919) in adjudicating what were essentially local conflicts, an involvement that to ministers was tedious at best, and politically dangerous at worst.

The inter-war governments had been keen to defuse the conflicts over county borough promotion. Following the report of a Royal Commission chaired by Lord Onslow, the Local Government (County Boroughs and Adjustments) Act of 1926 raised the population threshold to 75,000 and insulated the Ministry of Health from political entanglements by abolishing its power to create county boroughs by Order. It was henceforth left to would-be county boroughs to pursue their ambitions by sponsoring a private bill in Parliament. This process differs from public general legislation, involving close scrutiny by a select committee and the hearing of witnesses opposed to the change. In the case of local authority private bills – whether to extend boundaries or gain county borough status – strenuous efforts would be made by both sides:

> The county council opposes the bill. Both sides brief counsel, and fight it out in the committee rooms of the Lords and Commons. Counsel call witnesses, cross-examine and re-examine, as if they were appearing for the prosecution and defence; they stress the other side's deficiencies, and try to ridicule their arguments. The bill may or may not succeed, but in either case the local authorities are left with an account of ten thousand pounds or more to pay, and a lasting ill-will towards their opponents.[12]

Most, not surprisingly, did not succeed and, despite a number of attempts, no new county borough was created under the private bill procedure.

A later revision of the 1888 arrangements was intended to ensure that reviews of districts within counties were actually carried out, and the Local Government Act 1929 replaced the permissive power of counties with a mandatory duty to undertake an immediate review of their districts, submitting any proposals for change to the minister, and to undertake further reviews at ten-year intervals. The limitations on the effectiveness of this process were two-fold. First, alterations that impinged on county borough boundaries could only be made with the consent of the county borough concerned, placing off-limits any attempt to manage urban growth. Secondly, the amalgamation of smaller districts and municipal boroughs into more effective units heightened the risk of their reaching the qualifying population threshold and bidding for county borough status, encouraging county councils to be rather more cautious in their review proposals than might otherwise have been the case. Nevertheless, between 1931 and 1937 the number of urban and rural districts was reduced by this process from 1,606 to 1,048, which might again be considered testimony to the workability of the 1929 Act procedures.

By the outbreak of the war in September 1939, only limited progress had been made towards solving the three-fold problem of local government.

16 *The Spirit of Reconstruction*

First, while the number of very small authorities had been reduced, it remained an open question whether urban and rural district councils would prove sufficiently robust for whatever powers and duties they might be expected to exercise after the war. Secondly, urban growth had been dealt with by ignoring it, for nothing positive had been done to deal with the source of the pressure for promotion to county borough status. Channelling it within the private bill procedures merely served to underwrite the status quo. The third problem, that of effective action over larger areas, remained in the hands of the ministers and officials of the central government. Much would depend upon whether they chose to supplant the local authorities entirely, or to seek to strengthen them to carry additional responsibilities in the post-war world.

Unresolved, these issues would exercise the central government almost for the duration of the war, and certainly from the time when the reconstruction machinery was established, early in 1941. Great energy was brought to bear upon the detailed analysis of seemingly intractable problems. These efforts were bracketed by defensive reactions on all sides. The Whitehall departments scrutinized every proposal for its implications for their own responsibilities, moving to block anything that looked as if it might gain serious support at their expense. The local authorities, on the other hand, insisted on being brought into the picture, sniffing a threat of regionalized central government exercising dominion over them in peacetime as it had in war. Behind them stood the press and public opinion, wary of centralism, nervous of dictatorship, and quick to point out the irony of a war against fascism being fought by 'fascist' methods of centralization. In the meantime, local authorities in some of Britain's cities were having to cope with a hitherto unknown threat: the depletion of night-time population in response to the relentless attacks of the *Luftwaffe*.

Darkness falls from the air

London was the first and the prime target for aerial attack. Between September 1940 and May 1941 the capital was raided repeatedly with a total of 19,000 tons of bombs, the most serious damage being in the East End and the City. By the time the main period of bombing ended in the spring, almost 1.5 million Londoners had been made homeless, either temporarily or permanently. Central and local government worked together to organize repair squads for damaged houses and, by August 1941, more than a million homes had been made weatherproof and fit for occupation for the time being. The local authorities were not well prepared for what was to fall upon them, and few of London's borough councils had responded quickly enough to the emergency powers granted them in respect of the organization of air-raid precautions (ARP), the provision of shelters or the welfare of people made homeless by bombing. The administration of even a powerful county borough such as West Ham, competent enough in peacetime, could be found wanting under blitz conditions, with the council manoeuvring to protect their rights from official encroachment.[13]

Despite the magnitude of the attack on London, the scale of the city, the extent of the safer suburbs and the deep shelter available in the miles of the Underground system dissipated its worst effects. Inner London – the LCC area – also enjoyed a single well organized fire service, able to operate across the county. The provincial cities were in a different condition, being smaller in scale and more dependent upon joint action between neighbouring authorities. There were 1,666, largely volunteer, local fire services at the outbreak of war. Co-operation was sporadic, even under blitz conditions, with charging for services or, in some cases, refusal to attend a neighbouring area without prior charging agreements. Chief fire officers were sometimes loath to call for outside help in case this appeared extravagant to their councillors. And when reinforcements did come, incompatibilities of equipment and fittings could limit their usefulness. In May 1941 Herbert Morrison, Minister of Home Security, announced the creation of a single national fire service, divided into fifty unified regional commands, as a wartime expedient. The chief fire officer of the LCC was appointed to direct the new national service.

The inadequacies of localized, fragmented services had been exposed when, in October 1940, Goering's *Luftwaffe* launched the first night-time attacks on Britain's industrial heartlands. The attacks on Coventry, Plymouth and Southampton were more concentrated in their effects than those on London, so much so as to coin a new term: Coventration. A dense, compact city, Coventry on the night of 14 November was a place in which 'nearly everyone had heard the fall of nearly every bomb; nearly everyone knew someone who was dead, or missing, or homeless'.[14] The raid was the prototype for the attacks on the other second-rank industrial centres, the major conurbations of Birmingham and Glasgow escaping lightly. Local services were poorly prepared:

> The centre would be levelled by fire and high explosive. People would flee in great numbers to the fields and villages around. Organised evacuation would get under way slowly and inadequately. The rest centres, usually as bad as London's had been at the start of the blitz, would be overwhelmed. Feeding arrangements would break down. Local government would be as helpless as a boy with a feather duster attacking a tiger. Cities formerly puffed with local pride would become nerve-wrecked ghost towns.[15]

Nowhere was this more true than Plymouth. In a two-night raid in March 1941, more than 18,000 houses were destroyed or damaged, along with the municipal offices and the ARP control room. In the following month the bombers returned in force on five nights, leaving the city ablaze and scarcely a house untouched. Neighbouring fire services arriving to help found that their appliances would not fit Plymouth's hydrants. Thirty thousand were homeless, and another new term – *trekkies* – was coined for the 50,000 or so who left the city for the fields and moors each night. Whereas Londoners' resort to the Underground for shelter became a source of social solidarity, trekking from the provincial cities was the flight of helpless refugees, reflecting and amplifying a collapse of morale.[16]

There were lessons to be learned here for local government. The Lord Mayor of Plymouth, Lord Astor, enjoyed access to government ministers that no other municipal dignitary could hope to aspire to. During the winter of 1940–41, he had talked with Arthur Greenwood about his enthusiasm for the joint committees set up in the provincial cities to bring together the neighbouring local authorities for ARP purposes. Astor saw in this rudimentary and limited mechanism of co-operation the nucleus of larger units more suited to post-war administration. 'The war is breaking down the boundaries and the water-tight self-contained administration and activities of local authorities', he reminded Greenwood in June 1941, recollecting their earlier agreement that 'the present rigid boundaries of relatively small authorities frequently lead to inadequacies of staffing and so of [sic] relative inefficiency'.[17]

In May 1941, with his own city devastated, and the failures of localized administration exposed, Astor had written to Greenwood in his new capacity as minister leading the reconstruction efforts, sending a lengthy memorandum on the experience of local authorities under the blitz. He demanded regionalized fire services (which were then imminent), and pointed up the administrative and financial effects of population decentralization into surrounding areas. Local authorities were plagued by a 'granite rigidity which prevents inefficient and obstructive officials... being removed', by a propensity to 'slow, talkative committee rule' and to the stacking of committees with senior and retired 'worthies', while the passage of time 'is equally inexorable in its effects on aldermen and councillors'.

Writing with evident passion, Astor painted a picture of 'Hogarthian' conditions in which

> thousands of men, women and children move from a city into villages and towns for miles around – to live there for days or even weeks, overcrowd chapel halls, town halls, schools etc., where at times there are neither sanitary nor cooking nor sleeping arrangements or equipment or medical care or inspection . . . It must be realised that these buildings are located in different urban and rural districts [. . .] sometimes they are under the jurisdiction of the county council with a distant capital, that sometimes these various councils have foreseen nothing – are fearful of spending rates, their officers too often never had initiative, and are unaccustomed to co-operating and organising swiftly with voluntary bodies or with one another, because each local body's activities are limited to its own boundaries and no one is empowered to cross a neighbour's dividing line, or even is much interested in what happens there. . . .[18]

The answer to this chaos, in Astor's view, was regional direction of the local authorities, with executive joint committees of neighbouring authorities, headed by an appointed chairman, to bring together the provincial cities and their hinterlands, and the designation of evacuation areas. Only by these means could the lessons of Plymouth be learned, and 'serious panic, discomforts and loss of morale' associated with the 'uncontrolled and so disorderly trekking of blitzed people from the target city into the adjoining districts' be avoided.

Plymouth and Southampton were extreme examples – although the regional commissioner did not share Astor's gloomy view – and the British provincial cities were not to be put to the test in this way again. For the most part, the wartime framework of regional and local administration stood up well to the emergency. When Attlee met the county councils' leaders for dinner in January 1944, he praised the local authorities extravagantly, saying that 'if. . . Hitler had a secret weapon capable of knocking out London the local government of the provinces would enable the country to continue the struggle without dismay'.[19]

He flattered, perhaps, for the strength in the wartime machinery lay more in the regional framework of appointed commissioners than in the local authorities themselves. Astor's attempt to draw attention to the fundamental difficulties in the relations between cities and their hinterlands simply pointed up the long-standing problem in British local government, of a division between town and country made immutable by the county borough system. The attacks on the second-rank cities could not have drawn more vivid attention to this problem, and while civil servants and ministers alike deprecated too casual a projection of the stresses of war into peacetime, the view that something would need to be done about the machinery of government in post-war reconstruction was growing fast.

Planning for Reconstruction

It hardly needed the cities ablaze to bring home the intimate connection of local government structure, regional planning and strategic defence. It had been well recognized before the war, when *laissez-faire* urban development was seen as bringing about a terrible vulnerability in the age of the bomber aeroplane. The Barlow Commission on the Distribution of the Industrial Population reported only in 1940, by which time the lessons were too late to be learned. Its report voiced concern that

> the disadvantages in many, if not in most of the great industrial concentrations, alike on the strategical, the social, and the economic side, do constitute serious handicaps and even in some respects dangers to the nation's life and development, and we are of opinion that definite actions should be taken by the government towards remedying them.[20]

Inevitably, thoughts divided between the effective prosecution of a war in which Britain was already embroiled, and the development of a more effective framework for managing the peace that would follow.

A regional framework

The administration of home defence could not be left entirely to the local authorities. With war looming, the Regional Commissioners Act 1939 was passed to create a framework of eleven regions covering England and Wales, for each of which a regional commissioner was appointed by the Crown 'for the co-ordination of measures of civil defence'. Generally, the regional boundaries followed those of the existing counties, while the commissioners themselves were largely local notables, 'who accepted their posts from motives of patriotism'.[21]

The potential powers of the commissioners were formidable. The Ministries of Health, War Transport, Food and Home Security sent senior civil servants to each region, where the policies of their departments were co-ordinated by meetings under the chairmanship of the regional commissioner. Under normal circumstances, the reporting line for these officials was back to their ministry; were communications to break down, following an invasion, the regional commissioner would take charge, with the regional representatives of the ministries falling under his direct control. Many of the commissioner's powers were delegated from the appropriate ministers, and exercised under their supervision, while general guidance was provided by the Minister for Home Security; in time of crisis, a general power to make regulations for any purpose would devolve to the regional commissioner.

In relation to the threat of air attacks, the commissioners had a responsibility to co-ordinate the activities of the local authorities, the police and fire brigades, to organize emergency transport services, and to ensure that each authority made the appropriate plans for such an eventuality. In the event of invasion, the commissioner's task was to maintain an orderly civil government, and so avoid the necessity for complete control by the military authorities. The regional commissioner had the power under the Defence (General) Regulations to give directions 'for the purpose of meeting any actual or apprehended enemy attack' and to detain suspected persons.

Under stable conditions, their first function was administrative: to act as a link between central and local government, and between the local authorities themselves in respect of civil defence services. The commissioner's task was to secure co-operation between civil defence authorities and provide a bridge to other aspects of wartime administration. He operated 'to see that the collective wisdom and technical resources of the central government and of local authorities [were] used to the best advantage', and advised central departments on the giving or withholding of grants to local authorities, ensuring that local authorities attained the standards required by the central government.

The very existence of this powerful regional structure conditioned the ways in which ministers and officials thought about post-war reconstruction. An effective system in wartime, it could well provide a basis for a new system of sub-national government in which local authorities were subordinated – or even supplanted. Accordingly, in January 1941, Greenwood asked the Solicitor-General, Sir William Jowitt, to review

> the main peace-time problems of local government in England and Wales, in so far as they arise from the existing arrangement of local government areas and the existing distribution of local government functions,

and in particular to consider whether the regional system set up to co-ordinate civil defence could have a permanent role in bringing about a better system of local government.[22] This was, of course, a potentially explosive issue, and Jowitt's enquiries were intended to be discreet. He set off on tour, meeting regional commissioners and their staffs, before returning to London to hold a series of conferences in April with officials from all of the central ministries involved with local authorities. He asked those he met to report how far their normal peacetime functions had already been decentralized to the regions, and whether they thought it desirable to abolish, diminish, maintain or increase such decentralization after the war. In June, Jowitt met the central ministries again, this time to ask 'to what extent would it be advantageous to widen the areas within which local government functions are performed?' and whether 'the existing regional system suggest[s] any model on which local government areas and functions could be reorganised'.

The Jowitt enquiry

The underlying issue in the Jowitt enquiry was whether the regional commissioners should be kept in place at the end of the war, exercising supervision over the local authorities. Some in government – including Sir Ernest Simon – advocated this step, while much official opinion probably concurred with the view of one of Jowitt's staff that there can no longer be any question of return to local government by and through upwards of 10,000 local authorities. Regional organisation had begun to establish itself before the war; it has been largely developed during the war; and it will be further extended after the war.[23]

There could hardly be a more sensitive issue from the point of view of the local authorities themselves, and it was necessary to keep the Jowitt enquiry under wraps. When Greenwood faced a question in the House of Commons in June 1941, asking him to take account of 'the general view that there is a strong case for a complete revision of local government boundaries after the war' and to appoint an investigating committee, he stonewalled. Equally, Jowitt and his staff were in constant danger of trespassing upon departmental territory. In one incident, the reconstruction secretariat under Sir George Chrystal made the error of seeking advice on educational matters from the Workers' Educational Association, to the fury of the Board of Education officials, who thought that Greenwood and Chrystal 'naturally know nothing of the public system of education'.[24] In another, a trip by Jowitt to Cambridge to speak in favour of unification of the city and county was blocked by MoH officials citing their own minister's likely disapproval. In a third, the secretariat's proposed further enquiries into local government finance were headed off by the MoH with the somewhat patronizing warning that 'As you know, the subject of rating and valuation although – Heaven knows – a very technical one is also one of a highly political nature'. This intervention successfully shunted the enquiry into the innocuous siding of financial procedure.[25]

Jowitt's report was complete in August 1941. Its organization followed the twin themes of his consultations: whether the wartime machinery of regional government should be kept in being during peacetime, and whether it suggested any model on which local government could be reorganized. On the first of these issues, Jowitt was both decisive and definitive. After an exhaustive review of the workings of the wartime regions, he concluded that

> I do not think. . . that the experience of the Regional Commissioners or of the Commissioner for the Special Areas can be converted into a principle of general application. Local authorities which are willing to co-operate with a Regional Commissioner in the interests of national defence in time of war might regard such a personage with aversion in time of peace. The success of the Commissioner for the Special Areas was partly due to the fact

that he had inducements to offer in the shape of Exchequer money. It is doubtful whether, on major problems, the larger local authorities would in peace-time be willing to accept the decisions of any regional authority, however distinguished... My conclusion is that, while there is much scope for decentralising the work of individual ministers and strengthening their local staffs, and for increasing the local knowledge of departmental officials, the case for adopting a general regional system in peace-time is not proven.[26]

Even the very different Commissioner for the Special Areas could not, in Jowitt's judgement, 'be regarded as a precursor of a regional system of government', and this was a view in which Greenwood himself concurred.[27]

Jowitt, however, found the existing system of local government equally unsatisfactory. There were many services 'which must be dealt with on a wider basis than is compatible with local government boundaries as at present constituted'.[28] The great urban areas were governed by a multiplicity of authorities, precluding their needs being considered as a whole. There was a proliferation of small county districts. The ideal area for the administration of a particular service would often not correspond with local authority boundaries. The community of interest between town and country was insufficiently recognized. The distribution of functions between levels of local government was confused. Nor were these merely administrative matters. Jowitt valued 'the elective and democratic principles' of local government, which would only be maximized when local authorities commanded widespread public interest and participation. For this, they needed to be drawn into 'a single system conceived on comparatively simple lines'.

The number of people with leisure and public spirit was limited; a reduction in the number of authorities might increase the number of highly qualified people serving on each, while 'men of initiative and intelligence' could be attracted in proportion to the powers that an authority possessed; for to such men, 'responsibility is itself an attraction'. Jowitt accordingly

> sought for a scheme of local government reform which will produce a local government area which is (a) sufficiently large for the comfortable administration of most local services, and (b) which has sufficient internal cohesion to make it a suitable basis for a single unit of local government.[29]

This was the first statement of what would, in a few short years, come to be known as the 'unitary' principle. In practical terms, in would mean the creation of area-wide counties or boroughs in the large urban areas. Outside those areas, functions would need to be transferred from districts and boroughs to county councils, with few services remaining with rural districts. Urban and rural authorities should be amalgamated where their areas were inseparable. No county borough should be created if the effect would be prejudicial to the interests of the surrounding areas. And to define the appropriate boundaries for the new local authorities in line with these principles, a national commission should be appointed.[30]

In view of the sensitivities of the local authorities, it had been agreed that Jowitt would not talk to local authority representatives at either elected member or official level. But Jowitt himself sensed the handicap. His conclusions, the report noted, could only be 'provisional' without hearing 'the evidence of persons who have had experience as members and officers of local authorities'. Before going further, he advised Greenwood in a covering letter, 'it will probably be necessary to ascertain the opinion of those concerned in various local government activities to avoid the charge that they are being condemned unheard'.[31]

It was a lawyer's point, with no intuition that consulting local government might turn out to be of substantive, rather than merely procedural, importance. Officials at the Ministry of Health had opposed the Jowitt enquiry being taken as far as publication without prior consultation; they also blocked any investigation of local government finance 'in the absence of any knowledge of what post-war financial conditions are likely to be', when 'the material factors governing possible lines of reform' would be known. There was one thing that they did know: the nature of the enquiry was bound to change once Sir John Maude, Permanent Secretary at the Ministry of Health, was asked to invite the local authority associations to send representatives for informal discussions with Jowitt.[32]

Consultations began in October, when Jowitt met the representatives of the County Councils Association (CCA), and continued through November, when the representatives of the Association of Municipal Corporations (AMC) and the urban and rural districts attended. Each set of local authorities had their own clear views: they would accept any reform that enhanced their own status at the expense of their neighbours. The CCA welcomed the prospect of a very great reduction in the number of districts and the abolition of the smaller county boroughs. The others took the broadly contrary view, with the Urban District Councils Association (UDCA) subsequently protesting that the time was not ripe for reorganization, that any necessary action could be undertaken under the existing legislation, and that 'so far from there having been any failure of local government, local authorities have done wonderful work, and that the government should let well alone'.[33] Jowitt's secretary, Cooke, thought it unlikely that the associations could be induced to reach agreement even under the threat of regionalism. Backing away from the report he had helped to draft, Cooke urged that 'we must not hope for too much from a reorganisation of local authority areas and functions, and that we must concentrate rather upon the transfer of functions to joint bodies or to the central government'. He added that 'I am sure the Ministry of Health would agree with this general conclusion'.[34]

However, the cat was out of the bag. To have consulted at all with the local authorities meant that the Jowitt enquiry was now public knowledge. Although no reference was made to the Solicitor-General's labours, the *Financial News* had flown a spectacular kite in June with a leading article that suggested that if regionalism were the right framework for carrying out post-war reconstruction, its arguments applied equally to other local authority functions. The permanent establishment of the existing regions 'will provoke opposition which will need some courage to disregard in the relaxing days of peace, but the end will be worth the effort'.[35] Such speculations could only instil the deepest alarm in the local authorities, and Jowitt was warned that

> after your consultations with the wiseacres it has naturally become known that you are undertaking this investigation. As usual, busybodies have been at work, and conjectures are already being made as to the scope and contents of your report.[36]

The *Yorkshire Post* was the first to go public on the enquiry itself, reporting a heated discussion at Harrogate which demanded that any changes in local government should be a matter for a Royal Commission to consider after the war was ended. A Harrogate alderman protested that 'we do not like the method by which the Solicitor General and others in Parliament are seeking in these days to obtain views on what should be the form of local government after the war'.[37] Others were more agitated still. 'Hands Off our Local Councils' cried the *Yorkshire Evening News*, quoting the view of a Leeds councillor that the Jowitt enquiry, with its supposed flirtation with regionalism, represented 'a very dangerous tendency', signifying the disposition of people 'who got bureaucratic jobs because of the war to cling to those jobs when the war is over'. The CCA protested formally about 'grapevine allegations' about what Jowitt had said at the meetings. A flood of resolutions from district councils began to arrive, and Greenwood was forced to tell the House of Commons that there would be no changes in the system of local government without the consent of the authorities.[38]

During the next couple of months, Jowitt revised, finalized and signed his report, taking on board the extensive comments of the Whitehall departments. While he maintained his position on the unsuitability of the regional machinery for post-war, the brisk iconoclasm on the subject of local government reform of the August version was considerably tempered by the addition of detailed analysis and extensive qualification. He now offered alternative approaches, from wholesale reorganization to selective adjustment. This last was based on the 'plausible' argument that 'without completely recasting the local government map of England and Wales, it would be possible to effect certain amalgamations and adjustments which would be of definite advantage'. The contrast between the first and second versions of the Jowitt report could hardly be more striking. Prior to meeting the local authority associations, he could declare that

> If a general reorganisation of local government areas is to be effected at all, it is in my view essential that it should be effected as quickly as possible. I am satisfied that if the replanning and rebuilding of devastated and ill-developed urban centres is to be carried out through the agency of local authorities, it is urgently necessary that their areas and functions should first be re-organised on the lines which I am proposing. In my view, therefore, every effort should be made to complete the process of reform before the end of the war. I think it is only by the adoption of a procedure of the kind I have suggested that the work will be done with necessary rapidity.[39]

After meeting with them, and after being assailed by public criticisms and by the milder but no less insidious blandishments of the MoH officials, Jowitt's position changed. In his final version, he wrote of the 'selective adjustment' approach that

> Any alterations in the areas of the major local authorities must necessarily be preceded by long and careful examination of the evidence in favour of each adjustment. I see no possibility of starting such an examination during

the war or of concluding it within any reasonably short period thereafter. For these reasons, I have come to the conclusion that any selective review of the boundaries of counties and county boroughs must be regarded as impracticable during the reconstruction period.[40]

The report went to the Committee on Reconstruction Problems on 31 March 1942. By this time Jowitt had been promoted, taking over Greenwood's position with the title of Paymaster-General. It was decided not to publish the report, on the grounds that it might have proved embarrassing to Jowitt in his new role. In reality, the report had been emasculated by the local authorities' input, and by their Whitehall sponsor, the Ministry of Health. Jowitt had 'sought to advocate practical reforms which the Ministry of Health could support, judging it fruitless to make proposals which they would oppose'. That tactic had led him so to dilute his approach that he had little incentive to press the report.

However, as minister in charge of reconstruction he could have a second bite, assuring G. D. H. Cole that

> now that I am now in a different position I am able to put very much more pressure on the Ministry of Health and I look forward to reforms of a very much more drastic line than those I had advocated in my [August] report.[41]

Cole and his colleagues at Nuffield College had been working for some time on matters of post-war reconstruction.[42] They had earlier been warned off tackling local government in the light of the Jowitt enquiry; now Jowitt was all too keen to encourage the Oxford group (and even to offer Cole a desk), although the continuing opposition of the MoH meant that they would be expected to operate quietly, so as not to 'perturb' the local authorities: 'You are entitled, and indeed encouraged, to consider the reform of local government *in vacuo*, that is to say without consulting the local authorities'.

Further to encourage this new initiative, Jowitt sent a copy of his report for Cole and his colleague C. H. Wilson, who was to lead the Nuffield enquiry into local government. The Nuffield report would come to conclusions very similar to Jowitt's original view: the abolition of county boroughs, and unified administration for the conurbations. A new touch was added by the proposed abolition of rural district councils in favour of enhanced parishes.[43] But such back-room exercises were already overtaken by wider discussion as the debate on the future of local government, hitherto a private matter, slipped out of the control of the reconstruction team and became a matter of public contention.

Reform goes public

Once it was known that the government had considered restructuring local government, the issue gained a momentum of its own. In July 1942, the AMC held a special conference on the future of local government, publishing their proposals for a unitary system covering both urban and rural areas. The other associations naturally followed, but it was Lord Kennet who promoted a wider public discussion by commending the AMC plan in a letter to *The Times*, and rejecting any proposal for the continuation of the regional commissioners into peacetime. He called for a comprehensive inquiry to precede any change, and in response the AMC made a formal submission to Jowitt, calling for a Royal Commission to be established. When their friends in Parliament pursued this proposal, they were gently rebuffed by Attlee, who did not think 'that the procedure of setting up a Royal Commission now to begin work after the war would be a satisfactory one.'[44]

Jowitt now began to press hard for just such an inquiry, despite Attlee's discouragement, sending a soothing letter to tell him that proposals were still being worked upon.[45] He also faced the opposition of other powerful interests, including the Chancellor of the Exchequer, Sir Kingsley Wood, who thought that Jowitt's proposals went 'too far' in anticipating future needs and demands,[46] and Sir John Anderson, who let the Ministry of Health know his view that Jowitt's proposals should go no further than the reconstruction committee, 'on the assumption that any question of reform or changes in local government is still very much in the planning stage and there is no question of entering into any early commitment'.[47] The paper that Jowitt now prepared argued that a number of issues of post-war planning needed immediate attention: education, town and country planning, fire, police, medical and hospital services. 'I think it is difficult', he wrote, 'for the government to carry out any reforms of value without the backing of an impartial tribunal'. The problem remained of the Ministry of Health's interest in blocking such an inquiry. Their opposition was on the grounds that it would add to the pressure of work and hold up progress on planning for peace. Jowitt pressed a contrary view, that if we wait till the war is over we shall miss a favourable opportunity to deal with long-overdue reforms in the wartime atmosphere of co-operation. Other more insistent questions will monopolise our time when the war is won and we shall have to base our reconstruction plans mainly on the continuance of the status quo, thereby making ultimate reform even more difficult.[48]

On 17 March 1943, Jowitt put these views to the Committee on Reconstruction Problems, of which he was now the chairman. He recalled the sharp controversy spurred by his earlier report, much of which arose from the fact that it was conducted on a confidential basis. Now, with the question of reform very much in the air as a result of the AMC initiatives and *The Times* correspondence, the local authorities were as a result 'somewhat apprehensive and unsettled in their outlook' and, Jowitt continued, 'the view that there is a case for the drastic overhaul of local government is widely held. With this view I agree'. He urged that the opportunity be seized to capitalize on the wartime atmosphere of collaboration [sic] when 'the national outlook is likely to be less adverse to changes...'. Moreover, 'in the spaciousness of peace the deliberations of such a Commission are more likely to be unduly prolonged'.[49] Ernest Brown, the Minister of Health, opposed Jowitt's plan with a series or arguments against change. He had already tried without success to dissuade Jowitt from pressing for a Royal Commission, and had refrained from offering comments on the paper so as to oppose it more directly with his own.[50] His ministry officials doubted that any clear view could emerge, and were keen to avoid the local authorities coming to feel that 'the structure of local government is in the melting pot...'.[51]

As the ministry most concerned with local government, the MoH were loath to see the issue slip out of their own control. The Board of Education's officials were also deeply conservative on the question of restructuring, holding that the county boroughs would 'of course' remain, with 'no undue interference with the historic counties'. The support of the education officials was vital to block Jowitt, and the two Permanent Secretaries, Sir John Maude and Sir Maurice Holmes, conferred. Holmes ensured that his minister, R. A. Butler, supported Brown rather than Jowitt, the MoH having made the point that Butler's education reforms might be impeded by the establishment of a Royal Commission. Butler was of like mind: 'Yeah. Horse sense' he scrawled on the note asking him to oppose the scheme.[52] In the face of such opposition, and despite his advantage of the chair, Jowitt lost the issue in committee, where ministers agreed, after wide-ranging discussion, that there should be no Royal Commission. They did concede that the problems were indeed urgent, but it was Brown, as the responsible minister, and not Jowitt, who was asked to bring back fresh proposals for dealing with the problem of local government structure.

In July 1943, the first serious and extensive discussion was held on a comprehensive paper on local government reform to be put up by the Ministry of Health. Brown reviewed the history of attempts to bring about adjustment since 1920, alongside the now current proposals: those of the CCA; of the AMC; of the urban and rural districts (who were for no change); of NALGO; and of the Labour party. The previous approach taken by Jowitt – under considerable pressure from the MoH – was graciously commended, although the revelation of its existence had led to 'uneasiness'. Brown now had to contend with the fact that support for an independent inquiry was growing, leading him to re-examine the objections that he had put to the previous meeting. He was 'still of the opinion that on balance the disadvantages of appointing a Commission outweigh the advantages', deploying the canny argument that

> those who contend that a reform of the structure of local government should precede any change in the machinery for administering some new or extended service will, consciously or otherwise, be playing into the hands of the opponents of the policy which involves the change.[33]

He concluded by quoting back at Jowitt the same report which its author was now attempting to disown. The committee backed the Minster of Health, and agreed that consultations should be set in motion with the local authority associations, but with the limited aim of improving the machinery of rating valuation and instituting a more effective system of county reviews under a statutory commission.

This was very much less than Jowitt had hoped for. Yet it was in itself more than enough to whip up the worst fears of the local authorities. Jowitt received resolutions from fifty-three local authorities, fiercely resisting change. A typical resolution expressed

> serious concern at the drastic changes made and sought now to be made in the local government services and at the many proposals now emanating from the ministerial departments apparently with the support of the government, which seeks to reduce the powers and duties of local authorities.[54]

In September, Churchill fielded a question on the extent to which the government was contemplating change in local government, and was pressed for assurances that there would be either prior consultation or a Royal Commission; he dismissed the prospect of upheaval as 'highly prejudicial to the success of our post-war plans'.[55]

There the matter might have rested, had it not been for Brown's replacement as Minister of Health by Conservative Henry Willink in 1944. Willink came back to the reconstruction committee in July 1944, reporting that little progress had been made on consulting the local authority associations over county reviews, and predicting that 'it will be difficult, if not impossible' to delay for any substantial period after the end of the war the emergence of the problem of borough extensions', particularly in the highly industrialized areas of Lancashire and West Yorkshire. Private bills could be expected. While this – with a genuflection to his predecessor – was not the moment to 'throw the system into the melting pot', the government would be unable to resist ambitious county boroughs unless some conclusions could be agreed on the proposals made over the past few years.[56]

The only acceptable way out would be to establish a boundary commission with the power to alter, on its own initiative, the boundaries between counties and county boroughs, to create new county boroughs, to alter the boundaries between counties and to unite them when required. This it would do by framing Orders, much as the Local Government Board and the Ministry of Health had done between 1888 and 1926, but under the new Provisional Order arrangements soon to be more generally adopted. For so powerful a commission to be acceptable to Parliament, the responsible minister would need the power to issue guidance in the form of general directions, subject to Parliamentary approval. In approaching the question of boundary extensions, the government should promulgate the doctrine laid down by the Onslow Committee, that boundary changes should be a matter of calculating the balance of advantage, taking into account not just the interests of the urban residents, but also those of the surrounding county.

Willink won approval to open discussions on this basis, and announced in the Commons on 3 August that, while discussions with the local authority associations had established that 'there is no general desire to disrupt the existing structure of local government', the government now thought there was need for a mechanism for the adjustment of 'status, boundaries and areas'. In November he reported on the unexpected agreement among the local authority representatives on the desirability of a boundary commission. He was now ready to move forward to a draft white paper along these lines. He thought it important that the government should stress that a radical upheaval was neither necessary nor desirable; that in the future local government would be expected to play a greater, rather than a lesser, part in national life; and that it should 'dispel any remaining doubts as to the temporary nature of the regional commissioners'.[57]

Although Jowitt, Ede, Attlee and Bevin all ridiculed Willink's approach on the grounds that it was dealing with local government areas before functions had been settled, the white paper now had considerable momentum.[58] Much of the discussion that followed was confined to matters of procedure, aspects of which were dealt with in subsequent Willink memoranda that same week, in discussion within a subcommittee of the Machinery of Government Committee, and with officials of both Houses of Parliament.

Willink's white paper appeared as *Local Government in England and Wales During the Period of Reconstruction* in 1945, as a preliminary to the immediate introduction of a bill. An unusually discursive white paper, it rehearsed the arguments that had been put during the previous three years, and declared the government to be against 'drastic innovations'. Acknowledging that 'interest and apprehension' on the subject of larger administrative areas had been aroused by the appointment of the regional commissioners, the white paper finally buried the prospect of building upon that structure: 'it can be stated definitely that it is no part of the government's policy' to perpetuate the commissioners in being for the purposes of post-war reconstruction. Indeed, 'far from there being any ground for fear that the work of democratic local government may diminish', the white paper went on, the task for the future was to strengthen local government 'to bear greater responsibilities and fulfil new tasks'.[59] Foremost among these as components of the post-war social settlement would be the physical reconstruction of Britain's housing stock, and a comprehensive overhaul of public education.

Towards a New Settlement

During both world wars, politicians, administrators and commentators alike were exercised by the ambiguity of the term 'reconstruction'. The high profile given to reconstruction after 1917 had masked the dual meanings of the term, which signified to some no more than the putting right of war damage and deterioration and, to others, great schemes of social reform.[60] Something of that same division could be seen after 1941, but its effects were less marked. Reconstruction was seen by Churchill as a sideshow, a way of providing a safety valve for the overheated and untimely aspirations of social progressives brought into government under the coalition. The machinery put in place was therefore modest, taking the form of a powerless co-ordinating committee and secretariat, under a minister, Greenwood, whose influence was, by the time he took on the role, more modest still.

Some of the lessons of the Great War had been learned: there would be no histrionics about 'homes for heroes' this time, no inflated and unrealizable promises. Attention centred on the prospect of building the New Jerusalem not by housing programmes alone, but through the planning and control of development. The business of rehousing returned servicemen and workers under conditions of fairly substantial bomb damage was left to be settled by bureaucratic skirmishing within Whitehall. Here, the several ministries with a stake in reconstruction pursued short-term, temporary, solutions to the pending housing crisis, leaving the real thrust of the post-war programme to be settled by the incoming government working with and through the local authorities.

Preparing for the home front

The spirit of reconstruction owed its sustenance to apocalyptic visions of destruction by aerial bombardment. The Barlow report was the first official statement of concern over the vulnerability of Britain's overconcentrated and overcrowded cities, but 'the fear that London would be levelled to the ground on the outbreak of war was widespread'.[61] Air Ministry calculations led the government to expect 100 tons of bombs to be dropped daily on London, causing some 19,000 casualties a week. Policy and popular imagination alike ingested the grim doctrine that 'the bomber will always get through'. The reality was very different. Despite the worst horrors of the blitz, and its concentrated effects in such cities as Plymouth and Coventry, the entire wartime total of civilian casualties in London totalled some 49,000, a lesser number than died from cancer or tuberculosis.[62]

This is not to minimize the fact that a practical problem of physical reconstruction remained, in London and in a number of the provincial cities. The damage of the aerial bombardment in the war years had to be remedied, and inherent shortages provided for. While fears of aerial bombing in the months leading to the war had greatly overestimated the likely damage, the *Luftwaffe* and the V1 and V2 between them had destroyed 200,000 homes in Britain and severely damaged another 3.5 million, of which more than a quarter of a million were rendered uninhabitable. The pattern of population distribution had been changed, less by evacuation than by the deployment of workers to factories outside the main conurbations. Their anticipated return – 2.5 million to London alone – would lead to so dire a shortage that the Minister of Health was forced to take emergency powers under the defence regulations to requisition and re-let houses that had been declared as unfit. Because of the shortage of labour and materials, it was impossible to do more than patch these properties. It was clear that the total pool of post-war houses would be inadequate for the civilian population, and nearly all would require repair or maintenance.

In these circumstances, planning concentrated on short-term emergency measures to avert the immediate crisis. House building had virtually ceased during the war, with just 160,000 homes built.[63] The Rents and Mortgage (Restrictions) Act 1939 had frozen rents and mortgage repayments at their September 1939 levels in England and Wales. Over half of the population lived in private rented accommodation, and this freezing of rents led to such a constriction of supply that local authorities were obliged to intervene, using their powers to requisition properties and bring them into use. The end of the war would foreseeably accentuate these problems of supply. The Ministry of Health acknowledged in March 1944 that

> Our primary task must be to meet the urgent needs of those who have no homes of their own. These could not be fully met or met with sufficient speed by building new houses of permanent construction... we shall have to undertake a substantial amount of emergency housing both by adapting

existing buildings and by providing temporary accommodation of various kinds.[64]

For Churchill the priority was to allocate housing to returning servicemen, so avoiding the bitterness and social dangers of the 1918 armistice. Warning that 'The families of serviceman without separate homes provided the most pressing example of those living under unsatisfactory housing conditions', he pressed for short-term, highly visible measures to provide quick results.

'Quick results' meant prefabricated temporary homes, produced by industrial means for on-site assembly. Prefabrication techniques were well known to the Ministry of Works, which advocated them in the face of opposition from the Ministry of Health, the two departments fighting a running battle for control of the post-war housing programme. In 1943 the Ministry of Works had developed a prototype temporary house. The Ministry of Health responded by asking the Central Housing Advisory Committee critically to evaluate the 'prefab'. Their special subcommittee opposed the use of temporary houses of fixed construction as being less economical than they appeared at first sight, and having a shorter life expectancy – ten years – than conventional housing. The programme went ahead only when the reconstruction committee overrode the Ministry of Health's opposition and the concerns of the Treasury in June 1944, on the grounds that a programme of this sort was unavoidable.

It was decided to provide 100,000 prefabs in the first year of peace and a similar number in the second year. The Housing (Temporary Accommodation) Act 1944 provided the basis for the scheme: under the Act, finance was provided for between two and three hundred thousand houses, and the Minister of Health was empowered to enter into partnership with local authorities to provide these houses on their land, with the Ministry of Works overseeing the manufacture. Local authorities were to pay the government 10 shillings (£0.5) weekly for each unit, and to charge a similar rent to that levied on conventional houses. In September 1944 a Committee on Prefabricated Houses was appointed 'to make the best plan possible for the largest possible construction in the shortest time of pre-fabricated houses of all types'. It reported in two weeks, concluding that the programme was inadequate for the needs of the population. A working party was set up to review alternative systems of construction and, in October 1945, a white paper on the temporary housing programme was published, committing the government to providing 158,000 houses.

The Ministry of Health had since 1942 been working on a longer-term plan for post-war housing. In that year, its estimate of housing shortfall at the end of the war was 710,000. The government expected no more than between a quarter and a third of those houses to be built by local authorities. By March 1943 there had been a considerable switch of emphasis, with a Ministry of Health circular asking local authorities to begin work immediately on plans for a substantial post-war housing programme. Their function would be to cover the provision of houses for slum clearance, the abatement of overcrowding, and the provision of houses to meet general needs. The remainder of the field was expected to be left to private enterprise with a provision that, in so far as they failed to meet the needs, they would be displaced by the local authorities.[65] It was affirmed that local authorities, with their ability to monitor standards and provide at cheap rents, would be the main providers of social housing. Readily controlled by central government, local authorities could be part of a planned national strategy.

Linked to the emphasis on municipal building was the issue of the right of local authorities to dispose of their housing stock to sitting tenants. Between the wars, this had taken place on a small scale, with the consent in each case of the Ministry of Health, and subject to a requirement for the authority to obtain the best possible price. Sales were few, although Birmingham City Council had sold more than 3,500 houses by the outbreak of war in 1939. In line with the wartime emergency restriction on the sale of privately rented property, consent to the sale of council houses was withheld for the duration of the war. It was not envisaged that sales would be appropriate during the reconstruction period, and the Labour government was to continue the wartime ban.[66]

'Reconstruction' necessarily involved the repair of widespread devastation. To that extent, it provided a unique opportunity to rebuild to a new, more functional and more human pattern. The report of the Uthwatt Committee on Compensation and Betterment declared that 'the emphasis is on "reconstruction", not only as an immediate necessity for repairing the devastation caused by the war, but also as a long term measure', with the aim of transforming Britain's towns and cities to meet the needs of modern civilization and provide citizens with a healthy environment for work and leisure.[67] From 1943 this mood took hold, as the turning of the tide of armed conflict in the Allies' favour shifted attention to the home front and raised expectations of what might be achieved there. A daunting task had suddenly become a positive opportunity. 'Peace offers no more exciting and stimulating task than the reconstruction and positive planning of Britain's town and countryside' was the *credo* of one of a number of contemporary symposia on reconstruction.[68] An abrupt change in the whole climate of public opinion towards planning had been brought about by the bombing. As a result, the repair of war damage was seen as no more than an initial stage of a process that would sweep away the bulk of the older town property and replace it by new building 'planned for efficiency, health and attractiveness in design'.[69]

The cities would be renewed not through the medium of simple replacement building *in situ* but through creative land-use planning and decentralization, some of which might be to specially created garden cities. The 1944 white paper on land-use planning stated that

> Provision for the right use of land, in accordance with a considered policy, is an essential requirement of the Government's programme of post-war reconstruction. New houses, whether of permanent or emergency construction; the new layout of areas, devastated by enemy action or blighted by reason of age or bad living conditions . . . the balanced distribution of industry . . . for maintaining active employment . . . all these related parts of a single reconstruction programme involve the use of land, and it is essential that their various claims on land should be so harmonised as to ensure for the people of this country the greatest possible measure of individual well-being and national prosperity.[70]

The foundations of this policy were to be found in the three reports to government that were made during the period of the war: that of the Barlow Commission on the Distribution of the Industrial Population; that of the Scott Committee on the Utilization of Land in Rural Areas; and that of the Uthwatt Committee on Compensation and Betterment.[71]

It was no longer possible to consider housing matters in isolation from the broader issues of the location of population and industry.[72] The white paper set out the basic principle of the new regime: 'that there should be a universal requirement that consent must be obtained before any change is made in the existing use of any land'. The power to give consent would be vested in local planning authorities, the decisions of which would be consistent with development plans that they would draw up for ministerial approval. These powers would 'not only. . . control development and redevelopment, but also. . . . secure that approved development and redevelopment are carried out on the right land at the right time', and would represent one of the most significant accretions of local authority powers to emerge from the war. The public control of private development would be a key instrument in the making of contemporary Britain. And much of what was enacted in the 1943, 1944 and (after the war) the 1947 Town and Country Planning Acts was based on the work of the reconstruction secretariat which was, in turn, supported by a growing political consensus on the need for public control.[73]

The pattern of local government structure obviously impinged directly upon the exercise of the new powers. The control of development on the small scale by individual local authorities would be insufficient to meet the problem, and it was clear that planning powers would have to be restricted to county and county borough councils, although the counties failed to wrest the housing role from the districts. Given the endemic hostility between town and country, between county and county borough, local government could not be expected to tackle the wider issues of overspill or the continuous development of cities. For these matters central initiatives would be required, establishing green belts, providing for the construction of new, self-contained planned towns, and reconciling local development plans. The wartime period saw no final agreement on these matters, and the framework was not completed until the Labour government secured the passage of the New Towns Act 1946 and the Town and Country Planning Act 1947.

While local authorities were to lose out to special-purpose appointed corporations in the rehousing of people in the new towns, they could still look to a more central, and expanding role in remaking urban Britain. Comprehensive redevelopment – tackling local areas wholesale – offered a prospect of powerful multi-purpose authorities redeveloping on a grand scale. One of Abercrombie's Greater London Plan team caught this spirit exactly:

> The government and the local authorities had been the most important elements in the war situation, giving the directions. After the war we thought, why can't they continue, why can't they be the new patrons of the arts? They are going to be responsible for the housing programmes, for planning, for many of the things which previously the big aristocrats were the patrons. They provided the money originally for the building of great estates in London like Bloomsbury and Belgravia . . . But now the local authorities

were coming along it was necessary for them to improve their image, their understanding of people, so that instead of building great council estates or even little estates here and there, as the land became available, they had the responsibility to think in more comprehensive terms. So that they were not just putting a little house here or a block of flats there, they were building neighbourhoods.[74]

The war, and the bombing of the cities in particular, had greatly enhanced the capability of local authorities to respond to crisis. Using new powers, they had sheltered the homeless and carried out emergency repairs to damaged buildings regardless of their ownership.[75] Local authorities had exercised powers which, even when relinquished, left them in place as the principal agents to which government would look for the great post-war housing programme. And not just the government: people placed housing in the forefront of their concerns for the post-war world.[76] Housing programmes – building the largest possible number of homes through public action – would draw from this a powerful political impetus that would last a full ten years; until other, more complex, aspirations drew government in other directions, in which local authorities would not enjoy that same central role.

From Green Book to white paper

The best-prepared measure of reconstruction to emerge in the war years came not through the reconstruction machinery, but through the steady working of departmental officials at the Board of Education. They were already ploughing their own furrow towards a new education act from the earliest months of the war, although it needed R. A. Butler's skill and persistence to bring it off in 1944. In reorganizing the school system, Butler also changed the pattern of local education authorities, and established a strong a stable partnership between central and local government that was to last for two decades, into the very different world of the 1960s.

Education policy had received a great deal of political attention during the inter-war years. The great majority of children received only an 'elementary' education, leaving school at the age of fourteen without any qualifications. Only a small minority stayed on in full-time education, to the age of fifteen or even sixteen. There was growing pressure to abolish the distinction between elementary and secondary education, in favour of a single line of progression for all children over the age of eleven. The Labour party had for some time campaigned for the raising of school leaving age from fourteen to fifteen, and for a system of universal secondary education for all pupils over the age of eleven. The Hadow report of 1926 endorsed these aims, but the short lived Labour government of 1929–31 chose not to implement it, and so avoid having to confront the opposition of the churches. Since 1902, church-run schools had existed alongside local authority or 'maintained' schools under the so-called 'dual system'. Any move towards a single 'secondary' system would diminish the influence of the churches, with the Catholic church in particular fiercely opposed to any loss of control. In brief, the churches' loss would be the LEAs' gain.

In 1936 the Board of Education's consultative committee, chaired by Sir Will Spens, returned to the question of the school system. Charged with reporting on 'the organisation and interrelation of schools, other than those administered under the elementary code, which provide education for pupils beyond the age of 11', Spens affirmed the general principles of the Hadow report, and proposed 'a secondary code' to break down the existing divisions in education provision. His committee endorsed the view that education after the age of eleven should be regarded as secondary, and should be viewed as 'an organic outgrowth of primary education'. It also accepted the two main types of secondary school recommended by Hadow: the grammar and 'modern' school, but additionally proposed the establishment of selective 'technical high schools', to be accorded equality of status with the grammar schools. On this occasion the national government accepted the thrust of proposals, but the outbreak of war ensured that they were again shelved.

The impact of hostilities on the domestic front served to give educational reform an added urgency. The dispersal of children from urban centres not only created a seemingly insurmountable problem of the education of evacuees but also exposed the great variations in the standards of local education provisions. This was the context within which R. A. Butler began work in July 1941 on what was to become the Education Act 1944. Butler, offered a more prestigious diplomatic post by Churchill, showed characteristic insight in choosing instead the lowly Board of Education. The pressures for change, for bringing education provision and its organization into line with the needs of an advanced mid-twentieth-century

42 The Spirit of Reconstruction

economy, had been building for some time. A skilful minister, working in the back room of social policy, could bring far-reaching changes into being by astute tactics and a sharp sense of timing.

The war was an opportune moment, not just because the spotlight was elsewhere; the chaos of war made its own contribution. The scale of the disruption caused by the evacuation of children of school age made a wide-ranging debate on the future of state education inescapable. As early as November 1940, the Permanent Secretary, Sir Maurice Holmes, convened a group of officials to seize the initiative in the debate on post-war educational reconstruction. He wrote:

> I find that some of my colleagues, besides myself, have been considering whether we should not, now that we are working without constant interruption, be bending our minds to a study of the educational problems which will arise when the war is over . . . I think this is a matter in which the Board should lead rather than follow.[77]

It was an historic initiative. For the Board's officials to accept the lead role prefigured the powers of the new Ministry of Education, which the Education Act 1944 would bring into being.

Holmes operated with the consent and encouragement of the Board's President, Hereward Ramsbotham, whom Butler would replace, but the driving force was the deputy secretary, R. S. Wood. The Board's planning group, guided by Wood, produced early in 1941 a series of proposals, incorporated in the single document, which came to be known as the *Green Book*. The Green Book took a forward-looking stance, building on the report of the Spens committee and the longstanding commitments of the Labour party, whose ministers were expected to play the lead role in planning for reconstruction. This remarkable turn around on the part of Board's officials owed something to Wood's effective political antennae. He wrote confidently that the post-war government (which he imagined would be 'national' in character) would be 'prepared to face radical changes in our social and economic system' and approach the question of reconstruction as 'not merely restoration or a return to normality, but reconstruction in a very real sense'.[78]

The Green Book backed the raising of school leaving age to fifteen, and its proposals accepted for the need to provide 'secondary education for all' in different types of school on a selective principle. Holmes himself envisaged, in his foreword to the document, that secondary education would be provided in a tripartite system of secondary schools: grammar, technical and modern.[79]

The private and limited circulation of the Green Book was intended to collect opinion on the key proposals from a limited circle of educationists as a prelude to legislation. Despite the intention to limit the discussion to a small group of insiders, its existence and its proposals soon became widely known. Throughout civilian life and the forces, and through the medium of the BBC, the reconstruction of education was aired, with all-comers joining in.[80] The ensuing debate was an uncomfortably public one, with the high ground seized by such advocates of reform as H. C. Dent, the newly appointed editor of *The Times Educational Supplement*. In a series of four leading articles published in the summer of 1941, Dent argued that the principle of equality of opportunity 'demands total reform based on a new conception of the place, status and function of education in a democratic State, not a patching and padding of the present system', and attacked the proposals of the Green Book as failing to change the relationship between the educational system and the social order, criticizing the Board's officials' assumption that the post-war social order would be no different from that of the past.[81] This public airing of the issues pointed up the extent to which 'reconstruction' was thought of by those outside Whitehall as more than mere repair and reversion to the status quo *ante bellum* – the new agenda was true social reconstruction.

As such, the Labour movement, the teaching profession, the TUC and education administrators became widely engaged in debating policy and publishing pamphlets and leaflets. The result was 'a developing consensus around a radically progressive policy for educational change having very considerable social implications'.[82] The National Association of Schoolmasters argued for the abolition of the public schools on the grounds that 'schools that cater for "one caste" only cannot be included in a national system... the virtues of these schools are incompatible with democracy',[83] while the National Union of Teachers and the Grammar Schools Association campaigned for the integration of the public schools into the state system during 1942–3. The TUC, enjoying power as never before under the coalition government, endorsed these demands in its memorandum on *Education After the War*.

Whether or not the public schools were to be so absorbed, one common theme in this discussion was the need for greater egalitarianism in post-eleven education than had been envisaged by the authors of the Green

Book. The inter-war slogan 'secondary education for all' gained a new life with the revival of the demand that post-primary education should be regarded as secondary under a single code, with the separate status of 'elementary' education abolished. The Association of Directors and Secretaries – the professional education officials – called for all differences between types of school to be entirely eradicated as being 'relics of a system based upon class or social cleavage' and replaced by 'a unified system with all schools under a common code'. Secondary education should be free, with direct grant schools funded through LEAs, proposals which the Association of Education Committees was ready to support.

By the autumn of 1942, the idea of a single school system had gained sufficient ground for R. A. Butler to move steadily forward with plans for reform, supported by his experienced Labour Parliamentary secretary, Chuter Ede. Despite the discouragement of the Prime Minister, Butler was eager to produce a white paper and get its proposals on to the statute book. Churchill preferred all major reforms to wait until peacetime, and Butler was forced to work with discretion. However, he had the support of the Treasury, with the Chancellor, Sir Kingsley Wood, telling Ede that he preferred to put money into education rather than 'throw it down the sink with Sir William Beveridge'.[84]

For many in the coalition, education was the social investment on which the future strength of the economy would rest. Butler's white paper flagged this concern: 'upon the education of the people of this country the fate of this country depends'. The government's proposals set a new school leaving age of fifteen, with provision for its subsequent extension to sixteen 'as soon as circumstances permit'. The period from five to fifteen would be divided into two stages: primary, covering the years up to eleven; and secondary thereafter.[85] Secondary education would be provided for all children in schools of 'diversified types, but of equal standing'. Children would be classified at the age of eleven on the basis on an assessment of their individual aptitudes for progression into separate but equal secondary schools, warning that

> under present conditions the secondary grammar school enjoys a prestige ... which completely over-shadows all other types of school.... Inheriting as it does a distinguished tradition ... it offers the advantages of superior premises and staffing and a longer school life .... But ... an academic training is ill-suited for many of the pupils who find themselves moving along a narrow educational path bounded by the School Certificate and

leading into a limited field of opportunity. Such then will be the three main types: grammar, modern and technical schools. It would be wrong to suppose that they will necessarily remain separate and apart. Different types may be combined in one building or on one site . . . in any case, free interchange of pupils from one type of education to another must be facilitated.[86]

Immediately after the publication of the white paper came a report from a committee of the Secondary Schools Examinations Council, which had been established by the Board of Education in 1941 under the chairmanship of Cyril Norwood, former headmaster of Harrow, 'to review the existing system of school examinations'. The committee was encouraged to take a wider brief than its title and considered the patterns into which children grouped themselves by interest and aptitude, going on to urge that

> within a framework of secondary education, the needs of the three broad groups of pupils . . . should be met within three broad types of secondary education, each type containing the possibility of variation and each school offering alternative courses which would yet keep the school true to type.[87]

This was 'the essential ideological underpinning' for what came to be known as the 'tripartite' system.[88] The white paper had taken such a division for granted, and coming when it did, Butler judged that 'this well written report will serve our book very well – particularly its layout of the secondary world'.[89] That 'layout' was largely established in a series of steps: the Hadow and Spens committees, the Green Book, the white paper, the Norwood Committee and, finally, Butler's Education Act, which gave effect to the cumulative weight of their recommendations. Yet tripartism had a mixed reception, the egalitarian critics bridling at 'the suggestion of the [Norwood] committee . . . that the Almighty has benevolently created three types of child in just those proportions which would gratify educational administrators'.[90] Here was laid down the doctrine that would colour post-war education provision. It was also the main fissure that would in time divide one political party from another, and the Ministry of Education from many of the LEAs.

Although the debate that the Green Book had provoked was focused on school systems and educational issues, the longer-term significance of the wartime period lay in the espousal of a new (or rather revived) doctrine of partnership in education. Shaping the thinking of the Board's official team, R. S. Wood argued that the Board was charged by statute with the supervision of the public system of education, and for some time after 1902 it had been the senior and predominant partner while the LEAs learned their job. The authorities had now found their feet, and the Board's influence and control had come to depend on its prestige. The balance of power and the initiative had passed to the LEAs. Up to a point, this was both right and inevitable, but at times the process seemed to have gone to far, or rather there was a tendency for the Board to leave the field to authorities . . . The partnership with the local authorities needed to be put on a sounder basis, with more regular consultation . . . [91]

This need for the Board to assert itself and lead from the front was in tune with the growing consensus that the differences in provision between the various LEAs which had been exposed by the evacuation of children from the cities were no longer acceptable, and that far more emphasis needed to be placed on national policy. It was recognized that only greater centralization of control could redress the inequalities, and would provide for more purposeful national planning in education. The 1944 Act was to provide just that framework.

The war on the home front had not created the problems of local government. But the ways in which they had been handled left some new structures and a host of unresolved issues to impact upon the making of post-war Britain.

Notes

1   A. J. P. Taylor, '1932–1945', in *Coalitions in British Politics*, ed. D. Butler (Macmillan, London, 1978), p. 93.
2   J. B. Cullingworth, *Reconstruction and Land-use Planning, 1939–47* (HMSO, London, 1975), p. 5.
3   J. M. Lee, *The Churchill Coalition, 1940–1945* (Archon Books, Hamden, Connecticut, 1980), p. 118.
4   P. Addison, *The Road to 1945* (Jonathan Cape, London, 1975), p. 167.
5   CAB 117/224, Greenwood to Professor J. H. Jones, 10 June 1941.
6   CAB 117/27.
7   CAB 117/27.
8   For a full and thematically organized account of all the plans for the reconstruction of local government published during the war years, see 'Digest of proposals made by local authority associations and others for the reform of

The Spirit of Reconstruction   47

local government published 1941–45', in *Essays on Local Government*, ed. C. H. Wilson (Blackwell, Oxford, 1945), Appendix A, pp. 232–48.
9   V. D. Lipman, 'The development of areas and boundary changes, 1888–1939', in Wilson, *Essays on Local Government*, pp. 25–66.
10 K. Young and P. L. Garside, *Metropolitan London: politics and urban change, 1831–1981* (Edward Arnold, London, 1982), pp. 105–218.
11 Ministry of Health, *Local Government in England and Wales During the Period of Reconstruction*, Cmd. 6579 (HMSO, London, 1945).
12 B. Keith-Lucas, 'Three white papers on local government', *Political Quarterly*, 28(4) (1957), p. 333.
13 A. Calder, *The People's War: Britain 1939–1945* (Jonathan Cape, London, 1969), p. 192.
14 Calder, *People's War*, p. 204.
15 Calder, *People's War*, p. 205.
16 Calder, *People's War*, pp. 210–11, 219.
17 CAB 117/212, Astor to Greenwood, 3 June 1941.
18 CAB 117/212, 'Existing local government and blitzes' (Viscount Astor).
19 K. Jeffreys (ed.), *Labour and the Wartime Coalition: from the diaries of James Chuter Ede, 1941–1945* (The Historians' Press, London, 1987), p. 144.
20 *Report of the Royal Commission on the Distribution of the Industrial Population*, Cmd. 6153 (HMSO, London, 1940), para. 413.
21 CAB 117/214, Report to the Minister Without Portfolio, 22 August 1941 (hereafter Jowitt report, August 1941 version), paras 9–13. Angus Calder gives a portrait of the London commissioners – amongst whom was Sir Ernest Gowers – in *People's War*, p. 199.
22 CAB 117/214, Jowitt report, August 1941 version.
23 CAB 117/214, note by H. Stannard, 18 July 1941.
24 P. H. J. H. Gosden, *Education in the Second World War: a study in policy and administration* (Methuen, London, 1976), pp. 250–1.
25 CAB 117/222, Sir J. Maude to Cooke (secretary to the enquiry), 30 August 1941.
26 CAB 117/214, Jowitt report, August 1941 version, paras 19, 21.
27 CAB 117/212, Greenwood to Lord Astor, 27 May 1941.
28 CAB 117/215, Jowitt to Cooke, 18 November 1941.
29 Jowitt report, August 1941 version, para. 28.
30 Jowitt report, August 1941 version, para. 50.
31 CAB 117/214, Jowitt to Greenwood, 26 August 1941.
32 CAB 117/214, S. B. R. Cooke to Jowitt, 22 September 1941.
33 CAB 117/216, UDCA Secretary to Cooke, 13 January 1942.
34 CAB 117/214, Cooke to Jowitt, 15 November, 24 November 1941.
35 *Financial News*, 10 June 1941.

48   *The Spirit of Reconstruction*

36   CAB 117/215, Cooke to Jowitt, 13 December 1941.
37   *Yorkshire Post*, 9 December 1941.
38   House of Commons Debates, 15 October 1941, Col. 1362.
39   Jowitt report, August 1941 version, para. 33.
40   CAB 117/216, Jowitt report, January 1942 version, para. 55.
41   CAB 117/223, Jowitt to Cole, 2 April 1942.
42   Cullingworth, *Reconstruction and Land-use Planning*, pp. 7–8.
43   CAB 117/174, 'Nuffield College Social Reconstruction Survey: 1942 survey on local government reorganisation'.
44   House of Commons Debates, 19 January 1943, col. 35.
45   CAB 117/217, Jowitt to Attlee, 28 January 1943.
46   CAB 117/218, Tucker (Treasury) to Daish, 16 September 1943.
47   CAB 117/217, Bridges to Hurst (MoH) 2 February 1943.
48   CAB 117/217, Jowitt draft paper, February1943.
49   CAB 117/218, 'Proposed Royal Commission of Local Government in England and Wales: memorandum by the Minister Without Portfolio', 8 March 1943, paras 10, 14.
50   HLG 68/68.
51   CAB 117/218, 'Proposed Royal Commission of Local Government in England and Wales: memorandum by the Minister of Health', 11 March 1943. The Board of Education also opposed the Jowitt proposals as too late to help with the changes proposed in the education bill; see ED 136/353, 4 March 1943.
52   ED 136/353, Holmes to Butler, 12, 16 March 1943.
53   CAB 117/218, 'Local government reform: memorandum by the Minister of Health', 14 July 1943.
54   CAB 117/221, 25 November 1943.
55   House of Commons Debates, 22 September 1943, col. 196. The complete text of the government's considered response to the representations for an inquiry into local government was published in Hansard that same day as a letter from Jowitt to the chairmen of the AMC and CCA, at cols 196–8.
56   HLG 68/111, 'Local government reform: memorandum by the Minister of Health', 15 July 1944.
57   HLG 68/111, 'Local government reform: memorandum by the Minister of Health', 15 November 1944.
58   Jeffreys, *Labour and the Wartime Coalition*, p. 195.
59   Ministry of Health, *Local Government in England and Wales*, p. 2.
60   P. B. Johnson, *Land Fit for Heroes: the planning of British reconstruction, 1916–1919* (University of Chicago Press, Chicago, 1968); P. Abrams, 'The failure of social reform, 1918–1920', *Past and Present*, April 1963, pp. 43–64.

61 A. J. P. Taylor, *The Origins of the Second World War* (Penguin, London, 1964), p. 151.
62 K. Young and P. L. Garside, 'The prospect of war and its impact', in *Metropolitan London: politics and urban change, 1831–1981* (Edward Arnold, London, 1982), ch. 8.
63 B. Headey, *Housing Policy in the Developed Economy* (Croom Helm, London, 1978), p. 169.
64 HLG 101/216, 8 March 1944.
65 CAB 87/56, Official Committee on Post War Internal Economic Problems, 'The long-term housing policy', 25 November 1942.
66 R. Forrest and A. Murie, *Selling the Welfare State: the privatisation of public housing* (Routledge, London, 1988), pp. 42–3.
67 *Final Report of the Expert Committee on Compensation and Betterment*, Cmd. 6383 (HMSO, London, 1942), para. 9.
68 G. and E. G. McAllister, *Homes, Towns and Countryside: a practical plan for Britain* (Batsford, London, 1945).
69 M. A. Pink, *Social Reconstruction* (Nelson, London, 1943), p. 205.
70 Ministry of Town and Country Planning, *The Control of Land Use*, Cmd. 6537 (HMSO, London, 1944).
71 J. B. Cullingworth, *Housing Needs and Planning Policy* (Routledge and Kegan Paul, London, 1960), pp. 66–8.
72 Cullingworth, *Reconstruction and Land-use Planning*, chs 4, 6 and 7.
73 Cullingworth, *Reconstruction and Land-use Planning*, pp. 257–8.
74 P. Addison, *Now the War is Over* (Jonathan Cape, London, 1985), pp. 74–5.
75 Under the Housing (Emergency Powers) Act 1939, supplemented by later War Damage Acts in 1941 and 1943.
76 Addison, *Road to 1945*, p. 267.
77 Gosden, *Education in the Second World War*, p. 238.
78 Addison, *Road to 1945*, p. 172.
79 B. Simon, *Education and the Social Order 1940–1990* (Lawrence and Wishart, London, 1991), pp. 57–60.
80 S. J. Curtis, *History of Education in Great Britain*, 6th edn (University Tutorial Press, London, 1965), p. 377.
81 Simon, *Education and Social Order*, pp. 36–7.
82 Simon, *Education and Social Order*, pp. 37–8.
83 Quoted in Simon, *Education and Social Order*, pp. 44–5.
84 Quoted in A. Land, R. Lowe and N. Whiteside, *The Development of the Welfare State, 1939–1951* (HMSO, London, 1992), p. 141.
85 Board of Education, *Educational Reconstruction*, Cmd. 6458 (HMSO, London, 1943), para. 2.
86 Board of Education, *Educational Reconstruction*, paras 27–31.

50 The Spirit of Reconstruction

87 Board of Education, *Report of the Committee of the Secondary Schools Examination Council, Curriculum and Examinations in Secondary Schools* (HMSO, London, 1943), p. 14.
88 Simon, *Education and Social Order*, p. 61.
89 Gosden, *Education in the Second World War*, p. 380.
90 Quoted in Simon, *Education and Social Order*, p. 63.
91 Gosden, *Education in the Second World War*, pp. 239–40.

3 Building Jerusalem, 1945–1964

As the twentieth century advanced, the county borough and county councils acquired responsibility for an expanding range of social and personal services. Local authorities had long provided sanitary services, as well as police and highway maintenance. Some were providing services such as water, gas and electricity, buses and trams, docks, and libraries. The two major *ad hoc* authorities operating outside the local authority sector, the School Boards and the Boards of Guardians, were brought to an end in 1902 and 1929 respectively, the greater part of their duties being transferred to county boroughs and county councils.

At the end of the nineteenth century, local authority housing activities had been regarded as an aspect of public health, in which slum clearance predominated. The situation changed with the Great War of 1914–18, by which time the shortage of houses and problems of overcrowding had become more apparent. With the Housing and Town Planning Act 1919, the provision of homes was accepted as a social responsibility, and national financial assistance was provided towards the costs of council building. Local authorities began extensive house-building programmes and, by 1939, had built over a million homes. Education was another major area in which the role of local authorities steadily expanded. Since 1904, the local education authorities (LEAs) had been providing both elementary and secondary education. A new structure of primary, secondary and technical education developed, and between the beginning of the century and the outbreak of the Second World War, revenue expenditure on education increased six-fold.[1]

Under the Attlee government, the building of the Welfare State both withdrew functions from local authorities, and at the same time compensated for their loss by giving them new duties. The Education Act of 1944 widened the duties of LEAs in a number of ways and made them responsible for reorganizing their secondary education. The Town and Country Planning Act 1947 centralized responsibility in the hands of counties and county boroughs and introduced a comprehensive system for the control of development. The police and the fire services provide further examples of the transfer of functions to fewer and larger units of operation, the latter being transferred back to local authority control after 1945. After the Police Act 1946, the remaining non-county-borough forces were absorbed into the county police; subsequently, the process continued with the amalgamation of county and county borough forces. The Children Act 1948 gave counties and county boroughs an important responsibility for children in need. This service became the core of the post-war growth in local authority social services, and would merge with welfare services in 1973.

The overall pattern, then, was one of changing responsibilities and growing complexity, coupled with rising expenditure. Local authorities' current expenditure would grow from £949 million in 1949/50 to £10,733 million in 1973/74.[2] Despite the loss of services, the business of local government had become more important and demanding, and its national economic significance greatly enhanced. As a result, the spirit of partnership between central and local government which characterized the first part of the post-war period would come under increasing strain in the second. This development of increasing central control was most apparent in the two local authority services of greatest political visibility: housing and education.

Housing Policies and Programmes

With the end of the war in Europe, attention was urgently turned to the housing problem. As with 1918, popular expectations were running high. No 'homes for heroes' had been promised this time, but the extensive damage from bombing, not just in London but in Coventry, Plymouth and elsewhere, put the housing programme at the forefront of the post-war agenda. At first, the emphasis was on building for general needs to meet the acute housing shortage that resulted from wartime damage and low building rates. During the war a total of 475,000 houses were either destroyed or made permanently uninhabitable, while civilian building had come to a standstill.

The March 1945 white paper set out the coalition's view that 100,000 houses could be built in the first year of peace, and 200,000 in the second.[3] The caretaker government, that filled the interval between Labour's withdrawal from the coalition and their assumption of office after the general election, calculated that a programme of 750,000 new homes would be required to meet the wartime aspirations of separate home for each family, and another half a million to replace the worst of the slums.[4]

In the short term at least, local authorities were to be the vehicles for delivering the post-war housing programme. The role of the Ministry of Health was to advise and supervise the one and a half thousand local housing authorities in England and Wales, who were themselves responsible for licensing private-enterprise houses and for ordering, programming, subsidizing and, often, themselves building council houses and flats. The ministry's role had developed since its foundation in 1919 and, throughout the inter-war period, it had used subsidies as the principal means of encouraging local authorities' house-building. The post-war years saw an extension of this type of financial incentive, increased, reduced or withdrawn according to the apparent housing needs of the day, and the affordability of meeting them.

Subsidies were expected to remain high as long as costs continued to be high, but the underlying assumption was that high costs were a temporary reflection of post-war shortages. Even the Conservative election statement of policy in 1945 accepted that

> prices of materials must be controlled as long as supplies are short. Even so, building costs will be high at first. They must be brought down as rapidly as possible. Subsidies will be necessary for local authorities and for private enterprise alike.[5]

That these shortages continued over the next decade, and were amplified by the competing demands for industrial reconstruction, nationalization and welfare programmes, exposed that assumption as over-optimistic.

The flexibility of subsidy as an incentive gained particular importance from the high political profile that manifesto promises had bestowed upon housing. For the first time, the major parties were competing nationally on the basis of how many homes they could build. Under-performance spelled political exposure, and their fear of the opposition exploiting the housing statistics drove both Labour and Conservative governments to greater efforts as elections approached.

The effect was to create a powerful consensus as to both ends (mass house-building) and means (heavy expenditure on subsidies). Macmillan reminded the Commons, in the second reading debate on his housing bill, that

> houses should be provided for . . . new tenants at rents they can afford to pay and which may be regarded as reasonable in the prevailing conditions. To achieve this the deficit, after fixing what is a fair rent, has to be provided partly by Exchequer grant and partly out of the local rates, and it has always been, since the beginning of this system, in the proportion of three-quarters from the Exchequer and one-quarter from the local rates. This principle has been accepted as equitable ever since the war . . . [6]

This, from a Conservative Minister of Housing, exemplified the common ground between the parties on the provision of social housing.

A major novelty of the post-war period was the presumption, first made by the Churchill government, that private house completions, and not just those achieved by local authorities, should be reckoned in the total. When combined with the view that the market could, in favourable circumstances, deliver more, faster, than the local authorities themselves, this new perspective ensured that the instruments of policy developed in new directions. Conservatives now recognized that local authorities could, as major landholders, impede the private development process if they so chose. As landlords they could pursue low-rent policies, the consequences of which were inimical to the aspiration to home ownership. By the late 1950s, Conservatives were beginning to see the role that local authorities played as the problem, rather than the solution to Britain's housing needs.

The initial post-war consensus on housing foundered on the rock of municipal ownership. In time, a great divide began to open up between the two major parties. Labour increasingly became the party of large-scale public building and low-rent municipal landlordism. The Conservatives embraced the rhetoric of the 'property owning democracy', while increasingly seeking to break the grip that they imagined Labour councils to have on the electoral allegiances of their heavily subsidized tenants. Savage battles over rents were to ensue. Inescapably, as both parties pursued these competing visions, they tightened the grip of Whitehall upon the local housing authorities.

Pitfalls and progress

In October 1945, Aneurin Bevan, *enfant terrible* turned Minister of Health, reviewed the housing situation for the Cabinet.[7] Whereas between the wars a high proportion of new houses had been built by private enterprise for sale, the government would primarily rely on the local authorities over the next few years to build for rent. Within this programme the priority would be letting to lower-income groups. Local authorities would be allowed to issue licenses for the private construction of housing for other people only to the extent that such building would not 'interfere with the progress of the maximum programme which the local authority can carry out'. Even then, such licenses would be subject to conditions as to size, and selling price or rental.

Bevan's vision was a broad one. In his pamphlet *Why Not Trust the Tories?*, Bevan derided the coalition government's housing targets as hopelessly inadequate, compared with the potential production of half a million houses annually.[8] But faced with the stark realities of office, he concentrated on such qualitative aspects of the housing programme as could be realistically achieved. He wanted to see provision for both large and small families, for older and for single persons. The object was to achieve 'balanced communities', and local authorities would be encouraged within this programme to provide some larger houses for letting to middle income groups.[9] Bevan also sought an improved standard for local authority housing, in terms both of space and equipment. 'While we shall be judged for a year or two by the number of houses we build', he told a Labour conference, 'we shall be judged in ten years' time by the type of houses we build'.[10] Housing standards were raised, and local authorities instructed to build houses of an average 1,000 sq. ft, as against previous average of 800 sq. ft, houses which were also to be provided with the most up-to-date amenities. Raising standards was a bold move, and one which would not assist in achieving the crude numerical target of units built.

Within these broad objectives, Bevan offered a staged programme. The first phase was to repair the immediate destruction of war, providing 750,000 houses to re-house all of the families displaced by war damage. Of these, a proportion would have to be temporary prefabricated houses, while conversion and adaptation, and the requisition of empty houses, would also be necessary. This, is essence, was the policy that Labour inherited from the coalition. Bevan's Housing (Financial Provisions) Act 1946 added to it by increasing the amount that the government was authorized to spend on temporary accommodation beyond the limit set in 1944, raising the ceiling on the value of loans that local authorities could offer for house purchase, and empowering the Ministry of Works to control both the purchase and sale of building materials and the selling price of new houses built for sale under license. Local authorities would from now on be able to finance their building by borrowing at advantageous rates from the Public Works Loan Board.

In the second phase, the Labour government would move on to resume the attack on slum clearance and overcrowding that had begun before the war. For this purpose, another half million houses would be required. This target compared with the figure of something like half this number of local authority houses built in slum clearance programmes throughout the 1930s, since when housing conditions had deteriorated dramatically. Thereafter, a third phase would provide a large-scale continuing programme to meet persistent needs. Britain's decaying urban centres would be renewed. The aim would be to provide good permanent home for every family. The implications of this long-term objective were not quantified; but Bevan warned that even Labour's election promise to build five million houses would do no more than eliminate houses built for working-class occupation prior to 1865.

How was this programme to be achieved? Principally, of course, it was to be realized through the local authorities, although there were calls for some new *ad hoc* housing authority to be created in their place.[11] Apart from fresh legislation, measures to improve the output and productivity of building workers, to control costs of materials and to ensure that housing construction had a priority claim on both materials and components were all required. As before the war, the principal instrument of policy was to be the subsidy to local authority building, in this case one which could be varied according to the financial position of individual local authorities. Bevan introduced a new standard Exchequer subsidy to local authorities of £16 10s. annually per house for sixty years, to be matched by a compulsory rate subsidy of £5 10s., doubling the existing subsidy level.

Despite these measures, it proved no easy matter to build Jerusalem.

The grandiose house-building programme got off to a faltering start. Bevan's initial programme for the government's first year was to be no more than 15,000 permanent houses, and 150,000 in the second year. Progress was not helped by the tortuous relations between the government departments involved. 'Ten cooks are spoiling the broth' claimed *Picture Post* in September 1946:

> Mr Dalton, the Chancellor of the Exchequer, is responsible for providing the capital required to pay out the housing subsidies. Mr Arthur Greenwood, the Lord Privy Seal, has certain vague, over-ruling functions. No one quite knows what he does do. Mr Tomlinson, the Minister of Works, directs the building industry, licensing private builders, controlling building materials, and providing temporary and prefabricated permanent homes. Mr Isaacs, the Minister of Labour, has to provide manpower. The Minister of Town and Country Planning can decide against house-building on any site. The Minister of Agriculture must be consulted about rural housing. The Ministry of Supply deals with materials, and especially with the provision of house components, of which there is a serious shortage . . . The tenth cook is Sir Stafford Cripps, who, as President of the Board of Trade, is now calling upon all builders employing more than 50 men to reply to 90 questions.[12]

Shortages of materials, particularly of imported timber, high prices and the rising wages of building workers soon indicated that a review of the programme would be necessary. Additionally, the government's larger economic strategy demanded a greater priority to be given to housing workers in mining and agricultural areas and in the development areas. The vision of the great urban renewal programme to revitalize the cities had begun to fade; by 1947 a competing demand had been identified for 100,000 new homes for miners and agricultural workers for the next year. Industrial needs had hijacked Bevan's programme.

With the economic crisis of 1947, whatever remained of Bevan's original vision disappeared entirely. The Cabinet asked the central planning staff to review and recommend reductions in any projects which did not contribute to exports or to import saving.[13] In these terms, the housing programme was the most vulnerable of all the government's commitments. Cripps, now Chancellor of the Exchequer, told Bevan that 'control of capital investment was meaningless without some reduction in the housing programme'.[14] Bevan himself accepted the cutbacks with the deepest reluctance and had the sympathy of much of the Cabinet; the result was to moderate, rather than slash, the housing targets. In August 1947, Bevan cancelled existing licenses for the building of houses for sale, restricted approval of tenders for building by local authorities to rural and mining areas, and called for a ban on the establishment of new building firms. He hoped that the programme would still deliver 200,000 houses a year. But sensing that the urgency of housing as an issue had slipped, and might slip yet further, he asked that his colleagues should promise to adhere to any revised programme. Despite their concurrence, by October he was having to accept even greater limitations.

For the remainder of the lifetime of the first Attlee government, Bevan fought against pressures from the Investment Programmes Committee.[15] His room for manoeuvre was limited, and relaxing controls on the licensing of private building was one of the few steps he would reluctantly take to reduce the pressures on the local authorities' building programmes. Yet for a while the sheer momentum of the housing programme juggernaut worked in favour of his original plan. The difficulty of reneging on existing contracts, and the rising number of starts, ensured that – despite the reduced target – more than 227,000 homes were actually built in 1948. Also working to protect Bevan's position was the difficulty of bringing about too rapid a contraction without inflicting consequential damage and higher unemployment in industries related to house production, an issue of pressing concern to his Cabinet colleagues.

Yet by 1950 it was clear that the assumptions on which the post-war housing programme had been based were not well founded. Apart from the unforeseen claims on national shortages from other forms of development, which limited the resources available for meeting housing need, it was also clear that the wartime estimates of post-war housing requirements had been falsified by subsequent events. The 1945 white paper had promised 750,000 homes to house those left homeless by the blitz on British cities, on the simplistic assumption that achieving or building to beyond that number would clear the waiting lists. But this had not happened. Instead, demand had continued to grow as expectations rose. The first indications of the persistent post-war problem of satisfying the limitless demand for social housing began to appear.

But if the tide of support for an extensive housing programme had ebbed, it was to flow again, driven this time by electoral pressures. In 1950 the beleaguered Labour government, facing a general election, found itself politically exposed on the housing issue as Conservatives attacked its apparently poor record on house-building. Only in 1948 had the housing achievement anywhere near approached the target, and that fortuitously, as completions overran the government's planned cutbacks. Overall, Labour looked like delivering little more than half the number of new homes promised in 1945. Public dissatisfaction demanded a more extensive house-building programme, and the Conservatives were positioning themselves to satisfy it. In the final months before the 1950 election, Bevan was able to capitalize on the Conservative attack to resist the still further cuts in the building programme now being pressed upon him by Cripps. These, he argued, were now 'politically impossible'. It would be better for the government to take the initiative and restore the programme, 'rather than wait until they were forced to do so in response to political pressure'. With a general election looming, this argument proved decisive. The government accepted a commitment to giving housing a fixed priority in the capital programme and to make spending cuts elsewhere on grounds of 'easing political difficulties'.

Local authorities were inevitably affected by this continuous crisis in the housing programme. But Bevan's task was not simply to build more houses. As Minister of Health, his principal concern was understandably with the creation of the National Health Service. Housing, though an onerous duty, could only be a secondary concern. The episodic progress of house building highlighted the weaknesses of the ministry's ability to co-ordinate policy and secure the necessary resources when its attention was, for much of the time, elsewhere. In 1951, with Bevan no longer in the post, the Labour government took responsibility for housing policy away from the Ministry of Health, merging the housing division with the isolated Ministry of Town and Country Planning to form a new Ministry of Local Government and Planning. As minister, Hugh Dalton brought a new vigour to the housing drive, and succeeded in sustaining the programme in the face of the financial pressures occasioned by the Korean War. In the circumstances, the initial performance of the Labour government on housing policy was not insubstantial. The number of new houses completed rose steeply, from 55,400 in 1946, and 139,690 in 1947, to 227,616 in 1948, a considerable achievement in the context of the times.[16] With the separation of housing and health, a more effective instrument had been created. But it was the Conservatives who were to put it to use.

60   Building Jerusalem

An electoral talisman

The incoming Churchill government built upon the administrative changes introduced in the dying months of its predecessor. The 'planning' title was dropped from the new ministry, a symbolic gesture befitting both the spirit of the times and the new government's intention to dismantle much of Labour's land-use planning regime. An even more intensive focus on housing policies and programmes now became possible.

The contrast between Conservative ebullience and Labour defeatism on the house-building programme undoubtedly contributed to Labour's loss of office. The political commitment of the Conservatives – giving housing a priority 'second only to national defence' – exceeded that of Labour.[17] They had capitalized effectively on Labour's disappointing performance, although their own seemingly extravagant promises were not without risks. A small group of back-benchers had succeeded in securing a commitment by the party to build 300,000 houses a year. It was a high target by the standards of the recent past; indeed, a party policy group under Duncan Sandys had rejected such a target as unrealistic. However, vocal pressure from the floor at the 1950 Blackpool party conference had overwhelmed this caution. Churchill recognized the electoral advantage of such a promise, accepting the ambush gracefully in his end of conference speech.

It fell to Harold Macmillan to deliver this programme. Appointed to lead the new Ministry of Housing and Local Government, he was the first – though not the last – incoming minister there to harbour the mistaken impression that 'houses were produced by direct contract between the ministry and the builders, working hardly at all through local authorities'.[18] Disappointed not to have won a more powerful portfolio, Macmillan nonetheless exploited its possibilities to the full. The experience was to prove his making as a senior government minister.

Far from being a liability, the promise of 300,000 houses a year actually proved useful to Macmillan. Faced, like his predecessors, with Treasury demands for expenditure cuts and the restriction of imported timber, Macmillan proved implacable. As Chancellor, Butler was repeatedly defeated by his junior, the Minister of Housing, who more often than not had the Prime Minister's support. The 300,000 homes target was of such political significance for the party in the country that it proved 'a wonderful breastplate for any spending minister to have at his disposal, and Macmillan knew just when to buckle it on in any Cabinet dispute'.[19]

Similarly, the clear advantage of maintaining a high degree of stability in the housing programme worked in Macmillan's favour. Citing a 1950 ministry working party report, he argued on grounds of economic efficiency that the building industry ought not to be looked at as a tap which could be turned on and off for economic reasons.[20] When Butler proposed cuts in the housing programme on the contrary grounds that it was displacing investment away from more productive purposes, Macmillan's response emphasized the political costs of restricting the programme. The effects would be serious: 'the public as well as the building industry would be greatly discouraged'.[21] Moreover, 'slow progress was a matter of public criticism and would cause the government 'considerable embarrassment in Parliament.[22] These arguments were decisive, as Churchill judged it unwise to curtail the programme, pointing out that failure to rebuild the blitzed cities would leave the government dangerously exposed.

With such powerful backing, the housing drive was given a virtually unimpeded run.[23] The target was achieved and surpassed when, in 1953, 319,000 houses were built, Macmillan suavely announcing that 'we had done the job in the second full year of the government's administration'.[24] In the following year, the total reached 348,000. By 1957, a total of 2.5 million new houses and flats had been built, three-quarters of them by local authorities, who since 1954 had enjoyed a greater degree of freedom from central direction. Macmillan's success also owed much to more generous subsidies under the Housing Act 1952 and the stimulus to private builders of a relaxation of licensing, before licences were removed altogether in November 1954. Yet many in government thought the programme, with its single-minded insistence on sheer numbers, misconceived.[25]

By the mid-1950s, however, the apparent consensus on housing policy was disintegrating, as the two parties diverged from the shared position of 1945. The Labour party was moving towards a policy of municipalization of all privately rented accommodation, while the Conservatives increasingly supported owner-occupation. Two issues were to characterize this divide in the remainder of the post-war period: the increasing Conservative emphasis on private ownership; and the bitterly polarizing question of housing rents and subsidies.

Boosting private ownership

The Conservatives' questioning of the value of subsidies that benefited tenants at the expense of local ratepayers also lent support to the more fundamentalist strain of Conservatism. As early as July 1952, Lord Woolton had been urging the need to 'apply the principle of a property-owning democracy . . . instead of persisting in the Socialist policy of herding people into heavily-subsidised council houses'.[26] The promotion of owner-occupation was expected to foster Conservative rather than Socialist values and was thus part of a larger strategy of making Britain free and independent. Macmillan, who was sympathetic, pointed up the deterrents to private building, with high municipal subsidies and interest rates loading the dice against the prospective owner–occupier. As far as government was directly concerned, it was the licensing system that provided the most direct control over private house-building. Yet, while housing starts were picking up rapidly in the spring of 1952, the high costs of building precluded even the number of licenses granted from being taken up.[27]

Provided that these problems could be solved, there was clear scope for an expansion of the private-sector contribution. By September 1952 a total of 275,263 houses had been completed, with local authorities and housing associations providing 219,206 of these, the new town corporations 8,829, government departments 10,854 and the private sector 36,374 houses.[28] The attraction of private building was that, being unsubsidized, it represented no charge on the Exchequer.[29] And if the market could be encouraged, the politically sensitive national housing targets could be met without having to depend exclusively on the cumbersome apparatus of municipal building.

In June 1952, Macmillan argued for boosting private house-building from 40,000 starts annually to 70,000 or more, and for reforming the system of distributing licenses in order to overcome 'recalcitrant' local authorities, who 'on ideological grounds do not issue licenses at all'. As a legacy of the post-war controls, local authorities were supposed to have regard to the need for private housing, but it was a need which they themselves would assess. Macmillan proposed to abolish the needs test for licensing private building. Instead, local authorities should issue licenses to build at the rate of one for every house they built for let, as against the then ratio of one to five. They would be allowed to exceed this ratio where private building could be further encouraged, and it was anticipated that an additional 15,000 licenses would be issued in the remaining six months of the year.

In the event, the growth in private housing development exceeded all expectations. In July 1954, Macmillan reported 'a large and gratifying' increase in private house-building, and it became necessary to restrict local authority building both by administrative means and by applying a lower rate of subsidy to general needs building than for slum clearance. He intended that as private house-building increased, subsidies for local authority general needs building could be reduced further, and ultimately abolished. It was in part by this means – switching emphasis from social housing to the private market – that the house completion totals were able to rise as rapidly as they did (table 3.1), with all the resultant political credit for the Conservative government. This expansion of private building actually outran the capacity of the financial system to sustain purchases, prompting the government to intervene to support the building societies' lending programmes.[30]

Table 3.1 House-building completions, 1951–5

	1951	1952	1953	1954 est.	1955 est.
Local authorities, New Towns, housing associations and government departments	172,280	205,602	255,858	270,000	249,000
Private enterprise	22,551	34,320	62,921	93,000	133,000
Total	194,831	239,922	318,779	363,000	382,000

Source: Cabinet minutes, 20 July 1954.

So substantially had the government overshot its housing programme targets that a change of direction became possible in 1955. By the end of 1956, more than a million and a half houses would have been built in the lifetime of the Conservative government. Feeling that 'their political promises had been honoured, which gives great authority in charting their next course of action', the 300,000 houses policy could now be safely abandoned.[31] By now, the local authorities' position in the provision of housing was diminishing. They had lost their access to the Public Works Loan Board, and were forced instead to look to the money markets to finance their building.[32] Rising costs and debt charges were to sharply increase the polarization of housing policy, for the issue of 'who pays?' – the tenant or the ratepayer – became more acute under this greater cost burden.

For the moment, though, it seemed necessary only to reduce the size of the new build programme. For 1957, public-sector housing starts would run at a level 40 per cent lower than in 1954, with further reductions to about half the 1954 level foreseen for 1958/59 onward. Few noticed that the commitment to clear the slums was unlikely to be met on this basis, a matter which in time would come to prove a major embarrassment to the Conservative government.

Much had happened in the housing field since the end of the war, but there had been no chance to pause and take stock since Bevan had articulated his own vision in 1945. Macmillan now echoed the larger concerns of the Bevan programme when he brought to the Cabinet his 'grand design' in January 1953, hurriedly assembled over the recent Christmas break.[33] With home ownership accounting for just 3.75 million of Britain's 13.5 million homes, and private rental accounting for more than seven million, there was scope for bringing about substantial shifts in the pattern of housing to favour owner-occupation.

Macmillan's 'grand design' (no doubt an irritating title) took a three-part approach to the comprehensive reform of housing: the promotion of owner-occupation; the reform of private rents; and the reform of public housing subsidies. To promote owner-occupation, Macmillan proposed that local authorities should be encouraged to dispose of their housing to existing tenants, and be allowed to sell freehold sites for development. The building licence scheme should be liberalized, offered as of right to individuals and in small blocks to speculative builders. The rent proposals, which originally formed part of Macmillan's grand design, were put on ice for a while. The eventual white paper, *Housing: a comprehensive policy*, appeared equally grandiose in first draft, but a last-minute fit of modesty saw it re-titled as *Houses: the next steps*. The Cabinet hailed Macmillan's scheme as 'ingenious, courageous, equitable and right'.[34] It was certainly forthright: 'private enterprise', declared Macmillan,

> must play an ever-increasing part in the provision of houses for general needs, and will continue to be given every encouragement ... Any increase in private enterprise house-building, whether for letting or for sale, would in some measure lighten the ever-growing burden of housing subsidies, the rates of which cannot continue indefinitely at their present high level.[35]

Yet Macmillan was not oblivious to the political risks that his proposal to taper off the subsidies carried in the run-up to a general election. If restriction was too severe, it might depress local completions to below the level achieved in 1951 by the outgoing Labour government, and this would provide the opposition with powerful ammunition. Some ministers were even more wary. They saw the length of the housing waiting lists and the visibility of families in acute need as being of major electoral significance. In the event, they were to prove the more far-sighted.

The question of housing need also bore upon a policy which was to achieve prominence only in the 1970s: the sale of council houses to sitting tenants. The Attlee government had maintained the wartime policy of refusing consent to sales, on the grounds of the need to maintain the maximum number of dwellings available for letting. Conservative MPs had occasionally harried Labour over the refusal to restore the pre-war permission to sell, arguing from grounds of tenant choice and the need to reduce public borrowing. Labour ministers cited in reply the questions of equity, and their own hostility to public assets passing into private hands.[36] Macmillan's relaxation of licensing carried over to a general consent for local authorities to sell houses, notifying the ministry only on completion of the sale. The Housing Act 1952 established a general consent, removing the statutory requirement for authorities to obtain the best price, and providing a five-year right of reversion on re-sale. Despite continuous urging from back-benchers that the government should do more to override the reluctance of most local authorities to sales, the MHLG continued to stand aside.

As a result, the number of sales was initially negligible, running at just 5,825 between 1952 and 1956. Although sales levels picked up slightly after 1960, when a new general consent was issued, the national total for 1957–64 remained as low as 16,000.[37] The pattern appeared to be one of a fairly large minority of authorities selling relatively few houses each, on a more or less *ad hoc* basis. Sales as a policy still lay in the future.

Later Cabinets were undivided on the need to boost private ownership by whatever means, from promoting council house sales to aiding home purchase. In 1958, stamp duty was sharply reduced on cheaper houses, in an attempt to help young couples attain the first rung on the housing ladder. After considerable debate, a scheme for government support to building societies was introduced to boost their lending and so finance the incipient demand for private ownership. Between 1959 and 1962, the Macmillan government (as it now was) lent £100 million to building societies to encourage lending on pre-1919 housing. In 1962, owner–occupiers were freed from the hated Schedule A income tax liability, charged on the putative rental value of their houses. The success of the Conservative strategy first clearly articulated by Lord Woolton in 1952 soon became apparent. In 1951, only 29 per cent of households were in the owner-occupied sector. By 1964, when the Conservatives left office, that proportion exceeded 45 per cent.[38] Hailed as a success, that shift changed the pattern of political alignments, and could not be ignored by Labour. Less obviously, it was to imprison later governments in policies of lavish subsidy to owner-occupation.

Subsidies for whom?

The acute housing shortages in most areas of Britain had been relieved as the target of 300,000 homes in each of the years 1953, 1954 and 1955 was successfully met and exceeded. Bevan's notion that general needs could be met in time through the first phase of tackling shortages seemed – mistakenly, as it turned out – to have been vindicated. Attention now turned to the problem of the slums. More generous subsidies were available to meet the special needs of clearance re-housing, the relief of overcrowding and poor housing conditions, for housing the elderly, and for assisting the movement of population through overspill or town development schemes. Special compensation for well maintained houses, introduced in 1935, was revised in 1956; and authorities were empowered to 'patch' unfit houses to provide temporary accommodation in areas of local shortage.

The Conservatives' election manifesto for 1955 had promised to 'root out the slum at an increasing pace'. In order to switch resources from general needs building to slum clearance on a sufficiently substantial scale, it was necessary to abolish the general needs subsidies. The Housing Subsidies Act 1956 provided for subsidies to be given to only those requiring it. It was hoped that local authorities would be able to continue building the new houses that they required with less Exchequer assistance. As Duncan Sandys, Macmillan's successor, explained:

> Housing subsidies are granted with one object, and one object only, namely, to ensure that nobody, through lack of means, shall be prevented from having a decent, healthy home . . . the purpose is to bridge the gap between the full un-subsidised rent and what the tenant can reasonably afford to pay .... We on this side of the House do not agree that it is in the general interest

to keep the cost of housing artificially low for all council tenants regardless of their incomes. The justification for housing subsidies is need and, in our opinion, need alone. Housing need is no longer synonymous with financial need. There is no doubt that the rents of a large number of council houses are at present being subsidised to a greater extent than the financial circumstances of the individual tenants require.[39]

The Conservatives' concern over subsidy being used to support artificially low rents was as much about electoral politics as it was about public finance.[40] Weekly rents for pre-war houses could be as little as seven shillings, against an average manual wage of around £10. The total cost to the taxpayer of this subsidy amounted to more than £50 million annually in 1954/55 – up from £30 million in 1951/52 – with another third of this sum falling upon ratepayers.[41] The reduction of general needs subsidy agreed in 1955 as a means of diverting resources to slum clearance and the relief of overcrowding – although a success in terms of accelerating demolition – did not bite immediately, as it would only apply to new homes contracted from that date.[42] As a more immediate step, therefore, the statutory requirement to transfer any increases in revenue to the Housing Revenue Account (where they could be used to subsidize future rents) was abolished in October 1955. This was to permit local authorities, if they preferred, 'to use any savings they may make to reduce the rate burden, and will give them for the first time an incentive to adopt realistic rent policies'. It was the first move in an emerging polarization on the question of who should benefit from housing expenditure. Yet it was no more than a permissive provision. It would do nothing to challenge the more generous support given by Labour authorities to their tenants.[43]

The policies of Labour-controlled local authorities were by 1960 an increasing source of anxiety to the government. The use of subsidies to depress rents was understandably popular with actual and potential council tenants, and Labour's espousal of municipalization deepened the problem. It took the vigour of a Henry Brooke to challenge this development. Changing the subsidy system would help in the long term to eliminate politically inspired rent differentials, and would be welcomed 'by all ratepayers other than council tenants'.[44] Brooke stopped short, however, of proposing any action which would have immediate effect. His main contribution was to propose a new strategy for social housing. This was to provide public funding in order to finance the development, by

68   *Building Jerusalem*

housing associations, of homes for letting at cost rents. Brooke's immediate proposal was for a pilot scheme to demonstrate that there was an effective demand for new houses and flats at realistic rents and that the 'government have a policy other than munipalisation for the provision and management of rented houses'. Without such a breakthrough they would have 'no choice but to acquiesce in a position in which housing supply was increasingly divided between owner occupation and municipal subsidised housing'.[45]

The politics of squalor

The Conservative government juggled subsidies and dreamed of a 'third sector' of social housing. Meanwhile, a new housing crisis was emerging, with a growing problem of homelessness and scarcity of rented accommodation. In response, local authorities were granted new powers to lead 'the attack on squalor'. Brooke's white paper *Housing in England and Wales* of February 1961 conceded that

> So far, local authorities have not been in a position to do much to improve matters . . . The government wants to see an attack on the squalid living conditions to be found in these houses which are not only bad in themselves, but may also breed delinquency and crime. The government propose to provide stronger and more selective powers than those that have existed hitherto.[46]

As many as 600,000 slums remained to be cleared. Yet the problem was not just one of pockets of slum housing, but one of a general shortfall in the provision of housing of a satisfactory standard, easily accessible to the poorer families. The answer was to bring back the general need subsidy in a complicated formula which related the amount of support to the financial needs of different areas. The government affirmed that local authorities should 'continue to build for the needs which only they can meet'.[47] A further white paper from the enthusiastic Keith Joseph in 1963 emphasized the 'need for a larger local authority programme, building for those who cannot meet the full cost of housing, and tackling the comprehensive redevelopment of slum or other decayed areas'.[48] Policy was swinging back towards a revival of the local authority role.

The reason was not hard to find. Housing – and by extension the

Conservative government – was getting a bad, indeed worsening, press. The planned contraction of council house building, formerly opaque, was now 'becoming known and disliked', having 'dawned on many not previously interested'. New estimates of future housing needs 'have exposed both the massive character of the future problem and the sizeable shortfall of current accomplishments'.[49] The progressive switch of resources from municipal programmes to private construction left the expanding middle class better-housed; but the contrast with the squalor of the inner cities became the more pronounced. A new survey in 1965 was to show 824,000 slums, much the same as a decade earlier. Demolition was proceeding at the rate of between 60,000 and 70,000 houses a year, which, although a great increase on the earlier post-war record, was scarcely more than that attained in 1936. A huge problem of decayed, unfit houses still persisted in many areas, especially the older larger towns. Yet the nemesis of postwar housing policy lay not in the vagaries of the housing programme figures, but in the 'creeping de-control' of private rents under the Rent Act 1957 which released perhaps two million tenancies into the free market in a short space of time.[50]

The de-control of the rents of many private dwellings following the Rent Act – dubbed a 'landlords' charter' by Labour – had been accompanied by the arming of local authorities with numerous new powers for enforcement of standards, and the regulation of relations between landlords and tenants. But they were not adequate to cope with the pressures arising from creeping de-control whereby, under the Rent Act 1957, a letting ceased to be controlled when the existing tenancy was terminated. The facility to move lettings out of the controlled sector had encouraged unscrupulous landlords to lever out their tenants at an early date; the worst did not stop short of intimidation. When the activities of slum landlord Peter Rachman were publicly exposed, 'Rachmanism' came to symbolize the longer term failures of Conservative housing policy. Opposition leader Harold Wilson linked the rise of Rachmanism directly to the 1957 Act, which Labour pledged to repeal. It was an association that was hard to brush off. Joseph's establishment of a Committee of Inquiry into the housing situation in London could do little to save the situation. Nor did his last-ditch proposals to allow local authorities to take over multi-occupied houses for up to five years to provide for the safety, welfare and health of the residents, and to use their powers of compulsory acquisition in cases of tenants threatened with eviction or exorbitant rents. With three million people living in slum housing, the Conservatives were fatally tarnished. Despite a year of record housing output – 374,000 completions, of which 218,000 were built by private enterprise, and 156,000 by public authorities – the housing scandals of the early 1960s had so undermined their support that the only surprise was the small margin of their eventual defeat in October 1964.

Education in Schools

Alongside housing and town planning, education received considerable attention during the war, and produced the first legislative initiative of the period of reconstruction. Although education was a matter on which Butler led as President of the Board of Education, Churchill himself could be brought in to provide the occasional inspirational element: 'When the war is won', he promised, 'it must be one of our aims to work to establish a state of society where the advantages and privileges which hitherto have been enjoyed by the few shall be more widely shared by the men and youth of the nation'.[51] Such promises were largely tactical, however. In both wartime and during his 'Indian summer' of 1951–5, Churchill took little interest in the subject.[52]

Butler's white paper on *Educational Reconstruction*, published in July 1943, forecast the contents of the coming bill. The ensuing Education Act 1944 declared as its aim the 'complete overhaul of the statutory system of education' and came into immediate effect, with the exception of clauses dealing with universal free secondary education. In May 1945, with the coalition still in power, the Ministry of Education issued a pamphlet – *The Nation's Schools* – proposing a tripartite system of secondary schools – grammar, modern and technical – as the most appropriate way of implementing the 1944 reforms. The paper effectively headed off demands for more radicalism; 'It would be a mistake', Butler and Chuter Ede had argued, 'to plunge too hastily on a large scale into a revolutionary change... innovation is not necessarily reform'.[53] There was in any case little support for radical change, and the tripartite system represented the national consensus. Nevertheless, the existence of grammar, technical and modern schools presumed some mechanism of selection, and this was to prove the most contentious issue in the post-war history of British education.

The first step taken to establish the new system was to dissolve the Board of Education, and set up a national ministry. The Minister of Education would direct the national policy in education and ensure that it was carried out by the local authorities.[54] Section 1 of the Act set out the minister's duty

> to promote the education of the people of England and Wales and the progressive development of institutions devoted to that purpose, and to secure the effective execution by local authorities, under his control and direction, of the national policy for providing an varied and comprehensive educational service in every area.

In this, the minister would need advice. The relationship between local education provision and the central government had until that point been mediated through a consultative committee of the Board of Education. Now, two central advisory councils for education were established, one for England and the other for Wales, largely made up of people who had 'experience of the statutory system of public education'.

Other players were drawn in at the local level. Section 76 of the Act ensured a degree of parental participation while abstaining from laying down any means by which it might be obtained. The new requirement was highly general:

> In the exercise and performance of all powers and duties conferred and imposed on them by this Act the Minister and local education authorities shall have regard to the general principles that, so far as is compatible with the provision of efficient instruction and training and the avoidance of unreasonable public expenditure, pupils are to be educated in accordance with the wishes of the parents.

Although this concession to parents fell far short of the empowerment for which they were to wait for another three decades, it ensured that in the development of local education schemes neither central direction nor local initiative could be counted upon to win public support.

The abandonment of the Board of Education, and with it the permissive regime that had characterized education since 1902, was not without its critics. Some thought this an unwelcome *dirigisme*, and argued that the Act conferred excessive powers on the minister. Undoubtedly, the Act represented a greater subordination of the local education authorities, albeit one which presented in terms of a new partnership between central and local government. Butler promised to maintain the spirit of joint working which had developed since 1902, eschewing the role of dictator, but he was unapologetic about having taken the statutory powers to compel 'backward' or 'laggard' local authorities to carry out their duties.

Despite these powers, the approach which the coalition bequeathed to post-war Britain was one of coaxing towards consensus. In his inaugural message to the LEAs, Butler declared:

> The Education Act is now the law of the land. To convert legal phraseology into a living force will call for great and sustained exertion. I look, therefore, with confidence to authorities to join with the ministry in tackling the new responsibilities which the new Act lays on us. Let us see to it that the children and young people of our country derive real profit from this, the first measure of social reconstruction which has been passed in these historic days, and is born of a faith in the part that education has to play in shaping the future destinies of our country.[55]

Just what was that part, and what that faith, proved more contestable than Butler hoped. As Britain moved into the 1950s, different approaches to education, different values and different local programmes began to be articulated within this framework of the 1944 Act.

The structure of educational provision

Having established a strong central ministry, the Act in turn reconstituted the structure of local education authorities, abolishing the district councils as Part III authorities, and vesting all powers in 146 county and county borough councils. The Act also gave the power to the minister to combine small areas into joint education boards, a step taken only in the City and Soke of Peterborough. These changes were generally hailed as a major and long overdue rationalization of local education. The Part III authorities had been originally scheduled as LEAs in 1902. The subsequent Local Authorities (Education) Act 1931 prohibited the establishment of any new LEAs, which had the effect of side-stepping conflict between rapidly growing district councils and their counties on education matters. It nevertheless led in time to great anomalies. The 1944 white paper itself cited the contrast between Harrow UDC, with its 183,000 population (which was not an LEA) and Tiverton in Devon, with a population of under 10,000 in the same year (which was). In the first case, adaptation to suburban growth had been frustrated; in the second, adaptation to rural decline.

This centralization of education under a small number of powerful county and county borough councils did nothing to appease the recently expanded urban districts, which – like Harrow and its neighbours in Middlesex – stood to gain nothing. For their part, the demoted authorities stood to lose all. Their status was reduced to the mere provision of advice as district committees. This change generated such intense controversy as to force the coalition government to backtrack:

> instead of the proposal that district committee should be entrusted with the general duty of keeping the needs of their areas under review, and of making recommendations to the county education committee, there is substituted a system of delegation of functions to divisional executives representing individual county districts or groups of them. The divisional executives will ... prepare and submit their own annual estimates of expenditure.[56]

County councils were not obliged to establish these divisional executives. Those that were established – some 171 of them – gained wider powers than the former Part III authorities. Some larger districts were also able to claim the lesser 'excepted district' status, whereby they could prepare their own plans for primary and secondary education in consultation with their county council. Pressure from the local authorities forced further concessions, increasing the number of excepted districts. This then was the structure which was to sustain the provision of local education for the next thirty years: county and county borough councils as fully fledged LEAs; divisional executives exercising delegated powers on a district basis within a county; and excepted districts, with a local planning role.

The Act placed upon the local education authorities the duty of bringing about the 'spiritual, moral, mental and physical development of the community' by ensuring that efficient education was provided through the three stages of primary, secondary and further education. With this vision of education as a life-long process, the Act required a fundamental reorganization of local schools system. To this end, the minister required the preparation of local development plans, the approval of which would bring them about by a ministerial Order. The plans were required – and were mostly delivered – by 1 April 1946. Their implementation was to prove more difficult, as wartime shortages, and competition from the housing programme, precluded the rolling forward of the school building programme at the rate which the development plans envisaged.

The politics of educational provision

Ellen Wilkinson was Labour's first Minister of Education, and within six months had agreed the issue of a circular on *The Organisation of Secondary Education* which drew a clearer distinction between grammar schools, modern schools and technical schools, while leaving the door fractionally open for the introduction of non-selective common schools. This was a policy strongly advocated by the egalitarian elements in the Labour party, who had vehemently rejected the Norwood report's assumption of 'gold, silver and iron children'. In other respects a fierce egalitarian, Wilkinson nevertheless upheld the grammar school tradition. She had little knowledge of or interest in the case for the common school. A leading member of the National Association of Labour Teachers, the principal pressure group for comprehensives, judged that 'She didn't know her subject. She relied entirely on officials, when you went on a delegation, she was surrounded by officials and she tried to wriggle out of anything she could.'[57]

The divisions in the party on this issue were not reflected in the government itself, and it was from within the party that most of the opposition came. The National Association of Labour Teachers claimed that the tripartite system involved a rejection of the polarized belief in secondary education for all, for:

> The Ministry . . . implied that the majority of children were not capable of benefiting from a grammar-school education, so that access to the universities would only be through schools which were to be the preserve of a fortunate minority.[58]

An opportunity had been missed to plan education on Socialist principles; as the party conference heard in 1950:

> We are moving as Socialists to abolish the class method of entry into avenues of life and avenues of careers. It would be a supreme tragedy if in the years of Socialist government we threw out the devil of class snobbery and allowed the worse devil of intellectual snobbery to creep in its place.[59]

Wilkinson's last contribution to the development of education policy was to contribute a foreword to *The New Secondary Education*, a circular issued, after her death, in June 1947. This, the considered view of the Labour government on education to date, confirmed a rigid tripartism, apparently condemning three-quarters of the nation's children to an inferior, and wholly instrumental, education. Casting the Butler ideal of 'parity of esteem' cynically aside, the circular barred all but grammar schools from entering their children for external examinations, thus ensuring that the school certificate would be attainable only for the minority of children. It was an approach against which Wilkinson was to rail impotently, but only in private, as a triumph of official influence and political caution over social needs.[60] With Wilkinson's early death, George Tomlinson took over at education. His reforms to schools examinations set the pattern for the following decades, dropping the earlier prohibition on entry, but setting so high a standard of attainment that only the children who benefited from the selective system could hope to acquire qualifications.

If the issue of selection was to dominate the post-war politics of education, the basic lines of division were laid down in these first post-war years. But the most striking feature of the debate in retrospect was the scarcity of support for comprehensive schools. Promoting them had notionally been party policy since the 1946 and 1947 party conferences, but Labour ministers – and many ordinary supporters – took a meritocratic approach, favouring the grammar school system for the opportunities that it afforded to the bright working-class boy. That widespread view – it *was* the post-war consensus – had a decisive effect on the development of school systems by the LEAs.

The central issue was the selection process inherent in tripartism, and the harmful consequences that flowed from segregation. The rigidities of selection arose from the necessity of a break point from which children were routed into their grammar, modern, or technical schools at an early age. Such a decision was seen as shaping a child's life-chances once and for all. Some, moved by an egalitarian spirit, deplored the separatism of selection, which built barriers between those who attained that prize and those who had not. The only solution, it was argued, was to have 'a common school until the recognised leaving age' – the comprehensive school.[61] This conclusion was to mark out the principal battleground of central–local relations in the field of education.

Developing school systems

Other than specifying a transitional age of eleven, the Butler Act had been silent on the form of organization that LEAs might choose for their plans and provision. The relevant clause simply stated that secondary education – that is, 'full-time education suited to the needs of senior pupils' – must be provided, offering such variety of instruction and training as 'may be desirable in view of their different ages, abilities and aptitudes'. LEAs had been obliged to comply with the 1944 Act's requirement of a clean break at age eleven. In developing their school plans, most LEAs were influenced not only by the new Ministry of Education's guidance, but also by the philosophy of the Norwood report, and opted for its recommended tripartite arrangement.

How were these new school systems to be brought about? The 1944 Act laid down that the necessary reorganization of education should be accomplished by the usual methods of co-operation between LEAs and the ministry. Every local authority was required to submit, for approval by 1 April 1946, a development plan covering the next twenty years, setting out its proposals for secondary education. The plans, once approved, would be brought into effect by subsequent ministerial Order.

The great majority of LEAs managed to submit their plans on time, adopting the tripartite system as the basis of their proposals. Some, notably the London and Middlesex County Councils, that of the West Riding and the City of Coventry, decided instead in favour of a comprehensive system which drew no distinction on grounds of ability. To be effective, such schools had to contain at least 1,200 pupils, a requirement which itself drew criticisms of anonymity and the loss of the individuality of the child. It was also difficult to achieve in the circumstances of the day. The feasibility of educational experiments was limited by the shortage of building materials and labour, and the competition for their employment in the building of homes. Housing had greater political priority than education for Attlee's ministers, and sound finances greater priority than either. These shortages of resources mattered, because non-selective or 'common' schools would require large sites and extensive new buildings, to accommodate the size of intake required to sustain a sufficiently large sixth form in what came to be termed the 'comprehensive' school.

The LCC in particular was regarded even by some sympathizers as rash and doctrinaire for its decision to implement the comprehensive pattern across the entire capital.[62] Within the ministry itself, a clearer conception was beginning to emerge of what was involved in the idea of a common school. It became obvious that common schools and grammar schools could not coexist, and LEAs were told that selective schools should not share catchment areas with comprehensive schools. Indeed, the strict scrutiny to which the Ministry of Education subjected LEAs' plans was the principal factor in limiting the extent to which comprehensive schools could be introduced. When the Middlesex County Council submitted its county-wide scheme, Tomlinson approved plans for only two schools.[63]

Labour ministers had been hesitant, at best, in their willingness to accept comprehensive schools. They were anathema to Conservatives at the local level and their victory on the Middlesex County Council in 1949 brought about the prompt abandonment of the county's plans for comprehensive schools. Grammar schools, the Conservatives argued, had to be maintained, and one of their best defences was to impugn the motives of those who espoused the comprehensive system. Nationally, the party was quick to organize Conservative-minded teachers, encouraging them to 'exert proper influence where desirable and to report on the activities of LEAs'.[64] The Conservative and Unionist Teachers' Association affirmed its belief in 'the educational value of the separate grammar, technical and modern secondary school', and deplored 'any attempt to replace the tripartite system with comprehensive schools', which it saw as 'a calculated political move with no foundation whatever in educational expediency'.[65] The Association criticized comprehensive schools as too large and warned of the harmful effects of teaching together children of mixed abilities. It also ensured that its views shaped party conference agendas over the years; as when, in 1953, conference endorsed the view that 'Socialist proposals for destroying the grammar schools and undermining the position of the independent schools would result in a reduction of educational opportunities for all children.'

When the grammar schools themselves began to fight back against the comprehensive threat, they chose as their platform issue the submersion of the very bright child in the anonymous comprehensive. It was an effective case; a government committed to economic planning, as Labour was, could scarcely ignore the risks of a loss of talent, and at that stage the Labour market was envisaged as highly stratified, requiring just a handful of highly educated specialists. The government accordingly looked to grammar schools to maintain the 'highest academic traditions', and the minimum age of transfer to secondary school was lowered from eleven to ten, to facilitate the progress of children who, at a very early age, were considered exceptionally 'brainy' and 'intellectual':

> Somehow or other we must safeguard them, because we have to safeguard the nation. Brainy children developing into brainy, intellectual adults make a great contribution to the life of the nation; and without them . . . the nation will find itself in a very parlous condition in the decades which lie ahead.[66]

The grammar school continued to gain many powerful and eloquent friends: the secondary modern school had none.

The pro-grammar school stance of the Attlee government drew mounting protests and criticisms from within the Labour party. The party conference of 1950 sought to force the government to implement the Labour party's declared policy of comprehensive schools and to assist those education authorities which intended to develop this type of school. An *ad hoc* committee was given the task of preparing a report on comprehensive schools, which condemned the tripartite system as being 'out of tune with the needs of the day'. Tomlinson remained non-committal, arguing for a 'variety of approach' to the problems posed by secondary education for all. Freed from the constraints of office, the national executive pressed ahead with its declared support for comprehensive system, promising in 1953 to abolish selection at eleven-plus, and publishing a comprehensive *Policy for Secondary Education*, in July 1955. It was a proposal that electrified the grammar schools' defenders.[67] It would be another ten years before Labour could return, this time with determination and with the backing of the teaching profession, to push through comprehensive schemes nation-wide. Meanwhile, educational fashion and local authority practice were to converge steadily throughout the period of the Conservative governments.

Education under the Conservatives

Butler, now Chancellor, could not afford to be especially sympathetic to funding the implementation of his own Education Act: George Tomlinson unkindly accused him of 'the murder of his own child'.[68] The new Minister of Education, Florence Horsbrugh, enjoyed little standing in the

Conservative party, while as minister she operated in the shadow of her Permanent Secretary, Sir John Maud.

The post-war 'baby boom' meant that the pressure on the school system was bound to increase, and Horsbrugh was unable to win additional funds from the Cabinet, from which her initial exclusion clearly signalled the lower priority given to education. Resources were the key, for the problem of school building had plagued the implementation of the 1944 Act from its inception. The war itself had created shortages, for some schools had been handed over to the service authorities for stores or as hospitals and training establishments; often, schools were devoid of even everyday educational equipment. The post-war restrictions on development were just being eased when Labour lost office, to the extent that 1951–4 saw 1,500 new schools completed from the existing pipeline, giving a further 650,000 new places. By 1955 over 2,500 new schools had been built since the war, although these too were insufficient to cope with increasing school rolls.

Nor was the school building programme exempted from the expenditure cuts introduced by the incoming Conservatives. Economies were immediately implemented in 1951, and the building programme was drastically revised downwards in February 1952. Although new school completions would continue to rise as a result of the lags in the programme, between 1951 and 1954 the number of schools under construction fell from 1,204 to 193, at a time when the demand for places was continuing to rise. Education expenditure increased, but only at a modest rate, in the first post-war decade, growth being less than proportionate to the increasing numbers of children entering school.

Coping with numbers and with inadequate buildings at a time when resources were limited left little room for education experiment, not least when comprehensive schools were especially demanding of building resources. The incoming Conservative government pursued in full the very policy on tripartism on which the Labour party remained divided, although some Ministry of Education officials were agnostic on the subject, conceding that the fallibility of early selection constituted an argument for experimenting the comprehensives. When the Conservatives returned to office, there had been no more than a handful of comprehensive schools. By 1954, after three years of Conservative rule, there were still no more than thirteen comprehensives out of 5,000 secondary schools, with a further twenty-one under construction. Not that the Conservatives were engaged in stemming a tide: few among the 146 LEAs were actively promoting comprehensives, only twenty-three of them having proposed any such schools by 1955. Although their numbers were later to rise, the increase would be gradual, passing 200 only in 1964/65.

Nationally, Conservative policy was to defend the tripartite system against the comprehensive movement. Party conferences regularly deplored comprehensives, both on grounds of their size and anonymity and, more significantly, their dubious nature as social engineering. This last was what Horsburgh meant when reassuring the party conference in 1952 that she would deal with the question 'purely as an educational matter'.[69] On this basis, limited experiments were permitted. A Conservative Central Office brief around this time refers to

> a great deal of pressure being put onto the Minister by teachers of all parties to use his powers to prevent the expansion of comprehensive schools, except where they are obviously suitable, i.e., on new housing estates where Grammar schools are not in existence, and in country areas where there are a limited number of secondary school pupils who must, therefore be collected into a comprehensive school.

If Florence Horsbrugh is scarcely remembered – other than for her enthusiastic support for Church schools – her successor, Sir David Eccles, made a greater and more lasting impact upon British education. He promised on his appointment in 1954 never to agree to 'the assassination of the grammar schools'. They were instead to 'continue and flourish'. Eccles brought a new vigour to the Ministry of Education, promising to bring the Butler Act back to life.[70] To that end, he continued to permit experiments in comprehensive schooling, while bolstering the tripartite system with small reforms to permit 'second chance' transfers from secondary moderns and to allow the brighter children remaining there to enter for O-level examinations. At the same time, Eccles acknowledged that there was growing discontent, not about grammar schools, but about the secondary modern schools, on the part of disappointed parents.[71]

These experiments notwithstanding, the comprehensive issue was not really in the forefront of education politics during the mid-1950s. The problems of resourcing rising school rolls, building schools, and training and employing teachers eclipsed issues of doctrine and purpose. In that respect, education had to compete, with relative lack of success, against housing. Not only was it true that both parties would have faced the same crisis in the schools; both would also have placed solving it second in priority to housing until the late 1950s. With the shift in priority away from large-scale public housing construction in 1955, the stage was set for what was hailed as 'a new drive in education'. The growing public interest in education and belief in its value provided a significant political opportunity to the Macmillan government. A new building programme to improve dilapidated schools, and an expansion of teacher education to reduce class sizes, would have positive short-term effects if made in advance of the expected upturn in children staying on at school in the period up to the mid-1980s. Geoffrey Lloyd, who replaced Eccles at education, foresaw expenditure rising from £586 million in 1958 to £780 million in 1964. Hostility to selection was beginning to emerge as a political force, but through expansion the Conservatives hoped to avoid the issue.

For some years, the Labour party had set the agenda for the education debate by focusing on the shortcomings and apparent arbitrariness of the eleven-plus examination. Many natural Conservative voters at the margin of the middle class could be attracted by the reassuring promises of comprehensive schools. Rather than resist the local pressures that would follow, the Macmillan government instead chose expansion, a 'forward drive' to neutralize criticism by 'taking the sting out of the 11 plus examination', by expanding opportunities to 'reconcile national need with individual choice and achievement'. Eccles, returning to education in 1959, continued the expansionist impulse, seeking to convince the Cabinet of the political benefits of outflanking the Labour party. 'Public education is the most telling priority we have', he gushed, 'the best banner for a growth policy' that would outflank the Labour party and, by so improving maintained schools as to close the gap between the public and private sectors, to relegate the comprehensive issue to the sidelines.[72] Spending rose to provide the new schools and meet the demographic pressure. But the Conservatives were still thrown on the defensive, as expectations were rising - and faster than before.

By 1961, the growing reluctance of parents to see their children relegated to secondary modern schools was beginning to break through, leaving the mass of the Conservative party out of touch with popular desires. The Conservative teachers had convinced themselves that 'the comprehensive system of education had in the main been contained' and 'confined largely to an experimental basis during the last 30 years'. They congratulated themselves that they had played a part in ensuring that the general development of secondary education had proceeded 'less on political and more on educational lines'.[73] This sense of satisfaction was not shared the wider party, where the slow growth of comprehensives was seen as a more insidious and worrying process (see table 3.2).

Table 3.2 Development of comprehensive schools, 1961–5

Year	Modern	Grammar	Technical	Comprehensive
1961	3,872	1,284	228	138
1962	3,899	1,287	220	152
1963	3,906	1,295	204	175
1964	3,906	1,298	186	195
1965	3,727	1,285	172	262

Source: Ministry of Education and DES Statistics of Education, 1961–5.

The comprehensive system was gradually taking root as widespread disenchantment with secondary moderns encouraged LEAs – by no means all of them Labour-controlled – to develop reorganization schemes. Not the least of the deeper anxieties at the grass roots arose from the readiness of Conservative ministers – in particular Eccles and his successors – to take a pragmatic view of comprehensive proposals. Conservative activists looked to Central Office for guidance in resisting the growing readiness of Conservative LEAs to contemplate the common school: 'our own people are beginning to believe in the comprehensive system' grumbled one, appealing for help.[74]

That comprehensive proposals were increasingly coming forward reflected the changing opinions of parents and LEA members; that they were able to proceed with increasing ease was due in large part to the pragmatism of Sir David Eccles and, latterly, to the ambiguous stance of Sir Edward Boyle. Boyle, who took over as Minister of Education in July 1962, was inclined to give comprehensive schemes the benefit of any doubt while maintaining a smooth and pragmatic front: 'I should have thought that the right posture for the Conservative party', he wrote in 1963,

> was not to try to arrive at very generalised conclusions about the relative merits of the comprehensive system and the bi-partite system but rather to insist that all new proposals for secondary school organisation ought to be judged on their merits in accordance with the particular needs of the area.[75]

The tide of educational demand was flowing against the Conservatives, and neither Eccles' careful administration and enthusiastic expansion, nor the later progressivism of Sir Edward Boyle, was sufficient to rescue them. Labour had set the new agenda by linking education provision not just to equality and fairness, but to the efficiency of Britain's economy and society, arguing that the modern world needed a broader base of talent than selective schooling could supply. The reform of secondary education was to gain a new impetus when Harold Wilson entered Downing Street in October 1964.

Notes

1. B. Keith-Lucas and P. G. Richards, *A History of Local Government in the Twentieth Century* (George Allen & Unwin, London, 1978), p. 41.
2. M. Minogue, *Documents in Contemporary British Government*, vol. 2 (Cambridge University Press, Cambridge, 1977), p. 301.
3. Ministry of Health, *Housing Policy*, Cmd. 6609 (HMSO, London, 1945).
4. J. Campbell, *Aneurin Bevan and the Mirage of British Socialism* (Weidenfeld and Nicolson, London, 1987).
5. Conservative Election Statement of Policy in 1945, quoted in J. Udal, *Local Authority Housing*, Conservative Political Centre, Local Government Series No. 12 (CPC, London, 1964), p. 14.
6. House of Commons Debates, 22 April 1952, col. 229.
7. Cabinet minutes, 9 October 1945.
8. Campbell, *Aneurin Bevan*, p. 154.
9. The Housing Acts of 1946 and 1949 removed an important limitation under which local authorities could build only for the 'working classes'.
10. Campbell, *Aneurin Bevan*, p. 156.
11. K. O. Morgan, *Labour in Power, 1945–51* (Oxford University Press, Oxford, 1984), p. 167.
12. P. Addison, *Now the War is Over* (Jonathan Cape, London, 1985), p. 60.
13. C. Barnett, *The Lost Victory: British dreams, British realities, 1945–50* (Macmillan, London, 1995), p. 155.
14. Campbell, *Aneurin Bevan*, p. 161.
15. For a full account, see Barnett, *Lost Victory*, pp. 155–64.
16. Morgan, *Labour in Power*, p. 169. Other commentators have been less forgiving: for a view that the Attlee government had no real objectives in housing, but merely reacted to circumstances, see J. R. Short, *Housing in Britain: the post-war experience* (Methuen, London, 1982), p. 55.
17. A. Seldon, *Churchill's Indian Summer: the Conservative government, 1951–55* (Hodder and Stoughton, London, 1981), p. 248.

84 Building Jerusalem

18 Seldon, *Churchill's Indian Summer*, p. 249, n. 19.
19 A. Howard, *RAB: the life of R. A. Butler* (Jonathan Cape, London, 1987), pp. 184–5.
20 CAB 129/53, 'Housing – 1953: memorandum by the Minister of Housing and Local Government', 15 July 1952.
21 Cabinet minutes, 24 July 1952.
22 Cabinet minutes, 6 November 1952.
23 For the administrative arrangements developed to ensure the programme's effective implementation through regional housing production boards, see Seldon, *Churchill's Indian Summer*, p. 251.
24 H. Macmillan, *The Tides of Fortune* (Macmillan, London, 1969), p. 438.
25 Seldon, *Churchill's Indian Summer*, pp. 258–9.
26 Cabinet minutes, 8 July 1952.
27 C(52) 216, 26 June 1952.
28 C(52) 396, 7 November 1952.
29 Specifically, any house built without subsidy would save the Exchequer £577, and the local authority £192, a total of £769 in all.
30 C (58) 195, 26 September 1958.
31 Cabinet minutes, 3 September 1955.
32 Short, *Housing in Britain*, pp. 51–2.
33 Macmillan, *Tides of Fortune*, p. 446.
34 Cabinet minutes, 16 September 1953.
35 CAB 129/62, 'Housing: a comprehensive policy: draft white paper by the Minister of Housing and Local Government', para. 91.
36 R. Forrest and A. Murie, *Selling the Welfare State: the privatisation of public housing* (Routledge, London, 1988), p. 44.
37 Forrest and Murie, *Selling the Welfare State*, p. 45.
38 Short, *Housing in Britain*, pp. 49–50.
39 Quoted in Udal, *Local Authority Housing*, p. 16.
40 A subcommittee of the Central Housing Advisory Committee had reported in 1955 in favour of the marketization of council rents, with concessions available to low-income families.
41 CAB 129/71, 'Investment in housing: memorandum by the Chancellor of the Exchequer', 12 November 1954.
42 Short, *Housing in Britain*, p. 53.
43 CAB 129/101, 'Housing: memorandum by the Minister of Housing and Local Government', 17 June 1960.
44 CAB 129/102, 'Rating and housing policy: memorandum by the Minister of Housing and Local Government', 18 July 1960.
45 CAB 129/103, 'Housing Policy: memorandum by the Minister of Housing and Local Government', 29 November 1960.

46 Ministry of Housing and Local Government, *Housing in England and Wales*, Cmnd. 1290 (HMSO, London, 1961), paras 55–8.
47 The Housing Act of 1961 gave the Minister of Housing additional power to reduce by Order in Council the level or duration of subsidies on existing council houses built after 1961 if the existing level seemed unjustified. It also introduced a greater degree of flexibility in the application of subsidies as between one authority and another.
48 Ministry of Housing and Local Government, *Housing, 1963*, Cmnd. 2050 (HMSO, London, 1963), para. 42.
49 CAB 129/109, 'Housing: memorandum by the Minister of Housing and Local Government', 23 May 1962.
50 Cabinet minutes, 13 March 1964.
51 Quoted in S. J. Curtis, *A History of Education in Great Britain*, 6th edn (University Tutorial Press, London, 1965), p. 376.
52 Seldon, *Churchill's Indian Summer*, p. 270.
53 Cited in Simon, *Education and Social Order*, p. 105.
54 Curtis, *History of Education*, p. 378.
55 Quoted in Curtis, *History of Education*, pp. 378–9.
56 Board of Education, *Explanatory Memorandum to the Education Bill*, Cmd. 6492 (HMSO, London, 1943).
57 Addison, *Now the War is Over*, p. 150.
58 R. Barker, *Education and Politics, 1900–1951: a study of the Labour party* (Oxford University Press, Oxford, 1972), p. 87.
59 Labour Party Annual Conference Report, 1950, cited in Barker, *Education and Politics*, p. 88.
60 N. Timmins, *The Five Giants: a biography of the welfare state* (HarperCollins, London, 1995), pp. 151–2.
61 Barker, *Education and Politics*, p. 86.
62 See especially the remarks of H. C. Dent, quoted in Timmins, *The Five Giants*, p. 153.
63 The authority drew up a plan for transforming six secondary schools in one area on a comprehensive pattern using existing buildings, in the same way as the county of Leicestershire was to act in 1957. But in the case of Middlesex, between eleven and eighteen schools for some 850 pupils were envisaged and these, the ministry could argue, were too small to provide a viable sixth form. See C. Benn and B. Simon, *Half-way There: the British comprehensive school reform* (McGraw-Hill, London, 1970), p. 20.
64 CPA, CCO 505/1/1, Minutes of the Conservative and Unionist Teachers' Association, 8 March 1947.
65 CPA, CCO 505/1/1, Minutes of the Conservative and Unionist Teachers' Association, 11 July 1953.

66 D. R. Hardman MP, speaking in the House of Commons on 27 February 1948, quoted in Barker, *Education and Politics*, p. 91.
67 Joint Committee of the Four Secondary Associations, *The Organisation of Secondary Education* (n.d.); Incorporated Association of Headmasters, *The Grammar Schools: a reply to the Labour party's proposals*, September 1958.
68 Timmins, *The Five Giants*, p. 198.
69 Seldon, *Churchill's Indian Summer*, p. 277.
70 Timmins, *The Five Giants*, p. 199.
71 Timmins, *The Five Giants*, p. 240.
72 CAB 129/108, 'Education policy: memorandum by the Minister of Education', 4 January 1962.
73 ED 147/161, 'National Advisory Committee of the Conservative and Unionist Teachers' Association', 28 October 1961.
74 CPA, CCO 505/4/12, letter to CUTA secretary, 19 June 1958.
75 ED 147/641, Boyle to Secretary of CUTA, 30 January 1963. In April 1964 a major Whitehall reorganization created the Department of Education and Science under Quintin Hogg. Boyle was to remain in the Cabinet as Minister of State for Education.

4 A Structure in Tension, 1945–1964

Left unreconstructed in 1945, the struggle to modernize local government areas continued. It was a problem from which the Churchill coalition were said to have run away, their 1945 white paper being 'an escapist document'.[1] That successive governments compounded these failures by refusing to face up to the interdependence between the structure of local government, the functions exercised by the various authorities, and the means of financing them became the standard indictment for later critics. The truth was more complicated.

The coalition government had set its face against wholesale reorganization of local government, mainly out of fear that it would disrupt and delay, rather than expedite, the post-war reconstruction drive. In providing for the establishment of the Local Government Boundary Commission as an expert body with wide powers, the coalition had accepted that there was a need for some more effective method of adjusting the structure. The real point at issue was whether it would prove sufficient to the task. The pre-war procedures for securing change through private bills were cumbersome and uncertain. Before long, the independent Commission set up in 1945 was to reveal its own limitations, challenging the Labour government to introduce further legislation.

The root of the difficulty was political. While the 1945 white paper had been a bipartisan document, Aneurin Bevan, who, as Minister of Health, assumed responsibility for local government when Labour took office, had little time for the coalition and its doings. When, within the life of the first Attlee government, divisions opened up – as they had within the coalition itself – on how best to deal with the problem of local government structure, Bevan broke ranks. He forced the dissolution of the Commission, and pressed his own plan for radical and wholesale reform of the entire structure of local government. An interdepartmental battle on this subject was the last thing the dying government needed, and Bevan's critics successfully buried his scheme.

The underlying issue – the enduring conflict between counties and county boroughs – was less easily disposed of. Conservative ministers were in their turn forced to face it, as first Harold Macmillan, and then (with more vigour) Duncan Sandys, edged the local authority associations towards accepting change. However, the Local Government Commission set up in 1958 found the going no easier than its predecessor. Ministers were once again split, this time between those who wanted to demonstrate their 'modernism' by accepting the Commission's proposed changes, and those who preferred to soothe the susceptibilities of local interests by rejecting them. Impatient of 'adjustment', the next Labour government would consign this Commission to the fate of its predecessor, appointing the Royal Commission which had been persistently advocated during the coalition and 1945–50 governments. Tinkering was out. The call was for a grand scheme – albeit one shaped by the political priorities and electoral expediencies of the government of the day.

The post-war problem of structure was, then, a problem of finding a procedure that could deliver politically acceptable adjustments to the basic framework of local government. Had a workable procedure for adjusting to urban change and development and mediating the conflicts between counties and county boroughs been established by the wartime coalition, the post-war history of local government would have been very different. As it was, all attempts at change would founder on the rock of 'the county borough problem'.

Labour and Local Government Reform

On coming to power, Labour inherited a mechanism for local government reform that was not of its own making. It was true that Labour ministers had been party to preparation of the 1945 white paper and were thereby implicated in the Local Government (Boundary Commission) Act that followed it. But the Act's introduction had fallen to the caretaker government after Labour withdrew from the coalition, when political minds were on the coming general election. The proposals could hardly have appealed to Labour politicians, who had been privately scathing when they were first put forward by Henry Willink, the coalition's last (Conservative) Minister of Health.

It was left to *The Economist* to point out what those Labour ministers well knew: the government's proposals would do little to bring about improved administration in the 'human' services – education, health, housing and town planning – in which the post-war electorate would have the keenest interest. The weaknesses of the existing local government structure would be doubly apparent under the load of developing the new Welfare State. Clearly, the government did not wish to make the new Commission 'a serious instrument of reform'.[2] Others took the contrary view. A leading commentator writing at the time thought it 'a decisive point in the history of the development of local government', as the Commission would provide the machinery 'necessary for a complete revision... of areas and boundaries' raising the hope that 'an entirely new administrative map of local government may be the result'.[3]

The difference of view reflected uncertainties about how powers would be exercised in practice. The five-member Commission could operate as it chose, within the framework of general principles laid down by the minister, following consultation with the local authority associations, and approval by both Houses of Parliament. They would review the whole of English local government outside London, and while their programme could be determined by direction from the minister, and by requests by county or county borough councils, for most part it was left to their own judgement. If a municipal borough of 100,000 or more population requested elevation to county borough status, the Commission would have to give it consideration. That apart, they could unite or divide any area, promote to county borough status on their own account, or demote existing county boroughs as they saw fit. Importantly, the Commission's decisions were to be embodied in Orders which they themselves would draft for presentation to Parliament, together with an account of their proceedings and of their reasoning. Once an Order had taken effect, no further action could be taken in that local authority area for a further ten years.[4] Much, then, would depend on the commissioners themselves. Equally, much would depend on their relationship with the Minister of Health.

The Trustram Eve Commission

The membership of the Commission was effectively determined before Labour took office. The initial thinking had been to find a High Court judge for the chair. In late July, discussions were still under way with Sir Malcolm Trustram Eve, a baronet and experienced land expert, who was already chairman of the War Damage and War Works Commissions. Eve himself cleared the offer with the Treasury, pressing his candidacy for the job quite hard on the grounds that the three posts would make 'a nicely balanced full-time job for one man'.[5] The deputy chairmanship had already been arranged to the retiring Permanent Secretary at the Ministry of Health, Sir John Maude, who had played so restraining a role during the wartime enquiries.

When Bevan replaced Willink following the general election, the names were run past him for approval. Only two other names remained on the table at this point. One was Sir Will Spens, who had played an important role in the developments in education reform. But Spens had spent the war years as a regional commissioner, and the sensitivities of the local authorities were still raw enough on regionalism for both Herbert Morrison, and the outgoing Willink, to veto him. The remaining candidate was the academic constitutional lawyer and popularizer of local government matters, Sir Ivor Jennings. Jennings had nominated himself, the Permanent Secretary noting that he was 'a prolific writer but [with] no practical experience and the appointment would not be well received in local government circles'.[6] So the chair went to Eve's apparently safe pair of hands, and Attlee formally approved the Commission's membership in October 1945.

The Commission began work late in 1945 with a staff of around fifty officials, about a quarter of whom had been drawn from local government. With few applications for consideration under the special urgency provision, and with no formal directions from the minister, the Commission gave its first attention to proposed boundary extensions by county boroughs. By May 1946 the first investigation, of the city of Plymouth, was under way.[7] The Commission's first report for 1946 was a harbinger of things to come, in that it discussed the possible creation of new urban counties for metropolitan areas. Simply raising the issue drew a fierce response from the County Boroughs Association, warning that such a course would amount to the 'drastic' alteration in local government of the sort expressly ruled out in the 1945 white paper.[8] If the Commission's 1946 report was a provocation, that for 1947 was a bombshell. Making repeated reference to the 'general principles' laid down by Parliament that the Commission should secure 'effective and convenient' units of administration, the Commission reported that they had not found it possible on those grounds to make a single Order altering the status or boundaries of any local authority. The reason was simple. The Commission felt that if their consideration were to be limited for the areas of local government, without reference to the functions of local authorities those general principles could not be achieved:

> We have definitely reached the conclusion that in many areas – and these cover the great bulk of the population – our present powers and instructions do not permit the formation of local government units as effective and convenient as in our opinion they should be.[9]

They quoted in their support a recent remark by Bevan himself that 'every one who knows about local government feels that it is nonsense to talk about functions and boundaries separately. They have to be taken together...'. The Commission went on to make proposals for dealing with this shortcoming, proposals which would need new legislation to implement. The most controversial was for a new type of local authority, the 'new county borough', a most-purpose authority having a population of up to 200,000. This new type of authority would exercise substantial powers – including education – in its own right, but would otherwise fall under the jurisdiction of the county council. These proposals amounted to nothing less than the demotion of county boroughs as envisaged by Jowitt in 1941. The Commission called for an amendment of their general principles and for a new local government bill, the terms of which they spelt out in detail.

The weaknesses of the coalition's work on local government were now starkly revealed, although it was easier for Bevan, who had not been in government during the war, to face this than it was for some of his colleagues. The county councils strongly opposed the proposed creation of 'new county boroughs' as education authorities. The county boroughs protested 'in the strongest possible terms against the proposal to "strengthen" the two-tier system at the expense of existing county boroughs' and, pointedly ignoring the Commission, made their representations direct to the minister. They told Bevan that the Commission's 'ominous' report was based on 'startlingly slight arguments' and that 'no vestige of a case had been made to justify the demotion of three quarters of England and Wales' county boroughs', an act which would virtually destroy county boroughs on the slight grounds of 'sheer expediency'.[10]

Receiving no response over the next six months, Eve wrote to Bevan in November 1948, asking for an indication of the government's likely response. A further six months elapsed before it came – indirectly – in the form of an answer to a Parliamentary question in which Bevan curtly dismissed the Commission's 1946 and 1947 reports with the statement that 'it will not be practical to introduce comprehensive legislation on local government reconstruction in the near future'.[11] The work of the Commission continued, more than 1,300 local conferences having been held since 1946. Faced with rebuff on the main proposals, the commissioners decided to proceed in a conditional fashion, making Orders to deal with those few areas in which action was possible under the existing law, and not inappropriate were the law to be changed. The places that met these criteria would be few indeed. The ten-year rule, under which an authority affected by an Order gained immunity from any further changes for that period, greatly constrained what the Commission could do, unless that sterilization clause was itself changed in the new legislation for which their draft 1948 report called.

Confronted with that draft, Bevan summoned the Commission to see him on 10 March 1949.[12] It was a heated meeting, with personal antipathies scarcely concealed. Bevan told the commissioners of his 'distress' at the terms of their report. He was 'piqued' that they should have rebuked him for taking no action. True, he had encouraged them to go beyond their terms of reference and expose the weaknesses of the 1945 Act, but this had been in order to provoke discussion. He accused the Commission of seeking a much wider role than provided for under the Act. Their difficulties with the statutory procedure, and with the ten-year rule in particular, were largely invented; they held back from making Orders in the hope of wresting greater powers from the government. Eve objected that there 'was not a word of truth' in this allegation, which Bevan was forced to withdraw.

Eve justified the Commission's stance on the shortcomings of the Act in terms of an earlier meeting and correspondence with Bevan, which the minister affected not to recall. As to the wall of silence that Bevan had maintained over the past six months, he imperiously informed them that 'the Commission was entitled to expect a reply from the Minister only as regards matters within their statutory powers, and they had no right to ask to know the Government's attitude on other matters or complain if they were not informed'. After this stormy meeting the Commission, unmoved, signed off what was to be their last report with the declaration that 'we still remain of the opinion that neither we nor our successors can everywhere create effective and convenient units of local government without some amendment of local government legislation'.[13]

Clearly, the Commission had walked into a trap, and their fate was already sealed. Bevan had already taken proposals on the Commission's future to the Lord President's Committee of the Cabinet one week previously, on 4 March. At that stage he revealed to his colleagues that he had encouraged the Commission to express their views in broad terms, explaining that

> he had thought this would be useful because of the difficulty of dealing with boundaries in isolation from structure and functions, an it had seemed to him valuable that the issue would be publicly ventilated. The subject was, however, outside the statutory terms of reference of the Commission and that it would not be right or practicable to make major constitutional changes without reference to some body like a Royal Commission which could speak with great authority than the Boundary Commission.[14]

Bevan's tactics worked. The Commission had been used to highlight the limits of the existing legislation, but they were not themselves a body fitted for the larger task that they had identified. Nevertheless, some ministers, including Morrison, were sceptical of Royal Commissions. Memories of the wartime Jowitt enquiry, which had raised the same issues, were still sharp. Without agreement on the way forward, the next stage of the battle would be fought in full Cabinet.

On 12 May, Bevan attempted to persuade the Cabinet that a Royal Commission was needed and should be appointed without delay, to report by the end of 1950. He pointed out that the Commission's 1948 report would shortly be published and an urgent decision was needed on the way forward. He accepted the need for radical reform of what was still nineteenth-century local government, but this could not be based 'on the strength of a report of a small executive body appointed for a limited purpose who have made recommendations on a wide issue without hearing evidence'.[15] Morrison circulated his own paper, confronting Bevan head on, and showing how unlikely it was that a Royal Commission could be either timely – reporting early in the next Parliament – or predictable in its conclusions. He supported Bevan's past tactic of encouraging the Commission to expose the limits of their powers as one which had usefully 'drawn the fire' of the local authorities. He referred, approvingly, to the wartime interdepartmental enquiry carried out by Jowitt (now in the Cabinet as the Lord Chancellor), concluding that 'we might as well give up a little time now to thinking out more precisely what we would like to achieve'.[16] The Cabinet then took an historic decision to break out of the straitjacket of the coalition's approach to the problem, recognizing that

> a new situation in local government had been created by the transfer of the trading services to public boards, of hospitals to the Ministry of Health and of various functions from one class of local authorities to another. The situation had greatly altered since the Boundary Commission was set up in 1945.[17]

A new approach was needed, but the urgent business that remained was to deal with the Commission itself.

On 24 May, Attlee saw Eve, together with the deputy chairman, Sir John Maude, for an extended discussion. They asked for a government decision on their work, and came away feeling optimistic. Maude noted that the Prime Minister was 'friendly' and 'showed keen interest in the subject. He obviously had a fair acquaintance with our reports and sympathised with a good deal of what we had written'.[18] But when the Minister of Health asked for a further meeting with the Commission two weeks later, they were to receive a rude shock.[19] Bevan told them that post-war developments in local government had 'invalidated the foundation of the commission's functions'. The machinery of their operation by the drafting of Orders was 'cumbrous, complicated, and slower than private bill legislation', a surprising but apparently valid claim.[20] The Orders that the Commission proposed to make – extending the boundaries of Southampton, Plymouth, Liverpool, Hull and Bootle – would be 'deeply embarrassing' (in the electoral sense of the expression). The Cabinet would accordingly ask Parliament immediately to repeal the Act establishing the Boundary Commission. In future, any changes in status or boundaries would have to be sought through the private bill procedure.

Eve was shocked and angry. He wrote to Attlee:

this decision came as a complete surprise after my talk with you a week or two ago. Since I do not agree either with the decision or with the reasons given for it and I also feel that it will postpone for two or three years many alterations in local government areas which are already overdue, I ask that I may be released from my chairmanship of the Commission before the bill is introduced. Although the end is a sad disappointment I should like to express my thanks for the opportunity I have been given during the last four years to work with and for local government.[21]

On 27 June, Bevan made a statement to the House announcing the proposed dissolution of the Commission, justifying it in terms of how much had changed since the 1945 white paper, and intimating that the government would be carrying out its own review of the structure and functions of local government. On that same day the Commission met again to resolve that they 'profoundly regret[ted] the action of the government which [was] not in their view in the best interests of local government'.[22]

Meanwhile, Attlee had asked Eve and his fellow Commissioners to remain until the dissolution bill became law, a request to which they felt bound to agree.[23] Yet so angry was Eve with government's actions that he resigned all his public offices, including the chairmanship of the Central Land Board and the War Damage Commission. He explained his decision to the local authority associations:

I have thus been faced with the alternatives of continuing in public service until I am too old for anything else, or cutting adrift now into another sphere. I have chosen the latter although I do not as yet know what that other sphere will be.[24]

Perhaps the most surprising aspect of the Commission's dismissal was that it did come as a surprise to Eve. When Bevan met the Commission for that stormy meeting in March, Permanent Secretary Sir William Douglas had warned that the draft 1948 report, which they had met to discuss, read as 'a polemic against the minister'.[25] The warning was clear enough.

None of this, of course, was publicly known, and the government's action in dismissing the Commission was widely condemned. The *Manchester Guardian* on 28 June judged that 'local government needs a major reorganisation and Mr Bevan is running away from it, and throwing away the instrument with which he should be tackling it'. The county councils were not surprisingly appalled, praising the Commission for their initiative, regretting the 'unnecessary waste of knowledge, experience and time' and roundly condemning the return to private bill procedure.[26] Significantly, the CCA contacted Conservative Central Office and briefed Conservative MPs to speak against the dissolution bill, rightly judging that the counties would be the losers should a Labour government decide to take direct charge of local government reorganization. The CCA also made a last ditch attempt to get the bill withdrawn by joint representations of all four associations, on the grounds that a Commission would still be needed to bring about changes in the areas of local authorities under any broad scheme for change. Ominously, they warned that any future attempt to establish a similar body would encounter great difficulties in securing the co-operation of the local authorities.

The Bevan plan

In introducing the Local Government Commission (Dissolution) Act 1949, Labour ministers restated their own prerogatives in the matter of local government structure. But to what purpose were they to be exercised? Bevan had not found it difficult to get agreement on the abolition of the Commission, but it would prove another matter altogether to agree the way forward.

Bevan himself said no more than that the government had accepted that it had the responsibility to formulate its own proposals, rather than waiting upon a Commission.[27] But press and opposition filled the vacuum with speculation that Bevan intended to abolish all authorities of less than 100,000 population; and the spectre of regional councils appeared once again.[28] If speculation about regions was rife, and the anxieties of the local authorities widespread, the reason was not hard to find. The Labour party had produced its own plan for regional local government – decisively not based upon the existing regional commissioners – in 1945. More recently, the party's leading thinker on the subject, G. D. H. Cole, had published his own comprehensive study of local government areas and functions, the first such analysis to take into account the post-war realities. Cole's book mounted a thorough critique of the Boundary Commission's limited powers and argued that new legislation was required. He foresaw that the Commission might seek a widening of their terms of reference. However,

Cole was no enthusiast for the closed system of appointed Commissioners negotiating 'fixes' with central and local government:

> I do not want this [enhancement of powers] to happen, both because I believe the changes required go far beyond what could possibly be done in this way, and also because I want the problems of local government to be settled democratically, to the accompaniment of lively public comment, and not by a process of negotiation and agreement between the Commission and the local authorities . . . [29]

Given Cole's standing on the Left, and his prescience in anticipating the problems that the Commission would face, it was not surprising that many should suspect that Bevan was following his lead. But it was not in fact so; Bevan's own thinking was at odds with Cole's, and the immediate difficulty for the government was more mundane than this – the expected private bills had come flooding in. Bevan was obliged to go back to the Cabinet to get an absolute rule against promotion to county borough status – sought by Luton and Ilford – and a blocking of any bills to extend boundaries.[30] This new regime, under which private bills were the only route to change but would be opposed by the Labour government, was dubbed the 'freeze'.

Seeking to resolve the impasse on local government reform, Lord Astor now re-entered the scene. He induced his son, David, the editor of *The Observer*, to invite Eve to write regularly for the paper on local government matters, on the grounds that it would be 'a suitable vehicle for an assault on the public conscience of the two large parties on this matter'.[31] When Eve's first article appeared, it attacked the government's freeze, and warned that if it were not to be thawed soon, 'real and effective local government will become a thing of the past'.[32] Having contrived publication of the article, Astor sent a copy to Butler, urging that inter party talks should be held with a view to achieving an agreed scheme of reform. Meanwhile, he had been in touch with sympathetic Conservative backbenchers, and offered Eve a meeting with Walter Elliot, the shadow Minister of Health.[33]

Inter-party talks were a non-starter, as the dissolution of the Boundary Commission polarized the positions of the two parties. The Conservative party, fearing the worst from Bevan, began work on its own approach to the future reform of local government, building upon Eve's work, while Eve offered his services to the Conservative party as chairman of their

National Advisory Committee on Local Government.[34] Nor was he quiescent in public, firing off letters to *The Times* on local government matters, and lecturing frequently, despite his promise to drift off into another sphere. In May 1950 he addressed the local government group of the Parliamentary Labour party, calling on the government to define the outline local government framework, leaving matters of detail to a new Boundary Commission. He maintained that there was 'no likelihood of agreement among [the associations] now or ever. Nearly always a view is either "extend me or upgrade me" or it is "defend me from my grabbing neighbour"', although he found the private views of the individual association leaders closer than this.[35] The responsibility was the government's.

Bevan concurred in this at least. He had meanwhile set in motion an internal review of local government reorganization that surpassed anything that had gone before. Detailed work was done by all the concerned Whitehall departments, this time with co-ordination by a special Cabinet committee on local government reform, under the Prime Minister's chairmanship. At the first meeting of this committee, in May 1949, Bevan spelled out his reasons for believing that the Boundary Commission could not possibly work, being based on mistaken and short-sighted assumptions on the part of the coalition ministers that areas could be examined without reference to functions.[36] He asserted that 'the procedure under the Act of 1945 is unworkable even for the purposes for which it was intended', a claim that made some longer-serving ministers smart, but did not prevent their agreeing to abolition. Bevan was invited to work up more concrete proposals based on his proposed scheme of all-purpose (unitary) authorities of 50,000–60,000 population, encompassing both town and country. The ministers recognized that some parts of the country would need a two-tier form of administration, but this would be exceptional. So too would be the arrangements in and around the industrial conurbations, where larger unitary authorities would be required.[37]

For the second meeting in July, Bevan submitted a paper outlining the scheme for England and Wales to be divided into about 300 all-purpose authorities with populations varying from 50,000 to more than a million.[38] The scheme was intended to produce compact authorities and to bring as many people as possible close to the centre of decision-making. Neighbourhood councils could be created on the initiative of the unitary authorities, with possible delegation of functions in sparsely populated areas. The scheme was initially well received, although some ministers pressed for much larger authorities and there were some reservations as to the viability of the smaller authorities shown in Bevan's maps.

Throughout the autumn, Ministry of Health staff engaged in an exhaustive series of meetings, in which their opposite numbers from the Home Office and the Ministries of Education and Town and Country Planning began to stake out their positions. In the Ministry of Town and Country Planning, where Evelyn Sharp orchestrated official views, the proposed unification of town and country was welcomed as finally overcoming the divisions and conflicts endemic in the county borough system. Generally, though, Sharp sought much larger authorities for planning purposes, especially in the industrialized areas and in the home counties, where there was a need to keep in view movements of population and industry over a wide area. 'We have always hoped', she wrote, 'that in any scheme of local government reform the opportunity would be taken to provide for the implementation of large scale planning', which implied very large authorities with real development powers. Without the structure or strategic planning on at least a county-wide basis, 'we should... be worse off with the all purpose authorities'.[39] The Home Office and the Ministry of Education were less well disposed to the plan, the former thinking it 'most unfortunate'.

By the time Bevan's full plan was put to the November meeting of the Cabinet committee, the battle lines were well drawn. The plan had the merit of simplicity, and aimed 'to revive and maintain local government as a form of government which is truly local, which is near to the people and in which they would take an interest'. On the basis of the detailed study carried out by the civil servants, Bevan was 'more than ever convinced that the all purpose authority is the reform at which we should aim'.[40] Given that there was little more that could be done before the general election, Bevan proposed to have further research undertaken with a view to moving forward in the new Parliament. In the meantime, the utmost secrecy should be observed.[41]

Bevan stood by his plan in the face of widespread reservations, the only support for it coming from Lewis Silkin at Town and Country Planning, and Tomlinson at the Ministry of Education. Ede, the Home Secretary, circulated his own paper attacking the scheme as 'very retrograde' from the point of view of the police and fire services.[42] This much might have been expected; it was a responsible minister's job to fight his corner when proposals of this sort appeared. But Ede's more important objections came in a separate paper. The personal views of this doyen of the county councils were devastating: the Bevan proposals, he argued, do 'much violence to historic development and association', for

> The historic units of English Local Government are the parish, deriving from the manor, and the county. There is a local patriotism attaching the individual to both, varying in intensity but quite well marked in both cases. An examination of [Bevan's] map discloses that both these units disappear: parishes are combined in new aggregations and county boundaries are apparently regarded as of quite secondary importance . . . Historic association is not lightly to be disregarded and there are sometimes historic antipathies which have to be borne in mind when considering new groupings . . . I do not believe it is possible, over the country as a whole, to eliminate two-tier local government. I share the view expressed by the Minister of Agriculture that the scheme presented would greatly reduce the number of people participating in local government. In some of the present large towns, the councils may be unwieldy in size, but the lower authority in the two-tier system enables a very large number of people who have limited means, both of time and money, to participate actively in the development and control of their area. This is a valuable training ground, particularly for the Labour Movement and I fear that many of these people must disappear as active participants if the new scheme goes forward.[43]

Ede, well able to exemplify his every point from personal knowledge, had no rivals in the Cabinet when it came to this sort of argument. The Bevan plan could not be approved; and Labour had run out of options.

Deadlocked, the government decided to suspend any further examination of local government reform, on which the Ministry of Health would do no further work 'for the time being'.[44] In reducing Labour's majority to six, the 1950 general election effectively scotched any prospect of progress with any contested scheme. Bevan moved to the Ministry of Labour in February 1951, and a new Ministry of Planning and Local Government was created under Hugh Dalton. This energetic and effective minister instead on bringing Evelyn Sharp with him, having dismissed the local government officials at the former Ministry of Health, whom he inherited, as 'ageing duds'.[45] The scene was set for a new attempt at local government reform, but the government announced, in a July debate in the House of Commons, that it intended to pin its hopes on reaching agreement between the local authority associations. *The Economist* was scathing, criticizing ministers' 'unwonted anxiety for proceeding by general agreement' as a 'thin disguise for their wish to do nothing'. But whatever the potential for the Dalton/Sharp team, it was to be a short-lived Parliament, the Conservatives returning to power under Churchill three months later. From now on, events would move forward, albeit in steps so gradual as to be, at times, almost imperceptible.

Conservative Gradualism

Six years of Labour government had seen the rise and fall of the Boundary Commission, and with it the hopes of the reconstruction period. The pent-up demand for boundary extension and promotion to county borough status now revealed itself. The law permitted such changes. Policy could prohibit them only as long as there was an alternative object in view. Most commentators argued for a move in the opposite direction, to secure the demotion of most of the existing county boroughs, retaining just a handful of the largest among them.[46] Despite his dismissal, Eve's stock remained high, for almost every case made for strengthening local government short of 'drastic' – that is, Bevanite – change turned out to resemble his own proposals. He had indeed set the agenda, and the events of the next decade and a half came to resemble a slow-motion re-run of the 1940s, even ending on the same note, with Richard Crossman emulating his mentor by casting local government into the melting pot in 1966.

Towards a concordat

The adage that men, not measures, matter did not hold in the case of local government reform, as Eve was seen by many influential Conservatives as indispensable to any re-launch of the reform process. Bevan's veiled threat of imposed reorganization propelled the Conservative party to action, and the policy that it sketched out amounted to the implementation of much of Eve's own views. The 1951 election manifesto promised

> legislation to re-allocate the functions of local authorities and to create a new Boundary Commission to review boundaries on principles laid down by Parliament . . . only an independent Commission can remove the determination of boundaries from the squabbles of pressure groups. In doing this work, it must have regard to local conditions and traditions.[47]

Privately, Ian Macleod went further:

> There is a considerable case for setting up again the Local Government Boundary Commission, if possible under Sir Malcolm's chairmanship, and reconsidering its terms of reference. Most recent Conservative pronouncements, at any rate the unofficial ones, have tended to support this . . . The merit of such an approach is that urgent repairs to local government structure in England and Wales could be done without the expensive and dilatory method of private Bill procedure.[48]

Negotiating an agreement between the warring local authority associations was seen as a prerequisite of any change, as no plan – be it from a Commission or from government itself – was likely to succeed without it.

Once again, it was the presentation of a private bill – to gain county borough status for Luton – that stirred the government to action. In the spring of 1954, Harold Macmillan, Minister of Housing and Local Government, blocked the bill in Parliament. In doing so, he promised not to repeat the government's veto if he could not come up with a scheme of his own in the meantime, a position that looked likely to open the floodgates of municipal aspiration. Indeed, by this point, the government was being driven only by local pressures. Macmillan acknowledged the possibility of legislation following all-party agreement on reform, but it was something to be hoped for, rather than promised. As it happened, the county councils had been making the running in joint discussions since 1947, and by 1953 had achieved an agreed statement reconciling their views and those of the urban and rural districts and the parish councils.[49] This in itself was an achievement, but it left the AMC out in the cold. In April 1954, the AMC published their own proposals, identifying as the principal defects in the system the reluctance to extend urban boundaries and promote the larger boroughs, and calling for a universal system of single-tier local government.[50] It was stalemate once more.

This time, the opposing demands of the associations had been addressed directly to the minister. The ball was in the government's court, and there was really no choice but to play it. *The Economist* urged Macmillan to recognize that 'local government reform has made notable reputations for statesmen in the past – for Goschen in the last century and for Neville Chamberlain in the 1920s'.[51] *The Times* urged the need for a firm policy.[52] But Macmillan hardly aspired to emulate Goschen and Chamberlain, both of whom were renowned for their mastery of local government matters.

Instead, his own paper to Cabinet in March 1954 – entitled 'Operation round-up' – was characteristically flippant, summarizing the place of local government in the British political system as 'a poor thing, but mine own'. Local government reform was simply one of a 'large number of skeletons remaining in my ministerial cupboard'. The Cabinet might judge it best, 'after viewing the collection, to have it dusted and put away'. Should they not do so, then his advice was that the present mixed one- and two-tier system should be retained on the grounds that it was 'long-established and everybody is used to it', adding that 'it is obvious that if left to themselves the interested parties will never produce an agreed scheme'. Macmillan invited the Cabinet to 'decide now in principle on the retention of the present mixed structure', stipulating that London should be left alone, and that 'we would not willingly interfere with the government of the great cities'.[53] It was something less than a clarion call, and the Cabinet decided to do no more than promise some modest changes some in the next election manifesto. Bereft of ideas, it recognized that individual corporation bills – expected from Luton, Ilford and Poole – could no longer be held up.

Macmillan having failed to move matters forward in his remaining months in that department, it was left to his successor, Duncan Sandys, to do the hard work of advancing discussions. In a sense he benefited from Macmillan's failures, for having been so scathing about Macmillan's studied dilatoriness, the associations found themselves faced with the fact that their own mutual antagonisms were the principal obstacle to any government's action. When Sandys met them in October 1954, he reiterated the Macmillan line that he could not embark on any general reform without their agreement. 'Rather to my surprise', he reported subsequently,

> they immediately replied that, rather than see this problem indefinitely shelved, they would be prepared to make a fresh attempt to agree among themselves upon some more limited proposals for reorganisation, within the framework of the existing structure. I naturally welcomed this change of attitude; and, in order to facilitate the discussions between them, I agreed to take the chair at three further meetings.[54]

Between the autumn of 1954 and the spring of 1955, Sandys' skilful brokering led to compromise proposals being agreed between the four associations. He worked to hold the fragile '*concordat*' together, persuading the three would-be county boroughs to withdraw their bills in the interest of avoiding a renewed outbreak of arguments between the principal types of authority.

The Sandys position thus became the government's stance for the 1955 general election, Sandys telling the party conference that year that neither tier of local authority would be scrapped, that a sharing of powers between levels of government would continue, but with local authorities having 'as much discretion as possible to adapt national policies to local circumstances'.[55] Here was sufficient common ground for the work leading to a long-awaited local government act to be set in motion at last. The method by which this was achieved showed remarkable skill. Having placed the onus on the associations to start talking, Sandys was able to create a productive setting for the talks by effectively detaching the leaders of the associations from their constituencies, drawing them into a closed setting and insulating them by conventions of confidentiality that bound them to him. The AMC explained just how they had been neutralized: they had entered the discussions

> in the belief that they were acting in accordance with what would be the wishes of a large majority of the members of the Association and certainly in the interests of good local government in the cities and boroughs of this country. To have refused to continue the discussions would have lost an opportunity of securing a reasonable measure of reorganisation. The representatives were not prepared to accept the responsibility for this, but in entering upon the discussions, they did so expressly upon the basis that nothing they said or agreed to should commit the association or its members. The discussions were conducted throughout on the basis that the strictest confidence must be observed. Those taking part were pledged not to divulge, before the publication of a white paper, the nature and extent of the proposals resulting from the discussions....[56]

It was a classic example of the well known government technique of taking recalcitrant interest groups into the government's confidence, and imprisoning them in the mantle of 'responsibility'.[57] It enabled all sides to agree on a number of principles, of which the foremost was 'the need to ensure that all authorities (in all categories) are so constituted as to be individually and collectively effective and convenient units of local government'.[58] The presumption was that some authorities might not be effective and convenient; and that a means of adjustment was necessary to ensure that they were made so, thus preserving the effectiveness of the overall system. The agreement also registered an acceptance of the partic-

A Structure in Tension   105

ular need 'to improve the organisation of local government in the conurbations'.[59]

In July 1956, Sandys published the first of three white papers setting out the government's proposals.[60] In *Areas and Status of Local Authorities in England and Wales*, the Local Government Boundary Commission reappeared in a rather different form.[61] The proposed Local Government Commission would consider promotions to county borough status and extension of boundaries, the division, amalgamation, alteration and extension of counties, with district reviews being made by counties in the wake of the Commission's recommendations. Special powers to make more far-reaching proposals were envisaged for the conurbations.[62] Unlike the 1945 Commission, which had been given the politically dangerous power to make its own Orders, the body now envisaged would make reports and recommendations on their reviews to the minister who would, subject to such amendments as he saw fit, embody them in Orders of his own making, and lay them before Parliament for approval or rejection. The key decisions were, then, to be reserved to the minister, but he would act on authoritative advice.[63]

The second white paper, on the division of functions between counties and county districts, was not based on general agreement, but was published in order to take the discussions further. Its key proposal was to provide for the delegation of a wide range of functions from counties to the larger county districts. Those with populations in excess of 60,000 could expect to operate, on behalf of their county council, health, welfare, education, roads, town planning and public health functions.[64] The third white paper dealt with local government finance, and brought about an important shift from specific to general grant, a move readily presented as a major concession to local discretion in expenditure. The three white papers were given legislative form in the Local Government Bill, which put the seal on the *concordat* and was carried through the House of Commons by Sandys' successor, Henry Brooke.

The new review process

The 1958 Act established the new Local Government Commission under the chairmanship of Sir Henry Hancock, former Permanent Secretary at the Ministry of Food, and chairman of the Board of Inland Revenue. The

106 A Structure in Tension

Commission was to operate with two types of procedures. The first involved the investigation of boundary problems, receiving representations from the local authorities concerned and reporting to the Minister of Housing and Local Government with a recommendation for action, where the Commission considered it appropriate.[65] The second procedure permitted more radical change in the five conurbations which were designated as Special Review Areas (SRAs). Here the Commission was permitted to propose the recasting of the pattern of local authorities.

In undertaking reviews the Commission was required 'at all times [to] have in mind the general objective set out in the Act that any proposed changes should be in the interests of *effective and convenient local government*' (italics added), an aim which recurs throughout the history of the post-war Commissions.[66] Subsequent regulations made under the 1958 Act spelled out how the criteria of 'effective and convenient local government' were to be interpreted. *Effectiveness* was to be assessed in the light of the size and distribution of population and rateable values in relation to boundaries, and the extent to which they provided authorities with adequate resources and scope for the efficient operation of all their functions. *Convenience* was to encompass the number, size and boundaries of local authorities, travelling facilities and the access of council members and the public to administrative centres.

Nine factors were listed as specific matters that the Commission were required to take into account. Embodied also at the county level as the principles that county councils should bring to bear on reviews of their districts, these factors were identical to those formulated for the 1945 Act commissioners. Reviews were to focus on:

(a) community of interest;
(b) development and expected development;
(c) economic and industrial characteristics;
(d) financial resources measured in relation to financial need;
(e) physical features, including suitable boundaries, means of communication and accessibility to administrative centres and centres of business and social life;
(f) population – size, distribution and characteristics;
(g) records of administration of the local authorities concerned;
(h) size and shape of the areas of local government;
(i) wishes of the inhabitants.

The ministry was careful, in framing the regulations, to point out that these considerations were listed in alphabetical order, not in order of priority.[67] Under the Commission's procedures it was more difficult for local councillors and their political parties to shape the outcome of their reviews, as the 'wishes of the inhabitants' were now more broadly defined. The Trustram Eve Commission had been prepared to accept the view that 'the wishes of the inhabitants were most truly expressed by their elected representatives and their officials', while the 1958 Act guidelines required a wider process of consultation.[68]

In respect of proposals for extending the boundaries of county boroughs to unite the urban centre with suburban development, the ministerial guidelines made it clear that the county boroughs would need to make a strong case if the Commission was to recommend change, and while the suggested population minimum of 100,000 was not to be 'regarded as an indispensable requirement', the Commission was particularly directed to consider the effects of the creation of a new county borough on the remaining areas of the county, to determine where lay the balance of advantage, following the principle first put forward by the Onslow Commission in 1936.[69]

The Commission proceeded outside the special review areas by inviting written submissions, holding discussions and making visits to the areas under review. It then published draft proposals on which comments were invited and local conferences were held prior to submission of recommendations to the minister. It was 'a lengthy process giving maximum opportunities for public discussion and comment before the final decisions are taken'.[70] The bulk of the work lay in extension of county borough boundaries and the adjustment of the county councils. The changes in most cases were small. Northamptonshire lost 1.7 per cent of its area and 4.3 per cent of its population. Some county boroughs won much larger increases, with Nottingham's area being almost doubled, and a further 49 per cent being added to its population.[71] Some of the proposals – the creation of new county boroughs at Luton, Solihull and Torbay, and the demotion of Burton-on-Trent and Worcester – were controversial. None was to be more controversial than the proposal to merge tiny Rutland with neighbouring Leicestershire. The conflicts that attended the private bill procedure were not surprisingly played out, before the Commission and their assistant commissioners, at the local hearings.

The most formidable problems that the Hancock Commission faced were in the five conurbations designated as Special Review Areas (SRAs): Tyneside, West Yorkshire, South-East Lancashire, Merseyside and the West Midlands. Here the Commission could propose radical recasting of the pattern of local government, what Henry Brooke had described as 'a really wonderful opportunity... for trying to work out really practical arrangements which are suited to the individual needs of each of these great areas'.[72] Here the Commission made radical proposals, but quite apart from finding a workable structure to deal with the practical problems of the metropolitan areas, very considerable political difficulties were raised.

Conservative Central Office had expressed great concern over the political implications of the SRA provisions of the Act, and pressed without success to define their boundaries as tightly as possible to prevent the Conservative suburbs and the rural fringe falling under the control of an urban-based Labour party.[73] Whatever problems the Commission faced in formulating its proposals, the decisive question was one of their political acceptability. However well conceived the Commission mechanism, it could not supplant the political judgement of ministers. In July 1963, the Commission's proposals for three sets of amalgamations, between the Soke of Peterborough and Huntingdonshire, the Isle of Ely and Cambridgeshire and, most controversially, Rutland and Leicestershire, came to Cabinet. Rutland was the smallest English county, smaller than many rural districts and – importantly – smaller than some of the neighbouring authorities also scheduled for amalgamation under the Commission's proposals. It was also the site of a spirited campaign by local people.

Keith Joseph was determined to carry these changes through as a demonstration of the modernizing spirit of the government. 'Progress in a number of fields' he proclaimed, 'was impeded by the existence of antiquated and inefficient units of local government'. The government could be pleased with the bold decisions that it had already taken regarding local government in London and the Black Country (following the Commission's proposals there). 'A decision to give effect to the proposed amalgamations' he pronounced, 'would be clear evidence of the government's intention to promote efficiency in the administration of public services'.[74] He continued:

> I know of no reason which could be given with any conviction for deferring until after the general election decisions on issues as simple and clear-cut as these ... I feel sure we cannot do nothing. I am equally sure that our reputation for fearlessly seeking efficiency in the administration of public

services will be enhanced by decisions to carry through these amalgamations. Conversely, a failure to act now would be widely construed as weakness.[75]

Unfortunately for Joseph's reputation as a reformer, the argument cut the other way too, other ministers feeling that

> in view of the action which had already been taken in London and other urban areas it could hardly be said to be necessary that the government should endorse those recommendations in order to demonstrate their determination to carry through their policy of reorganisation.[76]

As to the politics of the thing, 'these decisions would be widely criticised in, and beyond, the areas concerned'. Indeed,

> there might be some political advantage in demonstrating that the government were prepared to take account of special historical and other reasons for leaving a small unit in being, provided that they made it clear, at the same time, that they intended to proceed firmly with amalgamations where no such circumstances existed.[77]

Rutland was saved.

The decision to perpetuate the anomaly of Rutland represented more than just a defeat for whole-hearted 'modernizers'. It highlighted the extent of ministerial discretion over the implementation of these reviews. Some – the new county boroughs such as Solihull and Luton, and the reorganization in the Black Country area of the West Midlands – were accepted with little change. Small though it may have been, the Rutland issue was widely viewed as a test of the machinery established by the 1958 Act, and thus of the *concordat* itself and, in turn, of the entire post-war approach to local government reform. That one failure of resolve had a disproportionate political consequence. Elsewhere, while a number of changes were successfully made, the administrative effort, time and cost of the process seemed hardly to justify the modest outcomes. The Commission's credibility was weakened by the unwillingness of ministers to accept their more unpopular proposals. The final crisis came when the government refused to extend its terms of reference so as to enable a more satisfactory approach to the problem of the territory lying between the two nearby conurbations of Greater Manchester and Merseyside. Before long, this Commission went the way of its predecessor, although few were to mourn its passing.

110 *A Structure in Tension*

Breaking the mould

Local government reform in England may have been difficult enough, but London was the great untouchable. Highly discreet discussions had taken place during the war with a view to tackling the weaknesses of the metropolitan boroughs, and a fruitless committee had been set up under the Liberal, Lord Reading, in parallel with the Trustram Eve Commission. Reading's wild-eyed advocacy of devolution of government powers to London ensured that he was swiftly silenced. In 1954, Enoch Powell, then director of the Conservatives' London Municipal Society, formulated a plan for breaking up the LCC in favour of strong 'county-borough' government within a loose regional framework, but his plan too would be quashed, in this case by borough Conservatives who had too much to lose.[78]

Yet Conservative gradualism would not suffice for London. Recognition was dawning that London's problems could only be tackled over an area larger than that of the LCC. Yet to even raise the issue was politically unthinkable for Labour, who faced losing control through any extension of the LCC boundaries. It was equally so for Conservatives, whose supporters would fight in the last suburban ditch to maintain their separation from the feared metropolis. Yet it was becoming more generally accepted that the area of Greater London needed to be treated as a whole. While the 1956 white paper on areas and status had envisaged that the proposed Local Government Commission would investigate the whole of England outside the County of London, partly because the size of the job and the political issues which would be raised appeared too formidable, and partly because there had been discussions with neither representatives of the LCC nor of the boroughs.

When Henry Brooke took over from Sandys as Minister of Housing and Local Government, he brought to the job a much sharper perception of the problems of London government; not for nothing had he been Conservative leader on the LCC. In July 1957, Brooke set out a different approach for the Home Affairs Committee of the Cabinet. The first problem was that of Inner London, where the LCC provided 'a highly centralised structure, with most of the worth-while responsibility concentrated in the county council'. Sooner or later, the question of devolution to the Metropolitan borough councils would have to be faced, and some among them were once again campaigning for a shift of powers from the county council to themselves. But whereas some of them were administratively strong, 'some are dangerously weak; and it is difficult to do much in the direction of shifting powers, so long as the pattern of boroughs remains untouched'. Outside the LCC area itself were more pressing problems still, and the area-wide issues in planning and transport and technical services would be impossible to deal with if county boroughs were to be created in the fringe areas. The white paper had envisaged that the Local Government Commission could, when looking at Outer London, make recommendations for issues to be considered over Greater London as a whole, but 'I do not think this a workable proposal'. The greatest of the problems lay in the LCC's adjoining county of Middlesex, where the eleven larger boroughs would claim their share of the county's powers: their claims to county borough status would be difficult to resist, with disastrous impact on the remainder of the county. The problems of Middlesex could not be settled in isolation:

> it is this emerging difficulty about a settlement in Middlesex, combined with the disadvantages inherent in the white paper's approach, which has led me to re-examine our policy and to consider whether the best course would not be to grasp the nettle now, and set up an inquiry.

Brooke commended the establishment of a Royal Commission in preference to some lesser special inquiry, and proposed some draft terms of reference, to cover the area of the Metropolitan Police District. He was under no illusions as to the difficulties: 'the body conducting this inquiry will need to be extremely pertinacious in order to arrive at the facts – the individual local authorities will not look beyond their own boundaries'. He expected that the inquiry would take two to three years and 'I could ensure, I think, that the report was not completed before the [1959] election, if the cabinet agrees . . . that this would be unwise' [79] Agreeing that it would, the government excluded the London metropolitan area from the scope of Part 2 of the Local Government Act 1958, and set up a Royal Commission on Local Government in Greater London in 1957 under the chairmanship of Sir Edwin Herbert, an appointment which attracted criticism due to his supposed political links with the Conservative party.[80]

When the unanimous report of the Royal Commission appeared three years later, it found that 'judged by the twin tests of administrative efficiency and the health of representative government, the present structure of local government in [Greater London] is inadequate and needs overhaul'.[81] It pointed up the lack of scope for government at the most local level in London. This, the Commission thought, should be the primary level of local government, exercising all the functions that did not need to operate over the whole metropolitan area. Some of the metropolitan boroughs

> were among the largest in the country, but instead of being allowed to run their own affairs as county boroughs do, they play a subsidiary role in uneasy partnership with the county council. Within the county of London the concentration of power in the hands of the London County Council leaves the metropolitan boroughs with functions more limited than those of the smallest urban district council.[82]

The Commission recommended a new metropolitan authority, the Council for Greater London, for the entire area within the green belt – an area of some 8.5 million population – and the creation of fifty-two strong boroughs with responsibility for, among other services, primary education. The government accepted the thrust of the report a year later, a period in which strenuous efforts were made to silence dissenting views within the Conservative party. The major change that the Macmillan government made to Herbert's plan was to reduce the number of boroughs from fiftytwo to thirty-two, so as to vest the whole of the education service – primary and secondary – in their hands. Special arrangements, however, were to be made for education in Inner London, and a new authority, the Inner London Education Authority, arose from the ashes of the LCC education service as a temporary, if remarkably durable, arrangement.[83]

The Labour party fought the London Government Bill tooth and nail, first in the confidence that they could defeat it, and then in the belief that they could repeal it when they took office. In this, they were mistaken. Labour's own success in the first election to the new Greater London Council not only produced a change of view within the party but, more importantly, forced Sir Alec Douglas-Home's government to postpone the general election to the latest possible date, in October 1964. Thus, when Labour did come to power, it was already too late to repeal the first truly comprehensive reform of local government since 1888. The mould had at last been broken, and with it the veto that the local authority associations had until now exercised in matters of local government reform.

Notes

1 W. A. Robson, *Local Government in Crisis* (George Allen & Unwin, London, 1966), p. 78.
2 *The Economist*, 24 February 1945, pp. 237–8.
3 V. D. Lipman, *Local Government Areas, 1837–1945* (Blackwell, Oxford, 1949), p. 249.
4 J. H. Morris, *Local Government Areas* (Shaw and Sons, London, 1960), pp. 12–15. The 1945 Act established a new population threshold of 100,000 for county borough status. With its repeal in 1949 the threshold reverted to 75,000.
5 HLG 68/112, Eve to Sir Alan Barlow (Treasury), 18 July 1945.
6 HLG 68/112, Sir William Douglas to Bevan, 15 August 1945.
7 Local Government Boundary Commission, *Report for the Year 1946* (HMSO, London, 1947).
8 County Boroughs Association for England and Wales, *Statement on Behalf of the Association in Relation to the First Annual Report of the Local Government Boundary Commission*, September 1947.
9 Local Government Boundary Commission, *Report for the Year 1947* (HMSO, London, 1948), para. 1.
10 County Boroughs Association for England and Wales, *Statement on Behalf of the Association Against Proposals Contained in the Report of the Local Government Boundary Commission for the Year 1947*, November 1948.
11 House of Commons Debates, 25 March 1949, col. 74.
12 Silsoe papers, 'Note of a meeting between the Minister of Health and the members of the Local Government Boundary Commission, 10 March 1949'.
13 Local Government Boundary Commission, *Report for the Year 1948* (HMSO, London, 1949), para. 11.
14 CAB 132/11, Lord President's Committee, 4 March 1949.
15 CAB 129/34, 'Local government: memorandum by the Minister of Health', 8 April 1949.
16 CAB 129/34, 'Local government: memorandum by the Lord President of the Council', 4 May 1949.
17 Cabinet minutes, 12 May 1949.
18 Silsoe Papers, Maude to Sir Frederick Rees, 10 June 1949.
19 Minutes of the 31st Meeting of the Local Government Boundary Commission, 21 June 1949.
20 Calculations by Ministry of Health officials quoted a typical time for a well prepared private bill to be seven to eight months, against the nineteen to twenty-one months required for a Local Government Boundary Commission Order. PRO, HLG 68/13.
21 Silsoe Papers, Eve to Attlee, 22 June 1949.

114 A Structure in Tension

22 Silsoe Papers, Eve to Attlee, 29 June 1949.
23 Silsoe Papers, Attlee to Eve, 27 June 1949.
24 Silsoe Papers, Eve to Secretaries of the Local Authorities Associations, September 1949.
25 Silsoe Papers, 'Note of a meeting between the Minister of Health and the members of the Local Government Boundary Commission, 10 March 1949'.
26 County Councils Association, Parliamentary and General Purposes Committee, 13 July 1949.
27 House of Commons Debates, 2 November 1949, col. 516.
28 House of Commons Debates, 2 November 1949, cols 457–77.
29 G. D. H. Cole, *Local and Regional Government* (Cassell, London, 1947), p. ix.
30 Cabinet minutes, 27 March 1950.
31 Silsoe Papers, David Astor to Eve, 25 March 1950.
32 Silsoe Papers, 'Local government: the freeze', May 1950.
33 Silsoe Papers, Waldorf Astor to Butler, 29 June 1950; to Eve, 29 June, 7 July 1950.
34 K. Young, 'The party and the English local government', in *Conservative Century, the Conservative Party since 1900*, ed. A. Seldon and S. Ball (Oxford University Press, Oxford, 1994), pp. 413–4.
35 Silsoe Papers, Notes by Sir Malcolm Trustram Eve, 11 May 1950. See also discussions of Eve's views in the *Estates Gazette*, 25 March 1950, p. 255.
36 HLG 68/13.
37 CAB 134/470, Minutes of the Cabinet Committee on Local Government, 31 May 1949. The committee also discussed the problem of London, where it was thought that a pattern of small neighbourhood councils would serve Londoners better than their existing metropolitan boroughs.
38 CAB 134/470, Minutes of the Cabinet Committee on Local Government, 13 July 1949.
39 HLG 68/13, Sharp to I. F. Armer, 8 September 1949.
40 CAB 134/470, 'Organisation of all purpose authorities in England and Wales: memorandum by the Minister of Health', 14 October 1949.
41 The Committee's business was classified as 'top secret' and the papers circulated to it were called in.
42 CAB 134/470, 'Organisation of all purpose authorities in England and Wales: memorandum by the Home Secretary', 15 November 1949.
43 CAB 134/470, 'Organisation of all purpose authorities in England and Wales: further memorandum by the Home Secretary', 18 November 1949.
44 CAB 134/470, Minutes of the Cabinet Committee on Local Government, 24 November 1949.
45 B. Pimlott, *Hugh Dalton* (HarperCollins, London, 1985), pp. 594–5.
46 *The Economist*, 11 October 1947, pp. 588–9.

A Structure in Tension 115

47 The Conservative Party, *Britain Strong and Free*, 1951.
48 Silsoe Papers, Iain Macleod, 'The reform of London's local government', n.d.
49 County Councils Association, Urban District Councils Association, Rural District Councils Association and National Association of Parish Councils, *Reorganisation of Local Government in England and Wales* (The Associations, London, 1954).
50 Association of Municipal Corporations, *Reorganisation of Local Government* (AMC, London, 1954). See also H. Maddick, 'Local government: reorganisation or reform?', *Political Quarterly*, 25(3) (1954), pp. 246–57.
51 *The Economist*, 27 March 1954.
52 *The Times*, 22 February 1954.
53 CAB 129/67, '"Operation round-up": a comprehensive scheme for local government: memorandum by the Minister of Housing and Local Government', 24 March 1954.
54 CAB 129/74, 'Local government reorganisation: memorandum by the Minister of Housing and Local Government', 14 March 1955.
55 CPA, NUA/2/1, Annual Conference report, 1955.
56 Association of Municipal Corporations, *Report of the General Purposes Committee of the Association*, approved 12 December 1956.
57 See P. Nettl, 'Consensus or elite domination: the case of business', *Political Studies*, 13(1) (1965), pp. 22–44.
58 Morris, *Local Government Areas*, p. 15.
59 Idem.
60 A. Alexander, *The Politics of Local Government in the United Kingdom* (Longman, London, 1982).
61 B. Keith-Lucas, 'Three white papers on local government', *Political Quarterly*, 28(4) (1957), pp. 328–38.
62 Ministry of Housing and Local Government, *Local Government: areas and status of local authorities in England and Wales*, Cmd. 9831 (HMSO, London, 1956).
63 MHLG, *Areas and status of local authorities*, para. 25.
64 Ministry of Housing and Local Government, *Local Government: functions of county councils and county district councils in England and Wales*, Cmnd. 161 (HMSO, London, 1957).
65 For a complete and detailed account of the procedures of the Local Government Commissions (for England and Wales), see Morris, *Local Government Areas*. Written primarily as a guide to local authorities and others, the need for such a detailed exposition arose from the English Commission's decision to proceed by means of comprehensive questionnaire to the local authorities.

116 *A Structure in Tension*

66 Circular letter from E. A. Sharp (Permanent Secretary to the Ministry of Housing and Local Government), 4 February 1959.
67 Statutory Instrument 1958 No. 2115: *The Local Government Commission Regulations, 1958*, para. 7. The nine factors are discussed at length in Morris, *Local Government Areas*, pp. 42–50.
68 Morris, *Local Government Areas*, pp. 49–50.
69 See G. W. Jones, 'The Local Government Commission and county borough extensions', *Public Administration*, 41(2) (1963), pp. 173–87, where Jones gives a detailed account of what the Commission proposed, their decisions and their approaches.
70 D. Lofts, 'The future pattern of local government in England and Wales', *Public Administration*, 37(3) (1959), p. 278.
71 J. Stanyer, 'The local government commissions' in *Local Government in England: 1958–69*, ed. H. V. Wiseman (Routledge and Kegan Paul, London, 1970), pp. 15–35.
72 Young, 'The party and English local government', p. 416.
73 CPA, CRD/2/22/7.
74 Cabinet minutes, 25 July 1963.
75 CAB 129/114, Memorandum by the Minister of Housing and Local Government.
76 Cabinet minutes, 25 July 1963.
77 Cabinet minutes, 25 July 1963.
78 K. Young and P. L. Garside, *Metropolitan London: politics and urban change, 1831–1981* (Edward Arnold, London, 1982), pp. 292–3, 310–12.
79 CAB 129/88.
80 M. McIntosh, 'The report of the Royal Commission on Local Government in Greater London', *British Journal of Sociology*, 12 (1961), pp. 236–48.
81 *Report of the Royal Commission on Local Government in Greater London*, Cmnd. 1164 (HMSO, London, 1960), para. 696.
82 CAB 129/105, 'Local government in Greater London: memorandum by the Minister of Housing and Local Government and Minister for Welsh Affairs', 26 June 1961.
83 G. Rhodes, *The Government of London: the struggle for reform* (Weidenfeld and Nicolson, London, 1972).

5 Paying for Growth, 1945–1964

The wartime schemes for reconstruction took it for granted that a major role would be played by the local authorities. Only by funding a range of locally devised and centrally approved schemes could the Attlee government bring about the expansion of public services. For local government to develop as the single most important instrument of the Welfare State would, however, entail an elaborate system of financial incentives and controls, arrangements which inescapably shifted the balance of expenditure on local services, and enhanced the prerogatives of central government. In time, this shift came to be seen as threatening the fundamental independence of the local authorities.

In actuality, something more subtle than money was at work. After 1945, there was a marked willingness on the part of local councillors to accept a degree of central direction in policy development. It was by such means that agreed post-war aims were to be achieved, and few carped. But the counterpoint was a growing tendency for the central government to regard all local activities of financial significance as a matter for central concern. The expenditure and borrowing of local authorities came to be seen as instruments of macro-economic control, as matters for ministers.

This evolving arrangement between central and local government continued to be described as 'partnership'. But it was not a stable partnership. Ministers increasingly sought to manipulate local expenditure in the national economic interest. Such central presumption (as it seemed to them) irritated the local authorities and they responded by pressing for change. They sought a new departure in local finance, new sources of local revenue and a new deal for local government. The tension inherent within the partnership prompted a search – a fruitless search as it turned out – for a healthier balance between central control and local initiative.

Any concern about the need for a new settlement of the financial relationship between central and local government, while of philosophical interest to a minority of ministers, was generally overshadowed by electoral considerations. As local authority expenditure, and local rates, climbed steadily in the 1950s and 1960s, governments sought to cushion their impact upon households.[1] As a result, the burdens shifted, on to industry and the national taxpayer. Such palliatives had their own drawbacks, and sharp differences of view began to emerge within the post-war Conservative governments. In encouraging the growth of locally provided public services, a generation of ministers had painted their successors into a tight political corner.

The Basis of Local Finance

The rise in the post-war expenditure of local government was sustained by three basic elements: locally raised rates, centrally provided grants and local borrowing, itself subject to degree of central control. Each was subject to a degree of change and adjustment as successive governments struggled to find a financial system that could meet the conflicting needs of local flexibility and central oversight. These dilemmas were made yet more intractable by the complexities of the rating system itself, and the ways in which variations in rateable resources and local behaviour influenced the call upon grant.

The rating system

The essence of the rating system was the levy of a locally determined tax upon the occupation and use of property – residential, commercial and industrial – according to its rateable value. The rateable value was itself derived from the notional *rentable* value of the property, until 1948 a matter of local assessment. The level of the charge, the 'poundage', was expressed as a sum relative to each pound of the assessed liability – the 'rateable value'.[2] Therefore, the lower the rateable value, the higher would be the poundage required for a given revenue product.

Still in operation at the end of the war, the Rating and Valuation Act 1925 provided for periodic assessment and the levy of a rate by some 1,400 local rating authorities: the boroughs, urban and rural districts. Outside the county boroughs, county councils obtained their finance from the district and borough councils through the levy of a 'precept', an additional charge added to that set for local needs.[3] Variations from place to place in the amount of rates in the pound (or diversity of poundage) arose from two principal factors: the total rateable value in that locality; and the total municipal expenditure falling on the rates, which in turn reflected local political priorities.

Originating in 1601, the liability for rates had been restricted to immovable property in the 1840s. Originally a plethora of local charges, rates had acquired their modern form of a single general rate levied to sustain the provision of all local services under the 1925 Act. The Act swept away a complex patchwork of rates and administration, produced by centuries of piecemeal legislation. The rating authorities were obliged to establish assessment committees with (in the county boroughs) not less than one third of their membership co-opted from outside the council. In the county districts these committees were in turn overseen by county valuation committees, consisting of members of the county council and of the assessment areas within the county area. Their purpose was to ensure uniformity in the principles and practice of valuation and to assist the rating authorities, but their powers were essentially advisory.[4] Just two national valuations were carried out under the 1925 Act, in 1929 and in 1934. The valuation due in 1939 was postponed, as problems in the likely incidence of assessment were foreseen. The coming of war made the postponement an indefinite one.[5]

The 1925 Act had also established a Central Valuation Committee, on which the various classes of local authorities were represented. It was the purpose of the Central Valuation Committee to keep the system under review, advise the minister and assist county valuation committees with the more difficult cases. But while this system represented an attempt to secure consistency, its results fell far short of uniformity. Local diversity, compounded by local judgement, ensured that this would be so, for local preferences and sentiments could only hinder objective valuation. And while the semi-independent county valuation committees were intended to iron out particular anomalies, they were scarcely able to challenge mass under-assessments.

More importantly, from central government's point of view, these local variations distorted, and were in turn perpetuated by, the grant system. Under the provisions of the Local Government Act 1929, and those of successive Acts, central government grants were based on an equalizing formula, the effect of which was to ensure that local authorities with relatively low rateable values per head received more money from the central government. Local authorities therefore had an incentive to maintain low rateable values so as to maximize grant and minimize rate levies at any given level of expenditure. County councils had an incentive to understate their real wealth so as to maximize their grant entitlements. Districts, for their part, had no interest in updating their valuations, which could only increase their liability to contribute to the financing of county expenditure.

The weakness of this grant-in-aid system was that it was built upon a variable local assessment. As long as the authorities themselves valued their hereditaments, they would be tempted to under-assess their value, in order to qualify for a larger grant. This problem had preoccupied the wartime coalition, for if central government was to influence local provision across the country, such perverse outcomes would render its measures unworkable. The Attlee government's Local Government Act 1948, which abolished local valuations, and introduced a uniform and national basis of assessment by the Inland Revenue Department, did no more than implement wartime plans. And the nationalization of valuation proved in time to bring its own difficulties.

The grant system

The regime under which central government funds local authorities effectively defines the central–local government relationship, and thus what might be called the 'political constitution' of local government. The grant regime in post-war Britain was both complex and subject to continuous change. Persistent instabilities followed directly from the tendency of any particular type of grant to give rise to unintended and unwanted consequences: too great, or too slight, a degree of independence; insufficient restrictiveness, or too much; distortions in the pattern of public expenditure; or a loss of initiative from Whitehall to town hall, or in the contrary direction. Of particular importance was the mix of percentage grants, unit grants and block grants.

Percentage grants were designed to meet a given proportion of the costs of providing a particular service, and so promote and encourage its development. As such, they had a long history, especially in relation to the police and fire services.[6] A characteristic of percentage grants was that they encouraged the local authorities to spend in the knowledge that each additional pound of expenditure would not be borne in full by their own ratepayers. From central government's standpoint, the drawbacks were several. First, the reduced local cost of certain percentage grant-aided services distorted the overall pattern of provision by stimulating those services at the expense of others. Secondly, central ministries were powerless to do other than respond to local initiative; expenditure commitments were open-ended, and depended on the amounts the local authorities themselves decided to spend on particular services. Thirdly, the control of public expenditure was frustrated by the inability to forecast expenditure under percentage grant systems, still less to actually restrict the sum spent to any budgeted total. The contrary effect was supposed to be produced by the *unit grant*. In making such a grant, central departments determined a fixed sum to be paid for every unit of the service rendered. If a local authority chose to provide a better and a more expensive service, it would have to bear all the additional cost itself. Both of these types of grants were given irrespective of the authority's needs.

Block (or general) grants provided for the distribution of a total sum amongst local authorities for their general needs, in place of various percentage or unit grants for specific services. While percentage grants had grown in both number and significance in relation to the expenditure of the local authorities in general, the financial resources of local authorities proved failed to keep pace with the expansion of services. The de-rating of agriculture, industry and transport in 1929 removed millions from the rateable values of local authorities, prompting the government to compensate them with additional general grant. Compensation took the form of a general subvention in aid of their revenues as a whole, and not earmarked to support specific services. Provision for it appeared in the Local Government Act 1929 in the guise of General Exchequer Contribution. The amount received by a particular local authority was not related to the expenditure of that authority, but only to its relative needs. It was not allocated to any particular service, but used as general income.

The principle of providing for an element of local authorities' expenditure to be met from some kind of general needs subvention from central government was extended and refined throughout the post-war period. From the outset, it was joined by a second principle, that this financial support should also be used to remedy the inequalities of local resources between areas of different types. The Local Government Act 1948 introduced Exchequer Equalisation Grants (EEG) as the new block grant. These grants were based on the ratio between the average rateable value per head in each local authority and the average rateable value per head throughout the country. The EEG formula attempted to ensure that no local authority should fall below a national minimum of financial resources.

The grant aimed to make up for the shortfall in rateable values by providing assistance to those authorities the rateable values of which fell short of the national average; this was the 'resources' element of the grant. It also introduced a 'needs' element through the curious step of 'double counting' children of school age. Additionally, in the more sparsely populated counties, a further 'ghost' population was added in where the population per mile of road was less than seventy, to bring them up to this figure.[7] It was the first appearance of an arbitrary mechanism for assessing need for grant purposes.

The control of borrowing

In 1945, the government had set out the capital decisions reached by central government on the amount of resources to be devoted to the development of the various sections of the nation's economy. These decisions fixed the initial framework within which local government services were allowed to expand or encouraged to develop. Up to 1945, councils had been free to invite the general public to lend, and free also to issue mortgage or stocks or bonds as security.[8] During the war, when there was little local authority building other than of air-raid shelters, municipal borrowing was in practice largely confined to the renewal or repayment of old debt.[9]

The end of the war brought fears of uncontrolled borrowing, and of confusion in the money markets as the wartime dreams were translated into reality. The Attlee government blocked this development by effectively shutting local authorities out of the money markets, introducing controls under the Local Authorities Loans Act 1945 for a period of five years, and extending them by the Expiring Laws Continuance Acts of 1950 and 1951. Under the Loans Act, local authorities were virtually obliged to obtain nearly all of their loans through the Public Works Loans Board – a state agency set up in 1897 to lend local authorities money for works of public utility. After 1952, the Churchill government gave local authorities a choice between borrowing from the open market at rates reflecting their own credit on the market, or going to the PWLB. The Treasury reasoning was that local authority borrowing under the Act had spiralled out of control, while steering them into the market would 'induce caution'.[10] The PWLB increasingly came to serve only as a lender of last resort, and advances to local authorities by the Board fell from £364 million in 1955/56 to £45 million in 1959/60. In the same period, net borrowings from the market went up considerably, to well over £400 million a year.

The initial liberalization in 1952, and a more general relaxation in 1955, led to local authorities being (in their own words) 'thrown onto the market'. The growth in borrowing that took place between 1955 and 1963 was predominantly of a short-term nature, a factor which, while initially reducing the cost to local authorities, increased their vulnerability. Additionally, competition among them for short-term funds had the effect of forcing up interest rates, subverting the government's monetary policy, and adding a further source of volatility to the balance of payments.[11]

The central department's power to approve or disapprove local borrowing was felt with great weight before the war, when the management of the national economy focused close attention on local finance. By 1950 loan sanction control was less direct, having become closely tied to the approval of capital projects. Achieving project approval from the Ministry of Housing and Local Government was effectively to obtain the (notionally separate) permission to finance the project by borrowing. Inevitably, this meant that the control of project approvals was itself used as an instrument of economic management, as government borrowing, central and local, came to be regarded as one, and as indivisible, for the purposes of economic management.[12]

While this control of the overall level of borrowing may have met Treasury requirements, the counter-argument was put by the Radcliffe report on the monetary system. Exclusive centralization was seen as undesirable, for 'local loyalties, local knowledge and local convenience all make it possible for an energetic local authority to attract to itself some local capital that would not otherwise find itself into the gilt-edged market'.[13] That Radcliffe deemed local authority borrowing to be effectively gilt-edged was based on there being 'no ultimate danger of default'. But ultimate recourse to government backing, coupled with concern over the economic effects of unregulated borrowing, led the Treasury to intervene in 1963, promising a staged return to the PWLB, as quid pro quo for a unified regime for loan sanctions.

Governing by grant

The total sum of grants by central government to local authorities steadily increased during the immediate post-war period. New grants had been introduced piecemeal as new or extended duties were thrust upon local authorities. But there was little questioning of the proper function of grants or of the services that should be grant-aided. As the post-war euphoria faded, the Conservatives began to search for ways of taking control of these new mechanisms of the state. That search implied shifting the initiative from local to central government, although this was a pragmatic rather than a doctrinal development. Percentage grants were a natural target, for as a later minister, Henry Brooke, summarized the standard ministerial view:

> the local authority spent the money knowing that whatever it spent, so much per cent would automatically be reimbursed by the Exchequer. The government departments looking after the taxpayers' interest inevitably had to keep tabs on each local authority's spending.[14]

In making the change away from percentage grants, it was convenient for Conservative ministers to ascribe to them a tendency to encourage extravagance. In practice, there were considerable checks within any percentage grant system: standards had to be met, and expenditure was subject to audit.[15] Nor was the open-endedness of the system untrammelled. As early as 1947, the Ministry of Transport had effectively cash-limited the sums available for distribution to local authorities in support of road expenditure. The effect was to reverse the usual dynamic, with the local authorities following, rather than leading, the Whitehall department.

Whatever the effect, the system was a haphazard one, with too many specific grants, the rates of which were fixed more or less by historical accident. The major part – about three-fifths – of the total grant support was paid specifically in respect of education. In the calculation of this grant there were three distinct elements: a fixed sum per school child (a unit grant), plus 60 per cent of net approved expenditure (a percentage grant), less a sum based on each local authority's rate yield (a resource adjustment). During 1955, a major internal review of local government finance was launched. The review was undertaken by the Home Affairs Committee of the Cabinet, under the chairmanship of R. A. Butler, Lord Privy Seal. It was noted that local authorities' rate yield was growing more slowly than incomes or taxes. The result had been a drift towards increasing central finance, and the consequential dependence of local government upon the centre. Butler thought this incompatible with sound local government. A favoured solution was to restore the liability of industry and freight transport to pay rates, thereby increasing the local rate base. Linked to this would be the replacement of as many specific grants as possible with a single general grant, fixed for three years in advance. Such a grant regime would 'give local authorities a real measure of freedom without freeing them from central control on essential matters'. Without it, there was a danger of 'the atrophy of local government and its degeneration into little more than an agent of the Central Government'.[16]

Whitehall departments were in fact divided over this proposal, most of them fearing that the loss of specific grant would deprive them of the means of ensuring adequate local provision, and weaken their prospects of securing improvements. This concern was pre-eminently that of the Ministry of Education, who contributed as much as £241 million of the £279 million distributed to local authorities in the form of specific grants for education. The ministry also argued that the nature of the service was such that specific grant was needed to give reality to the minister's statutory powers under the Education Act 1944. Nevertheless, the broader argument prevailed, with the government agreeing to introduce a broad-based general grant. It fell to Henry Brooke, Minister of Housing and Local Government, to carry these proposals through to legislation. Brooke was meeting the local authority associations throughout 1957 to win their support for the change. He met with no great resistance, other than from the London County Council, who foresaw their own situation – one of high spending attracting high percentage grant – worsening under the scheme.

The key political issue faced in changing the grant system arose from its linkage to the removal of industrial de-rating. The gains to local authorities' rateable resources from this step were in the order of £30 million. Just as central government had increased grant to local authorities to compensate for industrial de-rating in 1929, so now did the Treasury seek to reduce grant by the amount of the gain, while the local authorities themselves lobbied to retain some of the former level of grant. Brooke was thus in an ideal position to negotiate the change to general grant by holding out the prospect of his claiming back something less than the full £30 million saving in grant, and thus buying support for the change. He persuaded the Cabinet to withhold only £15 million of the saving, using the remainder to

> secure pretty general support for our plan as a whole, among the leading people in local government outside London. It will transform criticism into appreciation. What is however in my eyes equally important, it will greatly increase the number of individual local authorities which will in the end gain by the Government's proposals, and diminish the number which will, in the end, lose . . . . I consider that, if we were to make no concession, the scheme as a whole – however rational financially – would be politically impossible.[17]

The block grant proposals were incorporated, along with agreed changes in the distribution of functions and in the means of reviewing local authority areas, in Brooke's Local Government Act 1958. Most of the percentage grants earmarked for particular services were now replaced by a new block grant, paid in general aid of the receiving local authorities' finances. The new grant provisions were presented as a major liberalization of the former over-specific grant regime, giving greater freedom to local authorities to determine how they should spend their money, and reducing central checking and control of detail. Grant distribution was controlled by a formula, more flexible than those formerly used, and designed to take into account the needs of the recipients and the growth in the burden falling on them. Exchequer Equalisation Grant was recast as Rate Deficiency Grant (RDG), with the object of ensuring that no local authority failed to reach a national minimum of financial resources. In so far as this minimal level was not met by rateable resources – assessed on the basis of the product of a penny rate, rather than on total rateable value – it was to be made up by grant. A similar reorganization of the finances was carried out in Scotland at the same time, under the Local Government and Miscellaneous Financial Provisions (Scotland) Act 1958.

With the sweetener of grant retained, the local authority associations were happy to accept it in principle, although the actual operation of the new grant regime fell far short of their hopes. The opposition was almost wholly confined to the education interest, where the National Union of Teachers and the Association of Education Committees (AEC) launched a nation-wide campaign against the new grant proposals. In a widely circulated pamphlet, the AEC described the block grant as 'fundamentally hostile to the best interests of education – the largest and most important service administered by local authorities'. The essentials of their case were that block grants acted to reduce expenditure growth, and failed to take account of the special position of education within local government. They argued that increased local discretion was illusory, and (somewhat in contradiction) that block grant would make for a greater diversity in local standards of education provision. The AEC presented the government's 'tampering' with the grant formula as 'upsetting the delicate mechanism which controls the partnership between central and local government in education'. The effect was tantamount to 'tearing up the Education Act'.[18] The government were able to relegate the AEC to the margin of the debate by praying in their aid the larger world of local government. Education block grant nonetheless proved a serious political hurdle for the Macmillan government, and education minister Viscount Hailsham divided the Cabinet with a spirited defence of the service for which he had just become responsible.[19]

Partners or agents?

The increasing dependence on government grants and loan sanction naturally drew attention to the increasing degree of control over the local authorities that was coming to be exercised by the central government. That it would do so was readily foreseeable during the wartime planning period. One civil servant, flying a typical kite in 1941, even queried whether rates – apparently the only feasible source of local revenue – might be abolished. 'It seems to be assumed that local authorities must have the power to tax separately from the State' he mused, 'I suppose on the ground that he who calls the tune must pay the piper'. He continued:

> This maxim may be true of free agents, but do local authorities really call the tune? . . . [H]owever free the local authorities may be in theory they are in fact controlled to a very large extent by Whitehall. I do not suggest that

this is wrong; it is probably right and necessary; but I do suggest that the revolution would be more apparent than real if local authorities were to look to Whitehall for all their money which would thus come from general taxation not from rates.

Nor need the abolition of rates mean the end of local government. County and borough councils would still function 'as local Parliaments to direct policy within the limits of their grant'. 'After all', he concluded somewhat inaptly,

> no one suggests that the Colonial Office serves no useful purpose because it cannot impose direct taxation itself but has to obtain money either from the Colonies or from the Treasury.[20]

Such forthrightness was not to be heard in public, either during the war years or after, although the sentiment lingered on.

The tightening of central control was an automatic consequence of post-1945 service development. Its effects were amplified by the deliberate assumption of central responsibility for local *performance* through the medium of the grant system. For as long as percentage grants had existed, it remained open to a responsible minister to withhold payment on grounds of unsatisfactory performance. But the Local Government Act of 1948 had generalized that power and applied it to the distribution of the Exchequer Equalisation Grant itself. It was left to the minister to decide whether or not to withhold grant and, while the Act obliged him to seek Parliamentary approval for any such decision, the terms in which it could be justified were broad.

Grant could be withheld under the minister's duty to secure a 'reasonable standard of efficiency' in all branches of a local authority's work. But how was that standard to be understood? Some ministers would see it as requiring a rate of development of local services that compared with other, similar areas, thus implying the goal of a national standard service. Others thought that the 'reasonable standard' meant no more than not excessive or luxurious. Either interpretation raised the possibility that a minister might intervene to restrict expenditure, thus setting himself up as judge of the propriety and appropriateness of local service and rate level - matters that had hitherto been considered to lie with local ratepayers.

The 1948 Act therefore set the tone for the post-war relationship between central and local government. The increasing degree of central funding, and the terms on which it was now to be made available, undoubt-

Paying for Growth 129

edly represented a difference in kind for the relationship. But, for the moment, the reality of partnership was frequently re-affirmed, and its foundations unquestioned. The Manpower Committee of 1950 laid down the orthodoxy with its assertion that local authorities were

> responsible bodies competent to discharge their own functions and, though they may be the statutory bodies through which Government policy is given effect and operate to a large degree with government money, they exercise their responsibilities in their own right, not ordinarily as agents of government departments.[21]

'Not ordinarily': the reference was to the limited and constitutionally unimportant circumstances in which local authorities entered into agency agreements with central departments; for example, in trunk road maintenance. But this was a matter freely undertaken, and did not bear upon the powers and duties which local authorities held in their own right. Even here, the central ministries had a range of powers from that of *review*, in which they might call for information, disseminate 'good practice' and thus persuade the adoption of improvements, to *control* through sanctioning or veto powers over locally originated proposals and, ultimately, to the reserved power to *direct* and thus secure compliance with the minister's wishes.[22]

Yet these were textbook formulations, as readily trotted out at any time in the 1950s by the most seasoned central official as by the most jejune local committee clerk. They masked a deeper ambiguity as to how far the fact of the centre's financial dominance undermined the spirit of local independence. After all, a new generation of councillors had been elected after the war, many of them all too happy to play a role as the local agents of a centrally directed social revolution. The habits of independence were being sapped. In his 1952 Warburton lecture, Manchester City treasurer Sir James Lythgoe warned against this trend, and against the tendency of local councils, whether from 'sheer helplessness' or from a view that progress was better secured by central direction, to submit and surrender their autonomy:

> There are undoubtedly those who appear willing to accept these changes as the inevitable accompaniment of social progress in the modern state, and also see no real danger in the evolution of this increase in powers of the central government and its central executive over elected local councils. What matter, they say, so long as Parliament is elected by democratic

process. As the state assumes more responsibility for the welfare of the community, it must be recognised, they say, that the cost of maintaining minimum standards of subsistence is far beyond the resources of relatively small units of local administration. Therefore, local units should become the agents of the State ....[23]

Was it still possible to maintain a 'partnership' if one of the partners allowed the other to exert so pervasive an influence upon it? Had the point already been reached at which the relationship could be more accurately described as that between a principal and his agent?

It was their recognition of the question that led the Conservatives to launch their fundamental review of local finance in 1955; for in so far as the problem was one of financial (rather than political or psychological) dependence, changes in the financial relationship could reverse the trend. R. A. Butler, one of the principal architects of post-war Britain, was adamant that reform was needed:

> From the constitutional point of view, the fundamental issue is how far a Conservative Government should try to make local government more democratic and self-reliant and how far they should allow local authorities to become increasingly mere agents for the execution of social and educational policy nationally conceived and directed.[24]

But although the partner/agent dichotomy could still be discussed in these terms in the mid-1950s, they were the sentiments of the reconstruction generation. Those ageing figures would not long continue to define the terms of the debate. By the early 1960s a new conventional view, of the equalizing role of central government, was beginning to gain the upper hand:

> The fundamental reason why we in this country, at this time, do not accept this philosophy of local government is that we have very decided notions about equality, especially in the sphere of social services. Since the bulk of the activities of local authorities fall within this general field, this stress upon equality implies that as a nation we are not prepared to tolerate low standards of provision in certain key services, even if the majority of the local citizenry in any authority would be content with this state of affairs.[25]

Centralism would be the new orthodoxy.

The desire to eradicate the inequalities between areas and achieve a standard level of service across the country in the interest of 'territorial justice' grew in the later 1960s. The variations in local authorities' expenditure on the various services had long been recognized. In so far as these patterns could not be explained in terms of relative need, the temptation to force them to converge would remain strong. Seeking uniformity, then, would become a more prominent theme after 1964. Meanwhile, the struggle to contain local expenditure acted as a counter-pressure against the equally strong desire to expand local services, which characterized governments of both parties, throughout the 1950s and 1960s.

Containing local expenditure

Revenue expenditure had risen in the inter-war period from £148 million in 1914 to £533 million in 1939, while capital expenditure increased from £21 million to £142 million a year. A gross outstanding loan debt of £563 million in 1914 had increased to £1,595 million in 1939. In the immediate post-war years, the inter-war rate of growth in local expenditure was soon resumed and accelerated. With the expansion of the social services, particularly education, housing and health, the expenditure of local authorities increased year by year. This growth was foreseen in the 1945 white paper which, while conceding that 'it is impossible at the present moment to say definitely what the total increase in the money to be spent by local authorities is likely to be in five or ten years' time', nevertheless anticipated the doubling of expenditure on education within a few years, and the more than doubling of health expenditure at the outset.[26]

How was this expenditure to be financed? The proportion of local revenue expenditure financed by rates, while declining in pre-war Britain, still exceeded 52 per cent at the outbreak of war. It would not rise above 40 per cent again. In 1946/47 a total of £239 million was raised by means of rates, representing 40 per cent of local revenue. In 1963/64, the corresponding figures were £923 million, and 37 per cent of local revenue expenditure. As shown in table 5.1, grants soon came to provide a larger proportion of local revenue than rates, as a result of a national requirement to develop new services, and the need felt by the successive central governments to persuade and aid the poorer authorities to keep to a higher standard of provision through grants-in-aid. Rates declined slowly in relative importance as a source of revenue, while rents, dividends, profits and interest receipts increased correspondingly.

132   Paying for Growth

Table 5.1 Local authority expenditure and rates, England and Wales, 1950/51–1965/6 (£ million)

Fiscal year	Expenditure	Rates	Grants
1950/51	773	305	305
1952/53	932	351	385
1954/55	1,083	411	453
1956/57	1,335	514	568
1959/60	1,682	650	706
1961/62	1,986	747	831
1963/64	2,395	923	1,022
1965/66	2,997	1,132	1,260

Source: Rhodes, 'Local government finance, 1918–1966', p. 154.

The rate of growth in local expenditure, and the changing balance between rates and grant, became matters of concern as the social programmes of the post-war years gathered momentum. Throughout the first half of the 1950s, the single most contentious issue in local government expenditure was the cost of the housing programme, and the extent to which that cost was met by Exchequer subsidy. By the end of the decade, as the balance of housing investment shifted from the public to the private sectors, other local services began to take the pressure. An expanded school building programme was fought for with great doggedness by Sir David Eccles. Local authority health and welfare services began to grow rapidly, with grant aid jumping from £63 million in 1959/60 to £74 million in 1961/62; an ageing population was producing pressure for the development of more old people's homes; and the Royal Commission on Mental Health urged the rapid development of services with substantial incentive in the form of a generous percentage grant. The effect was a seemingly inexorable rise in both rate and grant-borne expenditure: general grant for 1959/60 increased by 9.9 per cent over the previous year, and for 1960/61 by a further 15.6 per cent.

Local authorities were at this point submitting annual estimates of their expenditure requirements to the MHLG, confident that they would be largely accepted. That this confidence was well placed created a sense among the Treasury ministers that spending had acquired an uncontrollable dynamic. Macmillan's Chancellors from time to time attempted to gain control of the situation, but with little apparent support from the Prime Minister, who tended to hold the ring between their imperatives and those of the spending departments. Some ministers were moved by deep anxieties about the affordability of limitless expansion. But for the moment it seemed as if they could be as readily intoxicated by social expenditure as their Labour opponents. The resignation in 1957 of Treasury ministers Peter Thorneycroft, Enoch Powell and Nigel Birch from the Macmillan government, in protest over the Cabinet's refusal to make cuts in public expenditure, was an exception, a warning sign, passed off by Macmillan as no more than 'a little local difficulty'.

Its underlying cause was less easily dismissed Selwyn Lloyd, Chancellor of the Exchequer from July 1960 to July 1962, persistently pointed out the tension between service expansion and economic well-being. Reporting on local authority expenditure in November 1960, he commented that the figures were

> a fair reflection of the policies to which the government have become committed. But these expenditures are growing faster than our resources. I am bound to ask my colleagues whether they would have accepted this rate of expansion if they had seen the bill in advance. Moreover, these expenditures have such a momentum that we are already heavily committed further ahead than 1963 by the way our policies are developing.[27]

In 1961, Lloyd was struggling to force education expenditure down by £17 million and housing down by £15 million, having persuaded Henry Brooke to reduce local authority housing approvals from 110,000 to 100,000 in 1962. The underlying worry was the relationship between public expenditure and the GNP and its implications for taxation. When the Conservatives came to power, public expenditure stood at 45.5 per cent of GNP. Conservative policies, in particular, the defence cuts and the reduction of local authority housing programmes after Macmillan's peak years of 1952 and 1953, brought it down to 40.1 per cent in 1957. Thereafter it started to creep up again, stabilizing at 42.5 per cent between 1959 and 1961. Projections from current expenditure plans would take it to 44 per cent in 1965. This forecast upturn in expenditure was bound to drive taxation, which had fallen steadily, upwards again.[28]

The most important new development at this time was the move towards the planning of public expenditure as a whole, with the publication of an annual white paper, following the proposals of the Plowden Committee. These new procedures, and their underpinning by the new public expenditure scrutiny committee system, helped Lloyd in his arguments with the spending departments. So great were the government's difficulties in coping with the upward trend in expenditure that followed from their own social policy decisions that some further reinforcement was needed. In October 1961, Macmillan created the new post of Chief Secretary to the Treasury, moving Brooke from Housing and Local Government to be the Treasury's first strong-arm man. The Prime Minister explained that the Chief Secretary would have full authority in any area that involved long-term public expenditure commitments. He would have the same powers of decisions as the Chancellor himself, to whom there would be no separate recourse for a minister dissatisfied with the Chief Secretary's decisions.[29]

The emergence of Brooke in this new role changed the balance of Cabinet's discussions. In November 1961, the Economic Policy Committee rehearsed the dilemmas of progressive Conservatism. The spending ministers argued that expansion of public capital expenditure was required in the public interest and for the healthy growth of the economy, and that the programmes should be carried forward even if they resulted in higher taxation. Against this, Brooke argued that while the development of services such as education and health might have a long-term effect on national productivity, they could not be expected to show such results in the next decade, while many of the other public services had a still more distant relationship with economic growth. On the other hand, the growth of the public sector was making it the employer of choice for the rising number of graduates, siphoning off the 'nation's best brain power from industry'. In the short term, the burden of the 'swiftly expanding' capital programmes and acceleration of current expenditure were damaging the economy by diverting resources from private investment, and leading Britain into economic crisis.[30]

In particular, Brooke homed in on the housing and education programmes. He well understood pressures on the Minister of Housing but urged further cutbacks, while asking that there should be no further increase in the Ministry of Education's already high rate of investment. 'I must seriously ask my colleagues', he wrote, 'to look at these figures as a whole to weigh the priorities and to see whether they can arrive at any other conclusion than that which I have reached'. They could indeed. David Eccles mounted a fierce defence of the education building programme, arguing for its protection from any cuts which would 'break pledges' that the government had already given.[31] The problem was that the decisions taken in 1961 had been made on what Brooke now saw as unrealistically optimistic assumptions, being some £100 million higher than the sum required to maintain public expenditure at 42.5 per cent of GNP. Brooke pleaded that he was trying to prevent the growth of public expenditure from 'altogether getting out of hand, not to pin it to an arbitrary ratio'.[32] It was not easily done, and in February 1962 Selwyn Lloyd was forced to tell the House of Commons that the government was unable to contain the estimates for 1962/63 within the limits earlier announced.

The arguments rumbled on through the summer of 1962 unabated by the replacement of one-third of the Cabinet in July. In June, Selwyn Lloyd made a final plea for economy before the axe fell, not upon the estimates, but upon the Chancellor:

> I must . . . warn my colleagues that I am much disturbed at the further expansion of public expenditure as at present envisaged by departments. To incur an even greater increase of public expenditure than that already contemplated would carry too great risks. I am horrified that even greater increase should be contemplated by some of my colleagues.[33]

The reconstructed Cabinet included Reginald Maudling as Chancellor, and John Boyd-Carpenter as Chief Secretary to the Treasury. The crisis with which they had to deal arose from the fact that in 1961/62 public service investment had grown at the rate of 13 per cent. The government determined on a 6 per cent target for 1963/64 to pull back the overspend in 1962/63. But bids for spending threatened to push the increase to nearly 12 per cent, something that was 'clearly unacceptable, both on its own merits, and politically'. Keith Joseph was pushing local authority housing approvals steadily upwards again to 115,000, safe in the knowledge that the Cabinet's feeling was in favour of special priority for housing. Education, Home Office and miscellaneous local government expenditure threatened to be substantially higher than planned. Public expenditure was slipping out of control for, even without the publication of the figures, 'local authorities are bound to see that they are getting authorisations more easily for housing, minor educational works and general local government loan sanctions'.[34]

The Cabinet agreed some improvements in public expenditure control, implementing the Plowden recommendations to a fuller extent. This would define 'blocks' of public expenditure, for a period of three to four years, and relate the whole to the resources of the national economy. Even so, Maudling warned the Cabinet,

> it will take time for such a system to have effect – in some fields there is limited scope for adjustments even five years ahead, because of the inexorable effect of decisions which have already been taken, and for some time expenditure may well go on increasing faster than the GNP.[35]

The fatalistic conclusion was that there was little that the Conservatives would be able to do this side of the general election. Labour would inherit the spiralling trend of public expenditure, seeking to add to it their own new policies and programmes. The Macmillan government had not managed to face up to the choices between public service expenditure and economic well-being, and the legacy that they left to their successors was one in which the post-war consensus on social expenditure, and on the role of local authorities, could scarcely be sustained.

The Politics of Rates

Paradoxically, the problems that the rating system posed for post-war governments were the direct result of their having tackled its pre-war deficiencies. The Local Government Act 1948 sought to promote uniformity and remove inequalities in the system of valuation by taking assessment away from the local authorities and entrusting it to the Board of Inland Revenue. The aim was to achieve national standards and single valuation, to eliminate variations within and between local areas, and to overcome the disposition to undervalue so as to maximize grant. Nationalization was intended 'to restore to the law of assessment some equity, logic and comprehensibility'.[36]

Yet adjusting unwarranted variations, and putting valuations on a rational and defensible basis, was to prove politically painful for the Conservatives. As with later reforms of local finance, re-writing the map created a large class of losers, and invested valuation for rating, and rate levels, with a political hypersensitivity that they had not hitherto possessed. Solving an administrative problem had created scope for the bitterest of political disputes.

Rates on the rise

Nationalizing the valuation function in 1948 was but a first step. Bringing it into effect entailed a new national valuation exercise. This was to prove unexpectedly difficult to achieve. Publication of the Inland Revenue's first comprehensive revaluation was due in 1952, to come into effect the following spring. The work was not complete, and the revaluation was postponed to 1953 by ministerial Order. It was further postponed by a second Order when it was discovered that the basis for valuing houses was not working well. Then it was discovered that legislation was needed both to deal with the complexities of nationalized Gas Board premises before the results of any revaluation could be implemented, and to give the Inland Revenue the statutory authority to provide relief for church buildings and charities. However, lack of Parliamentary time prohibited such a step, and forced Duncan Sandys to postpone once again the implementation of the changes to 1 April 1956.

Meanwhile, the Inland Revenue was stumbling along, using 1934 values as the basis for its exercise in a manner that was recognized as contrary to the provisions of the Act, but tacitly accepted by government and local authorities alike. There was no pressure from that quarter for early implementation, but the prospect of yet another postponement was regarded with alarm, and Butler, who as Chancellor took an interest in matters of local taxation, pressed the Cabinet to avoid it by all means. The problem was that some of the more enterprising cities – Liverpool and Sheffield among them – were hurrying to complete their own revaluations of their central business areas, so that the Inland Revenue would be forced to start from a higher baseline in valuing property for rating purposes in those areas. Further postponement would encourage other cities to follow their lead. More importantly, it could expose to public notice the fact that the Inland Revenue was actually acting outside the law.[37]

The Rating and Valuation Bill that Sandys introduced in 1955 was then greatly overdue. But it also had a second, political, purpose. The bill sought to harmonize the publication of the new valuation lists with that of the local authorities' own rates. Without it, the new assessments would become known as early as the autumn of 1955, while the countervailing reductions in rate poundage would not have been apparent for a further six months. In the meantime, there would be 'widespread apprehension, and the lodging of appeals on a large scale'. Attorney-General Reginald

Manningham-Buller feared that the appeals machinery would grind to a standstill.³⁸ Moreover, without synchronized publication, 'there will be a great outcry and the whole scheme may collapse' under the weight of political opposition.³⁹

Even with this pitfall avoided, revaluation conferred on the rating system a new sensitivity. Rates were a highly visible tax, a virtue in fiscal theory, but something of a liability for a government dependent upon the support of the more highly rated voter. During the decade to 1963, rate revenues rose from about 7 per cent to over 9 per cent of public sector revenues, and from three to 3.5 per cent of gross personal incomes. In theory, there was plenty of scope to continue, or even accelerate, this trend without straining the taxable capacity of local ratepayers. But was it desirable on economic, social or political grounds?

The economic effects were at best uncertain and did not feature much in the arguments, even when the rate burden on industry was deliberately increased. The social consequences of what was seen as a highly regressive tax came increasingly to the fore in debate as the Conservative government neared its end. But most important was the electoral consideration. During the run-up to, and aftermath of, revaluation, the political consequences of further rate increases proved too potent for a Conservative government to contemplate.

It was not just low-income families who felt the squeeze of the rates during the 1950s and 1960s. Their wider unpopularity – especially among the elderly middle-class home-owners – fed the supposition that local rateable capacity was subject to some kind of natural limit, beyond which local authorities could not be expected to sustain local expenditure. In the absence of an alternative and more buoyant source of revenue, the options could only be either continuously to increase the central government grant contribution, or to transfer local government functions to the central administration. Either course simply shifted burdens from the ratepayer to the taxpayer – in practice, of course, often the same individual.

In part, this bleak view of the options stemmed from the politics of poundage: the way in which rates were calculated and expressed inevitably called attention to the continuous character of post-war increases. Prior to the 1956 revaluation, many rate poundages were approaching the 20s. in the £ level. This figure had great symbolic significance, there being a public perception of a 'sound barrier' (as it was termed, in engaging period jargon) occurring at that level of poundage.⁴⁰ In reality, of course, the figure

Paying for Growth 139

had little real meaning, for periodic revaluation naturally pushed the figure down again, without reducing rate bills. For example, between 1955/56 and 1956/57, the average level of rate poundages in England and Wales fell from 22s. 10d. to 15s. 8d. (a fall of over 30 per cent), while the average amount of rates actually levied per head of population rose by nearly 20 per cent, from £8 19s. to £11 13s. The reaction was of even greater proportion, for angry ratepayers were well aware that their local authorities took advantage of the confusion of revaluation to reduce their poundages less than proportionately.[41] Rates began to acquire the status of a uniquely unpopular tax, leading *The Economist* to comment that 'if taxes are odious, rates are anathema'.[42]

One way of avoiding being anathematized by the voters was to shift more of the burden from domestic ratepayers to industry. In the late 1950s, industrial re-rating was proposed as a strategy of 'reducing the financial dependence of local authorities on the Exchequer and enlarging the scope for local initiative and enterprise in local government'.[43] It was expected that local authorities would welcome the removal of de-rating, as the benefits would accrue to the relief of their domestic ratepayers, an outcome which Henry Brooke was keenly pursuing in 1957. But the question divided the Cabinet. As President of the Board of Trade, Peter Thorneycroft opposed it vigorously, being unimpressed with the benefits to householders: 'Before we start to divide the spoils' he warned acidly, 'we should pause to consider the wisdom of the action'. He continued:

> British industry is already today perhaps the most highly taxed in all the world. It is living under the threat of higher taxes next April. It is in immediate danger of considerable dislocation due to fuel shortage and the interruption of vital transport facilities. It has just had to absorb price increases of 1s 5d on petrol and 6 per cent on steel. It is facing fierce competition in overseas markets. To tell it, on top of all this, that it is to bear another £25 millions in rates as a first step to a further £50 millions later will appear an odd sort of Christmas present... To court such unpopularity with industry for such minimal advantages to local authorities is surely a policy of doubtful wisdom.[44]

The arguments that all types of property should be assessed at their full values were ranged against the view that industry should not be further burdened. Neither view prevailed. Adjudicating a divided Cabinet, Macmillan took the view that the proposed re-rating would not prove an insupportable burden on industry. But in a classic compromise, industrial de-rating was to be reduced – 'as an interim instalment' – to 50 per cent.[45]

The government's thinking, including the desirability of doubling industry's liability for rates, were revealed in Henry Brooke's white paper on local government finance, published in July 1957. Its proposals were mainly directed to reconstructing the grant system; in particular, to the controversial shift to block grant. The 'system of local taxation... is traditionally the right of local authorities' and was left untouched.[46] Between the 1956 and 1963 revaluations, this unwillingness to do more than tamper with local finance plunged the Conservative party into a minor internal convulsion over domestic rates. The prospective impact of the next revaluation, due in 1963, echoed that of the mid-1950s, and began to kindle the first flames of desperation. Industry had proved the loser from the earlier adjustments, and the Federation of British Industry, fearing a squeeze on industry in the interests of the more vocal domestic ratepayer, mounted a campaign to secure concessions. When the Cabinet assessed the impact of revaluation, they concluded (wrongly as it turned out) that with industrial de-rating the overall rate burden would be marginally less than under the old values. However, the demand falling on industry itself was likely to increase by an average of 43 per cent, and in some areas would double. Although selective help for industrial areas was dismissed out of hand, there was prolonged discussion of possible action to soften the blow in seaside towns such as Blackpool and Bournemouth – where a new class of loser, the hotels and boarding houses, had been identified.[47]

The dilemma facing the Macmillan government arose directly from the nationalization of valuation in 1948. Having taken responsibility away from the local authorities, central government could hardly avoid the political consequences of that act. But should ministers now follow through the logic of the more rational and ostensibly fair system, or would the temptation to manipulate it for political ends prove too strong? Some argued that increases in valuation were the necessary consequence of any rationalization, and carried no entitlement to help from the Exchequer. Its object had been to produce fairness; arbitrary intervention should be resisted. Others looked for a way of avoiding the consequences. But before long it became clear that a national scheme of general relief, rather than a locally selective interventions, would be required.

The Conservative dilemma

When, during the late 1950s and 1960s, attention turned to finding new sources of local revenue, it was in order to strengthen the financial basis of local government, underwrite its independence, and produce a more equitable and affordable system. It seemed that the rating system had reached some kind of limit, for four reasons. First, the regressive character of rates imposed a disproportionately heavy burden on poorer families. Secondly, the pattern of local expenditure that the rating system produced displayed wide variations, by no means reflecting differences in the level of need. Thirdly, the visibility and political unpopularity of rates suggested that they had reached their natural ceiling, and lacked the buoyancy necessary to sustain future expenditure growth. Finally, these shortcomings seemed to presage a still greater assumption of responsibility by central government, the avoidance of which would require an entirely new system. A new system would come in time, although on its first appearance in 1953, the flat rate 'poll tax' received short shrift from Central Office, and was rejected outright on the grounds that 'of all the possible ways of raising local money, this... is certain to be the least equitable'.[48]

With hindsight, it is possible to see that the 1963 revaluation started the long slow disintegration that was to lead eventually to the abolition of rates and to the short-lived poll tax. What was apparent at the time was that it had provoked the first real crisis of confidence in the post-war rating system. Early in 1961, a Conservative party study group on rates reform and alternative sources of local taxation was appointed, under the chairmanship of J. M. Temple. Despite there having been a recent 'comprehensive review' carried out by the government itself, Henry Brooke welcomed this party initiative, as 'I don't think many people in our party have done serious study of this'.[49]

Serious study it certainly was. The group addressed the issues of the viability of local government, the tolerability of rates and the likely future trend of public expenditure. They concluded that in order for a meaningful system of local government to be maintained, a minimum of 30 per cent of its revenues should be derived from local taxation, a figure comfortably exceeded at that time. They also considered that there was an upper limit to the tolerability of rates, which they defined as 4 per cent of average earnings. The group argued that the rating system was capable of carrying the anticipated burden of local expenditure within this limit of tolerability until 1970. Just how much closer that limit was to being reached became uncomfortably clear when it was revised to 3.5 per cent of average earnings, a figure reached in the following year. Urgent action was therefore required, and internal party pressure came to be put on ministers.[50] With the exception of Sir Keith Joseph, ministers and party chiefs were opposed to publication, as airing the notion of there being a 'threshold of tolerability' in rates, but not in taxes, was seen as politically dangerous.

A more immediate political danger was that posed by the Liberal party, the success of which in attracting Conservative voters at Orpington – the Conservatives' second safest seat – had helped to precipitate Macmillan's 'night of the long knives'. Party sources close to the local finance discussions warned that the burden of rates was 'a matter which closely concerns our traditional supporters, some of whom feel very strongly about it'. Without decisive thinking, 'the Liberals will probably fill the gap, to their great advantage'.[51] Those who were concerned about the electoral effects of doing nothing foresaw that even after revaluation, the 'sound barrier' of 20s. in the £ could be reached frighteningly soon. By enabling a lower poundage to be charged on a higher valuation, revaluation was recognized as doing no more than defer the approach of the 'sound barrier'. The judgement was astute. Local authorities did indeed seize the opportunity to increase their revenues by making more than proportionate increases in the poundage they levied.

Sir Keith Joseph was seen within the party as largely indifferent to the rates issue. As the 1963 revaluation approached, he warned that the substantial increases in rateable values which the new valuation lists would show

> will make ratepayers everywhere particularly sensitive to the level at which next year's rate is fixed . . . The minister would therefore urge on local authorities that in framing their estimates for the coming financial year they should pay fully as much regard to the need for economy as in previous years. Expenditure which would have been regarded as excessive but for the revaluation cannot be justified by the fact that the revaluation has taken place.[52]

But this did not have the ring of firm government about it. Not that Joseph's critics within the party were any more specific. They only sought, rather feebly, to 'let the public know that the Party is worried about the unfair incidence of rates and is thinking what can be done to help'.[53] The popular suspicion that revaluation would not be neutral in its effects was confirmed by the trend in rates, which continued their upward climb. The total amount raised by rates in 1963/64 exceeded that raised in the previous year by £80 million. Domestic ratepayers' bills would rise by an average of 7.5 per cent, and some rises would greatly exceed this figure. The very basis of the system of local finance was beginning to unwind.

The Times added its voice to a growing debate, acknowledging that 'rates are a uniquely unpopular form of tax' and that a case could be made against them, as a means of raising taxes for expanding services, irrespective of revaluation.[54] Joseph responded to these party and public pressures by appointing a committee of inquiry, under the leading economist Professor R. G. D. Allen, to consider the narrower issue of 'the impact of rates on householders in different parts of Great Britain, with special regard to any circumstances likely to give rise to hardship'. This was a fact-finding exercise. The big questions were not for committees of inquiry. Transferring tax burdens from the ratepayer to the taxpayer 'was a matter of policy, which the government themselves must decide'.[55] For this, an interdepartmental scrutiny of the options was established under the Chancellor of the Exchequer.

The political crisis gathered pace in line with the rises in local authority expenditure, and faster than any independent committee or internal Whitehall inquiry could proceed. The rate rises foreseeable for April 1964 would provoke 'renewed resentment'. Joseph was thus forced to consider some interim measures of relief, pending the Allen report. But relief on the scale that any government could contemplate would be

> small beer in comparison with the £500 million or so which householders will have to find from rates next year, or the likely increase of around £100 million in the total rate levy, about half of which has to be found by householders.[56]

Intervention on this scale was also likely to be thought inadequate by back-bench Conservatives, to the extent even that Joseph was not confident about getting such proposals through Parliament. He foresaw (rightly, but for the wrong reason) a difficult party conference in the autumn of 1963, with resolutions calling for a remodelling of the financial structure of local government so as to make the rate burden more equitable. That conference had even more pressing concerns when Prime Minister

Harold Macmillan upstaged all other issues by resigning the premiership from his hospital bed.

A few weeks later, a new Cabinet assembled under the most unlikely of Prime Ministers, Sir Alec Douglas-Home. A general subsidy to hold rates at their then level was out of the question in terms of affordability and the dangerous precedent it would set. Failing that, there could be selective additional grant aid, a transfer of costs from ratepayer to taxpayer, or a degree of remission of rates in cases of hardship, with the costs borne in part or whole by the government. Joseph's preference was for an across-the-board increase in general grant, but his Cabinet colleagues demurred. The Treasury argued that to reduce average domestic rate bills by £3 would cost £100 million, or fourpence on income tax.[57]

The relief of distress as an interim measure was as far as the Cabinet was prepared to go in advance of the Allen report, in the form of a Rating (Interim Relief) Bill. Introduced in December 1963, the bill provided for increased central grants for areas with large numbers of people over sixty-five, and allowed for the remission of rates in individual cases of hardship resulting from revaluation. For the rest, more effective 'presentation' of policy would have to answer, and Douglas-Home invoked the help of Brooke – although Home Secretary, still a major voice on local government issues – and John Boyd-Carpenter, Chief Secretary to the Treasury, in making public an anodyne statement about the government's concern for the ratepayer. The government's announcement that 'the Government fully understand the apprehensions which many people feel about rates' and that 'many people fear that future increases in spending by local authorities may cause rates to go on rising' lacked conviction.[58] The new Prime Minister had been as concerned as his predecessor to press his ministers to continue their expansionist policies.

The postponement of the general election date to the autumn of 1964 raised the question of what more, if anything, need be done in the meantime. Maudling, the last Conservative Chancellor of that era, pacified his troubled colleagues, arguing that the heat had gone out of the politics of rates, that the timetable of reform meant that nothing could in any case be done before 1967/68, and that the Cabinet 'must decline to be rushed into premature decisions. And we need to bear in mind that there is no solution to the rates problem which will please everyone.'[59] It was hardly an electorally potent position. In this, as in other key areas of policy, the Conservatives had allowed themselves to be outflanked by a reformist and exuberant Labour party who, notwithstanding their reputation as high spenders, entered the 1964 general election with a clear pledge to reform the rates.

Notes

1. G. Rhodes, 'Local government finance, 1918–1966', in Department of the Environment, *Local Government Finance: Appendix 6 to the report of the Committee of Inquiry under the chairmanship of Sir Frank Layfield, QC: the relationship between central and local government: evidence and commissioned work* (HMSO, London, 1976), pp. 102–73.
2. N. P. Hepworth, *The Finance of Local Government*, 7th edn (George Allen & Unwin, London, 1984), pp. 69–104.
3. H. Finer, *English Local Government*, 4th edn (Methuen, London, 1950), pp. 405-449; W. Thornhill (ed.), *The Growth and Reform of English Local Government* (Weidenfeld and Nicolson, London, 1971), pp. 122–52.
4. Appeals from the decisions of the assessment committees were to Quarter Sessions or, in the counties, to specially constituted committees of Justices. See Finer, *English Local Government*, pp. 443ff.
5. G. Block, *Rating Revaluation*, Local Government Series No. 8 (Conservative Political Centre, London, 1963).
6. M. Schultz, 'The development of the grant system', in *Essays on Local Government*, ed. C. H. Wilson (Blackwell, Oxford, 1945), pp. 113–60.
7. J. Maud and S. E. Finer, *Local Government in England and Wales* (Oxford University Press, Oxford, 1953), pp. 157–9.
8. M. Schultz, 'The control of local authority borrowing by the central government', in Wilson, *Essays on Local Government*, pp. 161–203.
9. Sir H. Page, *Local Authority Borrowing: past, present and future* (George Allen & Unwin, London, 1985), p. 176.
10. Cabinet minutes, 14 October 1952. Significantly, Macmillan, as Minister of Housing and Local Government, initially opposed the move on the grounds that vitually the entirety of local authority borrowing was to finance projects undertaken at the behest of the central departments.
11. Page, *Local Authority Borrowing*, pp. 176–89.
12. L. T. Little, 'Radcliffiana', *Local Government Finance*, October 1959, p. 1.
13. *Report of the Committee on the Working of the Monetary System*, Cmnd. 827 (HMSO, London, 1959), para. 597.
14. Quoted in A. Williams, 'Local authorities and the national economy', in *Local Government Today . . . and Tomorrow*, ed. D. Lofts, reprinted from *Municipal Journal*, (1962), p. 48.

146 *Paying for Growth*

15 D. S. Lees et al., *Local Expenditure and Exchequer Grants* (Institute of Municipal Treasurers and Accountants, London, 1956).
16 CAB 129/84, 'Local government finance: memorandum by the Lord Privy Seal', 14 December 1956, paras 22, 19.
17 CAB 129/87, 'Local government finance: memorandum by the Minister of Housing and Local Government and Minister for Welsh Affairs', 21 June 1957.
18 Association of Education Committees, *The Threat to Education* (Councils and Education Press, London, 1957).
19 CAB 129/85, 'Local government finance: the general grant: memorandum by the Minister of Education', February 1957; Cabinet minutes, 7 February 1957.
20 CAB 117/214.
21 *First Report of the Local Government Manpower Committee*, Cmnd. 7870 (HMSO, London, 1950), p. 6.
22 Maud and Finer, *Local Government in England and Wales*, pp. 171–88.
23 Sir J. Lythgoe, *Local Government Reform: a Warburton Lecture delivered in the University of Manchester on 24th April 1952*, p. 4.
24 CAB 129/84, 'Local government finance: memorandum by the Lord Privy Seal', 14 December 1956, para. 24.
25 Williams, 'Local authorities and the national economy', pp. 38–9.
26 Ministry of Health, *Local Government in England and Wales During the Period of Reconstruction*, Cmd. 6579 (HMSO, London, 1945), p. 7.
27 CAB 129/103, Memorandum by the Chancellor of the Exchequer, 16 November 1960.
28 CAB 129/104, 'Public expenditure: memorandum by the Chancellor of the Exchequer', 23 March 1961.
29 CAB 129/107, 'Memorandum from the Prime Minister on the duties of the Chief Secretary to the Treasury', October 1961.
30 CAB 129/107, 'Memorandum on civil public investment by the Chief Secretary to the Treasury', 18 December 1961.
31 CAB 129/107, 'Educational expenditure, memorandum by the Minister of Education', 21 December 1961.
32 CAB 129/108, 'Memorandum by the Chief Secretary to the Treasury on public expenditure 1962/63 to 1965/66', 4 January 1962.
33 CAB 129/109, 'Memorandum by the Chancellor of the Exchequer', 7 June 1962.
34 CAB 129/110, 'Memorandum by the Chief Secretary to the Treasury', 27 July 1962.
35 CAB 129/113, 'Rates of growth of public expenditure: memorandum by the Chancellor of the Exchequer and the Chief Secretary to the Treasury', 26 April 1963.
36 Finer, *English Local Government*, p. 446.

Paying for Growth 147

37 CAB 129/74, 'Memorandum by the Chancellor of the Exchequer', 21 February 1955.
38 Cabinet minutes, 24 February 1955.
39 CAB 129/74, 'Memorandum by the Minister of Defence', 21 February 1955.
40 Williams, 'Local authorities and the national economy', p. 41.
41 Hard evidence on such perceptions is hard to come by. In a survey following the Scottish revaluation of 1985, respondents attributed their increased rates in the greater part, and correctly, to changes in grant, revaluation and local rating decisions, in that order. See A. Midwinter and C. Mair, *Rates Reform: issues, arguments and evidence* (Mainstream Publishing, Edinburgh, 1987), p. 168
42 *The Economist*, 26 November 1960.
43 Cabinet minutes, 29 January 1957.
44 CAB 129/84, 'Local government finance: memorandum by the President of the Board of Trade', 19 December 1956.
45 Cabinet minutes, 5 February 1957.
46 Ministry of Housing and Local Government, *Local Government Finance (England and Wales)*, Cmnd. 209 (HMSO, London, 1957), para 3.
47 Cabinet minutes, 6 March 1962.
48 CPA, CRD 2/22/10, Herbert Brabin to Peter Goldman, 5 November 1953; Goldman to Brabin, 6 November 1953.
49 CPA, CRD 2/22/12, Henry Brooke, 14 July 1961.
50 CPA, CRD 2/22/12. The group's calculations were checked by Treasury officials, who pronounced the exercise to be valuable and realistic. J. M. Temple, the group's chairman, commended the report to Butler, expressing his own worry about local government expenditure 'taking a greater and greater share of the GNP'. Temple to Butler, 28 June 1962.
51 CPA, CRD 2/22/13, Gilbert Longden MP to Butler, 19 September 1962.
52 Ministry of Housing and Local Government, Circular 65/62, December 1962.
53 CPA, CRD 2/22/13, Longden to Butler, 20 November 1962.
54 *The Times*, 1 March 1963.
55 Cabinet minutes, 7 March 1963.
56 Cabinet minutes, 3 October 1963.
57 Cabinet minutes, 27 February 1964.
58 Cabinet minutes, 5 March 1964.
59 CAB 129/118, 'Rates: memorandum by the Chancellor of the Exchequer', 19 May 1964.

6 The Consensus Crumbles, 1964–1979

The period of thirty years following the war was a period of expansion in the provision of local services, punctuated only by periodic economic crises. Both major parties were committed to growth, and the first act of Sir Alec Douglas-Home, on succeeding Macmillan as Prime Minister, was to urge his depleted Cabinet to continue to bring forward plans for the further development of services. Agreement on the desirability of the provision of public services characterized an entire political generation. It was a received belief in the political class prior to 1980 that

> palpable injustices and differences in the life-chances of the well-to-do and of the poor could be diminished by public expenditure and redistributive taxation: and that the agents to bring about change were the bureaucracies of central and local government, under the control of elected ministers and councillors.[1]

Sustained by this powerful consensus, local government became the deliverer – rather than the originator – of a wide range of services, from public infrastructure and housing, to education and social welfare.[2] The consequence was a period of continuous expansion in services, expenditure and employment, much of it in the local authority sector.

Growth did not come cheap, and from around 1960 onward successive governments found themselves torn between wishing to expand local services, and containing expansion in the national economic interest. The conflict almost always took the form of a contest between Treasury ministers and those responsible for the major local government services, with the Minister for Housing and Local Government, and later the Secretary

The Consensus Crumbles 149

of State for the Environment, acting as the principal spokesman for local authority expansion. Expansionism reached its zenith in the decade that followed the election of a Labour government in 1964. Thereafter, while both parties continued to pay homage to public services, they became increasingly uneasy about paying for growth. By 1975, when Anthony Crosland foreclosed on expansion with his brutal warning 'the party's over', there were already stirrings on the right of a new approach, foreshadowed in a series of speeches by Sir Keith Joseph in 1974. The consensus crumbled as Conservatives turned their backs on the spirit of 1945

None of this could be foreseen when Labour won the general election in October 1964. The party's appeal was characterized by a breezy optimism, a young, technocratic approach that mirrored the new leader himself. After 'thirteen wasted years', Labour activists were looking for big results. Housing and education were, once again, areas in which local authorities would be looked to for the implementation of nationally formulated policies and programmes. The new mood of institutional reform turned the spotlight on local government itself, and, with the example of the creation of the Greater London Council before them, politicians of both parties embraced a new programme of enforced restructuring.

At the same time, it was becoming increasingly apparent that central government control was stepped up with each new initiative. Ministers were not especially fastidious about local discretion; in that respect too, the mood had changed since the post-war Attlee and Churchill governments. In both housing and education, the Wilson/Callaghan period, and the Conservative interlude under Heath, were marked by ministers looking for results. They were not notably successful. Labour's lack of success in pursuing its social policy aims was dispiriting to its supporters, while the similar failures of the Heath government produced a brisker reaction. In 1975 Heath was deposed as Conservative leader by Margaret Thatcher. Few at the time could have foreseen that the victor, a youngish woman who had featured so far only as a rather ineffectual Education Secretary, would transform the political landscape and, in time, rewrite the place of local government in the political constitution.

Housing Polices and Programmes

Rachmanism and its associated scandals of homelessness did much to shape housing policy in the early 1960s. The temptations of political opportunism were considerable, and the years of scandal propelled the Labour party into exploiting the Conservatives' discomfiture. They made firm commitments to solve the housing problem, commitments which the Conservatives themselves, now on the defensive, readily echoed. Labour came to power in 1964 with a commitment to build 500,000 houses a year by 1970. When, due to the worsening economic climate and devaluation in 1967, this ambitious target was dropped, it marked the end of an era in which 'grand, rounded national figures, dreamed up on somebody's doodling pad, were the main deciding figures in national housing policy'.[3]

This time, the Conservatives would not follow Labour's lead. They took the opportunity of opposition under Edward Heath to rethink housing policy, bringing to it a distinctively anti-municipal bias. This too was 'reconstruction' in a sense, as the party's thinkers had a clear vision of the ways in which patterns of housing provision shaped the kind of society Britain would become. Their policies would be driven by a desire to foster independence and break Labour's hold upon the publicly housed urban working class. The Conservatives' white paper *A Fair Deal for Housing* signalled the end of bipartisan policies, and the politics of housing was infused with a new spirit of bitter contention. But for all their demonization of new Conservatism, Labour had lost the initiative on housing policy to their opponents and, when they returned in 1974, they appeared bereft of ideas. Time had run out. After 1979, there would not be another opportunity for local authorities to regain their role as the providers of large-scale social housing.

Targets and subsidies

Having made housing needs and conditions a central feature of their attack on the Macmillan/Home government, Labour was bound to pitch high on housing targets.[4] Wilson himself had no illusions as to the importance of meeting the expectations that his own pre-election speeches had done so much to raise. 'On housing', he told the new housing minister, Richard Crossman, 'we win or lose'.[5] Crossman urged upon Wilson an immediate target of 150,000 council houses for the coming year. When his 1965 housing white paper upped the overall annual target from 400,000 to 500,000. Wilson dubbed it 'not a lightly given pledge – it is a promise'.[6]

How was the promise to be delivered? Clearly, only through a 'mixed economy of housing' in which the private sector would have to make a major contribution. In fact, the Conservatives had already succeeded in winding the housing programme up to the level that Labour had envisaged, and little or no additional action would be required to achieve the 400,000 target set in the election campaign. During 1964, 144,000 council house approvals had been given and private sector completions ran at well over 200,000. Indeed, when the housing programme was discussed in Cabinet in February 1965, the Chancellor, James Callaghan, attempted to force the local authority housing target down to 135,000, well below that actually achieved in the Conservatives' last year.

Crossman's approach to achieving Labour's housing goals was three-fold. First, he pressed for a switch in the balance between private building for sale, and local authority building for rent, in favour of the latter. He told the Cabinet:

> Our pledge was to increase the building of new houses, both for rent and for sale. Under the previous government houses for rent lagged well behind houses for sale; and rented houses are now the great need. It is only public authorities who can and will build rented houses on any scale; in addition to which most of the many hundreds of thousands of families at present in wretched housing conditions can only afford a subsidised rent.
>
> Local authorities have been held down from building all that they want – and knew that they needed – to build. Last year's programme was their biggest for some years, but given encouragement they will do more; and I propose now to settle a four year forward programme with them. For years they have concentrated on slum clearance, old people, overspill and relieving the worst squalor and overcrowding. Though households have been increasing fast, they have been allowed to build very little to meet general needs. They must now be allowed to do more.[7]

Given the high level of housing construction that Labour inherited, the building industry could not readily cope with a major increase in activity. Crossman's first answer, then, was to squeeze private building in order to free resources for public-sector construction: 'If the private sector shows signs of getting out of hand we shall have to consider ways and means of ensuring a properly balanced housing programme.' Although the Cabinet explored ways of controlling private house building – including a ban on the building of more expensive houses – such a return to the spirit of 1945, with the legislative and administrative controls that it would require, did not find much favour. Callaghan pointed out that the government was equally committed to making private house purchase easier, as aspiration which could be expected to lead to further increases in private building. Should the government take powers to control private building, the knowledge that they *intended* to do so would itself stimulate a surge in housing starts to beat the ban.

The underlying problem – if problem it was – was that Labour had moved from being a party of the council tenant to being a broader based party. They had accepted the shift in the ground rules of the housing debate that enabled private house building to count equally with local authority programmes as a measure of success. The long period of Conservative rule had brought about such marked shifts in the tenure pattern (of England in particular) that the new government was bound to accommodate the needs of the owner–occupiers. Labour was more ready than before to acknowledge the widespread desire for owner-occupation. The party's traditional supporters were gradually becoming richer, and more of them could afford to buy their own homes. Changing tenure patterns meant that it had become politically feasible for Labour to recognize home ownership as the natural form of tenure. The housing programme for 1965–70 acknowledged building for owner-occupation as 'normal' and as reflecting 'a long term social advance which should gradually pervade every region'.[8] There was no way Labour could hope to meet their targets without a major private-sector building contribution.

Crossman's second move was to attempt to increase the productivity of local authority house construction. This he did by espousing industrial building. Having already agreed to continue housing approvals at the level of 150,000 annually, the government endorsed the 1965 white paper with its commitment to 250,000 council houses as part of the new half million annual target; a total of 200,000 starts were expected for 1966. Crossman was a complete convert to industrialized building. Indeed, he argued with some success that the advantages of industrialized building were so great that an increasing programme of local authority housing construction was needed in order to realize their benefits. 'Nothing could more effectively show our determination to promote efficiency in all sectors of the economy', he enthused, 'than a dramatic increase in the use of labour saving methods in house building. We cannot achieve this unless we can authorise bigger programmes where the authorities will use these methods.'⁹

The essence of industrialized building was on-site fabrication of the panels and other structures needed to erect the tall flats and linear blocks that were to become the hallmark of 1960s public housing. Huge sites were needed to reap the advantages of large-volume production that such systems needed, as well as providing space for the production process itself. Large-scale redevelopment, especially of derelict sites, offered the main opportunity, and Crossman thought that as much as one-third of the municipal housing needs of London and Birmingham could be met in this way. In approving targets he would advise the local authorities that he expected them to make increased use of industrialized building methods. In London, junior minister Bob Mellish strong-armed neighbouring local authorities into forming consortia to reap the advantages of industrialized building methods.

In 1967, a new Housing Subsidies Act altered the basis of Exchequer grant, until now a flat sum per dwelling, to a low-interest loan which, in effect, enabled local authorities to borrow at a maximum of 4 per cent. As the interest rate rose so also did the amount of subsidy, protecting local authorities from the burden on excessive debt charges. As a result, the rate of new building under the Labour government continued at a high level, 1967/68 recording the highest level of council house building since the early 1950s. Yet this new approach to subsidy proved uncomfortably open-ended. The Exchequer subsidy set at £24 per house under the Conservatives on the long-standing contribution-per-unit built basis reached £110 per house under the new scheme. It made the housing programme all the more difficult to protect from the Treasury.

Less controversial within the government itself was Crossman's third plank - tackling the private rented sector. The commitment to the municipalization of rented property had been watered down under Hugh Gaitskell's leadership on cost grounds. The revisionist policy document *Signposts for the Sixties*, published in 1961, had trimmed the commitment to take private rented accommodation into municipal ownership. This was far from welcome to much of the party, however, especially in London, where the housing problems were at their most intense; considerable tension ensued between the national party leadership and the London Labour party. Attacking private landlordism was no less insistent for that.

The antipathy to private landlords ran deep, having been stoked up by the experience of the Conservatives' 'wasted years'. Labour's commitment to repeal the hated 1957 Rent Act was quickly honoured with one of their own, a framework of 'fair rents' and rent tribunals replacing the former mix of controlled and decontrolled tenancies. The security of private tenants, and the costs of their housing, were immediately stabilized. There was no positive effect, however, on the condition of their housing, as no incentive was given to investment by landlords. On the contrary, the combination of large-scale, low-rent, municipal housing and lavish encouragement to private house purchase – itself carried over from the Conservatives – ensured that private tenants continued as the most neglected of all the so-called housing classes.[10]

The public expenditure cuts made in the aftermath of devaluation in 1967 broke the essential continuities of post-war municipal housing. The new-build programme was trimmed rather than curtailed in January 1968, but of greater importance was the switch of resources away from building, towards the rehabilitation of existing, older property with more generous grants in General Improvement Areas (GIAs). The 1968 white paper on housing declared that 'within a total of public investment in housing at about the level it has now reached, the greater share should go to the improvement of old homes'. Behind the policy switch lay a renewed belief that the numerical shortage of homes was coming to an end. The priority was to improve standards, not build more units of a quality which was for the first time coming to be seen as inadequate, and as containing the seeds of a slum problem of the future. The subsidy system that had promoted high-rise building in the mistaken belief – persistently and patiently challenged by the Town and Country Planning Association – that building higher meant building more, and cheaper, was abandoned at this time, just before the Ronan Point disaster conferred scandal status on high-rise public housing schemes.

The principal instrument of the new policy was, as before, financial incentives. The take-up of improvement grants rose dramatically after the Housing Act 1969, while the GIA scheme, under which local authorities could make environmental improvements to support the availability of grants, was responded to with alacrity. Not the least significant aspect of this new approach to housing was the convergence it represented between Labour and Conservative thinking. Indeed, part at least of the impulse behind area improvement was an awareness of how large-scale urban renewal under Labour councils could destroy both the physical and the social fabric of stable, if dilapidated, urban communities.

By this point, the prospects for that type of large-scale municipal development were in any case severely curtailed by the new political realities. The Wilson government, suffering an unprecedented degree of unpopularity after devaluation, suffered catastrophic electoral defeats in the 1967 and 1968 local elections. The safest of Labour councils were swept away and replaced with solid Conservative majorities. In areas of Inner London, the political infrastructure of local Labour parties was destroyed, opening up opportunities for a new generation of middle-class socialists to take over the party and, before long the local council. Neither they, nor the Conservatives who for the present held sway in town halls across Britain, were especially friendly to the old-style municipal house building machine.

Despite their hopes of a recovery, Labour lost the 1970 election to Edward Heath's Conservative party. And the Conservatives proved to be unusually well prepared for office, having totally rethought their housing policies during their years in opposition. When Heath came to office, Peter Walker headed the new Department of the Environment, which had absorbed the old Ministry of Housing and Local Government. His white paper *A Fair Deal for Housing* set out the new approach, the essence of which was to 'subsidise people, not bricks and mortar'. This was to be achieved through a new national rent rebate scheme for council tenants (with rent allowances being paid to those in private renting) and a new form of deficit subsidy to local Housing Revenue Accounts (HRAs). This was a radical departure in housing subsidy, and one which thrust the local authorities' HRAs into a central place in the politics of housing, where it was not only to be subjected to a close scrutiny, but was to be manipulated by both central and local government in the battle over resources.

In place of a general housing subsidy that local authorities used to keep rents down, or to reduce the rates, assistance would in effect be directed at individual households, in proportion to their financial need. Walker presented the proposals as a measure of redistribution from the better-off council tenant to the less well-off. The new regime was intended to contain the growth of subsidies, which had been so rapid and uncontrollable under Labour, with a view to reducing them after 1975/76. Subsidy would also be redirected to areas of greatest housing need; and the aim was to enable long-term planning by making provision for 1981/82 and beyond.

Apart from a subsidy to the HRA, which was to be paid in the proportion 80 : 20 from the national Exchequer and local ratepayers to meet the costs of rebates, a new subsidy was payable when costs on the HRA rose faster than rent income. This would be paid only for a limited period, as it was expected that 'fair rents' would eliminate deficits on the HRA. The corollary of this subsidy regime was that local authorities would be subjected to much closer scrutiny and control, to prevent their expenditure on management, maintenance and improvement increasing under the impetus of an open-ended form of subsidy. In this one respect, the new government's proposals did not survive unscathed, and a House of Lords amendment to the subsequent Housing Finance Bill ensured that increased local expenditure during 1971/72 would be met in the greater part by the government, the resultant impact being to *increase* the actual subsidy paid rather than allow it to reduce.

The most striking feature of the short period in which the Housing Finance Act applied was the rapid increase in both local expenditure and national subsidy. Because the 1971/72 spending was the base for 'reckonable' expenditure for subsidy purposes in subsequent years, it was in the interest of local authorities to maintain as high a level of expenditure as possible in that year. There was also an additional incentive to persist in a high level of deficit-inducing expenditure, for the Act provided for subsidy to be withdrawn as soon as the HRA moved into profit. If the Act wholly failed to control the total amount of subsidy, it was more successful in redistributing it, particularly to high-cost areas such as Inner London. At the level of the individual tenant, the steady growth in the proportion of subsidy being applied to rebates signalled the extent to which the less well-off tenant was benefiting.

While Labour were committed to repealing the Act when they returned to office (as they did in 1974), the new close controls and detailed scrutiny would be retained. Under Environment Secretary Anthony Crosland, a far-reaching review of housing finance was set in motion; in the meantime, the system of rent rebates and allowances and other subsidy arrangements were left intact. The rebate system, with its 75 : 25 division of cost between the Exchequer and the ratepayer, was unpopular with local authorities, who looked to a Labour government to deal with poverty through the income maintenance system. The government's response was to hold the line pending the results of the review: 'We shall have to examine our definitions of housing subsidy and housing finance' Crosland promised, 'and consider rebates and rent allowances in future as part of the cash social security scheme'.

Labour's Housing Rents and Subsidies Act 1975 brought with it a new subsidy system, with the aim to restore local authorities' autonomy in determining their own rent levels, and to enable them to maintain higher levels of investment in housing without imposing additional burdens on tenants and ratepayers. It was also intended to raise the total subsidy to equal that granted to house-buyers on their mortgage payments, providing 'fairness' between the sectors. While the government were prepared to accept a high level of subsidy support to municipal housing, they were well aware of the escalating tendencies of open-ended subsidies. In practice, it was impossible to control the steady rise in subsidy, as the subsidy scheme provided a dynamic to increasing expenditure, at a time at which rents were being strictly controlled and prices and costs were rising rapidly. Between 1973/74 and 1978/79 subsidies, excluding rebates, increased from £237 million to £1,055 million, a five-fold increase. This was not a situation that any incoming government could have tolerated.

Conservatives rethink rents

Following the 1966 election, when Labour was clearly going to be in power for a full Parliament, Edward Heath established one of his numerous policy study groups under the chairmanship of Sir Keith Joseph.[11] Almost alone among these policy groups, that on housing was to have a major impact on party policy and, eventually, on housing legislation. It differed in another respect too. The membership of the group owed little to past orthodoxies and everything to the coming, free market oriented Conservatism. Apart from Joseph himself, and Hugh Rossi MP, it included two of the leading architects of the new right thinking on municipal housing: Horace Cutler of the GLC, and Frank Griffin of Birmingham.[12] Between them, they could vie for the title of being the most strenuous advocates of selling council houses to sitting tenants. Among the other members was Margaret Thatcher, the rising MP for Finchley, who chaired the group in Joseph's absence.

The group's approach was as distinctive as its membership. It attributed the widespread obsolescence in Britain's housing to 'decades of misguided housing policies, based on Socialist prejudice, and Tory inability to escape from the shackles imposed on it'. The overall aim was 'to release the self-renewing mechanism of our towns and to satisfy the desire of the vast majority of people for home ownership or for a decent dwelling for rent. This will involve some people paying more for their housing than they do now.' Setting out in December 1967 to provide a full review of 'party policy on housing in all its aspects', the group began with a speculative policy paper by Joseph himself, defining ten key problem areas that needed to be addressed. Some of these were highly specific: Was there in any sense a national housing target? What steps might be taken to accelerate owner-occupation? What provision was appropriate for elderly people? But there was no mistaking where the centre of gravity of the housing issue lay: with over-subsidized, low-rental council housing. A vindication of Joseph's later reputation as the Conservatives' key policy thinker, this paper drew heavily on recent academic work and was fully referenced. Later, as important academic writings on relevant issues emerged, they were fed into the group, which also had sitting with it Professor J. Parry Lewis, one of Britain's foremost housing researchers, who on one occasion presented three separate papers to the same meeting.

One of the key problems for the group was the substantial number of households who were prosperous enough to become owner–occupiers. The Conservative strategy should be to entice them out of local authority housing by making it less financially comfortable. Those who could be attracted to home ownership should be targeted with grants and loans, for

> these prosperous households remain council tenants partly because of inertia; partly because there seems in many towns to be a right of inheritance regardless of need; and partly because council rents are in general well below the market value of the accommodation...

While one reason for low rents was historic – the presence in some areas of large number of pre-war houses and flats built at the prices then obtaining, and no longer incurring interest charges – the fundamental problem was that subsidies were attached to dwellings rather than households. A system of 'fair rents' and the elimination of unnecessary subsidies was required. Beyond that, councils should be encouraged to consider selling off complete estates to housing associations, while 'the sale of individual council houses to their sitting tenants [was] unlikely to have much impact on solving the housing problems'.

The policy group's report fully reflected this approach. To declare that 'owner occupation is the form of tenure we would like to see as widespread as possible' was no novelty in post-war Conservative politics. What was novel was the determination with which this aim was to be pursued, with local authorities pushed to release their land-holdings for private building, as well as giving land free of charge to housing associations 'on the lines of the GLC scheme'. Municipal tenants would be liable to pay fair rents in order to encourage them into private ownership. There would be no further general needs building by local authorities. And, significantly, it accepted that as 'the alleviation of need [was] a national rather than a local responsibility', local authorities would accordingly need to 'accept curtailment of their financial independence'.

That transfer of responsibility, and the consequential curtailment of local autonomy, was high on the agenda when the Conservatives returned to power in May 1970. With the work of the housing policy group behind them, the task of preparing the rent proposals of the white paper *A Fair Deal for Housing* was soon accomplished. Its presentation was made all the easier by the anomaly of private rents having been regulated by Labour on a 'fair rent' basis under the Rents Act 1968, while municipal rents were subject only to such adjustments from year to year as would barely avoid a deficit on the HRA. Few could argue that local authority rents met the statutory requirement of 'reasonableness', although both 'fair' and 'reasonable' rents were essentially a matter of political judgement. The white paper, however, could also claim to be seeking fairness as between the sectors:

> These reforms are based on the principle of fairness. They will establish a fair balance between owner occupiers and tenants and parity of treatment for council tenants and private tenants. They will do justice between landlord and tenant. They will have due regard to the reasonable claims of the citizen as a tax payer and as a rate payer, without placing on either the inflationary burden of unnecessary taxes.[13]

Aimed principally at local authority tenants, the government proposals sought to move rents towards market levels. This was to be a major departure from the provisions of the successive housing acts which required local authorities to charge reasonable rents. A body of case law had done little to clarify what constituted 'reasonableness', which might refer to the rents paid by municipal tenants in similar properties, or to a comparison between those in public and private housing.[14] The principal difficulty facing the government was that the National Board for Prices and Incomes proposed a quite different basis for determining local authority rents. The Board had become involved when the Labour government had referred to it the rent policies of the GLC which, being based on the fair rent principle, were seen by the Conservatives as a pilot project for their eventual national scheme. The Board had rejected the concept of the fair rent and proposed in its place the historic cost rent advocated by the Labour party.

The historic cost rent was derived from the debt charges on the construction of a property, with the current cost of maintenance and management added in. In the case of older pre-war council houses, especially for those where the capital costs had been fully amortized, the historic cost rent would be a very low figure, probably well below what a council would charge in practice. The historic cost rent, then, would usually bear no relation to market rent, nor indeed to the actual rent charged. Nevertheless, the Conservative espousal of the fair rent principle gave the historic cost rent some short-term political credence in Labour eyes, thus ensuring a complete polarization of the debate.

The Housing Finance Act 1972 carried the fair rent principle into law and, for the first time, divorced the basis of rent from the actual cost of providing, managing and maintaining council dwellings. The basis for determining fair rent was largely that used for the private dwellings under the Rents Act 1968 and reflected the age, character, locality and state of repair of the dwelling. Scarcity was to be disregarded, as was any claim to a social role on the part of the local housing authority. The Labour party bitterly opposed this approach but, having already adopted the term 'fair rent' for the rent regime they had introduced into the private rental market, the party 'had some difficulty in denying its relevance to the public sector; their clothes had been stolen'.[15]

Local authorities were given six months from the date of the Act coming into force from July 1972 to fix and publish provisional fair rents. During the next two months the tenants could make representations, which the local authority was obliged to consider while finalizing its proposals for submission to a Rent Scrutiny Board. These Boards, the members of which were drawn from local Rent Assessment Panels with additional members appointed by the Secretary of State, were to determine the rent, paying attention to the comparability between different authorities. The Board's decision became the 'fair rent' for the dwelling. Because the move to fair rents would involve substantial rent increases in many cases, the Act provided for a gradual move towards fair rents in the interim. Immediately, across-the-board annual increases of £26 per dwelling were to be made, and twice that figure upon the Act's coming into force, until the fair rent level was reached. One escape clause only remained: amendments to the bill during its passage enabled local authorities to apply to the Secretary of State for a lower rate of increase.

Although the origin of the Housing Finance Act in Sir Keith Joseph's preelection policy group testify to its real intent – to tackle the artificially low rents charged by Labour councils – the great increase in the central government's powers that it represented fell equally on local authorities of all political colours. The problem for some Conservative authorities, who had traditionally charged high rents, was that the fair rent scheme was balanced in the Housing Finance Act by a system of rent rebates, the cost of which fell in part upon the ratepayer. In such councils, the Housing Finance Act was greeted with outrage, as the cost of rebates would necessitate a substantial rate rise. Tory authorities, it was claimed, were being 'penalised for good housekeeping'.[16]

The affronted pride of these authorities, however, bore little comparison with the rage and determination of many Labour councils, a large number of which vowed to oppose the Act and frustrate its implementation. The government had anticipated such a response. The Secretary of State for the Environment was given powers to place a default order on any authority which his enquiries revealed to be impeding the Act and, if remedial action was not taken within a specified period of time, to appoint a Housing Commissioner to take over the operation of the local housing service. All the expenses of the Commissioner would fall upon the local authority, and officers and members would have a duty to assist him, on pain of a fine.

With as many as seventy local authorities originally committed to nonimplementation, that number fell to around forty as the traditional Labour stance of compliance with unwelcome laws began to operate. By November 1972, five months after the Act came into force, just a dozen continued to hold out. Some of these soon gave way under the pressure of default orders, having made their stand, and their point. Two Welsh districts had Housing Commissioners appointed to take over their housing service. Some other protesters were curbed by the threat of the withdrawal of all housing subsidy. Just one housing authority, Clay Cross District Council in Derbyshire, continued to hold out.

The tactical ingenuity of the Clay Cross councillors and their delight in tweaking the government's tail was to make them heroes of the Labour movement. With a pre-existing reputation of militancy gained over their earlier refusal to deny free school milk for primary school children, Clay Cross had a record of very low rents and a history of threats of surcharge from the district auditor. The district had a large proportion of municipal properties and the Labour group, themselves all council tenants, had been elected on a promise of no rent rises. On the publication of the white paper itself, the council declared its outright opposition to implementation of the Act and refused to make the interim rent increases. They challenged the government to appoint a Housing Commissioner, a ploy to which the government initially refused to respond, deciding instead to hold the council personally responsible for the loss of rent income. Following an extraordinary audit, the district auditor surcharged the councillors, who retaliated by orchestrating a rent and rate strike and by appealing to the High Court.

The appeal was dismissed in July 1973. The councillors were disbarred from office and a new council formed, only to take an identical stance. The Environment Secretary, Geoffrey Rippon, at last acted to appoint a Commissioner. The council refused to co-operate, denying the Commissioner both office space and access to their staff, until such time as the Commissioner ordered the council staff to collect the higher rents. Fearing that their staff would comply, the council suspended them, leading to a strike by NALGO. It was in this condition of chaos that the Clay Cross District Council ceased to exist, becoming part of the larger North Derbyshire district on 1 April 1974.

In reality, Labour local authorities and the Labour party itself were deeply divided. Anthony Crosland, the Shadow Environment Secretary, advised local authorities to comply with the Act while applying for lower levels of rent increases. While Clay Cross sent shock waves through the Labour movement, the Labour leadership had no intention of endorsing unlawful behaviour. This stance led to a stand-off between the leadership and the party conference, which resolved that a future Labour government would absolve the 'Clay Cross Eleven' from all penalties and, in March 1974, councillors appealed to the NEC of the Labour party, who asked the newly elected Labour government to indemnify them. A special party conference on the Clay Cross issue was held in June 1974, which put further pressure upon the government. In the event, the government went part way to meeting these demands in the Housing Finance (Special Provisions) Act 1975. The changed basis of housing rents may have seemed an overdue reform to most commentators, but the transition to universal means-tested benefits engendered a political earthquake. The Labour government had done little to inspire its supporters, and new fissures had arisen within the party itself. The Housing Finance Act drove a wedge into these tense divisions. Undoubtedly, the new Conservative rent policies did much to rally the more militant forces within the Labour party, pitching them in a trial of strength against the government and, incidentally, against their own more moderate comrades. For the far Left, the struggle against the Act 'was one in which the Labour party and the affiliated trade unions went part of the way towards breaching the principle of '"constitutionalism"'.[17]

It was that principle that had characterized the entire period of the postwar consensus. During the Attlee period, and – perhaps less willingly – under the Wilson governments, Conservative councillors and activists accepted the most disagreeable of measures, tempering their bitterness with the hope of future repeal. The same spirit had infused Labour throughout the long years of their exile from office, even in times when their tolerance was tested to the limit. What was new about the response to the Housing Finance Act was the ferocity of the opposition, the extent of direct action against the government and local councils alike, and the willingness of some to defy the law altogether. The relations between central and local government had entered a new era of polarization, the full force of which would not be seen until the 1980s.

Labour comes to terms

The right of local authorities to sell houses to their existing tenants had been restored in 1952 when the Conservatives returned to office, and enhanced in 1960. Demand, however, remained at a low level. Not until 1966, when the Conservatives took control of Birmingham City Council, did a major local authority commit itself to large-scale disposals of municipal housing. The Birmingham example provided ready inspiration to those Conservative groups who took power in the landslides of 1967 and 1968; not least in London, where the incoming GLC Conservatives sought confrontation with the Labour government. The policy received a warm press as its appeal quickly became evident. The ideal of a property-owning democracy was lauded as 'the soundest of all. . . . To destroy it would be to reduce the British people to a herd level' declared the *Daily Mail.*

Labour had not revoked the general consent on taking office in 1964, but confined themselves to general admonitions about the value of the capital assets disposed of by sales, and the need to maintain a sufficient pool of houses for letting.[18] This passive disapproval was no longer sufficient once the new Conservative majorities confronted the government with their active sales policies. In July 1968, Minister of Housing and Local Government Anthony Greenwood, under pressure from back-bench MPs and from party conference, intervened to impose a quota on local authority sales, set at a quarter of one per cent of an authority's housing stock. For even an authority as large as the GLC, the quota amounted to no more than 600 sales. Greenwood had been under strong pressure from London Labour politicians, who had been lobbying the minister since June 1967, and generally attacking this 'erosion of the housing stock'. The government had initially been reluctant to intervene, Greenwood declaring at the 1967 Labour party conference that 'it would be wrong for me to step in and stop a council doing something simply because you and I thought they were wrong to do it'. Yet the political costs of ignoring the new Conservative initiatives were too high, as selling council houses had the hallmark of an electorally popular scheme. Even Greenwood's limited intervention had its risks, as Conservative councils campaigned on the slogan 'Labour government against local government', in a conscious echo of the old Wooltonian slogan, 'Town Hall, not Whitehall'.[19]

The unexpected defeat of the Wilson government in the spring of 1970 had immediate effects on local authorities' freedom to sell council housing. As early as June 1970, the Conservative government's Circular 54/70 gave a general consent, restoring to councils 'the right to dispose of council houses to their own tenants or prospective owner occupiers as they think fit'. This satisfied the Conservative critics. But something more was required to bear down upon those authorities that were falling once again under Labour control, as the landslide losses of the late 1960s were reversed. To this end, a further circular in June 1972 noted that 'many authorities continue to adopt policies which frustrates [sic] their tenants' desires to own their home', and warning that a local authority who deny their tenants the opportunity to own their own home would be failing to exercise their powers under section 104 of the Housing Act 1957 in a manner which is appropriate to present circumstances.[20]

Such exhortations and veiled threats, however ineffective, were as far as the Heath government was prepared to go, despite mounting pressure from successive party conferences.

The Conservatives had set out their strategy for sales in *A Fair Deal for Housing*, which extolled owner-occupation as 'the most rewarding form of house tenure'. Despite this general endorsement, and Peter Walker's enthusiasm for a property-owning democracy, the government was actually rather cautious in its approach to sales. While Julian Amery won a standing ovation at the 1971 Conservative conference for his assertion that the government regarded 'the selling of council houses as the best way of providing a healthy mix on council estates', in practice ministers kept their distance from the more flamboyant local advocates of council house sales.[21] It was left to a private member to introduce a bill during the 1973–4 sessions to give tenants a statutory right to buy. Although the bill made no headway, the outgoing Heath government adopted the proposal for future action.

Returning to office in February 1974, the Labour party was more inclined even than before to accept the desirability of owner-occupation, their manifesto simply promising to end the 'free for all market' in housing. The continuing spread of home ownership meant that to do otherwise would have undermined their electoral base. In other respects, too, they built upon the recent past. Their 1974 Housing Act extended the provisions of area improvement, increasing the levels of improvement grant, and providing extra aid for housing action areas. Rehabilitation of the existing stock was affirmed as a major priority in housing provision.

Traditional Labour policies were also followed. The squeeze on the detested private landlord continued, with furnished tenants being brought under the scope of the Rents Act, the consequence of perhaps 100,000 units being withdrawn from the market being compensated for by a corresponding expansion in municipal building. Specifically Socialist initiatives were pursued with the modest promotion of co-operative housing.

Additionally, some of the Heath reforms of the previous four years were countermanded. Circular 70/74 re-affirmed the role of the municipal rented sector in meeting housing need. There was no alteration in the general consent to sell of two years before, but local authorities were required to take into account local housing conditions before offering council properties for sale:

> In areas where there are substantial needs to be met for rented dwellings, as in the large cities ... it is generally wrong for local authorities to sell council houses. There may be areas where the sale of council houses into owner-occupation is appropriate, in order to provide a better housing balance, but this should not be done so as to reduce the provision of rented accommodation where there is an unmet demand.[22]

This essentially permissive line enabled Labour councils to stand firm against local pressures from ambitious tenants.

Equally, it did not stand in the way of Conservative councils developing an active sales policy where they chose to do so. Some developed special arrangements to promote sales, including high rates of discount and, as economic conditions changed and more councils began to fall under Conservative control, council house sales began to take off.[23] In the last three years of the Wilson/Callaghan government, sales rose steadily with new incentives, one authority contemplating giving trading stamps to completing buyers. These activities eventually provoked the reluctant intervention of Peter Shore, Labour's last Environment Secretary. Shore introduced new restrictions on 'indiscriminate and irresponsible sales'. But the fact that the government was acting to stem a popular demand was an electoral gift to the Conservatives, who responded with a still more enthusiastic advocacy of sales. Peter Walker advocated giving council houses free to long-standing tenants, and in 1976 the Conservative party conference voted in favour of the early implementation of a statutory tenants' *Right* to Buy. Labour's own attempts to reconcile social and private ownership came to little, and their pilot 'shared ownership' schemes found few takers (see table 6.1).

On rents, Labour's February 1974 manifesto promised to repeal the Housing Finance Act and to return to local authorities the power to set their own rent levels, subject only to the 'reasonableness' requirements of the Housing Acts. The Housing Rents and Subsidies Act 1975 swept away the concept of fair rents, together with the Rent Scrutiny Boards. But the freeing-up of rents could not be allowed to lead to further increases. Labour's 'Social Contract' with the trade union movement in 1973

Table 6.1 Sales of local authority dwellings, 1967–9 (actual to 1977; estimates thereafter)

1967	3,200	1971	16,851	1974	4,153	1977	12,495
1968	8,571	1972	45,058	1975	2,089	1978	29,538
1969	7,530	1973	33,720	1976	4,879	1979	41,095
1970	6,231						

Source: DoE Housing and Construction Statistics.

committed the government to freeze rents as part of a general policy of price control, in return for wage restraint. Crosland acted immediately to freeze residential rents, for an initial period of eight months, later extended for a further four-month period. However, rising costs and a high rate of inflation, coupled with rising private rentals, meant that this position could not be sustained. Labour had no positive policy on rents, what their levels should reflect or how they should be determined by local authorities.

Having scrapped fair rents, Crosland had taken a general power to limit rent rises by Order, dealing by this means not with individual authorities, but with broad classes of authority or classes of dwelling. These powers could only be used if a significant number of unduly large and frequent increases materialized. It was hoped that this threat would be sufficient to restrain authorities from rent increases higher than necessary to maintain an (undefined) working balance. But while the powers were there to control high rents, there was nothing the government could do when faced with artificially *low* rents, as the scrapping of the Housing Finance Act removed all mechanisms for tackling the long-term problems of insufficient rent.

The situation was one of considerable confusion, and during the passage of the 1975 Act, Crosland announced the establishment of a wide-ranging review of housing finance to sort out 'the dog's breakfast' that had resulted from decades of accretion, amendment and deletion. However, the review became trapped between electoral realities, Labour's manifesto promises, and bitter clashes between officials and advisors. Its main result was simply to point up how difficult the choices were for any government.

Education in Schools

The essence of the post-war settlement in secondary education was that each LEA would be left to choose for itself between comprehensive and tripartite systems. Most LEAs developed their school systems on tripartite lines without much pause, partly for reasons of administrative convenience, partly because it involved the least change from the past, and partly because both government policy and educational opinion at the time favoured selection, and accepted the separatism that it entailed. While LEAs were legally free to go comprehensive, in practice, this often involved steps – for example, the closure or enlargement of particular schools – which themselves required ministerial consent. There were other obstacles which an obstructive Minister of Education, vested with wide powers over finance and planning, could erect in the path of a LEA which desired a comprehensive system. These were powers that some Conservative ministers did not shrink from using, for while the Labour government of 1945–51 had not been sympathetic to comprehensive schools, Conservative governments, at first emphatically hostile, remained at best suspicious.

Labour and education

By the time Labour returned to power in October 1964, the climate of educational opinion had swung progressively towards the comprehensive school. In particular, selection methods no longer commanded expert confidence. As early as 1957, a study by the National Foundation for Educational Research (NFER) established that as many as 12 per cent of children were allocated to the 'wrong' school at age eleven, and that even the most stringent form of selection testing would not reduce this error below 10 per cent.[24] In the same year, the British Psychological Society pronounced against intelligence tests. Although pioneers such as Sir Cyril Burt continued to defend them, the advocates of tripartism increasingly had to take their stand not on the efficacy of the elevenplus examination itself, but on the existence of transfer mechanisms for older children misplaced at eleven.[25]

Ministers, civil servants and local education authorities themselves were beginning to absorb a new consensus. To the charge that Labour frontbenchers were latter-day converts to the comprehensive ideal, Michael Stewart could only reply that 'all of us, except for a few pioneers, were wrong about the virtues of separatism in the years immediately after the war'.[26] The conversion may have been a recent one, but it had come about gradually in response to changing social and educational circumstances. It was Anthony Crosland himself who had captured the new public mood almost before it became discernible to others, and had expressed it in the egalitarian terms that were especially welcome to Wilson's modernizing programme. 'The object of having comprehensive schools' he wrote in his influential *Future of Socialism*,

> is not to abolish all competition and all envy, which might be rather a hopeless task, but to avoid the extreme social division caused by physical segregation into schools of widely divergent status, and the extreme social resentment caused by failure to win a grammar . . . school place, when this is thought to be the only avenue to a 'middle class' occupation.[27]

This idea of the comprehensive school as an instrument of social engineering converged conveniently with a longer-standing Christian Socialist strand in Labour thinking, which held it to be morally good for people of different interests and intellectual gifts to work together, dissolving the mutual contempt that characterized so many of the encounters across the class barriers in Britain's divided society.

Underlying Labour's acceptance of the comprehensive school was a recognition that the claims made for tripartism in 1944 – claims which the Attlee government had so vigorously upheld – had shown themselves to be hollow. Indeed, it was now fashionable for the advocates of comprehensives to speak of 'separatism', rather than 'tripartism'. The essence of the claim for separate schools was that separate grammar and modern schools could, taken together, give better education to all children. The more academic child would benefit by being in a school that concentrated on intellectual achievement, set high standards of work and attainment, and in which the efforts of specialist academic teachers were devoted entirely to the kinds of pupils that they were best suited to deal with. In the modern schools (the argument went) children of middling ability would not be discouraged by the presence of those of first-class ability. They would have a chance to gain a sense of achievement, and often blossom into success in various directions, which they might never do in a school which included the most able. Secondary modern schools could be much smaller than comprehensive schools, giving the least able and the most difficult children the benefit of direct personal supervision by dedicated teachers.

In practice, few secondary modern schools could claim to realize these aims, and it was their failure, rather than any deficiency of the grammar school as such, that undermined support for tripartism. The prospect for the majority of school leavers was unskilled work. The predictions of the critics at post-war Labour conferences, pointing to the role of secondary modern schools in reproducing low-skill, low-wage labour, had been proved accurate. Moreover, what was deemed generally acceptable in 1948 became a source of discontent to ambitious working- and lower-middle-class parents in the more open and more demanding social climate of the 1960s. Their discontent was further exacerbated by the well known variations between areas in the proportion of grammar school places available, which ranged from 8 to 34 per cent in English county boroughs, and from 13 to 29 per cent in the English counties; in some Welsh authorities, the proportion was as high as 40 per cent.[28]

Table 6.2 Development of comprehensive schools, 1965–71

Year	Modern	Grammar	Technical	Comprehensive
1965	3,727	1,285	172	262
1966	3,642	1,273	150	387
1967	3,494	1,236	141	507
1968	3,200	1,155	121	745
1969	2,954	1,098	109	962
1970	2,691	1,038	82	1,145
1971	2,464	970	67	1,373

Source: Ministry of Education and DES Statistics of Education, 1965–71.

A slow drift of opinion towards comprehensive schools had been running for some years, with close to half the LEAs in England and Wales introducing or devising schemes of comprehensive organization by the time Harold Wilson reached Downing Street (see table 6.2). However, the schemes were varied, and often partial; few were truly 'comprehensive'. Many related to only part of the LEA area, or applied only to the county schools, church schools remaining outwith such schemes. All reflected the variable local circumstances in which they were introduced, in which the existing pattern of school buildings was the most powerful factor. Labour's stance was unequivocal – at least in public. The manifesto for the 1964 election pledged that 'Labour will get rid of the segregation of children caused by 11-plus education. Secondary education will be re-organised on comprehensive lines.' At the same time, however, Harold Wilson – the first grammar school boy to become Prime Minister – grandly promised in a pre-election television programme that 'the grammar school will be abolished over my dead body'.[29] The Labour party, it seemed, was confused.

Moreover, the commitment to comprehensives would not be easily achieved. The key problem was to fit a comprehensive system into an existing pattern of school sites and buildings. This pattern was more firmly set than might have been supposed, for around two-thirds of the total secondary provision – 3,383 of England's total of 5,891 existing or planned schools – was either newly built or in the building programme. The very successes of the post-war drive for physical renewal of school buildings had served to set tripartism in concrete, giving the new government less room for manoeuvre. The rate of replacement of the remaining buildings would be slow, as the worst schools had been tackled first, and few really pressing needs remained. There was little prospect of having many purpose-built comprehensive schools for years to come. Any acceleration of comprehensives would therefore mean accepting a proportion of split-site schools.

Nor were the educational issues as clear-cut as had been supposed. The Crowther report of 1959 and that of the Newsom committee in 1963 had counselled caution. The first called for a 'non-dogmatic' approach to comprehensives which 'neither condemns them unheard nor regards them as a prescription of universal application'. The second called for a longer period of assessment, arguing that a reasoned judgement on the performance of comprehensive and rival systems of education was 'premature'. The case for comprehensives would have to make headway against this kind of reservation.

Although comprehensive schools had long been an article of faith for the egalitarian wing of the Labour party, the issue had been considered largely out of the context of the wider setting in which schools existed, particularly in urban areas. Poor schools were generally to be found in deprived urban areas. The selective system enabled the bright working-class child to escape to a grammar school and, sometimes with ambivalence, from his or her own community.[30] The 'ladder of opportunity' thus provided had been an important factor in welding Labour commitment to tripartism in the immediate post-war period. A universal comprehensive system would in effect be a neighbourhood school system, locking in bright children from deprived backgrounds to those same residential communities, for while 'in theory it would be possible to compel parents living in Hampstead to send their children to school in, say, Hackney or vice versa', in practice this was 'too drastic an attack on the rights of parents to choose the best and most accessible school which has room for their children'.[31]

The objection had obvious force: a neighbourhood school system would reflect more exactly than in the past the actual pattern of poverty and deprivation. The prospects of mobility through success at school would be reduced, and the incentive to parents with the ambition and the wherewithal to acquire educational success for their children by moving house would be the greater. In time, this would drive a still greater degree of residential – and thus class and educational – polarization, especially in Inner London. The objection was anticipated when Labour came to power in 1964. The reply that they offered – that the overriding task was to eliminate poor social conditions altogether – had a hollow ring, even then.

Leaving aside the social consequences, the comprehensive policy could scarcely hope to eliminate selection altogether, even in the local authority funded sector. Three per cent of all secondary school pupils were in direct grant schools; the majority had their fees paid by their LEAs under the Assisted Places Scheme. These would remain, although the ministry could hold the line against paying increased fees over time, and could control any growth in direct grant schools themselves, with the long-term objective of bringing them under LEA control. Additionally, parents who had been frustrated in their attempts to get their children into grammar schools could be expected to turn to private education, for which Labour would have to devise other plans.

In the face of these difficulties and complexities, the incoming Labour government had just three potential resources to support its policy. The first was the ability to commit resources to the achievement of the policy through an expanded school building programme, although the historic rate of increase of education spending – around 6 per cent annually – meant that this would not appeal to other Cabinet Ministers. The second was the ability to require a change to comprehensives through legislative means, although again any such bill would have to compete for space in the legislative programme. The third was the moral authority that it enjoyed by virtue of its election on a manifesto commitment to a policy that seemed widely favoured. Given that the implementation of any comprehensive plan depended on the responses of the LEAs, these resources were in reality less substantial than appeared at first sight.

The bark, not the bite: Circular 10/65

Although the 1965 push for comprehensive education is indelibly associated with Anthony Crosland, it was Michael Stewart, former schoolmaster and Wilson's first education secretary, who brought proposals to the Cabinet in January 1965, following a difficult Commons debate on the future of grammar schools. The issue was given a greater urgency by the fact that the new Outer London borough councils – the first new education authorities to be created since the war – would be taking over their new responsibilities in April. Here was both a need and an opportunity to shape local education provision.

It is now time', Stewart informed the Cabinet, 'to give a national lead, indicating the principles to be observed'. It would, he acknowledged, be a contentious step to impose a central government requirement. The practical problems would require a case-by-case approach, for

> It is of the nature of these difficulties that there is no one general answer to them. They have to be dealt with by scrutiny of each local authority's plan for reorganisation. In some areas these difficulties are absent, or slight; in others we must accept that re-organisation can only proceed slowly. The complete establishment of comprehensive secondary organisation will take a considerable time. I believe, however, that in five years such progress could be made that the comprehensive system would be accepted as the normal pattern, towards which all local authorities were working, though necessarily at different speeds.[32]

The initial plan was to issue an early circular to LEAs, calling upon them to submit schemes for approval, and to follow this with legislation in the 1966–7 session. Some thought was given to providing financial incentives as an enticement to formulate comprehensive plans. Given the complexities of local school systems and the still deep division of opinion on selection itself, it was not difficult to foresee a wide variety of responses: 'there will be enthusiasm; moderate enthusiasm; cautious acceptance; reluctant acceptance; delaying tactics; and, perhaps, in a few cases, outright refusal', Stewart told his Cabinet colleagues. To cope with this last response, legislation would be needed:

> I think that absolute refusal would be rare; but if there were no mention of legislation many authorities would delay action in the hope of a change of policy and a few awkward authorities might be encouraged not only to refuse themselves, but to try to recruit supporters among authorities who would otherwise be willing to co-operate.

The Cabinet were, however, more relaxed about the need for legislation. 'It would be preferable at the outset,' they assured themselves,

> to emphasise the government's confidence, based on the growing acceptance of the comprehensive principle, that local authorities should respond voluntarily to the request to submit plans for re-organisation and to indicate that the government did not intend to introduce legislation unless it proved to be needed.[33]

That was, it turned out, a momentous decision, and one that has been portrayed as a victory for civil service opinion.[34] Some of the more farsighted players in this game foresaw that the government's policy would not work. Junior education minister Reg Prentice thought it would be impossible, and at any rate constitutionally improper, to veto selective plans prior to legislation, warning that hard-line LEAs could challenge the government in the courts. He saw 'strong persuasion', a propaganda effort by the Labour party in the country, and continuing contact with LEAs at official level as the most useful interim measures pending a new Education Act, which he saw as the strongest card that the government had to play.

Strong cards might have done something to cover weak arguments; behind the scenes, the work on the proposed circular showed it to be full of holes. Michael Stewart had tried to find the best of all worlds by eliminating selection while denying that grammar schools would disappear as a result. A good deal of effort went into trying to find a line of argument that covered up the impending destruction of the grammar schools. Although this was essentially a presentational and political issue, civil servants did not shrink from pointing up the consequences for the grammar schools:

> many people for respectable reasons will deplore their passing or their transformation into something they will regard as vitally different; and I believe

that in the end – and sooner rather than later – to prevaricate in dealing with an assertion that grammar schools as now known cannot exist under a national comprehensive policy will do more harm than good.[35]

A similar confrontation between pronouncements of principle and private reservation centred on the 'community schools' issue. Schools in predominantly working-class neighbourhoods would be less likely to provide good educational opportunities due to 'the attitude to school and learning of the generality of the pupils there' than those in better areas. The losers would be the very children whom past Labour ministers had been so keen to promote:

> The children likely to suffer from this state of affairs will be the able children in these 'poor' neighbourhoods who, under the selective system, have been and still are being sent to grammar schools . . . One is forced to the conclusion that there is no escape from the dilemma and that a comprehensive school must involve some loss of educational opportunity for bright children in poor neighbourhoods . . . Many people would regard it as a particularly serious one because it detracts from the main purpose of the policy, viz. counteracting the educational disadvantages arising from a poor social background.[36]

Concerned to put on a brave face in spite of these dilemmas and reservations, the government took the opportunity of an Opposition debate on grammar schools on 21 January 1965 to announce its plans. The battle lines were already drawn, as the government's manifesto commitment had driven the opposition front bench into a die-hard defence of the grammar schools, calling on the government to 'discourage local authorities from adopting schemes of reorganisation at the expense of grammar schools' and deploring 'any proposal to impose a comprehensive system upon local authorities'.[37]

However, imposition was not an option. Although the original intention was to require LEAs to submit plans for secondary reorganization following the comprehensive principle, the circular merely requested such plans. This change was perhaps more one of form than substance, a concession made following consultation with the LEAs' representatives.

Problems of implementation

The idea that a comprehensive policy could be imposed turned out to be something of a fantasy. For, despite the fanfare with which the policy was launched, it actually amounted to little more than exhortation. The Secretary of State – by now Anthony Crosland – had no legal power positively to shape the particular form of secondary school provision in any one area, but only that of preventing the adoption of a scheme which he disapproved on some ground which his powers under the 1944 Act addressed. The policy had no teeth. It was a statement of national policy without the means to enforce it. Even the further Circular 10/66 that gave effect to the limited building programme to encourage the shift to comprehensives remained a negative control, for while it could prevent the building of new selective schools, it could not bring comprehensives into being where they were not the local choice.[38]

Such political resources as the central government possessed came to look rather threadbare in the face of those of the hostile local authorities. They could procrastinate, consult excessively, and reconsider locally. They could wilfully submit unsatisfactory plans, or recall those that were under consideration. Some of the schemes submitted had no timetable for local implementation, or left out of consideration large areas of the authority. Some chose not to re-submit schemes following their rejection by the ministry. Some simply ignored Circular 10/65. The initial response – of regarding the circular as embodying a mandatory requirement – soon faded as the realities became clearer. A mere circular from a minister in a shaky-looking government with a small majority could in fact be safely ignored as long as there was local public support for the LEA's stance.

The second major impediment to local adoption of the government's wishes was the shifting political control of the LEAs themselves. Because the circular had itself led to a party polarization of attitudes, the loss of control of any LEA to the Conservatives could be expected to set back the comprehensive programme. And, as it happened, the local elections of 1967 and 1968 brought about the greatest losses of Labour seats to have occurred since 1949 – and in London the losses were still greater. In some parts of the country, long-standing Labour strongholds passed to Conservative control. By 1970, 115 LEAs had plans either implemented or approved. Of these, only seventeen had uninterrupted Conservative rule, and the great majority had been Labour controlled for all or most of that five-year period. A further sixteen that had their plans rejected had been Conservative controlled for most of that time. More than half of the Labour county boroughs submitted plans on time, but only a third of the others did so. The five authorities that submitted plans outside the required period were all Conservative, and seven of the ten that chose not to respond to Circular 10/65 were either Conservative, had no overall control or were only briefly Labour.[39]

The report of the Comprehensive Schools Committee summed up the prospects bleakly:

> Most of the areas that changed hands in the spring of 1967 have changed before; most (before 1980) will change again. Others will be added. In areas that changed, comprehensive reorganisation featured in many party political programmes and speeches. Those who won control had promised certain action in respect of schemes (usually withdrawal of grammar schools from comprehensive plans) and, naturally enough, regard their electoral majority as mandate for these changes. Secondary school planning is already subject to the national electoral process; now it will inevitably be subject to the local process as well. With all the certainty built into the British political pattern that these two will often conflict, it is clear that the planning of secondary education will be handicapped in certain fundamental ways in many areas where local political changes take place.[40]

Despite Crosland's earlier warnings about perils of clumsy reform, the haste with which the government moved tended to encourage the submission of ill-supported and potentially unpopular local schemes.[41] Those Labour authorities that chose to go comprehensive in one single operation in September 1966 – thus meeting in full the government's aspiration – were very likely to have by-passed the consultation with teachers that Circular 10/65 required. Proposals by the teachers' associations to give the LEAs more time to consult did not appeal to the ministry, partly because they did not relish delay, and partly because they knew that the LEAs themselves were hoping to evade any prior consultation. Instead, assessment of the adequacy or otherwise of local consultation was deferred until the plans were submitted and examined.[42]

Although the opposition of Conservative controlled LEAs was stiffening, public support for comprehensives appeared to be growing. A report by the Comprehensive Schools Committee in 1969 claimed that the tide of public opinion had clearly turned in favour of comprehensives:

The staple item of the press diet, the angry grammar school parents marching to 'save' their school, is less in evidence these days. Indeed it has been replaced in many areas by the march to County Hall (and . . . by representations to Ministers and MPs) demanding to know about the likelihood of ever having the comprehensive school that has so long been promised.[43]

Not all parents were of this view. In the London boroughs of Enfield and Ealing, parent groups challenged the LEAs' decisions on the creation of comprehensive schools. In the Enfield case, parents used their right to lodge objections under section 13 of the 1944 Act to challenge the LEA on procedural grounds. The court judged in favour of the parents, and the DES quickly issued Circular 12/68 to relieve the situation. In the Ealing case, a group of local parents made a substantive objection under section 76 of the Act, arguing that the introduction of comprehensive schools vitiated their rights to have their children educated according to their wishes. This case was lost, the court ruling that the rights of parents did not extend as far as the conditions of entry to a school. The LEA's duty was to provide schools adequate in number, character and equipment, not of a particular grammar, or secondary modern, type.[44]

Meanwhile, impatience was mounting amongst the government's supporters. In 1969, the NUT annual conference called upon the government 'to make the necessary legislative changes to bring about comprehensive education by abolishing selection for secondary education', adding that 'the continued existence of the grammar school completely nullifies all attempts to create a fully comprehensive system' and calling on the Secretary of State 'actively to intervene forthwith and demand that local education authorities present comprehensive schemes of secondary reorganisation immediately. . . '.[45]

These calls were intended to strengthen the government's resolve to deal with the recalcitrant LEAs. At the Labour party conference in October 1968, Minister of State Alice Bacon had announced the government's intention to bring forward a bill to compel LEAs to reorganize on comprehensive lines. In the following autumn a short bill was introduced but, due to mismanagement by the whips, it was lost in committee shortly before the general election. The bungle provided the Conservatives, and Shadow Education Secretary Margaret Thatcher in particular, with an unexpected fillip.[46]

The attempts to implement the comprehensive policy, first by exhortation and latterly by legislation, went to the heart of the relationship between central and local government. The Labour government had to acknowledge that Circular 10/65, even in its watered-down final form, implied a fundamental change in the balance of power between the minister and the LEAs, a balance that had settled into a comfortable partnership since 1944. The DES officials saw themselves as the guardians of that partnership. As one civil servant summed up the proposal when the draft circular first went to Cabinet committee, 'the Secretary of State envisages a situation in which the initiative is taken by the government where before it rested with the LEAs'. Another warned of 'a constitutional change of a sharp centralising type' which could only be achieved 'by changing the law to the disadvantage of two out of the three partners who have conducted English education on a basis of shared powers since 1870'. Such a move would only bring in its train 'other and undesirable centralising tendencies' which would 'diminish and weaken the quality of local government'.[47] The education bill, had it not fallen, would certainly have brought about just such a development.

The Conservatives naturally made much of this compulsion as a feature of the policy. They had from the outset presented themselves as the defenders of the established education partnership, of the rights of parents and of the continued existence of fine schools. Now they could become the champions of local government itself.

The Conservative response

The Conservatives' initial response was to present a reasoned argument against 'the rapid and universal imposition of comprehensive school education ... involving the loss of integrity of established schools of real excellence'.[48] Edward Heath (who was yet to become leader of the party) promised that a future Conservative government would repeal any legislation to compel LEAs to go comprehensive. The architect of the 1944 Act himself, R. A. Butler, reproached Labour for their centralism:

> I always envisaged that in secondary education the experiments would come from the circumference, that is from the Local Education Authorities. I never expected that the centre would give instructions as to a particular type of secondary education.... It would be a great pity to take away from the

LEAs an interest in education, because it binds education to local government, and thereby binds it to the district and makes it the responsibility of every resident.[49]

Standing firm in defence in defence of diversity, Conservative spokesmen equated the managerial autonomy of the school with the policy autonomy of the LEA:

> it goes without saying that LEAs should be free to decide on the form of their own secondary structure; likewise, schools should be free to decide on their own local organisation. The diversity of our educational system has itself formed a powerful progressive force.[50]

If the first line of defence was to stand up for the LEAs against central government, the second was actively to support Conservative councils in their resistance to the circular. Central Office was asked to give 'all possible assistance to Conservative LEAs opposing the circular', and the local government department there was asked to produce an advice note on the legal implications of Circular 10/65 and the powers of the Secretary of State for education.[51] As the party gained increasing success in local elections, Conservative councillors found themselves assuming responsibility for unpalatable reorganization plans. They were urged to keep their nerve, for the grammar school could survive only if Conservative councillors were 'prepared to uphold and fight for the selective principle in secondary education'. In many areas, however, local Conservatives were unwilling to unscramble Labour plans to abolish selection.

The problem with holding the line locally was that there was remarkably little support from the national leadership. Even the new party leader appeared ambivalent about Labour policy. Heath reiterated the need for choice in a free society, and attacked 'the bogus hotchpotch of so-called comprehensive schemes', but would not set his face against change and even – astonishing as it must have seemed to many supporters – portrayed the Assisted Places Scheme as an indefensible creaming off of the best pupils into private education. His overall line was one of even-handedness between the two sectors.

The leadership's judgement was that this position could be defended, and that the grammar school's supporters would increasingly be found only among a shrinking group of die-hards. For his part, Boyle thought that 'party opinion on this general subject of secondary re-organisation has got considerably more peaceful' enabling the modernizers to become 'a little more forthright in support of those who... have been in full agreement with the general approach adopted by Mr Heath and myself'. As Boyle explained to the 1967 party conference, that approach was one of accepting comprehensive schools for largely technocratic reasons:

> The days have long gone by for this country, and I beg this conference to remember this, when one could say that so long as the top 10 or 20 percent were catered for, the rest did not matter so much. In Britain today we want more technicians, and higher standards of professional training, if I may so put it, for the Betas in our society, but not at a cost of a system which discourages the Alphas... Let us remember that our party has long recognised the dangers and the unfairness of too early and too final selection and categorisation of children. Many LEAs, Tory controlled no less than Labour controlled, were making changes in organisation to overcome these problems long before Mr Crosland issued his circular 10/65.

His reading of the situation was that

> the trend of educational opinion in many Tory controlled areas (no less than Labour controlled ones) has now set in against rigid segregation in different kinds of school at the age of 11 or 12 – and increasingly I find Tories are coming to realise this, and also to accept that there must be an element of continuity in the planning of secondary schooling in any area.[52]

This line ensured that Boyle had a rough ride at party meetings whenever comprehensives were discussed. At the 1967 party conference he urged that Conservatives should accept 'the trend of educational opinion against selection into different kinds of school at the age of 11'. The parties, he asserted, did not differ about 'the general trends of secondary organisation which do away with the need for early separation into different kinds of school' but only over 'the way in which the government have carried out their comprehensive policy'.[33]

This was not what the party activists were looking for. A more full-blooded opposition would be necessary, and Central Office was persistently urged to provide support to the resistance. One response was to convene meetings of Conservative education committee chairmen. Some at least of these turned into unscheduled discussions on the extent to which the national spokesmen could be counted upon to assist local resistance. Statements of future policy were demanded: 'If it is a fact that Conservatives believe that there is still room in secondary education for systems other than comprehensives, is it not time that the Shadow

Minister of Education made our views known to the general public?' inquired one embittered member. At that same meeting 'there were strong expressions of opinion and requests for more definite and decisive guidelines from central office'. Further meetings were demanded, and Boyle's presence rather tartly requested.[54]

Opposition, even resistance, was no substitute in the longer term for a Conservative policy which would arrest, and at best reverse, the changes brought about by Crosland. Boyle was initially pressed to produce a draft of a circular that a future Conservative Secretary of State would issue, and to circulate it widely within the party. The actual response was more measured, and typical of Heath's leadership: a party policy group on education was established under Richard Hornby MP to provide the Shadow Cabinet with a platform for the future manifesto.

Like other groups set up on this model, the policy group on education made little impact on party policy. It largely reiterated the generally accepting line that Heath and Boyle had taken towards comprehensives, while respecting the autonomy of LEAs. Despite the expectations of a new Conservative policy for secondary education, its report contained little that was new, and was very poorly received by the Shadow Cabinet and by Central Office. Tactically, there was a 'danger of firing off all our ammunition... in the next few months, and that we will then be left with 18 months before the election with nothing much new to say' thought one party official, 'although my memory of the education report is that it is a pretty soggy cannon ball'.[55] Peter Walker was fiercer in his denunciation. He found the report 'positively encouraging to a theme of eliminating the role of the grammar school as opposed to the comprehensive'.

In one important respect, Walker's opposition pointed up a vital strategic issue that the party was yet to face. The Labour government had appointed a Public Schools Commission in 1965, and extended its remit to the direct grant schools in 1967, in response to the failure to draw them into LEA comprehensive schemes by local negotiation. To Walker's way of thinking, only the grammar school stood in the way of an outright assault on private education itself, by a government motivated to a desire to eradicate social divisions. 'If this report's findings on the subject of secondary education were taken to their logical conclusion', he warned, and many of the remaining grammar schools were transformed into comprehensives, there can be no future for the independent school. For no democracy would tolerate a system whereby the great majority were educated at comprehensive schools, whilst a small wealthy minority were able to enjoy the benefits of public school education. Such a system would be socially dividing, and would result in political action against the independent schools within a very short period of time.[56]

This recognition that the creation of a wholly comprehensive system would deepen the social divide came curiously late to Conservative politicians, although it was a commonplace in the grammar schools' own defence of their interests. And by late 1968 the climate within the party was changing to allow a more robust defence – and, in time, a more robust defender – of the grammar school to emerge.

The theme that the grammar schools were the last bastion of defence for independent education obviously had an appeal to the fundamentalist tendency within the Conservative party. And there was at that point no more eloquent spokesman than Enoch Powell, liberated from the constraints of collective responsibility by his ejection from the Heath Shadow Cabinet. Linking the comprehensive policy to Labour's hostility to private education – manifest in the approach of the reconstituted Public Schools Commission – he warned that the government's aim

> involves not only the absorption of the existing selective schools in the state system – such as the municipal grammar schools – but leads on inexorably to the attempt to eliminate, in one way or another, the direct grant schools and the public schools, and other independent schools outside the State orbit, since these are selective too.[57]

Alongside the austere logic of Enoch Powell was to be found the more flamboyant rhetoric of a Rhodes Boyson. For this former headmaster, the urge to comprehensivization was an aspect of 'the modern neurosis', on a par with 'British Summer Time, metrication, decimalisation, the cult of youth, all-number telephones, postal codes, the Radcliffe Maud [sic] report, the campaign to enter the Common Market', changes which seemed to have 'very little justification to the ordinary voter'.[58] As this new spirit gained ground, Edward Boyle's days were more clearly numbered. In 1969, to the relief of many in the party, he left politics to become Vice Chancellor of the University of Leeds, and Margaret Thatcher was promoted to replace him as front-bench education spokesman.

Mrs Thatcher swims upstream

When Mrs Thatcher replaced Sir Edward Boyle as Shadow Education Secretary, she brought a sharpness of approach for which the defenders of the grammar schools had long waited. Opinion within the party was divided, less on the merits of grammar schools than on the degree of vigour with which the battles for their retention should be fought. That division had become acrimonious, and the party leadership had been on the defensive since 1965.

With the Conservative victory in the general election of 1970, Mrs Thatcher became the Secretary of State for Education. Her first political initiative, taken immediately on assuming office, was to withdraw Circulars 10/65 and 10/66. The new Secretary of State made it clear why urgent action was required:

> I, for my part, knew that the pledge to stop pressuring local authorities to go comprehensive was of great importance to our supporters, that any delay would be taken as a sign of weakness, and that it was important to act speedily in order to end uncertainty.[59]

Unlike Circular 10/65, Mrs Thatcher's own contribution was constrained by neither consultation nor consent. She overrode the education officials, to whom she had an almost instinctive antipathy, only to be rebuked by Downing Street for being hasty.

Circular 10/70 was issued in June 1970, within days of the Conservatives assuming office. It called for 'local needs and wishes' and 'the wise use of resources' to be the main principles determining the local pattern, while making clear that the presumption was against any upheaval. Where a particular pattern of organization worked well and had the support of the Secretary of State, there should not be any cause for further change without good reason. Schemes under consideration could be withdrawn and new schemes need not be submitted. Taking closer scrutiny of local schemes than her predecessors, Mrs Thatcher insisted on giving or withholding approval on a school-by-school basis, instead of endorsing LEA-wide schemes. The essence of the new circular was to encourage variety and choice rather than seek to 'plan' the system. The immediate aim of reassuring the party's supporters was achieved: the party's National Advisory Committee for Education praised Mrs Thatcher for scrapping the 'infamous' directive of the last government, and welcomed the reaffirmation that all pupils should have full opportunities for secondary education 'suitable to their needs' -a coded reference to the bipartite system.

Elsewhere, reaction to Circular 10/70 was hostile. The education establishment, the majority of local authorities, and the main teacher union condemned it, although the local authority associations themselves were more concerned about consultation than about the substance of the issue, a factor that had helped to promote acceptance of comprehensives under the Labour government.[60] One of the principal criticisms directed against the new Secretary of State's approach concerned the difficulties that comprehensive and grammar schools would have in coexisting in the same area. It had long been orthodoxy that such coexistence was unworkable. Now the criticisms were directed both from Left and Right. The principal advocate of comprehensive schools observed: 'The selective school gets more selective, the comprehensives get less selective. That is the law of coexistence.'[61] From the other end of the political spectrum, Enoch Powell had pronounced, with characteristically remorseless logic, that

> selective and non-selective schools cannot be justified side by side as parts of the same system, since the existence of the selective schools automatically and inevitably deprives the comprehensive schools of their comprehensiveness: they too become selective willy-nilly, by default, or by elimination.[62]

Indeed, just such an argument about incompatibility had been used to retard schemes for partially comprehensive schemes in the past. But whereas this logic had in the past worked against the comprehensive school, it would begin to work in its favour once a threshold had been crossed, beyond which comprehensive schools predominated.

That threshold was fast approaching, for while the circular would lift a requirement to prepare comprehensive schemes, it could not stem the gradual tide of opinion in their favour. In that same year, the National Association of Head Teachers, at their annual conference at Scarborough, stated their acceptance of 'the principle of comprehensive education', although they were prepared to support only those schemes that provided single-site schools. Thus the struggle to resist the comprehensive school had already been largely lost. Plans continued to come in, notably from Conservative councils harried by middle-class parents who saw the eleven-plus examination as a threat to their children. The former resistors among them could now afford to adopt comprehensive schemes without seeming to have been bullied into compliance, while the Labour party started, in 1972–3, to regain control of the LEAs that it had lost in the late 1960s.

In fact, the sheer rise in the number of schemes coming forward from the LEAs obscured the actual effects of Mrs Thatcher's tenure at the DES. Kept in place for the full four years of the government by a Prime Minister wary of the effects that she might have in another department, it fell to Margaret Thatcher to approve or reject a greater number of schemes than all her post-1965 predecessors put together. She was thus an easy target for those who wished to point up the irony of her creating more comprehensive schools than any other minister, in the face of her own predilections. This she did, but no minister could have done otherwise when presented by schemes that were sound in themselves and locally supported.

The other side of the balance sheet was that she could claim to have saved nearly 100 grammar schools between 1970 and 1972. Balancing her large number of approvals with decisive interventions, Mrs Thatcher used her powers under section 13 of the 1944 Education Act to prevent their closure, and in 1970 made rare use of section 68 to force Surrey to retain selection in the first phase of that county's comprehensive scheme.[63] The outcome of all these interventions was that a few grammar schools – about 150 in all – survived in a few local authorities. But that too was politically significant. The grammar school had lasted long enough to provide not just a memory for the true believers but a base on which to rebuild the idea of selection when the Conservatives returned in 1979.[64]

First, Labour had to mount their final assault. Following their return in the two 1974 general elections, Reg Prentice, now Secretary of State for Education, again countermanded Mrs Thatcher's circular with one of his own. Circular 4/74 was sent not only to LEAs but also to the managers and governors of voluntary aided and direct grant schools, threatening a loss of status and of funding if they resisted incorporation into a non-selective system. In August 1975, a limited additional school building programme was announced to facilitate a swifter implementation of the policy.

By this time, despite Mrs Thatcher's own efforts to stem the tide, comprehensive schools had become commonplace across the country. By early 1975 there were more than 2,500, catering for 68 per cent of the secondary school population. The number of grammar schools had fallen by more than half, from 1,285 to 566 in the course of the ten years since Circular 10/65. Only one LEA – Kingston upon Thames – had no comprehensive school. As many as forty-four LEAs in England and Wales were totally comprehensive or had plans soon to become so. By the end of the decade, 83 per cent of the secondary population would be educated in more than 3,000 comprehensive schools. Only fifty of Britain's LEAs would have any grammar schools left, and their numbers would fall to 253.[65]

Meanwhile, the Prentice circular was a stop-gap measure, as there were still seven LEAs that openly refused to consider comprehensive reorganization, and it was to deal with these that Prentice re-introduced the failed education bill of 1968 which, on this second try, was to become law, as the Education Act 1976. In addition to limiting the powers of LEAs to support the Assisted Places Scheme, the new Act required comprehensive schemes to be submitted by a specified date; if the schemes were unsatisfactory, resubmission was required. LEAs would be obliged to implement approved schemes. The Secretary of State's new powers were used against as many as twenty-nine LEAs during the remaining years of the Callaghan government.

Because of the 'mopping up' nature of the exercise, this last phase of comprehensive reform proved the most contentious in the relations between the central government and the LEAs. Its epicentre was to be found in Tameside metropolitan district in Greater Manchester. A comprehensive scheme had been approved by the Labour council there, for implementation in 1976. When control of the council changed in the spring of that year, the new ruling Conservative group sought to withdraw the plans, and reintroduce selection for 240 places at two local grammar schools. Labour Secretary of State Fred Mulley used his powers under section 68 of the 1944 Act to direct them to reverse their decision. The Court of Appeal ruled that the Secretary of State was acting unlawfully, in that his action was unreasonable, and the House of Lords upheld their judgement. Conservatives were jubilant: 'never again will an education minister be able to behave with dictatorial arrogance to parents and councillors', crowed Norman St John Stevas, the former Minister of State under Mrs Thatcher at the DES. The ruling shook the confidence of the DES officials, who found their powers over aspects of education in schools to be more limited than they had imagined.

While the Labour government's powers were enhanced when the 1976 Act came into force, the tactical skills of their opponents had meanwhile been honed still further. Conservative education animateur Stuart Sexton co-ordinated behind-the-scenes machinations between the seven last-ditch resistors, meeting secretly to share schemes for defeating the DES.[66] However, the heat had gone out of the comprehensive issue, even if it continued to burn brightly for some. But this endgame coincided with a deeper crisis in local education. The post-war assumption that a steady expansion of education would produce an increasing satisfaction with the schools had fallen apart. A battle over standards was soon to be joined.[67]

The politics of educational standards

The battle over comprehensives effectively over, educational thinking entered a new phase in its development. The demographic downturn spelt falling primary school rolls, while still-rising secondary school numbers clashed with tightening public expenditure, and growing controversy over teaching methods and educational standards. The issue of comprehensive schools came to be displaced by questions of educational standards, and by the allegation that the state system had failed. There were two distinct but related concerns voiced at that time. The first was about the standards being achieved by pupils and the relevance of what was being taught. The second was about the neglect of the economic well-being of the UK, the educational system of which seemed unable to respond effectively to the changing demands for skilled labour.

'Standards' had become a rallying cry for the critics of post-war education. Conservative spokesmen were naturally attracted to 'standards' as a stick with which to beat the Labour government, scorning Labour for 'plenty of talk about class and equality, about privilege, but nothing about quality, about standards...'.[68] This vague concern gained coherence in a stream of vigorous pamphlets – the 'Black Papers' – the authors of which argued for the existence of a 'fixed pool of ability', which meant that any attempt significantly to increase educational opportunity would merely lower standards. One of the leading contributors was Rhodes Boyson, a comprehensive school head-teacher and former Labour councillor, and a vocal critic of what he described as 'low standards of discipline and academic work'. These he attributed to modern teaching methods, and to the failure to meet the preconditions for success in the comprehensive school.[69] His proposals, notably the testing of all pupils at seven, eleven and fourteen, were eventually to become party policy, and he himself a Conservative MP and education minister.

Behind the call for standards lay the demand for education to become more responsive to the needs of employers. Yet the detail of the curriculum itself lay outside the influence of government. Earlier attempts to gain a grip over it had misfired for, in the creation of the Schools Council, teacher influence had been effectively consolidated, and that of the DES neutralized. But a new and determined attempt was made by Prime Minister James Callaghan's in his Ruskin College speech in October 1978, in which he portrayed curriculum matters as a 'secret garden' not to be entered by non-educationalists. Deliberately violating this taboo, Callaghan called attention to the need for more centralized control of education with the creation of a core curriculum and the testing of pupils' attainment, closer involvement of parents and industry in schools, and more technological teaching. Warning against favouring creativity at the expense of the 'three Rs', of formal instruction at the expense of the acquisition of employable skills, Callaghan urged the monitoring of performance against national standards, with testing and national inspection. His remarks, he claimed, were not a 'clarion call to Black Paper prejudices' which had simply sought to defend old privileges and inequalities, but to a new debate based on facts and rational inquiry. When Callaghan sat down, 'a new more centralising, more accountable era had dawned for education'.[70]

Callaghan's strong views on education arose from his suspicion of the vested interests of the professions. He had earlier asked the then Education Secretary Fred Mulley to produce a brief on what had gone wrong with the schools. Leaked just before his speech – to the annoyance of Mulley's successor, Shirley Williams - this document, immortalized as the 'Yellow Book', claimed that 'child centred learning and informal teaching methods had, in 'less able and experienced hands', gone too far in some primary schools; a 'corrective shift of emphasis' was needed. The 'Yellow Book' judged that insufficient emphasis was being placed on preparing children for employment. The time was ripe for change and the DES should seize the opportunity to give a firmer lead. Following the Ruskin speech, a series of regional conferences on what was now billed as the 'Great Debate' were held, from which emerged a green paper in July 1977. The green paper emphasized the productive goals required of education: 'Young people need to reach maturity with a basic understanding of the economy and its activities, especially manufacturing industry, which are necessary for the creation of Britain's economic wealth'.

Meanwhile, pressure mounted for wider public participation in the education service and for parent representation within the system. The Taylor report on the management of schools, published in 1978, recommended that governing bodies should now include equal representation from parents and the local community, alongside local authority representatives and teachers, and that these governors be given more powers and limited oversight of the curriculum. The committee's proposal for parents to gain a powerful voice in their children's schools was endorsed by its inclusion in the Conservative election manifesto the following year.

While Shirley Willams' education bill of 1978 contained much of this thinking, there was no mention of a national or 'core' curriculum. The bill provided for each school to have its own governing body. Parent governors would be appointed, and community governors, to provide a tentative link to industry. Parents would gain the right to more information and, within limits, a degree of choice in the school their children attended. While it was bitterly contested by the Labour Left and the NUT, the bill provided the basis of a new direction in education policy, despite its progress being terminated by the 1979 general election.

That new direction was one which emphasized greater central intervention, and the bypassing of the old 'partnership' between central government and the LEAs in the interests of value for money and greater public accountability. It focused on two issues: the raising of standards, and the enhancement of parental choice. These issues were to dominate British politics once the Conservatives returned to office in 1979. They not only gathered momentum, but brought in their train other transformations of the education scene, culminating in the changes of Mrs Thatcher's third administration, and of that of John Major, who replaced her in 1990. The educational consensus of the 1940s and 1950s had indeed crumbled. The Butler Act was finally laid to rest. Buried with it was the notion of desirable social changes brought about through the agency of central and local authorities, working together in harmony.

Notes

1 N. Annan, *Our Age: portrait of a generation* (Weidenfeld and Nicolson, London, 1990), p. 12.
2 R. Lowe, *The Welfare State in Britain since 1945* (Macmillan, Basingstoke, 1993).

3 B. Lapping, *The Labour Government, 1964–70* (Penguin, Harmondsworth, 1970).
4 J. Short, *Housing in Britain: the post-war experience* (Methuen, London, 1982).
5 Quoted in N. Timmins, *The Five Giants: a biography of the welfare state* (HarperCollins, London, 1995), p. 233.
6 Timmins, *The Five Giants*, p. 234.
7 CAB 129/120, 'The housing programme: memorandum by the Minister of Housing and Local Government', 8 February 1965.
8 Ministry of Housing and Local Government, *The Housing Programme, 1965–70*, Cmnd. 2838 (HMSO, London, 1965).
9 CAB 129/120, 'The housing programme'.
10 For an indictment of Labour policy in this regard, see Timmins, *The Five Giants*, p. 233.
11 CPA, CRD 3/15/7.
12 The approach of Joseph's group closely corresponded with the 'pincer' strategy adopted by Horace Cutler as chairman of the GLC's housing committee from 1967 to 1970, whereby incentives to home ownership were combined with a rents squeeze occasioned by the progressive shift towards market rents. For a detailed account of the policies pursued by Cutler, see K. Young and J. Kramer, *Strategy and Conflict in Metropolitan Housing* (Heinemann, London, 1978), pp. 67–92.
13 Department of the Environment, *A Fair Deal for Housing*, Cmnd. 4728 (HMSO, London, 1971), para. 86.
14 J. P. Macey, 'Housing policy and its implications, with particular reference to economic rents', paper to the Public Works and Municipal Services Congress, 16 November 1966.
15 J. B. Cullingworth, *Essays on Housing Policy* (George Allen & Unwin, London, 1979), p. 56.
16 Young and Kramer, *Strategy and Conflict*, pp. 137–8.
17 L. Sklair, 'The struggle against the Housing Finance Act', *Socialist Register* (1975), pp. 250–92.
18 R. Forrest and A. Murie, *Selling the Welfare State: the privatisation of public housing* (Routledge, London, 1988), pp. 47–50.
19 Young and Kramer, *Strategy and Conflict*, pp. 89–91.
20 Department of the Environment, Circular 56/72, 13 June 1972.
21 For the party leadership's use of their influence to displace Horace Cutler from the housing chair of the GLC, see Young and Kramer, *Strategy and Conflict*, pp. 113–4.
22 Department of the Environment, *Local Authority Housing Programmes*, Circular 70/74, para. 35.
23 For a detailed study of the development of sales policies in one London

borough, see Young and Kramer, *Strategy and Conflict*, pp. 107–9, 136–8, 196–9.
24 A. Yates and D. A. Pidgeon, *Admission to Grammar Schools: third interim report on the allocation of primary school leavers to courses of secondary education* (NFER, Slough, 1957).
25 For general discussions of the development of intelligence testing, see A. Weeks, *Comprehensive Schools: past, present and future* (Methuen, London, 1986), pp. 9–11; and I. G. K. Fenwick, *The Comprehensive School, 1944–1970: the politics of secondary school reorganisation* (Methuen, London, 1976), pp. 30–33.
26 House of Commons Debates, 27 November 1964, col. 1789.
27 A. Crosland, *The Future of Socialism* (Jonathan Cape, London, 1956), p. 202.
28 House of Commons Debates, 21 January 1965, col. 431.
29 Cited in B. Shaw, *Comprehensive Schooling: the impossible dream?* (Blackwell, Oxford, 1983), p. 40.
30 For a discussion of the experiences of working-class children in the grammar school system, see B. Jackson and D. Marsden, *Education and the Working Class* (Routledge and Kegan Paul, London, 1961).
31 CAB 129/120, 'Comprehensive secondary education: memorandum by the Secretary of State for Education', 14 January 1965. The choice of examples was perhaps typical of the Wilson Cabinet's London-centred approach to the issue; Stewart himself was MP for Fulham.
32 CAB 129/120, 'Comprehensive secondary education'.
33 Cabinet minutes, 19 January 1965.
34 For such an ascription of opinion to the Ministry civil servants, and for a view that the Labour government's plans were fatally damaged by their political naiveté at this point, see C. Benn and B. Simon, *Half-way There: the British comprehensive school reform* (McGraw-Hill, London, 1970), p. 87. The education files at PRO support Benn and Simon's judgement that the civil servants were indeed opposed to legislation.
35 ED 147/827A.
36 ED 147/827.
37 House of Commons Debates, 21 January 1965, col. 413.
38 P. H. James, *The Re-organisation of Secondary Education* (NFER, Windsor, 1980).
39 James, *Re-organisation of Secondary Education*, p. 28.
40 Survey Report of the Comprehensive Schools Committee, 1968/69, p. 8.
41 Crosland had earlier written in *The Future of Socialism* that a premature move to comprehensives without the necessary resources being in place would produce a decline in educational standards and discredit the whole experiment.
42 ED 147/827D.

43 Survey Report of the Comprehensive Schools Committee, 1968/69, p. 8.
44 R. Saran, *Policy-Making in Secondary Education: a case study* (Clarendon Press, Oxford, 1973), pp. 69–70.
45 Benn and Simon, *Half-way There*, p. 51.
46 M. Thatcher, *The Path to Power* (HarperCollins, London, 1995), p. 158.
47 ED 147/827.
48 Speech by Sir Edward Boyle to the Central Council of the National Union, 6 March 1965.
49 CPA, CCO 505/4/104.
50 CPA, CCO 505/4/104.
51 CPA, CCO 505/1/3, Report of the National Advisory Committee of CUTA to the General Purposes Committee of the National Union, 2 February 1966.
52 Sir Edward Boyle, speech to the Annual Conference of the Conservative National Advisory Committee on Education, 17 June 1967.
53 Sir Edward Boyle, speech to Conservative Party Conference, Brighton, 1967.
54 CPA, CCO 505/4/27.
55 CPA, CRD 3/8/5, Brendan Sewill to Sir Michael Fraser, 18 October 1968.
56 CPA, CCO 505/4/81.
57 J. Enoch Powell, MP, Speech at Thornaby, 29 March 1969.
58 R. Boyson, *Case for Comprehensive Schooling: 'Not Proven'* (National Education Association, Barnet, Herts, 1970), p. 1.
59 Thatcher, *Path to Power*, p. 168.
60 M. Kogan, *Educational Policy-making* (George Allen & Unwin, London, 1975), pp. 221–2.
61 C. Benn, *Comprehensive or Coexistence – We Must Choose Which We Want* (National Union of Teachers, London, 1976), p. 41. Generally, see Shaw, *Comprehensive Schooling*, pp. 74–7.
62 Powell, speech at Thornaby.
63 James, *Reorganisation of Secondary Education*, p. 30.
64 Timmins, *The Five Giants*, p. 320.
65 James, *Reorganisation of Secondary Education*, p. 53.
66 Timmins, *The Five Giants*, pp. 319–20.
67 H. Judge, 'After the comprehensive revolution: What sort of secondary schools?', *Oxford Review of Education*, 5(2) (1979), pp. 137–45.
68 Sir Edward Boyle, speech to Conservative party conference, Brighton, 1967.
69 A useful survey of the series, and of the responses to them, is given in C. R. Cox and A. E. Dyson, *The Black Papers on Education* (Davis-Poynter, London, 1971), pp. 9–34.
70 Timmins, *The Five Giants*, p. 326.

7 Into the Melting Pot, 1964–1995

The problem of local government structure, apparently resolved by the *concordat* and the 1958 Act, returned to centre stage in 1966. Confounding all expectations, it has remained there ever since. The Wilson government, fatigued and irritated by the painstaking procedures of the Local Government Commission, cut through all the constraints of the past and appointed the Royal Commission that Jowitt, and later Bevan, had fought for. After an exhaustive inquiry, lasting three years, and backed by a large number of commissioned research studies, Redcliffe-Maud eventually produced the expected radical redrawing of the map of England based on the 'unitary' principle. Yet, despite the time expended and the research commissioned, despite even the generally laudatory press and public reception, Redcliffe-Maud's brave new England came to naught. The episode was memorable less for the Royal Commission's proposals themselves than for their abrupt rejection by the incoming Conservative government, and their replacement by a more limited reorganization aimed at preserving the existing counties.[1]

With comprehensive change at last accomplished, local government was now truly in the melting pot. The old fixities of structure and purpose belonged to an unrecoverable past, for the 'settlement' of the Local Government Act 1972 proved to be no such thing; within three years the former county boroughs were straining to break out of the constraints of county government. Yet another Labour minister strove to persuade his colleagues of the benefits to be gained from undoing the structure again, and while Peter Shore was superficially successful – a white paper was published in 1979 – there was never a realistic chance of making such contentious changes after so short an interval.

With the advent of Mrs Thatcher, there began the long period of Conservative rule. But any hope of stability in local government structure soon began to fade. The 'un-Conservative' reforms carried through by the Heath government in 1972 excited little admiration in the new regime, and by 1983 the fundamentalist view of the new metropolitan authorities – and of the not-so-new GLC – as wasteful and politically threatening was in the ascendant. Abolition was forced through, and in 1986 Britain's largest and most powerful local authorities were brought to an end after only twelve and twenty-one years of life respectively.

Nor was that the end of the matter. The spectacle of 'unitary' authorities managing the separate parts of the conurbations where there had formerly stood a two-tier structure excited the ambitious county districts to try again for that same status. It took the advent of John Major to make this a practicable hope with the establishment of (yet another) Local Government Commission in 1991, thus initiating another round of the complex and exhausting reviews and recommendations, rejections and acceptances, to which English local government was becoming accustomed. As ever, Scotland and Wales experienced different treatment, the niceties of inquiries by Commissioners being deemed unnecessary there, when executive action could do the same job.

The structure of local government provides no more than a framework of governance. Contained within that structure is the process of local decision-making within which national priorities are roughly reconciled with local preferences, budgets set and services managed. Ministers have been far more wary of venturing into that territory with their proposals for reform, although from 1940 there was no dearth of private critiques of the quality of councillors and of the ways they made their decisions. By 1960, the notion was gaining ground that the 'modernization' of these internal structures and processes – of the *political management* of local government – was worth attempting.

The events that followed – beginning with the Maud committee in 1964 – spoke of a desire to make local government more like some other institution, the private company, perhaps, or central government itself. But attempts to streamline the decision-making process by involving fewer people and concentrating executive authority in them brought its own dangers as first the old (financial) and then the new (political) corruption showed the risks of power without corresponding accountability. The pattern familiar from the history of structure repeated itself: first, an authoritative committee whose deliberations were supposed to settle the matter with some sensible reforms; then a re-opening, after scarcely a decent interval, of those same issues by ministers with a zest for change, in this case holding up the prospects of Westminster-style cabinet government or Chicago-style mayoral government for Britain's major local authorities.

All the while, elected local authorities were losing ground to new, government-appointed bodies. The rise of this 'new magistracy' saw the disappearance of the last vestiges of the consensus on the role of local authorities in modern Britain.

Local Government Reorganized

The return of a Labour government in October 1964 was to begin a new and wholly unexpected chapter in the history of structural change. The incoming Minister of Housing and Local Government, Richard Crossman, was initially content to follow the established line that local agreement, reached under the auspices of the Local Government Commission, was the right way to adjust existing structure. Before long, he came to a different view; that the present mechanisms of piecemeal adjustment through boundary review were

> very unsatisfactory since it means accepting the war between county councils and the county borough authorities as endemic in our national life, something I find one of the most stultifying things in our whole governmental system.[2]

Crossman also knew that the Commission's method of adjusting to urban growth by extending the boundaries of county boroughs threatened Labour's control of those authorities and, indirectly, of the Parliamentary seats the boundaries of which would be later realigned to match them.

Despite the reservations of his civil servants, who believed the Local Government Commission to represent the most suitable means of achieving change, Crossman determined on a new review. He was critical of the present system, the efforts of which had so far brought about nothing more than a few new county boroughs and some minor adjustments elsewhere. Taking advantage of Permanent Secretary Dame Evelyn Sharp's absence on holiday, Crossman announced to the AMC conference in September 1975 that

> the whole structure of local government is out of date ... our county borough and county councils as at present organised are archaic institutions whose size and structure make them increasingly ill-adapted to fulfilling the immensely important functions with which they are charged. The greatest obstacle, in fact, which prevents efficient councils from retaining public confidence is the obsolete constitutional framework within which they have had to operate.[3]

The sentiments were familiar. No-one had yet managed to act on them. Crossman did so, proposing a small, quick-acting body that would deal with the whole country authoritatively within two years.

In May 1966, a Royal Commission on Local Government in England was established under Sir John Maud (soon to become Lord Redcliffe-Maud), former Permanent Secretary at the Ministry of Education and chairman of the still-sitting committee on the management of local authorities. The '*concordat*', itself largely the work of Dame Evelyn, was thus declared dead and buried. The Local Government Commission, crippled by deaths and resignations, lingered for a year or so while ministers considered whether there was still a job for it to do, eventually deciding not.[4] The 1945 Trustram Eve Commission had offended with its presumption and its persistence. The 1958 Hancock Commission 'failed' only in so far as it did not deliver the sweeping reforms that some wanted (but still others would have abhorred), and because by the mid-1960s it seemed to be out of tune with the supposed spirit of the times. The fate of both Commissions testified to the difficulties of independent bodies with a statutory duty to advise, and thereby embarrass or irritate, the responsible ministers on matters where the political stakes were high.

The new Royal Commission had at least a chance of avoiding this fate, if only because of its status and authority for, unlike the 1945 and 1958 Commissions, which had statutory powers to make proposals, the Redcliffe-Maud Commission was a commission of inquiry, the sole purpose of which was to investigate and report. Its terms of reference were

> to consider the structure of local government in England outside Greater London and to make recommendations for authorities and boundaries and for functions and their division, having regard to their size and character of

areas in which these can be most effectively exercised and the need to sustain a viable system of local democracy.⁵

Its members were a powerful and respected group, significantly numbering among them Dame Evelyn Sharp, recently retired as Permanent Secretary at the Ministry of Housing and Local Government. But despite Crossman's initial reference to a short sharp inquiry devoted to a few key principles, it soon became clear that little could be expected from the new Commission before the middle of 1968 at the earliest.

At the same time, the government sought to be truly comprehensive in its reform of local government. While Wales and Scotland were not covered by the Redcliffe-Maud inquiry, they were dealt with separately in processes which ran in parallel. The Local Government Commission for Wales, established under the 1958 Act in parallel with the English Commission, had made proposals for rationalizing Welsh local government which were wholly unacceptable to the Conservative government.⁶ Following the Labour government's election in 1964, the newly established Welsh Office undertook its own process of consultation and consideration, and produced a new framework, with a striking resemblance to that eventually introduced in England. In 1967, the Secretary of State for Wales published the outcome of these deliberations in a white paper that proposed the creation of new and larger county and district councils throughout the Principality. The new system was to be based on two tiers of local authorities; only Swansea, Cardiff and Newport were to be retained as all-purpose authorities.⁷

Scotland needed a different approach. Under the Conservatives, the Scottish Office had been working up proposals during 1962–3 for a reorganization into fewer, larger units. These, while far-reaching, were superseded by the appointment of the Wheatley Royal Commission on Scottish local government, which the Wilson government set up in parallel to Redcliffe-Maud. The Wheatley report, when it came, was dismissive of the existing system:

> From the start, we recognised . . . our work had to be thorough and radical. The defects of the present structure were so deep-seated that surface patching would not do.⁸

In what many considered to be a better-argued report than that of the Redcliffe-Maud Commission, Wheatley identified a new structure of

Into the Melting Pot 199

regional and district councils, proposals which in broad terms were to be followed in the Local Government (Scotland) Act 1973.

Brave new England

It was to be 1969, with a general election approaching, before the Redcliffe-Maud Commission would finally labour to its conclusions.[9] It would have needed to have been an unusually independent-minded body for its conclusions not to have been predictable from the evidence put before it by the several Whitehall departments, which spoke with one voice in favour of reorganization into a much smaller number of authorities. In their evidence to the Royal Commission, the Ministry of Housing and Local Government spoke for Whitehall in complaining that government departments

> have found it increasingly unsatisfactory that their relationship with local government should, in a number of fields, and in particular in the administration of loan sanctions and Exchequer grants, take the form of a relationship with nearly 1,300 English local authorities . . . There is a clear need to reduce drastically the number of authorities with major financial responsibilities, so as to secure an improvement in their budgeting and control arrangements and in their relationship with central government in these matters.[10]

The Redcliffe-Maud report was delivered in 1969. The majority report provided a vigorous criticism of the defects of the existing structure. 'Local government areas no longer correspond to the pattern of life and work', it declared. The failure to recognize the interdependence of town and country, together with an unsatisfactory division of responsibilities and inadequate size, were judged 'a fatal defect'.[11] The report proposed a drastic reduction in the number of local authorities, with a single tier system of unitary authorities across the whole country, with the exception of the three metropolitan areas of Greater Manchester, Merseyside and the West Midlands, where a metropolitan county would be complemented by more local district councils. Above all of these authorities, metropolitan and unitary, would be a structure of eight provincial councils.

The Redcliffe-Maud inquiry was notable for three features, each of which echoed Bevan's 1945 attempt drastically to restructure English local government. First, there was intense debate within the Commission as to whether boundaries should be redrawn from the basis of existing units, or whether a radically different approach based on socio-economic linkages should be adopted. This debate was decisively won by supporters of the first approach, with lone dissenter Derek Senior publishing a voluminous minority report advocating city regions.[12]

Secondly, despite the decision to proceed by aggregating existing authorities as far as possible, solving town and country conflicts was to be tackled by the expedient of creating a single tier of unitary authorities everywhere except in the metropolitan areas. The unitary principle was paramount, and all the old arguments for single-tier authorities – first put by Jowitt – were rehearsed as if they were only now being conjured into existence.

Thirdly, the Redcliffe-Maud Commission accepted a conventional belief that fewer, larger authorities would be more effective. This was on the basis of 'evidence' – that is, submissions of convenient opinion – that would not stand up to critical scrutiny and which were largely orchestrated by the Whitehall machine. Research set up and funded by the Commission was discounted wherever it pointed in another direction.

On publication of the report on 11 June 1969, the Prime Minister immediately accepted its main principles. The Commission had been expected to produce a report acceptable to the Labour party, which could expect to benefit from any future changes, provided that its urban strongholds were left reasonably intact. The membership of the Commission had been constructed to ensure just that. One of the civil servants involved in handling the report thought that

> the report ran very well with the Labour government in the last year of their administration . . . it chimed rather well with the government's political preferences in that what it meant in many areas were bigger county boroughs which in a good year would be Labour areas. It would also provide room for the cities to grow where they needed to. So it had the right sort of political flavour.[13]

Labour's regional and local government committee had a draft policy for its implementation ready within the month. The Conservatives, on the other hand, were caught on the hop, having neither a firm policy of their own, nor time to create one within the short period allowed for consultation. In the first weeks of 1970, the Labour government published a white paper largely embodying and building upon the Commission's proposals, finding the report 'sound in its broad essentials' and providing 'the best basis for re-organisation'. The government accepted the proposed abolition of counties and districts and their replacement by a new framework of unitary authorities, 'the advantages of making a single authority responsible for all services in a particular area' as 'successful local government depends to a significant extent on the ability of authorities to co-ordinate a wide range of functions and services, and to develop links between them'. It was also accepted that the new unitary authorities should bring together the 'complementary' areas of town and country, for

> the social and economic interdependence of the towns and countryside has increased to a point where only a single authority responsible for both can undertake the planned development of the main services to the maximum advantage of both.[14]

The government also endorsed the two-tier system for metropolitan areas, identifying these as needed in parts of the country – West Yorkshire and Southampton/Portsmouth – where the Royal Commission had not thought them appropriate. In consequence, Redcliffe-Maud's proposed fifty-eight unitary authorities reduced to fifty-one under the Labour government's scheme.

These proposals were subject to an even more compressed consultation period, during which Conservative anxieties rose to new levels. But all was not well within the Labour party. Regional consultative conferences had shown opinion at the grass roots to be split on the Redcliffe-Maud proposals, which were deeply disliked in some areas. Special efforts had to be made to sell the government's acceptance of Redcliffe-Maud to Labour councils, for it was recognized that

> Many councillors do not realise the considerable extent to which the white paper reflected the [National Executive Committee's] proposals, and unless this was made clear to them, opposition to reform could be increased.[15]

Activists and councillors in neither party were happy. The perennial problem of local acceptability already threatened to corrode whatever new structures were put in place, by whatever party.

A new architect

The consistency of the departmental submissions to Redcliffe-Maud had underlined the extent to which the Labour government held the initiative in pushing towards fundamental change, exposing what a Conservative party official judged to be the 'bare bones' of their own position. The Conservatives could well expect to form the next government and shape the future of local government, so what they did – or did not do – would be a matter of some importance. Here, as in other matters, Heath's approach was to appoint a study group, this time to formulate policy on local and regional government. In doing so, Heath was driven not by the need to think out a position on local government as such but by his anxiety about the political consequences of nationalist movements. Responding to nationalism led him to countenance far-reaching measures of devolution for Scotland and Wales, a course of action which would also have had implications for sub-central government in England. But it was a short-lived concern. When the study group, which was chaired by Geoffrey Rippon, began to coalesce around a radical scheme of regional authorities, it started to be ignored by the party's leadership and officials. The official position was that no decisions should be taken in advance of the Redcliffe-Maud report, a line insisted upon by Peter Walker from the moment he became shadow spokesman on local government.[16]

Believing that the Redcliffe-Maud report would be much delayed, the Conservatives persuaded themselves that they had ample time to formulate their own approach. When a Research Department paper (by future Environment Secretary Chris Patten) predicted that the Labour government would shelve making any response to the Commission's report until well into the next Parliament, the Shadow Cabinet agreed that the best line was to do nothing. There was some political sense in this position, even if it misjudged what the government would do. The Conservatives had, during the life of the unpopular Wilson governments, made steady gains in the political control of local authorities. By 1968, the party could claim to be 'the party of local government', controlling the great majority of local councils in England. Almost any line on future reform was certain to upset some interests within the party, as any change in the structure of authorities would threaten some group of Conservatives. Their very successes had 'created and encouraged the development of a powerful local government lobby within the party', within which there were strong and diverse views on reorganization.[17]

The Conservatives were bound to have difficulties with radical change. Unwilling simply to wait for Redcliffe-Maud and respond to whatever was proposed, Peter Walker sought to regain the initiative by urging his party to accept the idea of local government reform. His main card was the offer of devolved powers from central government as an inducement to accepting change, although his canvass of Shadow Cabinet colleagues revealed no widespread willingness to relinquish the reins of power. And beyond the generalities of devolution, there were no specific proposals. Indeed, although the still-to-be-revealed proposals of the Royal Commission could be expected to harm the Conservative interest, remarkably little was done to formulate an alternative policy. 'We have plenty of time' reassured Walker, who did not anticipate a general election before late 1970 or even the spring of 1971. The Shadow Cabinet also assumed that a Labour government would not have moved far towards formulating legislation by that time, while an incoming Conservative government would have priorities other than local government reform. It was necessary to do no more than promise that the question would be addressed 'within the lifetime of the next Conservative government'; that is, possibly not before 1975 or 1976.

The other plank of opposition policy, to refrain from comment on the Redcliffe-Maud report, also went drastically wrong. The Labour government issued an immediate acceptance of the report and invited comments from the local authorities, allowing only three months for this consultation; it was now open season for Conservative councils seeking to protect their interests. The tone of their representations was generally defensive and deeply critical of the Commission's approach and conclusions. Party chairman Anthony Barber's plea for them to avoid 'acrimony and snap decisions' fell on deaf ears. The party leadership remained silent, but the only result of this was to sour relations with local Conservatives who longed for clear guidance. The unitary authorities and the metropolitan councils were deeply unwelcome to Conservatives, and Walker quickly promised that a Conservative government's reforms would be 'based on the principle of the existence of a bottom tier to look after genuinely local amenities', with full consultation over boundaries.[18]

As a result of their 'wait and see' policy, the Conservatives had been drastically unprepared for Labour's prompt response to Redcliffe-Maud, leaving Walker to complain lamely that the government had not waited for the Kilbrandon report on the constitution. It was the more damaging that they were unprepared for the realities of early office under conditions in which they had no substantive policy whatsoever. There was no option but to leave it to Peter Walker himself to assume the role of architect of the new system after the Conservatives' surprise win in May 1970.

On taking up the reins first at Housing, and then at the new Department of the Environment which absorbed it, Walker found himself with neither a party policy position nor an acceptable inherited commitment. Considerable progress on drafting a new local government bill had already been made by the civil servants who were, as is sometimes the case, strongly committed to the streamlined and rational structure that they hoped to put in place. Walker immediately stopped work on the bill:

> It was rather a shattering moment for the Local Government Division of the Department, both because the Conservatives, as it turned out, were committed against the Redcliffe-Maud reorganisation but also because I think it was the first moment, as I saw it, of a considerable change in the way ministers behaved in relation to the system. Peter Walker . . . didn't want to implement the report. [The Permanent Secretary] reported 'they are not going to do it, they want to do something else'. It took us right back to the drawing board. It was a new style where ministers were going to decide very much more by themselves what was to be done on this matter. We weren't going to have any more Commissions and committees working it all out . . . . Peter Walker himself wrote a large part of the Conservative white paper . . . .[19]

The key principle that Walker enunciated marked off the Conservative approach from that of the Wilson government:

> there will always be conflicts between those who argue for large-scale organisation on grounds of efficiency and those, on the other hand, who argue for control by a body close to the people for whom the service is designed. The government must obviously seek efficiency, but where the arguments are evenly balanced their judgement will be given in favour of responsibility being exercised at the more local level.[20]

Outright rejection of Redcliffe-Maud could have been embarrassing, but Walker was lucky, in that Maud himself – ever the civil servant at heart – was prepared to desert his own Commission colleagues and speak and write in favour of Walker's own line.[21]

Walker's Local Government Act 1972 built upon, and largely preserved, the existing structure of county councils in England. Labour had favoured

Redcliffe-Maud's proposed structure of unitary authorities, because it fitted well with the pattern of existing county boroughs, most of which were Labour controlled; indeed, the northern industrial county boroughs were Labour's electoral heartland. The Conservative strength lay in the shire counties, and the Act was so framed as to make the least possible impact upon the county councils. Indeed, during the legislative process, Walker readily made concessions to local sentiment and historic ties, allowing many areas to remain in their historic counties despite having proposed their incorporation into adjacent counties with which they had stronger economic ties.

The main exception was in the plan for metropolitan government, where in six areas – not the same as Labour's – powerful metropolitan county councils, modelled on the GLC, were created. The metropolitan counties in the West Midlands, West Yorkshire, South Yorkshire, Greater Manchester, Merseyside and Tyneside were complemented by a total of thirty-six metropolitan districts with substantial powers. This was the least conservative aspect of the Walker Act, and one that occasioned deep alarm within the Conservative party. So too did Walker's adoption of Redcliffe-Maud's proposed new county councils for Humberside, Cleveland and Avon, new entities that both lacked historical roots and had to endure considerable local antipathies.

Here, within the Local Government Act itself, were sown the seeds of its own destruction. Most of what would have been implemented by either party would have been unpopular, and there was no prospect of a new cross-party consensus on the best pattern for local government. Yet in one respect the parties were in concurrence with one another and with established opinion. The 1972 Act greatly reduced both the number and the size ranges of local authorities throughout England (see tables 7.1 and 7.2). Orthodoxy at last came into its own, although D. N. Chester's warning of twenty years before was more pertinent than many imagined:

> Criticisms of the structure of local government and proposals for its reform have been a popular pastime for many years now ... The impression is given that if only the area problem were solved, by which is usually meant the creation of a number of larger units, then everything would be well with local government ... There is no evidence to show that this is the case.[22]

This new pattern was not expected to be immutable. Despite the political problems and abrupt termination of the two prototypes, the advantages of a standing commission to keep boundaries under review remained. It placed between Parliament and the locality the area of which was to be changed a process of scrutiny by a disinterested party, while still leaving it to ministers, with their responsibility to Parliament, to make the final decision as to what changes, if any, were to be adopted. For these purposes, and in order to define the initial boundaries of the new districts (those of the counties being scheduled in the Local Government Act 1972), a Local Government Boundary Commission would be once again set up for England, and another for Wales.

Table 7.1 Type, number and size ranges, pre-1972 English local authorities

Type	Number	Smallest	Largest
Counties	45	29,680	2,428,040
County boroughs	79	32,790	1,074,940
Boroughs, urban and rural districts	1,086	1,490	100,470
London boroughs[a]	32	134,000	318,000

[a] Thirty-two London borough councils were established by the London Government Act 1963.

Table 7.2 Type, number and size ranges, post-1972 English local authorities

Type	Number	Smallest	Largest
Counties	39	337,000	1,396,000
Metropolitan counties[a]	7	425,000	1,142,000
'Shire' districts	296	24,000	425,000
London boroughs	32	134,000	318,000
Metropolitan boroughs	36	174,000	1,096,000

[a] Including the Greater London Council which, together with the six metropolitan county councils, was abolished by the Local Government Act 1985.

A house of cards

Before long, such support as there was for the 1972 Act began to collapse. Redcliffe-Maud's own director of research commented that

> Never perhaps in the modern era has a structural change in British government become so unpopular so quickly as the Walker Local Government Act of 1972. Apart from occasional defensive utterances by Mr Walker himself it is hard to find anyone to defend it . . . For many the Act is seen as the root of all the major problems that are thought to beset local government, including over staffing, over-spending and over-taxing as well as the actual malfunctioning of the new system itself.[23]

The Local Government Act 1972 was also to prove politically disastrous to the Conservatives. The abolition of the county boroughs placed the second-rank urban centres within the counties and thereby destabilized the political control of the county councils. The abandonment of rural weighting took away the electoral advantage that Conservatives had long enjoyed in the more sparsely populated parts of the counties. More important still, the extension of party competition to the whole of England had the effect of forcing out of politics the independent and Conservative-sympathizing county notables, some of whose families had long dominated the counties. The old links between social leadership and political power were fractured and county politics would not be the same again.[24]

During the next decade, two separate movements began to destabilize the new system of local government. The first was a renaissance of independent ambition among many of the former county boroughs, who fretted under the constraints of mere district status within an often hostile county. The entire point of the long struggle to reform local government had been to eradicate the tensions and the instabilities that arose from the separate interests of counties and county boroughs. What became clear almost on the inception of the new system was that the conflicts remained, and were simply fought out in different arenas. The former county boroughs had lost much of their power but nothing of their ambition, and had added to it a sometimes bitter resentment. The chief executive of one spoke for more than just his own authority in expressing that spirit:

> We are a great city and we will always be so, and whatever the local government institutions, it is imperative that we should be able to talk to the county

on equal terms . . . If you can't do that, you might as well have parish council's status.[25]

The issues that fuelled these hostilities were the exercise of concurrent powers and the operation of agency arrangements, whereby district authorities provided county services under agreements which were exploited by the former county boroughs.

In November 1975 the larger district councils met jointly to express their 'dissatisfaction with the restricted powers available to them as a result of local government reorganisation' and to urge the Secretary of State to grant them much wider powers. As there was now a Labour government, these Labour authorities could expect a sympathetic hearing. The Labour party itself was struggling to define a viable policy on devolution to Scotland and Wales, a concern that brought in its wake consideration of the possibilities for greater devolution within England. The party's policy document on devolution picked up the issue of the tensions arising from the 1972 Act and, while it ruled out 'wholesale reorganisation', proposed a re-examination 'to see what improvements could be made without tearing up local government by its roots: to embark in short on a process of local government reform'.[26]

While Anthony Crosland, the first Environment Secretary in the 1974 Wilson government, had rebuffed any pressures for further change in the system, his successor, Peter Shore, was more sympathetic to the idea that the larger cities should be restored to their former power. Shore set out to convince his colleagues that the existing 'absurd' division of power should be changed in order to 'save the city'.[27] The Labour leaders of some of the cities had begun to lobby Shore immediately on his appointment, but it was the prospect of widespread Conservative gains in the 1977 county elections that added urgency to their case. Jack Straw, Peter Shore's political advisor, reputedly coined the term 'organic change' to refer to the devolution of power from the counties back to the cities. At the Labour party Local Government Conference at Harrogate in January 1977, Shore announced an impending policy change:

> We have the situation of former large county boroughs outside the metropolitan counties – Bristol, Norwich, Leicester, Nottingham, Plymouth and Hull to mention only a few – the great cities with their own individual character and traditions which once provided all local services and which on reorganization suffered a traumatic reduction in functions and status to not

more than urban district councils and whose citizens may still be wondering just how they have benefited from the reorganization that took place.[28]

The Association of District Councils responded to these signals and made the running in an new campaign for devolution of power from counties to districts and for the ending of concurrent functions. The county councils, naturally enough, called for 'a period of stability'. As many as half of the nearly 300 districts supported such a change, as it was clear that once the largest among them regained many of their former powers it would be difficult to draw the line to prevent a more widespread devolution. Some authorities – Bristol was one – wanted the virtual restoration of county borough status as a unitary authority. Most wanted education powers, the *sine qua non* of municipal muscularity.

The 'organic change' movement towards a redistribution of power received a considerable setback when, in July 1977, the Labour party published its own paper expressing doubts about anything so incremental and gradualist, fearing that 'the opportunity to create a new system of elected regional authorities and new district authorities may be lost for several generations. Piecemeal reform may be the enemy of radical reform.'[29] This did not prevent the Conservatives from attacking 'organic change' as being motivated not by a desire to strengthen local government or enhance its efficiency but 'to give a better chance for the Labour party to have greater control over larger sections of local government'. Just three years had passed since the new system had come in operation on 1 April 1974. Already the political and governmental divisions were beginning to undermine its foundations.

Contested even within the government, where some ministers thought that Shore had 'bounced' them in his Harrogate speech, organic change began to bog down. An interdepartmental committee of officials provided a forum for differing Whitehall views, while the several local government and professional associations lobbied a range of concerned ministers for or against change. Shore continued to edge towards a decision, but progress was slow until, in November 1978, the Queen's Speech announced that proposals would be brought forward in that Parliament 'to secure the better functioning of local democracy in a number of large towns and cities in England'. Celebrations by the would-be beneficiaries would have been premature, as the Callaghan government was now staggering through its final months and few expected the Parliament to run its course.

Nevertheless, the government pressed on, and in January 1979 published the white paper *Organic Change in Local Government*.[30]

Yet firm proposals were still lacking. The white paper was floated as a consultative document, a range of issues having been left unresolved. Education continued to be a major stumbling block, as it was the one service most earnestly desired, and the one the transfer of which was bound to be most strongly opposed by the DES officials. Linked to the range of functions was the question of the size threshold at which a district would qualify for the transfer of power, an issue that was predictably hard to resolve. The thorniest question was that of the right of a county councillor serving a devolved area to vote on (say) education policy in the county council at large. And still left open was whether devolution would come as of right to those districts above the size threshold, or would be a matter for case-by-case scrutiny by DoE officials.[31]

There was not the remotest prospect of early settlement of these issues, which could be fought over for many months more. This was a policy that 'contained the seeds of its own delay'.[32] And delay was bound to be fatal. On 28 March, the Callaghan government lost a vote of confidence in the House of Commons, and a general election was called for 3 May. Organic change, Peter Shore-style, would not happen.

The election of a Conservative government could not forestall the progressive collapse of the 1972 local government system. The discussions on organic change over the past two years had established one thing: that the Walker settlement could fairly be regarded as temporary. Ambitions fired up would not be readily quenched. And at this point another unravelling began, driven by a separate impulse that would, in time, converge with the unconsummated desire for unitary status for the powerful districts.

The GLC had long been a deeply unpopular body within Conservative circles, and the metropolitan counties did little to redress the suspicion with which such large and powerful authorities were regarded. The first serious moves to abolish the GLC were made as early as 1972, just as metropolitan counties were at the point of being created. Since 1965 the outermost London suburbs, all Conservative controlled, had struggled to fend off what they saw as the predatory actions of both Labour and Conservative controlled GLC administrations. The source of the contention was the acquisition of land for housing purposes, where the GLC had been seen as the instrument for equalizing housing opportunities between the inner city and the leafy suburbs. Once the suburban political leaders began to co-ordinate their opposition within the Conservative party, they found that they were able to defeat government ministers as well as the GLC itself. But their fear of a Labour GLC acting with the support of a Labour government was sufficient threat for them to garner support for GLC abolition.

At just this point, Edward Heath, as opposition leader, came under pressure to appoint a party figurehead for London to rally the party faithful and define a coherent policy for the capital. Reluctantly, Heath was persuaded to appoint Geoffrey Finsberg, the MP for Hampstead, and the Conservatives' leading authority on London matters. Finsberg was in fact the most hostile of all the GLC's critics, as he had been of the LCC before it. In his first act as front-bench spokesman on London affairs, Finsberg published *A Policy for London* in October 1974, proposing to strip the GLC of most of its housing powers and promising a review of London government.

A strong abolitionist lobby was already developing among London Conservatives. Finsberg prepared a draft GLC abolition bill, which would have been brought forward had the Conservatives won the second 1974 general election. That they did not win the election only held back the prospect of abolition. But Heath's defeat also propelled Margaret Thatcher into the party leadership. Under Mrs Thatcher, Finsberg retained his responsibility for London but was promoted to a deputy chairmanship of the Conservative party. The 1977 GLC election saw the Conservatives committed to an immediate inquiry into London government, and so broad-based was anti-GLC feeling by this point that an 'Abolish the GLC' campaign, led by a former Labour GLC alderman, fought thirty-one of the GLC's ninty-two seats. In opposition nationally, but in power at London's county hall, there was little that Conservatives could do for the moment. Any public expression of desire to see the GLC abolished would weaken the position of the GLC's leader, free-market Conservative Sir Horace Cutler.

Once they were in power nationally, the abolitionist Conservatives had to hold back in deference to Cutler's position, while the GLC's own review of London government misfired badly. The inquiry was entrusted to Sir Frank Marshall, the former Conservative leader of Leeds, but Marshall lost control of the process when he brought in a large number of academic experts, and his report argued the case for a powerful, strategic

Greater London Council. He was overwhelmed by his own advisers.[33]

What drove GLC abolition to the top of Mrs Thatcher's agenda was the Labour victory there in May 1981, and the confrontational policies pursued by its leader, Ken Livingstone. But the government would have remained aloof had it not been for the polarization of London's local and Parliamentary opinion. During a prolonged battle over the GLC's public transport policy, pursued through the courts to the House of Lords, an unbridgeable gulf opened up between the Labour boroughs, some of whom supported the GLC, and the Conservatives who opposed it. The result was a split in the London Boroughs' Association after the LBA majority had voted in favour of GLC abolition, with the Labour authorities seceding to a new Association of London Authorities, a split which was to last until 1995.

Conservative MPs were themselves beginning to line up behind GLC abolition. They were led by John Wheeler, MP for Paddington, with tacit encouragement from Geoffrey Finsberg, now a junior minister at the Department of Health and Social Security. The Greater London Area organization of the Conservative party set up its own policy group on London government which, after bitter arguments and changes of tack, swung behind abolition, a position that it claimed was supported by 'the overwhelming body of opinion in the party'. In January 1983, London's Conservative MPs formally supported the abolition of the GLC, with the press reporting that such a proposal would feature in the Conservative manifesto of the coming general election.

Although the abolition of the GLC, together with that of the metropolitan county councils, was by now publicly supported by the Institute of Directors and the Confederation of British Industry (the West Midlands branch of which had made the running in opposition to the industrial strategies of the metropolitan county council there), ministers themselves were deeply divided. The Cabinet committee set up to consider local government finance also looked at the abolition of the GLC and the MCCs as a cost-saving option. The Prime Minister favoured it; Michael Heseltine opposed it; Tom King, the Environment Secretary, was deeply sceptical, publicly dismissing speculation that abolition would be included in the manifesto. When the Cabinet met in April to approve the manifesto, the proposal to abolition the GLC and the metropolitan counties was not discussed. Yet immediately after the meeting Mrs Thatcher met Geoffrey Finsberg and Ian Gow to draft a passage dismissing this 'wasteful and unnecessary tier of government' and giving an unequivocal commitment to abolish it. Cabinet Ministers were startled and few of them were pleased. But London's Conservative MPs and borough leaders were triumphant. Some uncharitably interpreted this surprise manifesto promise as compensation for there being nothing of substance to be said on rates reform. In fact, the long-running tide of London opinion against the GLC within the Conservative party was in tune with Mrs Thatcher's own sentiments, and her unilateral action rightly captured the spirit of the London party.

Three months after Mrs Thatcher's 1983 election victory, the white paper *Streamlining the Cities* was published to a derisive and generally disbelieving reception.[34] The GLC's highly effective campaign against abolition had far more impact and public sympathy than those of the metropolitan county councils; and the Labour opposition, aided by substantial cross-bench sympathy in the House of Lords, inflicted a series of defeats on the government. For all their efforts, the bill could not be stopped, and the Local Government Act 1985 abolished all seven authorities. The government substituted for them a pattern of single-tier local government, making the unitary principle a reality at last, if only in London and the provincial metropolitan areas.

Redrawing the map

The abolition of the GLC and metropolitan counties had powerful repercussions on local government outside the conurbations. The principle of the unitary authority had been accepted, if only by default, and the opportunity arose to again press the case for the former county boroughs to regain their power. From 1985 the leading district councils returned to the campaign that had brought them success in the argument over organic change, although events had derived them of the fruits of that victory. At the ADC annual conference that year a debate was staged on the abolition of the county councils, a proposition directly inspired by the working through of the GLC and metropolitan county abolition.[35] Once again, government would have to respond to these pressures.

It was not that ministers were unsympathetic, as the passage of time had dimmed even residual attachment to Walker's 1972 Act. Conservative environment secretaries were not well disposed towards the Labour controlled artificial 'counties' of Avon, Cleveland and Humberside. In fact, they already possessed the means to press for their dissolution. The Local Government Boundary Commission established by the 1972 Act operated through guidance laid down by the Environment Secretary. Nicholas Ridley was the first to use this power, directing the Commission to reconsider its view of Humberside, and lowering the threshold at which it could recommend abolition of the county council. But this review process was laborious, and its outcome uncertain. The temptation to seek more immediate and certain results, and to do so across the country, was compelling.

Converging with this tendency was Mrs Thatcher's persistent opposition to unnecessary levels of local government and her search for stronger mechanisms of financial accountability. The counties were big spenders, and the Conservatives were controlling fewer of them. A new generation of Conservative MPs, devoid of county connection, began to demand the dismantling of the 1972 Act in favour of a single tier of unitary authorities. What appealed to Mrs Thatcher was that unitary local government, the pattern now found in London and the metropolitan areas, offered clear accountability in comparison with the county/district system. There the division between revenue collection (at the district level), and the greater proportion of spending (through precepting, at the county level), was thought to confuse the electorate.

Mrs Thatcher did not remain in office long enough to pursue any such scheme. Her defeat in November 1990 triggered the latest round of change. Returning to the Department of the Environment, Michael Heseltine launched the reconstruction of local government that he had promised during his election campaign and in the publications of his wilderness years. He set up a three-part review, covering finance (where his task was to replace the poll tax), structure and internal management. At the same time, the Secretaries of State in Scotland and Wales published proposals to rationalize local government in both countries into a smaller number of single-tier or 'unitary' authorities. The abolition of the Scottish regions, especially the huge and powerful Strathclyde regional council, would be particularly gratifying to Conservatives north of the border. The proposals published in January 1992 were firmed up for Scotland in October 1992, and for Wales in March 1993. Legislation was introduced that autumn.

In contrast with this speedy executive action, characteristic of the way in which successive governments have tackled Scotland and Wales, the proposals for England once again envisaged an independent Local Government Commission, working gradually and laboriously to review the entire country (outside London and the metropolitan areas) in stages. The presumption was in favour of a unitary structure, so that

> people can identify one authority which secures services in their area. Having a single tier should reduce bureaucracy and improve the coordination of services, increasing quality and reducing costs. This argument holds even if both the county council and the district councils in a county are efficient and if the two tiers co-operate closely with each other; there can still be benefits in a clearer and more streamlined structure. Such a structure is also important for proper financial accountability on the part of local authorities to local taxpayers: people must know who is responsible for setting a budget and achieving value for money in services in their area, and how the size of their local tax bills relates to what is spent on local public services.
>
> Introducing unitary authorities in shire counties would also offer the opportunity of relating the structure of local government more closely to communities with which people identify . . . This should increase interest in local affairs, and make for more responsive and representative local government.[36]

The aim of the review was, then, to achieve the structure 'which best matches the particular circumstances of each area'.

Heseltine made extensive use of consultants to formulate guidance for the Local Government Commission and appointed CBI Director-General John Banham to lead it. By the time the Banham Commission began work in earnest, Michael Heseltine had moved to the Department of Trade and Industry. His successors at the DoE were far from enthusiastic, and although its continuation was announced in May 1992, the review had already lost its momentum, together with the sense of purpose that had originally driven it.[37]

For the first phase of its work, the Banham Commission was given some easy targets including the Isle of Wight, where the case for a unitary authority was almost self evident, and the artificial counties of Avon, Humberside and Cleveland. Thereafter, a rather leisurely process of review in a further series of four '*tranches*' was envisaged, the end-date of 1997 lulling some authorities into the belief that the tide of change was unlikely ever to reach them. The Commission's procedure was to make an outline proposal for each area, taking account of 'community loyalties and local opinion'. Local authorities and other affected parties within an area were asked to make proposals for the Commission's consideration. The

Secretary of State would then come to a decision on the Commission's recommendations and seek Parliament's approval by means of Order to bring it into effect.

If this starting point for the review process seemed uncontentious enough, it nonetheless soon began to disintegrate under the pressure of its own contradictions. Either unitary authorities were everywhere appropriate or they were not; and either it was for the Commission to judge where they were appropriate, or it was not. In May 1993 the Commission proposed replacing Cleveland with four unitaries, and in June the twenty-three authorities in Avon, Gloucestershire and Somerset with eight. In November, the Commission proposed a mixture of two-tier and unitary authorities in Derbyshire and in Durham, claiming that the unitary model was inappropriate to the more rural parts of these counties. Although the government would eventually accept proposals made at this point for thirty-eight new unitary authorities, local government minister David Curry warned of a 'strong chance' that the Commission's recommendations might be 'some distance' from the government's wishes. In December, Environment Secretary John Gummer tossed the Avon/Somerset/Gloucestershire proposals back to the Commission, asking them to think again.

By mid-1993 the review process had few friends. It was indelibly identified with Michael Heseltine, so few other ministers took much interest in the review when it was launched. Some would have gladly consigned it to oblivion as soon as Heseltine had moved to other pastures. But once the decision had been made to continue, the Commission would continue to exercise its own judgement. The resulting conflicts between John Gummer and Sir John Banham – who was reported as hovering on the brink of resignation – were well publicized. The Commission was accused of misleading MPs. *The Guardian* reported that Conservative backbenchers were calling for the review to be abandoned. But when the 1993 elections virtually wiped out Conservative control in the English counties, leaving them with the sole bastion of Buckinghamshire, there was little left for Conservatives to fight for in county government.

Recognizing a losing hand when he inherited one, John Gummer sought to wind down this unpopular and uncontrollable initiative by putting the review on a voluntary basis, with councils opting in. However, in September 1993 *The Independent* reported that Major had over-ruled Gummer; instead, the timescale was to be foreshortened, and the

Into the Melting Pot 217

Commission asked to complete its work by the end of 1994. New guidance was issued, instructing the Commission to consider whether or not the areas under review met the criteria for unitary status. Retention of the two-tier system was expected to be an exception, although very large unitary authorities were to be avoided.

To the critics, to revive the review was to compound the initial error. The Association of County Councils, speaking for the most obvious losers, warned that the end result of the review would be a loss of efficiency and higher costs. Unlike organic change, which threatened only to remove some of the urban centres from the county's jurisdiction, an insistence on creating unitary authorities would spell doom for the county councils.

In 1995, the Commission launched its review of a further twenty-one districts in twelve counties. The outcome was that unitary authorities were proposed in just eleven areas. Following the representations after the publication of the Commission's proposals, the plans for unitary authorities in Northampton and in the Dartford/Gravesham area of Kent were withdrawn, leaving just nine proposed unitaries to be placed before the Secretary of State in December 1995. The result was a patchwork. Local government in England would now be characterized by the term 'hybridity', much used in the Commission's report to capture the mixture of new unitaries, existing unitaries (in London and the metropolitan areas) and the older two-tier structure.

This did not look to be a particularly stable mix. Norwich, for example, once in the vanguard of organic change, was to remain a district within the jurisdiction of Norfolk County Council. Nevertheless, the Commission made a brave attempt to contain the volatility that had so destabilized local government since Peter Walker's ill-fated 1972 Act:

> The appetite for unitary status will not have been extinguished, particularly in councils which have failed to convince the Commission, the Secretary of State, and Parliament of their case. But if they remain in the two tier struc ture, that means that, when compared with current statute and guidance, their circumstances are not convincing. Only with a different vision of local government and fresh legislation could the outcome be different. Some of the new authorities to be established as a result of the 1992 Act introduce unitary local government into settings where it has not previously operated. It would be advisable for the progress of those new unitary authorities to be monitored and evaluated before any further comprehensive change is

contemplated. In the meantime, councils owe it to their communities to make the present two-tier system work as efficaciously as possible, rather then persisting in decrying its failings.[38]

This was hardly a clarion call for a new beginning, for the Commission sensibly recognized that the old tensions remained, and were no less potent than before. The county borough ghost would continue to haunt the English shires.

Reshaping Political Management

The compulsion to tinker with local government did not stop short at structure. Largely taken for granted since the creation of the framework of modern local government in the closing years of the nineteenth century, the ways in which councils were managed came under closer scrutiny from around 1960. Attention was to be paid to two issues: the personal qualities of councillors, relative to the tasks that they had to perform; and the decision-making framework within which they operated in their local authorities. As councillors themselves came to seem both less relevant and less effective, a search for a more accountable local politics was launched.

The growth and expansion of local government had often raised concerns about the ability of elected representatives satisfactorily to cope with the new demands. The question of whether they had the capability to take on the expanded responsibilities envisaged by the age of reconstruction had received some attention during the war, the coalition government placing its faith in 'the capacity and public spirit' of the members and officers of the local authorities.[39] That faith was put to the test as the work of local authorities acquired a more technical and professional character. The individual councillor faced an increasingly difficult task in understanding the rationale of policies and the minutiae of schemes proposed by the central government for local adoption.

Official concern with the problem of 'people in local government' emerged only in the 1960s, when local government – in common with many British institutions – was faced with a major problem of declining public confidence. 'Parliament, Ministers and the Whitehall departments have come increasingly to lose faith in the responsibility of locally elected bodies', it was claimed, while 'there is often too wide a gulf in local government between the governors and the governed'.[40]

The theme gathered impetus. The report of the Royal Commission on Local Government in Greater London in 1960 commented on the need to attract people of 'high standard of intelligence, experience, personality and character' to council service.[41] A clear signal was given of an emerging orthodoxy when Dame Evelyn Sharp, Permanent Secretary at the Ministry of Housing and Local Government, pronounced that 'the work of local authorities is often not good enough' and that 'most people engaged or interested in local government agree... that the calibre of local government is not equal all round to its responsibilities'.[42]

In keeping with the spirit of an age that celebrated youth, this elusive quality of 'calibre' was seen as something denied to people of more mature years, which most councillors then (as now) were.[43] 'Our councils are filled with retired people, with women whose children have grown up, and with a few others who can afford the time, or see some particular advantage in being on the council', wrote one commentator: 'There is a need for more life and energy; for more people in their thirties and forties; even in their twenties'.[44] Similarly, Dame Evelyn thought the average age of councillors 'a great deal too high', and confessed herself 'an unrepentant believer in an age limit, as with the magistrates'. Life and energy were not qualities of youth alone. The elixir of experience in the quite different world of business and commerce were also seen as vital, for too few people 'from business, from industry, from agriculture, from the professions' were taking an interest in local government, less still serving as councillors.[45]

For some time this problem was addressed obliquely, with an assumption that the reform of local government structure would itself draw in a better class of person as councillor by offering greater opportunities and responsibilities (although this sat uneasily with the proposition that councillors were not coping with their *existing* responsibilities). The Herbert Commission was the first, but by no means the last, to justify the increasing the size and scope of authorities in terms of the need to attract better councillors:

> If we are to encourage a sufficient supply of councillors of ability, the scope and size of the authority on which they serve must be such that the arena in which their talents are displayed is wide enough to require (and indeed to stimulate) their qualities and to satisfy their ambitions; there does seem to

be some relationship between the size and scope of the authority and the capacity of the councillor and official attracted.[46]

So 'a certain minimum size and scope of authority seems to be needed to attract councillors and officers of the right calibre'. But in this one instance, the circularity of the argument was conceded: 'it is useless to create too many "outsize" jobs' mused the Commissioners, 'when one knows there will not be enough "outsize" people to fill them'. This latter, arguably vital, qualification would be discounted by the reorganizers of the 1960s and 1970s: they simply anticipated that large units would attract more capable people from outside the system to stand for election as local councillors. When the Macmillan government came to decide on the London proposals, Herbert's conception of the medium-sized authority as optimal was dismissed in favour of the supposed benefits of a more substantial increase in scale.

Dame Evelyn Sharp in particular pressed the argument that larger authorities provided greater scope for councillors, for part of the difficulty in getting good enough people to serve arose 'from the fact that the areas and status of local authorities are often too cramped or too small to enable a satisfactory job to be done'.[47] By the mid-1960s, it had become a commonplace that more powerful local authority units would do much to attract 'people of calibre' to the service of local authorities'.[48] In 1967 Peter Walker, contributing to the Conservative party's own review of the future options for local government, argued the potential of local government reform in just these terms.[49]

After 1965 there was a tendency to approach the problem more directly by reforming the internal decision-making structure of councils. This was expected to yield two benefits. First, it would create a speedier and more efficient decision-making system, and thus modernize the local authorities and make them more business-like. Secondly, by attracting to local government the 'better' type of councillor, it would tackle at source the barrier to service as a councillor.

Sharpening-up decisions

Increasing dissatisfaction with the internal working of local authorities led the Conservative government in 1964 to appoint two parallel committees, under the chairmanship of former senior civil servants, to review the management and personnel of local government. The first of these, under Sir John Maud, was given the task of investigating problems of managerial efficiency of councils and their members and 'to consider in the light of modern conditions how local government might best continue to attract and retain people of the calibre necessary to ensure its maximum effectiveness'.[50] The second, under Sir George Mallaby, investigated the paid local government service.[51]

The Maud Committee criticized the existing local authority system as leading to waste of time, delay, frustration, excessive paperwork, resistance to delegation to officers, lack of discrimination between major and minor issues, excessive demands on councillors' time and acting as a deterrent to the recruitment of 'policy-oriented' councillors. The too-close association between service committees and departments led to departmentalism and an absence of unity, scattering responsibility, and inhibiting co-ordination and a clear focus of responsibility.

To meet this considerable indictment, Maud proposed an executive *management board* of five to nine members to lead and co-ordinate the work of the authority, while committees as decision-making bodies would be abolished. Residual committees would become mere deliberative bodies, advising the management board, reviewing performance in the services with which they were associated, and channelling the views of the public. They would be few in number, and not all councillors would have a committee place.

Maud's proposals, presented as a means of finding attractive opportunities for able people, were widely attacked. Committee member Sir Andrew Wheatley's own dissenting opinion took a diametrically opposite view, arguing that changes that privileged a minority of decision-makers would necessarily exclude the participation of many councillors. 'Unless the members as a whole are given a worthwhile part to play', he warned, a function which 'must inevitably involve direct participation in formulation of policy, local government will not attract members of the quality that are needed'.[52] For the like-minded D. N. Chester, the formidable warden of Nuffield College, Maud's proposals would give most members 'little or no responsibility – only to criticise and be active at Council meetings – a pleasant but not very responsible activity', while committees would be so downgraded as to make it unlikely that councillors would want to serve on them.[53]

The response to the report from local authorities was equally condemnatory, with councillors rejecting the proposals for a management board on the grounds of their impracticability. One authoritative commentator concluded that the Maud Committee had failed to 'provide an authoritative analysis of the problems set by its terms of reference'.[54] The Redcliffe-Maud Royal Commission had already been established under the same chairman, and would take the discussion further. While its report abandoned the management board in the face of the earlier wave of criticism, it otherwise largely endorsed the earlier committee's analysis.

The two themes of structure and internal organization came together after the structural reforms of the 1972 Local Government Act. A working group on local authority management was set up under the chairmanship of Laurence Bains, a retired local authority chief executive, to consider the management structures appropriate to the new authorities. Here the focal concern was once again that particular types of individual were excluded from serving on councils. In this case this was largely attributed to local authorities' time-consuming procedures. Some potential members, 'particularly professionals and businessmen', were deterred from putting themselves forward for election 'because of the amount of time traditionally occupied by Council affairs'. This down-to-earth working group hoped that the proposals that they put forward for streamlining the decision-making structures – far less radical than those of the Maud Committee – 'will result in more of these potential candidates being willing to play an active part in local government'.[55]

The search for 'new conventions'

The new management structures recommended by Bains were almost universally adopted, although concern remained about the 'calibre' of elected representatives. By the early 1980s, concern about the kind of people who became councillors remained, but was exacerbated by unease about how they acted once they came to be in control of the new local authorities. The election of the Conservative government in 1979 led to a deterioration of the relations between central and local government, and between the two political parties, giving rise to new and more confrontational patterns of councillor behaviour.

The growing intensity in political relations between the parties arose at first sight from conflicts over the Conservatives' new legislation.[56] At the same time, something more than just policy was involved here, for it seemed that the very tone and style of local government was being transformed. For many councillors, the context within which policy was made became one of heightened conflict and personal rancour:

> The vigour of the debates produced by such radical policies as privatisation on the right or equal opportunities on the left often reflected the mutual incomprehension of polarised parties. Relations between such parties were hard to manage; mutual loathing was not unknown, with no suspension of hostilities outside the council chamber . . . Polarisation was accompanied by an intensification of the party battle as the temper and tempo of conflict increased.[57]

More insidious in the eyes of hostile ministers and wary civil servants was the way in which new councillors sought to reassert the political nature of local government by adopting a 'hands on' approach, intervening in the day-to-day management of council affairs rather than leaving the execution of policy to officers.[58] These developments in turn gave rise to a confusion over the respective roles of councillors and officers, and a controversy about the trend to appoint politically aligned officers. The polarization of party politics in local government led to allegations of the abuse of political power in the (more numerous) Labour controlled councils.

Margaret Thatcher, whose political career was marked by a deep suspicion of local government, became increasingly incensed by what appeared to be growing evidence of entrenched opposition to central government in the Labour strongholds. Reports of Labour 'abuses' made good copy in Central Office, and fed the Prime Minister's own predispositions. Her demands that the Department of the Environment 'do something' drew a blank as civil servants demurred from any overtly partisan intervention. Recognizing her frustration, senior figures in the government and party took their own steps to privately commission an inquiry by Charles Goodson-Wickes, a prospective Conservative Parliamentary candidate. Goodson-Wickes worked under the auspices of Keith Joseph's Centre for Policy Studies, and was fed with reports and anecdotes about Labour councils' misdemeanours through the Conservative party's constituency network.

The publication of his pamphlet, *The New Corruption*, coincided with the 1984 Conservative party conference, fuelling a heated debate. The report claimed to reveal an increasing politicization of officers, and documented instances of local government officials in one authority serving as councillors in a neighbouring one, a practice which, he claimed, would inevitably be detrimental to local government.[59] Goodson-Wickes also produced evidence of local authorities using public money for political campaigning purposes. The report commented that 'a whole new subculture is showing signs of emerging, quite out of tune... and running contrary to the tradition of those committed to voluntary service to the community'.[60] It was this last comment in particular that would have chimed with Mrs Thatcher's hostility to Labour local government. The basis for action was now in place, and Minister of State Kenneth Baker announced at the conference that the government would appoint a committee of inquiry to tackle 'abuses'.

Within six months, the inquiry was beginning its work, under the chairmanship of former Labour Parliamentary candidate David Widdicombe, QC. Although established as a partisan move, the scope of the committee's inquiry soon broadened, as Environment Secretary Patrick Jenkin found it necessary to carry with him the Labour front bench on both the membership of the committee and its terms of reference. Before very long, the committee was making officials nervous with its evident refusal to accept the Goodson-Wickes starting point. An additional appointment was made of a leading Conservative to balance what was increasingly seen within the DoE as a 'left-wing' committee, but to little avail: the committee's analysis demolished the wilder claims of 'abuse', was even-handed in its criticisms, and attributed much of the turmoil in local government to the tensions of change.

Recognizing the process of politicization that underlay these developments as progressive and irreversible, the Widdicombe Committee set out to propose a new system to fit these new circumstances.[61] In doing so, however, it took the view that the system of decision-taking in local government should continue to be one in which the authority remained a corporate body with decisions taken openly by, or on behalf of the whole council. There should be no separate source of executive authority such as existed nationally – the 'cabinet' model was a matter of much debate – and officers should serve the council as a whole. The committee reaffirmed that the traditional model was still appropriate to the needs of local government in the late twentieth century, and well capable of bearing both the impact

Into the Melting Pot 225

of party political organization, and the growing emphasis on popular participation.

Reporting in June 1986, Widdicombe argued that ultimate responsibility in local government rests with the elected members, acting within the law and accountable to the electorate. It therefore recommended the abolition of the co-option of outsiders to decision-making committees to avoid political balance and political accountability being upset, and responsibility blurred. Local government officers should be disbarred from council service elsewhere, and their political activities restricted in a manner analogous to that of civil servants; councillors' financial compensation should be reformed. The realities of party politics should be acknowledged by statutory recognition of political party groups on local councils, in return for which parties would gain the right to proportionate representation on all committees.

By and large, and despite a report the account of which of contemporary developments in local government distanced itself as far as possible from the Conservative government, these conclusions were what ministers wanted to hear. In July 1988, over two years after the publication of the Widdicombe report, a white paper setting out the government's response was published.[62] The government had broadly accepted the Widdicombe Committee's recommendations, including the Committee's principle that 'those who take decisions on behalf of the council must reflect the decisions of the electorate'. The proposals outlined in the white paper formed the basis of Part I of the Local Government and Housing Act 1989.

A new wave of change

The Widdicombe Committee's attempt to create 'new conventions for new circumstances' soon came to be seen as inadequate. The source of the supposed 'abuses' had been stemmed by compliance with the 1989 Act, but the longer-standing problem – of a system of local decision-making that lacked any clear focus of accountability – still remained. By the end of the decade, concern about councillors' roles showed no sign of abating, despite the Widdicombe report and the subsequent legislation. The ground covered by Maud and Widdicombe would be traversed yet again, as the Audit Commission turned its attention to the problem with a sustained critique of the ways in which councillors spent their time, provocatively published as *We Can't Go on Meeting Like This*.[63]

Michael Heseltine's return to the Department of the Environment reintroduced his distinctive approach to local government. His review of the political management of local authorities reopened issues that Widdicombe had hoped to have settled. Heseltine's consultation paper on *The Internal Management of Local Authorities in England*, published in 1991, set out his objective of promoting more effective, speedier and more business-like decision-making; strengthening scrutiny and enhancing public interest in local government; and enabling councillors to devote more time to their constituency role.

Among the several options for change that local authorities were invited to consider were: retention of the present system; adaptation of the committee system with delegated decision-making to committee chairs; and a 'cabinet' system, with a small group chosen from among elected councillors with authority to run the council on a day-to-day basis, without reference to the council as a whole. In this last, the majority of council members, whether in the party forming the executive or in opposition parties, would not take part in day-to-day decision-making. Central to Heseltine's initiative was his challenge to the committee system, the mechanism by which council business had been conducted since before the 1835 Municipal Corporations Act, and which was considered to be the heart of the local government system.[64] It could not be denied that the committee system was cumbersome. An extended cycle which, when elaborated through subcommittees, entailed at least three stages of consideration, with the possibility of referencing back to further extend the cycle, provided slow, and sometimes tortuous, decision-making. Various proposals for streamlining the system were offered, including a full 'cabinet' system of executive councillors with distinct portfolios, exercising powers on behalf of the council, and holding office on the confidence of its members.

The second challenge focused on the inadequacies of council leadership, which failed to provide a clear focus of responsibility. Although 'boss' or strong leader systems developed readily enough in local government from the late nineteenth century onward, there was still no statutory recognition of the realities of leadership. The office of leader still lacked formal authority, and council leaders were no different from other members, in that they could not take decisions themselves, but could only recommend courses of action to their fellow councillors. In the classic (but fast-vanishing) local authority of independent members, this formal position may have approximated to reality, but in the party-controlled authority, it was a travesty. Indeed, the legal fiction of council approval or ratification of recommendations from its subordinate bodies had led the Widdicombe Committee to adopt a distinction between *decision-making* by party groups and (formal) *decision-taking* by the council and its committees. The Heseltine paper urged new approaches to leadership, including the adoption of an independently elected US-style executive mayor system.

There was little enthusiasm for change among the responses of the local authorities, and the main outcome of the consultation was the establishment of a joint working party on internal management in June 1992. This body comprised representatives of the DoE, the local authority associations, the Audit Commission and the Local Government Management Board, to 'investigate current practices and propose possible experimental models of internal management'. In its report, published in July 1993, the working party made recommendations intended to strengthen the role of the councillor and develop effective leadership within local authorities by building on existing developments.[65]

Yet, by the early 1990s, these proposals had an almost curious air of irrelevance to what was actually happening to local government. Since 1980, the Conservative governments had progressively sidelined local authorities by establishing new *ad hoc* agencies composed of nominated people, largely with a private-sector background. Some with statutory powers, occasionally taken from the local authorities that they displaced, and some without, these new bodies took a leading role in urban regeneration and employment development.

The Urban Development Corporations – themselves modelled upon the New Town Development Corporations of 1946 – were constituted in a number of inner-city areas, most significantly in the London docklands, and had the planning powers and land holdings of the local authorities vested in them. The City Action Teams, Inner City Task Forces and Training and Enterprise Councils (TECs) that accompanied them were not statutory bodies, but the government increasingly looked to them to take the lead from the local authorities in promoting investment and employment growth. The overall result of these developments was to push councillors out of the frame, for they were to play scarcely any role in setting UDC and TEC policies.

Moreover, these transfers of functions threatened to destroy local government's capacity for integrating local service provision, displacing them from the lead role to which local authorities consistently aspired. That displacement was reinforced by the actual or proposed cutting back of councillor representation on other bodies, ranging from health authorities to police authorities. Meanwhile, the number of appointed bodies, the number of appointees and the share of public expenditure controlled by them, steadily increased. Some 4,500 bodies were now operating locally under appointed (or self-appointed) committees of people, often with a business background. An estimated total of around 55,000 of them could be compared with the 22,000 councillors in England and Wales, although there was probably a considerable degree of double-counting due to their multiple memberships.[66]

The importance of these appointed bodies lay in their dominance by the very businessmen and other local notables whose under-representation on local authorities had drawn forth such persistent complaint since 1960. 'Quangos' had succeeded in drawing them into local public life, but at the expense of popular accountability. Some dubbed them the *new magistracy*, denoting a return to those nineteenth-century structures of local power and forms of government that predated local democracy. And this was not the only semantic shift that their presence provoked. By 1995 it had become commonplace for commentators to use the term 'local governance' in preference to the mono-institutional term 'local government'. Local government no longer seemed to capture the reality of political life in urban and rural Britain. The melting pot had claimed not only the structure of local government, but its infrastructure: the belief in the value of local democracy.

Notes

1 A. Alexander, *The Politics of Local Government in the United Kingdom* (Longman, London, 1982).
2. R. Crossman, *The Diaries of a Cabinet Minister* (Hamish Hamilton/Jonathan Cape, London, 1975), vol. I: *Minister of Housing and Local Government*, p. 65.
3 Cited in P. G. Richards, *The Reformed Local Government System*, 2nd edn (George Allen & Unwin, London, 1975), pp. 37–8.
4 The process that started with the 1954 Sandys discussions was ended by the Local Government (Termination of Reviews) Act 1967.

5 Royal Commission on Local Government in England, 1966–1969, *Volume I: Report*, Cmnd. 4040 (HMSO, London, 1969), para. 3.
6 B. C. Smith and J. Stanyer, 'Administrative developments in 1967: a survey', *Public Administration*, 46(3) (1968), pp. 239–79.
7 B. Wood, *The Process of Local Government Reform, 1966–74* (George Allen & Unwin, London, 1976).
8 *Report of the Royal Commission on Local Government in Scotland*, Cmnd 4150 (HMSO, Edinburgh, 1969), para. 9(a).
9 G. Smith (ed.), *Redcliffe-Maud's Brave New England* (Charles Knight, London, 1969)
10 Royal Commission on Local Government in England, *Volume I: Report*, para. 88.
11 Royal Commission on Local Government in England, *Volume I: Report*, paras 85–94.
12 *Report of the Royal Commission on Local Government in England, Volume II: Memorandum of Dissent by Mr Derek Senior*, Cmnd. 4040-1 (HMSO, London, 1969).
13 Derek Osborn, Local Government Division civil servant in 1969, in *Contemporary Record*, 3(1), Autumn 1989, p. 37.
14 Department of Local Government and Regional Planning, *Reform of Local Government in England*, Cmnd. 4276 (HMSO, London, 1970), para. 18.
15 Labour Party Regional and Local Government Advisory Committee, 'Local government reform in England and the white paper', March 1970.
16 K. Young, 'The party and the English local government', in *Conservative Century, the Conservative Party Since 1900*, ed. A. Seldon and S. Ball (Oxford University Press, Oxford, 1994), pp. 432–6.
17 CPA, LCC/68/209, Conservative Research Department paper on local government reform, 28 November 1968.
18 CPA, LCC/70/269.
19 Osborn, *Contemporary Record*, p. 37.
20 Department of the Environment, *Local Government in England: government proposals for reorganisation*, Cmnd. 4584 (HMSO, London, 1971), para. 13.
21 G. W. Jones, 'The Local Government Act 1972 and the Redcliffe-Maud Commission', *Political Quarterly*, 44(2) (1973), pp. 154–66.
22 D. N. Chester, *Central and Local Government: financial and administrative relations* (Macmillan, London, 1951), pp. 332–3.
23 L. J. Sharpe, '"Reforming" the grass roots: an alternative analysis', in *Policy and Politics: essays in honour of Norman Chester*, ed. D. Butler and A. Halsey (Macmillan, London, 1978), pp. 82–110.
24 C. Game and S. Leach, 'The county councillor: 1889 and 1989', in *New*

Directions in County Government, ed. K. Young (Association of County Councils, London, 1989), pp. 22–62.
25 A. Alexander, *Local Government in Britain Since Re-organisation* (George Allen & Unwin, London, 1982), p. 62.
26 R. A. W. Rhodes, *The National World of Local Government* (George Allen & Unwin, London, 1986), p. 207.
27 Rhodes, *National World of Local Government*, p. 209.
28 Quoted in Rhodes, *National World of Local Government*, pp. 210–11.
29 Quoted in Rhodes, *National World of Local Government*, p. 218.
30 Department of the Environment, *Organic Change in Local Government*, Cmnd. 7457 (HMSO, London, 1979).
31 J. D. Stewart, S. Leach and C. Skelcher, *Organic Change: a report on constitutional, management and financial problems* (Institute of Local Government Studies, Birmingham, 1978).
32 Rhodes, *National World of Local Government*, p. 229.
33 Sir F. Marshall, *The Marshall Inquiry on Greater London: report to the Greater London Council, Sir Frank Marshall, MA, LLB* (GLC, London, 1988); R. Freeman, 'The Marshall plan for London government: a strategic role or regional solution?', *London Journal*, 5(2) (1979), pp. 160–75.
34 N. Flynn, S. Leach and C. Vielba, *Abolition or Reform? The GLC and the Metropolitan County Councils* (George Allen & Unwin, London, 1985), pp. 1–18.
35 Association of District Councils, *Closer to the People: a policy for future local government structure, functions and finance* (The Association, London, 1987).
36 Department of the Environment, *Local Government Review: the structure of local government in England: a consultation paper* (DoE, London, 1991).
37 S. Leach, 'The local government review: a critical appraisal', *Public Money and Management*, January–March 1994, pp. 11–16.
38 Local Government Commission for England, *Final Recommendations on the Future Local Government of: Basildon and Thurrock; Blackburn and Blackpool; Broxtowe, Gedling and Rushcliffe; Dartford, and Gravesham; Gillingham and Rochester upon Medway; Exeter; Gloucester; Halton and Warrington; Huntingdonshire and Peterborough; Northampton; Norwich; Spelthorne; The Wrekin* (HMSO, London, December 1995), para. 4.13.
39 Ministry of Health, *Local Government in England and Wales During the Period of Reconstruction*, Cmd. 6579 (HMSO, London, 1945), p. 2.
40 Committee on the Management of Local Government, *Vol. 1, Report of the Committee* (HMSO, London, 1967), para. 5.
41 *Report of the Royal Commission on Local Government in Greater London, 1957-1960*, Cmnd. 1164 (HMSO, London, 1960), para. 235.

42 Dame E. Sharp, 'The future of local government', *Public Administration*, 40(winter) (1962), p. 383.
43 N. Rao, *The Making and Un-making of Local Self-government* (Dartmouth, Aldershot, 1994), ch. 5.
44 B. Keith-Lucas, *Mayor, Aldermen and Councillors*, Unservile State Papers, No. 3 (Liberal Publications Department, London, 1961), p. 7.
45 Sharp, 'The future of local government', p. 383; L. J. Sharpe, 'Elected representatives in local government', *British Journal of Sociology*, 13 (1962), pp. 189–208.
46 Royal Commission on Local Government in Greater London, 1957–60, *Report of the Commission*, cited in W. Thornhill (ed.), *The Growth and Reform of English Local Government* (Weidenfeld and Nicolson, London, 1971), p. 256.
47 Sharp, 'The future of local government', p. 383.
48 A study of local authority members by the Robinson committee in 1976, comparing results with those of the Maud Committee in 1966, revealed that the effect of reorganization was marginal in terms of altering recruitment patterns of local councillors. For a comparison of evidence on the willingness of people to stand for election in 1965 and 1994, see K. Young and N. Rao, 'Faith in local democracy', in *British Social Attitudes, the Twelfth Report*, ed. J. Curtice, R. Jowell, L. Brooke and A. Park (Dartmouth, Aldershot, 1995), pp. 91–118.
49 CPA, LCC/67.
50 Committee on the Management of Local Government, *Report of the Committee, Volume 1* (HMSO, London, 1967), p. 1.
51 See W. S. Steer and D. Lofts, 'The Mallaby Committee', in *Local Government in England*, ed. H. V. Wiseman (Routledge and Kegan Paul, London, 1970), pp. 71–95.
52 Sir A. Wheatley, in Committee on the Management of Local Government, *Report of the Committee, Volume 1*, Section A, p. 155.
53 D. N. Chester, 'Local democracy and the internal organisation of local authorities', *Public Administration*, 46(2) (1968), pp. 287–98.
54 J. Stanyer, 'The Maud report', *Social and Economic Administration*, 1(4) (1967), pp. 3–19.
55 *The New Local Authorities: management and structure* (HMSO, London, 1972), p. 30.
56 Committee of Inquiry into the Conduct of Local Authority Business, *Report of the Committee* (HMSO, London, 1986), p. 33.
57 J. Gyford, 'Local politics in the 1980s', *Politics*, 9(1) (1989), p. 26.
58 S. Lansley, S. Goss and C. Wolmar, *Councils in Conflict: the rise and fall of the municipal Left* (Macmillan, Basingstoke, 1989).
59 Lansley et al., *Councils in Conflict*, p. 15.

60 C. Goodson-Wickes, *The New Corruption* (Centre for Policy Studies, London, 1984), p. 6.
61 For a summary and analysis of reactions to the Widdicombe report, see C. Game, 'Widdicombe: some considered responses', *Local Government Policy Making*, 14(3) (1987), pp. 3–28.
62 S. Leach, 'Strengthening local democracy? The government's response to Widdicombe', in *The Future of Local Government*, ed. J. Stewart and G. Stoker (Macmillan, Basingstoke, 1989), pp. 101–22.
63 Audit Commission, 'We can't go on meeting like this: the changing role of local authority members', Management Papers, No. 8, September 1990.
64 Sir K. C. Wheare, *Government by Committee: an essay on the British constitution* (Clarendon Press, Oxford, 1955).
65 *Report of the Working Party on the Internal Management of Local Authorities in England, Community Leadership and Representation: unlocking the potential* (HMSO, London, 1993).
66 S. Weir, 'Quangos: questions of democratic accountability', in *The Quango Debate*, ed. F. F. Ridley and D. Wilson (Oxford University Press, Oxford, 1995), pp. 128–44.

8 The New Accountabilities, 1964–1995

Stress and uncertainty seem to run through the post-war history of local government in Britain. During the period of consensus – roughly the first twenty years after the war – the search for structural solutions continued, even when it was none too clear what problem it was supposed to address. With the 1972 Act in place, it would have been reasonable to suppose that the restless search for something better would have come to a pause, if not to an end. But it was not so. Even before the structure imposed by Peter Walker started to come apart at the seams, the urge to 'reform' had begun to gnaw at other aspects of the local government system.

The foremost focus of concern was the set of arrangements under which local authorities were financed. The short-lived Conservative government of Sir Alec Douglas-Home appeared bewildered and ineffective on the question of rates. Labour had taken power under Harold Wilson with a clear and unambiguous commitment to relieving the ratepayer. But in no time at all, it became apparent that shifting the burden from the ratepayer to the taxpayer actually exacerbated the underlying problem: the gradually weakening link between those who advocated spending, and those who would foot the bill.

This was the problem that Mrs Thatcher and her advisers saw clearly enough after only a few years of contending with local government finance. Each step taken by the Department of the Environment after 1979 to control local expenditure had seemed to draw it still deeper into local financial decision-making, and weaken still further that fragile link of financial accountability to the local electorate. It was in order to re-establish a direct link between voting for, and paying for, local services, that the poll tax (or community charge) was introduced. The simplicity of its underlying assumption appealed to Mrs Thatcher: those who benefit should pay.

The third area in which a new framework of accountability was sought concerned the protected workforces of large-scale local government. Labour councils had built up chronically inefficient direct labour forces, providing local services with little regard for cost, and none for competitiveness. In housing construction and building maintenance, where a hard-pressed private-sector alternative existed, the criticism from industry was continuous.

During the late 1960s Conservative party strategists delved into the mysteries of direct labour workforces and contracting practices, but not until 1979 did a government come to power committed to exposing local authority operations to the disciplines of the market through Compulsory Competitive Tendering (CCT). After a slow start, and a prolonged period of manoeuvring by Labour councils seeking to evade the new requirements, CCT began to bite in the late 1980s and early 1990s.

Financing Local Government

The sustained growth in local government functions and expenditure during the twenty years after the war led to a growing crisis of financial accountability. The problem lay in the system of local government finance itself, where successive central government initiatives steadily transferred the burden of expenditure from local to central government. At the local level, the problem was amplified by the rating system which, being intrinsically regressive, led to a continuing search for ways of cushioning the poorer ratepayers against the financial demands of their local authorities. In time, this would produce a situation in which it seemed, at least to Conservative critics, that local expenditure decisions were shaped by the demands of an electorate, only a minority of whom had actually to foot the bill. The poll tax, or community charge, was a radical attempt to address that problem by ensuring that every individual paid something towards the costs of local services. When that experiment failed, bringing the Thatcher era to an end, something at least of its underlying principle was carried forward into the new council tax, a true hybrid of both the old and the new regimes.

Tackling the problem of rates

By the 1960s, the argument that further increases in rates were socially undesirable, due to the regressive nature of rates as a tax, were increasingly voiced. The true limit on taxable capacity of the rating system, on this view, lay in the effects of rate increases on poorer households. There was a desire to reduce the burden of payments upon the poorer households by finding instead a more progressive local tax, or by limiting the impact of the rates. It was by no means a novel concern, and the problems of regressiveness had been reviewed in connection with the reconstruction plans in 1942.[1] The problem was to reduce the burden of rate payments upon the poorer households by finding some way of making it a less regressive local tax.[2] One solution – the simplest – was to provide for the remission of rates among poorer households. The weight of the burden on different classes of ratepayer – domestic, industrial and commercial – received far less attention after the war.[3]

The Allen committee, set up by Sir Keith Joseph, fastidiously averted its eyes from the larger problems of the rating and confined itself rigorously to its brief, 'to ascertain the facts and provide an objective and balanced account' of the impact of rates.[4] Its report confirmed what was already common knowledge, but buttressed it with detailed statistical analysis. It found the relationship of rates to income to be generally weak. However,

> This does not imply that the relationship fails to be firmly established. On the contrary... we find income is very closely associated with rate payments. What it means is that, as income increases, the rates paid grow very slowly ... an extra £1,000 of income adds little more than eight pounds a year to rates. The consequence of this slow growth in rates with income is that the *proportionate* amount spent out of income on rates declines quite markedly as income rises. This is a measure of the regressive nature of rates as a tax.[5]

As a result, most householders were well able to pay the rates demanded of them. For the lower income groups, however, rates did constitute a significant burden. And, in striking confirmation of the Conservatives' fears for their natural supporters, retired people constituted as much as 61 per cent of the lowest income group, for whom the relative burden was the greatest.

The election manifesto of Labour party for the general election of October 1964 promised 'early relief to ratepayers by transferring a large part of the burden of public expenditure from the local authorities to the Exchequer'.[6] The new minister, Richard Crossman, argued that the rates situation was so serious that immediate reform was called for. As with his predecessors, Crossman found it easier to define the problem than to solve it. Like them, he was to fall back on interim measures. Labour's Rating Act 1966 introduced rate rebates, provided for the payment of rates in instalments and introduced the rating of empty property, as recommended by the Allen committee. The subsequent Local Government Act of the same year introduced a 'domestic' element in the new Rate Support Grant. This gave relief to domestic ratepayers on a rising scale, so that as local expenditure grew, government grant was geared to outpace it. The amount of grant in the domestic element would be calculated as sufficient to subsidize domestic ratepayers to the extent of a fivepenny rate in the first year, tenpence in the second, and so on.[7]

This was admitted to be no more than patching the system until such time as the new Royal Commission on Local Government could produce a new map, one on which a new financial framework might be erected. Crossman could only accept the weakening of local democracy implied by the progressive shift from rates to taxes if it were a temporary measure. As Gerald Rhodes summed up his predicament:

> In truth, he was caught between his desire to break out of the dilemma by some bold radical move – abolish the rates, give local authorities a better local tax – and the need, in the face of departmental scepticism about the practicalities of any fundamental change, to keep the system going . . . Everyone could agree that the problem might look different if and when a new structure were devised. But meanwhile rates and grants would have to continue to share the burden, and if rates were reaching the limit of what they could bear more would have to be provided by way of grants. The 1966 'package' would at least help to keep things going, and one suspects that by the departments, if not by the minister, it was seen as likely to last longer than five or six years.[8]

The search for independence

Labour and Conservative ministers alike seemed to be exhausted by the problems of devising even their 'interim' measures for local finance. Meanwhile, the search for radical alternatives continued under the stimulus of an unsatisfactory rating system. The prospect of a local income tax had been explored in depth during the wartime reconstruction period, and the argument in favour of a more progressive tax had been officially considered as early as 1901.[9] Among the arguments put at that time was that while basing local finances upon personal incomes would eradicate the inequalities of burden between individual, it would nonetheless perpetuate, and possibly accentuate, the inequalities of resource between localities.

When in 1956 the Royal Institute of Public Administration set up a special study group to examine alternative sources of local revenue, it concluded that a local income tax on wages and salaries, at a simple proportional rate not exceeding 1.25 per cent of gross income would be both feasible and desirable. The study group also considered that the proceeds of certain other taxes should be transferred from central government to local authorities. The professional body of local authority finance officers, the Institute of Municipal Treasurers and Accountants, likewise devoted itself to the problem. Their proposals were silkily praised, before being dismissed outright, by Henry Brooke's white paper on local government finance. The government 'did not think it practicable to devise a satisfactory new source of local revenue by authorising the collection of a local income tax or such other impost on top of the national system of taxes...', nor would they transfer the proceeds of other taxes to local authorities.[10] The rating system was to stay for the foreseeable future.

A Royal Commission with a wide remit of inquiry was bound to force the issue of radical change on to the agenda. When the Redcliffe-Maud report was published in 1969, it predictably called for a new system of local finance robust enough to sustain the new framework of local government. Without financial reforms, local government would be 'cramped and handicapped' as a self-governing institution.[11] When Labour lost the 1970 general election, the Redcliffe-Maud proposals were ditched for a more conventional scheme of two-tier local government. The Heath government set up a corresponding review of local finance, which resulted in a green paper in 1971.[12] No new solutions were proposed, but a number were reviewed. Among them, the idea of a per capita surcharge was floated and dismissed, while a fixed levy or 'poll tax' received a brief mention.

Just as the 1956 and 1963 revaluations stoked the fires of dissatisfaction with the rating system, so too did the long-postponed revaluation that took place in 1973. Large rate increases followed from the reorganization of local government, forcing the incoming Labour government further to increase short-term relief to domestic ratepayers. The cycle of interim measures accompanied by a search for some grand panacea was completed when Anthony Crosland established a committee under Sir Frank Layfield QC, to inquire into the entire structure of local finance.

Perhaps the most telling criticism made by the Layfield committee in their report of 1976 was of the confusion of roles and responsibilities between central and local government. Their call for clarification, and thus clearer accountability, through adoption of a clear localist or centralist approach was no doubt bound to be rejected. The need for a simple and principled approach rarely seems compelling from inside government, where all seems too complex; and a blurring of lines of accountability more often suits government's own purposes by maximizing its freedom of manoeuvre.

Layfield's rarefied debate on the nature of government did have implications for local finance. In opting for local responsibility as the preferred alternative to centralism, the committee called for an enlargement of the share of local taxation in the totality of local revenue, for which the best available instrument was a local income tax.[13] It was neither a new proposal nor one calculated to commend itself to government. Its rejection by Peter Shore, Crosland's successor as Environment Secretary, was brusque. His 1977 green paper commented that the disadvantages of both the centralist and the localist approaches were obvious, and 'the government do not think there is a case for the adoption of either'.[14] Rejecting all the proposed new sources of local revenue, Shore instead favoured a shift to capital value rating, as Layfield had proposed.

Meanwhile, the choices had become polarized, with the Conservatives' October 1974 commitment that 'within the normal lifetime of a Parliament' they would abolish the domestic rating system 'and replace it by taxes more broadly based and related to people's ability to pay'. Not that there was a clear view on the alternatives: a Conservative party policy group set up in 1975 and chaired by Keith Speed MP examined, only to reject, the possible replacements for rates, including the local sales tax favoured by Shadow Environment Secretary Margaret Thatcher. Accordingly, the 1979 manifesto, framed under Mrs Thatcher's leadership of the party, eschewed all promises on local finance in favour of a broad commitment to reducing public expenditure and cutting income tax.

The matter of local government finance was bedevilled throughout the post-war period by a further, less often recognized confusion concerning the nature of the rating system and its alternatives. Were rates in fact a local tax or a charge for services provided? One reason why the arguments for local income tax made so little headway within government circles was that the criticism of regressiveness, or lack of relation to the ability to pay rates, was seen as missing the point. Rates were not *meant* to be progressive, but to reflect the consumption of the services that they sustained. A War Cabinet paper, largely dismissive of the various proposals for a local income tax, had claimed that 'the principle of "benefit received"... in addition to "ability to pay" has generally been accepted as the basis of our rating system'.[15] The traditional view, then, was that were the basis of local taxation to become more progressive, the element of 'charge' for services rendered by local authorities to householders would be lost. The liability for rates was based on the occupancy of fixed property; the benefits of local expenditure – providing for the infrastructure, maintaining law and order – naturally flowed to householders. Rates represented an appropriate charge for those benefits.

It was more difficult to adhere to this view after 1945, as the post-war growth in the role of local authorities shifted the balance away from basic public services towards personal services to individuals with needs or entitlements. It was hard to discern a generalized provision to ratepayers at large (as distinct from parents) in the burgeoning expenditure on education, or in the foundation of the new children's service. Arguments about 'benefit' were transformed by this development from providing roads, drains, lighting and police, to the new personal services. The AMC maintained that such arguments were redundant, and that a tax needed no particular justification other than its ability to raise revenue. If a basis in benefit of some sort had to be identified, then the rate could be said to recognize a generalized or community benefit flowing from social investment. The Allen committee had met the argument head-on, albeit on a narrow front, recognizing that while the post-war development of the social services provided benefits to particular client groups, and not to ratepayers at large, these services should rightly be heavily subsidized and non-contributory. Rates, on their view, had the characteristics not of a charge but of a tax.[16]

Contrary to appearances, these arguments were more than mere scholasticism. The answer to the question of whether rates and their alternatives should be properly seen as a tax or as a charge dictated how their reform should be approached. The matter scarcely surfaced prior to the 1980s. It was a subterranean issue, inconvenient and seemingly insoluble if addressed directly, and on those grounds best left to lurk unnoticed. With rising social expenditure and the agreed need to protect poorer households, the Allen committee view held sway. But the issue was to come to the surface again in the very different public expenditure climate of the mid-1980s. Margaret Thatcher's affinities with ratepayer politics and her unequivocal view of rates as an insufficiently explicit charge for services were to lead her into the most bitter of all the conflicts over local government – the abolition of rates and the introduction of the 'poll tax' or *community charge*.

Poll tax and after

Mrs Thatcher's elevation to the leadership of the Conservative party marked the beginning of the end of the rating system. The pledge to abolish domestic rates, although one of dubious wisdom in her view, and one which she had opposed at the time, was to haunt the entire period of her premiership. Far from being content with the rating system, she saw it as a system of local finance that was 'unfair and un-Conservative'.[17] At her behest, the 1979 Conservative manifesto firmly asserted that 'cutting income tax must take priority for the time being over abolition of the domestic rating system'. Following the Conservatives' 1979 election victory, events moved forward quickly. Minister for Local Government Tom King had revealed that the government was considering a flat rate tax as an alternative to the rates in November 1979, and by 1981 a private member's bill had been introduced to test the water. But such a tax was only one of the options when at the end of that year environment secretary Michael Heseltine published a green paper *Alternatives to Domestic Rates*. The green paper acknowledged the dissatisfaction with the way in which local people contributed to the cost of local services through the present system of domestic rates. Some domestic ratepayers believe that they pay too large a share of that cost, pointing out that other local people who are not householders are not required to pay rates at all.[18]

The problem that the government sought to address was, then, primarily that of fairness, judged by the broadness of the tax base. But there were other criteria: accountability, practicability, financial control and implications for other taxes, ease of administration and suitability for all tiers of local government. Against these criteria, a local income tax, a local sales tax and a per capita or poll tax were considered. None were judged sufficiently robust and effective to replace the rates. None would be easy to implement and 'no tax is popular'. The House of Commons Environment Committee made its own study of the same issues, and came to much the same conclusion, that a poll tax 'would have some limited merit as supplementary tax', but it was 'persuaded by the much greater weight of evidence to the contrary and recommends strongly that a Poll tax, even at a low level, should not be introduced'.[19]

A Cabinet subcommittee was established in June 1982 to consider local government expenditure, rates, structure and transport.[20] Chaired by William Whitelaw, the subcommittee included Leon Brittan, the Chief Secretary to the Treasury, and other senior ministers with local expenditure responsibilities. Although the committee considered a system of statutory rate limitation proposed by the civil service advisers, Michael Heseltine resisted it firmly on the grounds that it would be complicated and unconstitutional. The subcommittee recommended only minor changes in the rating system. Mrs Thatcher was not satisfied. With Tom King replacing Heseltine at the DoE, a new opportunity arose to consider the abolition of rating.

Soon after the 1983 general election a white paper, entitled simply *Rates*, announced the government's reasons for keeping the rating system, and set out the arguments against poll taxes and other novel sources of local revenue. The government recognized that

> rates are far from being an ideal or popular tax. But they do have advantages. They are highly perceptible to ratepayers and they promote accountability. They are well understood, cheap to collect, and very difficult to evade. They

act as an incentive to the most efficient use of property . . . The government have concluded . . . that rates should remain for the foreseeable future the main source of local revenue for local government.[21]

There the issue rested for some time, until Patrick Jenkin, who had taken over from Tom King as Environment Secretary, pushed to re-open discussion of the rating system. It fell to Jenkin to administer the controversial capping system, the political and legal problems of which were all too apparent to him. When his officials began to press for a new comprehensive review of local finance on the grounds that 'the grant system was falling to bits', Jenkin was amenable. He had told a party meeting in March 1984 that the search for an alternative to the rates had been abandoned for that Parliament.[22] But a combination of continuing struggle with Labour local government, and a flood of motions calling for the abolition of the rates, submitted for discussion at the 1984 Conservative conference, forced rates reform back on to the agenda.[23]

'Selective rate limitation' – more generally known as rate-capping – had already been introduced at the second attempt in the 1984 Rates Act. It bore, however, only upon individual authorities, where the size of their budget and the degree of their 'overspend' could lead to their being prohibited from levying a higher rate than that determined by the Secretary of State.[24] The rating ystem was so unpopular in the party that a universal measure was needed, and the imminence of the Scottish rates revaluation in 1985 lent renewed urgency to the problem. Jenkin pressed the Prime Minister for her agreement to mount a new full review of local finance, to be announced at the conference itself. Mrs Thatcher was cautious about raising expectations that could not be met, insisting that a workable alternative had to be in view before starting work.

The seriousness with which the government approached the issue was seen in the establishment of a Cabinet subcommittee comprising senior ministers to consider policy on local finance. Within the DoE itself, responsibility passed from Jenkin to Kenneth Baker, the Minister for Local Government, and William Waldegrave, the Parliamentary Under-Secretary. Despite the prominence of the subcommittee, it seems that the real thinking took place in an informal review group chaired by Waldegrave, and including a number of notable external advisers. Among them was Professor Christopher Foster, a lone voice among economists in thinking a poll tax feasible. The team moved at breakneck speed, prepared to cut corners by avoiding consultation with other experts, relying instead on the intellectual power of its own members.[25]

While the review group was well under way, the debate on a possible options shifted markedly towards the poll tax. The Adam Smith Institute, a free-market 'think tank', commissioned the Scottish economist Douglas Mason in 1985 to work on a universal '*per caput tax*, or as it is popularly known, a poll tax'.[26] While the Institute were later to discount their possible influence in bringing about the acceptance of the poll tax within government circles, it appeared in public that the government had been influenced by this latest brainchild. The poll tax gained greater political credibility in governing circles when Michael Forsyth's Conservative Political Centre pamphlet, *The Case for a Poll Tax*, was published in order to test feeling within the party.[27]

The review group aimed to complete their work for March 1985, and by that time they had eliminated the other contenders and come down in favour of a poll tax levied at a flat rate on all adult residents, to be known as the 'residents' charge', or the 'services charge', and only in its ultimate form as the 'community charge'. At a Chequers meeting that month, Waldegrave presented the poll tax scheme to Mrs Thatcher, ending his presentation with the 'vigorous and seductive words, "And so, Prime Minister, you will have fulfilled your promise to have abolished the rates"'.[28] It was here, recalled Margaret Thatcher, 'that the community charge was born'.[29] Baker, as Environment Secretary, approved the general thrust of the review, but warned that 'controversy was inevitable' and that 'the community charge would be costly and difficult to collect'.[30]

Importantly, Chancellor of the Exchequer Nigel Lawson, who had not been present at the crucial Chequers meeting, thought the poll tax to be 'a political disaster'.[31] Lawson resolved to oppose it vigorously, and circulated an attacking paper at the next meeting of the Cabinet subcommittee in May 1985.[32] In that paper, Lawson pointed out that 'The report recognises that a flat rate poll tax would be politically unsustainable; even with a rebate scheme the package would have "an unacceptable impact" on certain types of household.'[33] The difficulties of collection and the problems of registration, taken with the radical shift in the distribution of the burdens of local taxation, promised an administrative and political nightmare.

When the proposals went to full Cabinet in January 1986, only three weeks remained before the publication of Baker's green paper in which the poll tax proposals would be aired. Decision could not be deferred. Although the English rating revaluation had been postponed to avoid the political backlash of 1963, that due for Scotland in 1984 had gone ahead. The political backlash there was intense, and Scottish ministers were keen to find an alternative to the rates north of the border. William Whitelaw's intervention in favour of change for Scotland coincided with the Cabinet decision on the poll tax; it sailed through.

The poll tax proposals, launched by Kenneth Baker in the glossiest of green papers, *Paying for Local Government*, were accorded an enthusiastic reception within the Conservative party.[34] Scarcely a voice was raised against it at the 1986 party conference. The next major decision was on how it should be introduced. The green paper proposed what came to be known as 'dual running', a mechanism by which the poll tax would be gradually phased in to take over from rates over a period of years, during which time they would run in parallel. The Cabinet was deeply split on the length of that transition, the more cautious and sceptical favouring the longest possible period, not least because it would be the easier to abandon if it proved too unpopular.

In the event, dual running was abandoned, and the new tax introduced in one single simultaneous operation, first in Scotland, and the following year in England and Wales. The responsibility for what was later to be seen as a fatal decision rested with Nicholas Ridley, who replaced Baker as Secretary of State for the Environment in 1986, and who favoured the briefest possible period of dual running. Ridley and Michael Howard, his Minister for Local Government, lobbied against the planned four-year phasing-in, and argued that a clean switch from rates to poll tax was preferable. Whether orchestrated by Ridley or not – the memoirs disagree on this – an apparently spontaneous gush of enthusiasm at the 1987 party conference propelled the audience into demanding its immediate introduction, rather than a phased transition.

In the autumn of 1987, Mrs Thatcher returned to power in her third successive general election victory, still with a majority of more than 100 seats. The election manifesto promised that the Conservatives would, if re-elected, 'abolish the unfair domestic rating system and replace rates with a fairer Community Charge'. In November Mrs Thatcher pressed a decision to abandon dual running, overwhelming the opposition of those such as Kenneth Baker, now Education Secretary, who sensed that immediate introduction would spell the party's political doom. The key issue was that a once and for all switch from rates to poll tax would produce the maximum number of winners and losers. Losers would be vocal and virulent in their opposition, while there were few votes to be won from those who gained from poll tax.[35]

The poll tax had by now become the issue on which the Prime Minister's opponents within the party had begun to take up their positions. In the debate on the Queen's Speech in 1987, Michael Heseltine, now free of Cabinet constraints, adroitly recalled that

> twice I have advised Conservative cabinets and shadow cabinets against this form of local authority finance and twice, at least, they have accepted my advice. I must say that I have not yet seen any reason to change my mind.[36]

When the Local Government Finance Bill received its second reading, the government's majority slumped. Heseltine was a notable abstainer. Seventeen Conservatives, including Edward Heath, voted against the government. When the Commons considered an amendment to relate the tax level to charge-payers' ability to pay in April 1988, thirty-seven Conservative MPs went through the division lobby against the government; this time their number included Heseltine himself. The presence among these rebels of experienced former ministers dropped by Mrs Thatcher, and talent whose rise had been blocked by her, was to prove potent later.

The effects of the introduction of the poll tax in April 1990, the huge expense of transitional relief at £3 billion, the vigour – even violence – of the reaction against the tax, and the wild inaccuracy of its predicted levels all served to demonstrate that its proclaimed virtues of fairness and accountability were largely discounted by the public, if they were perceived at all. Within the party many of those who, like Sir Rhodes Boyson, had originally applauded the poll tax scheme were, within eighteen months, pushed by the mechanics of its introduction into opposition, leading deputations to the Department of the Environment to press for relief. Less attention was paid to a related change, long advocated by the CBI and by some Conservatives; the removal of non-domestic properties from liability for local taxation via the nationalization of the business rate. The cumulative effect by 1984/85 of the domestic rate relief introduced by the Wilson government in 1965 had been such that non-domestic ratepayers now paid 60 per cent of the total rate levy, the share paid by business being some 38 per cent. Rather than give non-domestic ratepayers a direct voice in local decisions (over and above the ineffective requirement that local authorities consult with industry and commerce before setting their rates), they would now be taken out of the ambit of locally determined taxation altogether.

With at most two years to run to the next general election, a sizeable minority of Conservative MPs came to believe that their political futures were linked inextricably to the poll tax. The question came to permeate the mounting speculation over the alternative to Mrs Thatcher. When, in 1990, she was forced to defend her leadership of the Conservative party, her challenger, Michael Heseltine, went on record as promising a review of this Thatcher 'flagship'. By the second ballot there was nothing between the three candidates – Heseltine, Major and Hurd – on the need to replace it, and the fate of the poll tax was sealed with that of Mrs Thatcher herself.

Heseltine himself accepted the offer of a Cabinet post under Major as the price for withdrawing from a punishing and unwinnable third ballot. Returning to the Department of the Environment, he thus became directly responsible for delivering a more acceptable alternative to the tax he had so long opposed. Other notable poll tax rebels were to join the Major government then, or soon afterwards. The first problem was to bridge the period of transition until a new system came on stream. In January 1991 the government announced a further £11 million support to keep poll tax levels down in what was hoped to be its second and final year of operation in England. This stop-gap move was followed by the budget statement in March, which announced an across-the-board reduction in poll tax bills of £140, to be funded by a 2.5 per cent increase in Value Added Tax. The sting was drawn, if at the price of a further shift in the balance between the central and local sources of revenue in favour of the centre.[37] A week after the budget, Michael Heseltine unveiled his proposals in *A New Tax for Local Government*. Significantly, the illusion of a 'charge' was dropped. A hybrid of the rating and poll tax systems, the new council tax would consist in equal parts of a property and a personal tax, the former based on capital value and the latter on a presumed two-person household, with a discount for single persons. The business rate, already nationalized and redistributed to local authorities as grant, would remain unchanged.

The strongest objections to the poll tax were met at a stroke by this announcement. There would be no need for a register. The notion of a universal charge with a fixed 'floor' was abandoned in favour of rebates.

The property basis gave an element of stability and predictability, while easing collection. Michael Heseltine made considerable play of these virtues in his 21 March announcement, urging that the new tax met the requirements of accountability and fairness better than its short-lived predecessor. Yet it was not to be all plain sailing. The banding of property values did rough justice, and reproduced some of the earlier anomalies of the rating system, with high valuations in the Conservative south. In April the government announced a seven-band scheme; at the end of the month it abandoned consideration of a possible nine-band scheme; in July the scheme was finalized at eight bands.[30]

So rapid a pace of policy development was bound to leave the government exposed to criticism. The transition, with introduction in 1993 coming on top of increasingly desperate efforts to collect the residue of the vanishing poll tax, would be predictably difficult, although this was not a point which had much electoral force. Neither did the overall outcome – an 80 : 20 division of central and local funding of local government – even though it recognizably locked the government into a system of virtual direction of local expenditure.

The doubts soon set in, in part because the council tax enjoyed the advantages, and suffered the disadvantages, of both the systems – property and per capita tax – of which it was a hybrid. Michael Heseltine made much of the by-now obligatory claim of enhanced accountability when announcing the changes, although the council tax was not evidently superior to the rather purist, universalist, doctrine that underlay the poll tax. As to his second criterion of fairness – by which he had consistently implied relation to ability to pay – the new tax, while preferable to poll tax, nevertheless had less margin of superiority than at first appeared. The value of property occupied is a poor indicator of personal resources, while the banding of values provided for only modest progessiveness. The Institute of Fiscal Studies judged council tax to be a highly regressive system, made palatable only by virtue of the system of benefits. Yet these were specialists' points; in reality the debate was over. Heseltine's council tax had finally buried the rating problem that had bedevilled Conservative governments since the mid-1950s.

Controlling local expenditure

Central government grants to local authorities supplement the income raised from, in turn, the rates, the poll tax and the council tax. They also provide an important measure of control. The Rate Support Grant (RSG) introduced in the Local Government Act 1974 accounted for about 85 per cent of central government grant aid to local authorities. The RSG was divided into three elements: a domestic element, intended to subsidize the rate bills of domestic ratepayers; a resources element, intended to compensate poorer authorities for deficiencies in their rateable resource; and the needs element, which compensated for differences between authorities in expenditure per head of population due to variable costs of providing a standard service.

Michael Heseltine's Local Government, Planning and Land Act 1980 changed the principles of grant distribution to provide for a greater degree of equalization and to eliminate the incentive to higher spending in the RSG. It was also intended to simplify a highly complex system, eliminate the sources of volatility in the grant formula and provide for greater clarity in the division between centrally and locally determined services. The overall aim was greater accountability. The need for such changes had been recognized for some time and had been recommended by the DoE in their evidence to the Layfield committee, while the Labour government's 1977 green paper had looked favourably on a new *unitary grant* to replace the RSG.

The *block grant* system introduced by the 1980 Act was essentially the same proposal, in that it combined the former needs and resource element into a single grant. The aim of block grant was to enable local authorities to provide a common standard of service at an equal rate poundage cost to their ratepayers. To this end, a large number of statistical indicators of need were defined and weighted for their relative importance in driving local authority expenditure. A formula was then used to apportion the national total of grant for each service to individual authorities. These service-by-service apportionments were then aggregated into a single sum: the Grant-Related Expenditure (GRE) of the individual authority. At the heart of the process by which these allocations were made was a calculation intended to equalize the rate poundage charged to local ratepayers arising from the differences in rateable values between authorities. The block grant arrangements also discouraged high spending by authorities through a system of 'tapers' and 'multipliers', where the Secretary of State's powers were limited to prevent him from taking arbitrary action against a particular authority.

Block grant did succeed in producing a greater equalization effect at a lower level of grant than the RSG system that it replaced. However, it quite failed to produce a simpler system of grant assessment. The principal claim made for block grant – that it would promote accountability – soon came to be seen as hollow. The theory was that expenditure above GRE represented either a desire to exceed a common standard of service, with more lavish provision, or an inability to provide that common standard at an appropriate degree of efficiency. Such expenditure was the responsibility of the local authority and its marginal cost should fall upon local ratepayers to whom the authority was accountable. A major difficulty in practice was that the choice and weighting of the indicators in the GRE calculation were essentially subjective and political rather than objective.[39]

The block grant system ran into serious difficulties as soon as it was introduced in 1981/82. Estimates of local authority expenditure indicated a total spend of more than 5 per cent above the government's projections. The local authorities had clearly chosen to maintain service levels rather than reduce expenditure. Michael Heseltine responded by setting a new total expenditure target requiring all authorities to reduce their expenditure by 5.6 per cent compared with that in 1978/79, the last year of the Labour government. Any authority failing to comply would be subject to the holding back of grant. Additionally, he announced that any authority which, while exceeding its 1978/79 expenditure, was nevertheless spending below its GRE, would not be subject to hold-back. Such authorities were generally the Conservative controlled counties, while those spending above GRE, and therefore exposed to the hold-back of the grant, were mainly Labour controlled London boroughs and metropolitan districts.

The legal difficulties involved in these manipulations and the limited effect that they had in controlling actual expenditure soon led to a new finance bill, which not only provided for statutory authority for the hold-back arrangements, but also – and most controversially – proposed a new power for the Secretary of State to set a ceiling on local rate levels. The combined powers would have meant that the DoE would effectively have determined the expenditure of every local authority and, following angry protests by Conservative back-benchers, the rate-limiting powers were withdrawn. A new bill, which was to become the Local Government Finance Act 1982, incorporated the hold-back powers and prohibited the raising of a mid-year supplementary rate by over-spending local authorities.

These changes to the system of block grant eclipsed the basic principles of the system, which was now driven only in the most general sense by the GREs and the tapering system, not by apparently objective formulae, for 'the targets and their penalties became the key variables in local authority budgeting'.[40] And those targets and penalties were altered year on year as the Conservative government struggled to control local expenditure. The penalties, with their strong gearing effect on local rate demands, were themselves deliberately increased on the grounds that once a single year's penalty had been absorbed into the budget baseline, an authority could choose to continue to spend at that level without a further rate increase. To prevent this, a further device, the ratchet, was added to the armoury of tapers, multipliers, thresholds and targets: the rate poundage effects were to be tightened in successive years, to produce the increasingly punitive penalties for expenditure above target shown in table 8.1. Under this system, the grant penalty associated with a 10 per cent 'overspend' in 1981/82, the first year of the system, would require a rate increase of 9 per cent to make good; in the following year this would increase to 15 per cent, and thereafter to 42, 77 and 87 per cent. Such severe penalties provoked a number of unsuccessful challenges in the courts by local authorities on whom the penalties would fall the hardest.[41]

Despite the severity of the penalties, local authorities seemed willing to

Table 8.1 Rate poundage effect of grant penalties (pence/pound)

	Expenditure above target				
	1%	2%	5%	10%	15%
1980/81	1	–	–	–	–
1981/82	2	2	9	9	9
1982/83	3	6	15	15	15
1983/84	1	2	17	42	67
1984/85	2	6	32	77	122
1985/86	7	15	42	87	132

Source: Loughlin, *Local Government in the Modern State*, p. 43.

transfer the financial burdens that they imposed on to their local ratepayers, while the retrospective nature of targets encouraged them to maintain high expenditure levels in the early years. National average rate rises were as high as 27 per cent in 1980/81 and 19.4 per cent in 1981/82, and were moderated by this punitive regime only to a limited extent, running at around 10 per cent in 1985/86. Some individual authorities, of course, maintained very much higher levels of rate increases, with 75 per cent of the national overspend being generated by just 12 authorities in 1984/85.[42] This increasingly *ad hoc* system had failed to control local expenditure, did nothing to limit the overall level of grant support, and had adverse effects on the efficiency with which local authorities managed their finances.[43] Its defects invited local authorities to mount legal challenges to its apparent arbitrariness, while developing skills of 'creative accounting' with which to evade grant losses.

These factors all served to drive the government towards further change in the system of local finance in the mid-1980s. Complicated as the block grant regime had been, its underlying failing seemed to lie in the rating system itself, and in the lack of real financial accountability in the system which first poll tax, and then council tax, were intended to remedy. Any system of grant aid from the centre raises issues of local accountability, which could only be secured – if at all – by the marginal costs of expenditure decisions falling upon the general body of local electors. 'Effective local accountability', declaimed the green paper *Paying for Local Government*, 'must be the cornerstone of successful local government. All too often this accountability is blurred by the complexities of the national grant system' and by the lack of correspondence between the body of ratepayers and the larger electorate.[44]

Block grant was presented as an improvement on what had gone before, but the green paper did not shrink from presenting fundamental criticisms of its working. Basing grant on the GRE presented 'a temptation to make GREs over-complicated by introducing new factors and by continual refinement. This leads to instability'.[15] The block grant system's focus on 'grant-related poundage' reflected the central assumption that the purpose of the national grant regime was to secure notionally equal rate *poundages* across the country, under conditions of standard levels of service and a common level of efficiency. This could be thought a curious objective in Conservative terms, as the wide variations in rateable values ensured that the actual rate *bills* would vary roughly in line with the values of the properties in different areas. This point was now confronted, and not before time:

> There is no obvious justice in saying that a household living in an area where houses are expensive should pay more for their services than if they lived in the same house in an area where housing was cheap. But that is what happens. To pay for a similar increase in spending, local authorities in areas where rateable values are low need to increase their rate bills by a smaller amount than high-rateable value authorities.[46]

The new goal was to equalize rate bills on the basis of a common standard of service.

A new grant regime was therefore introduced to complement the poll tax. The abandonment of domestic rates and the nationalization of the business rate freed government from having to maintain a measure of resource equalization, while taking business rates out of local taxation also removed the need for an element of domestic relief. The business rate – now the National Non-Domestic Rate (NNDR) – was to be distributed back to authorities in proportion to their population, giving a national standard per capita sum. As with the poll tax itself, however, the best intentions of simplicity and transparency were lost in the implementation process. The basic problem was to cushion Conservative supporters in marginal seats against the effects of much higher poll tax levels than had been predicted earlier. This required a very much higher level of grant than formerly, and led to strenuous struggles between the Treasury and the DoE. Ridley tried and failed to win the 'extra billion' that the DoE reckoned necessary to keep poll tax bills at acceptable levels. His successor, Chris Patten, did rather better, but still won far less than his officials judged to be needed. The key decision from an electoral point of view, announced at the party conference, was that the cost of a transitional 'safety net' would be met by the Exchequer, and not by clawback from the 'gaining' areas. The safety nets were to run for three years, were put in place and then considerably modified, and a further 'extra protection grant' added to compensate those who would lose most heavily from the modification. New transitional grants were introduced for Inner London, to help the boroughs adjust to taking education responsibilities over from the abolished, and high-spending, ILEA. The total cost of the transitional relief for 1990/91 was estimated at £572 million.

The next problem was to determine the distribution of the new Revenue

Support Grant, by calculating the Standard Spending Assessments (SSAs). Community charge levels would be crucially affected by the SSA, where, as before, central government determined how much a local authority should spend, service by service, to provide a standard level of service nationally. From this total was subtracted the distribution of the NNDR and the Revenue Support Grant. The result gives the level of poll tax necessary to achieve the standard spend. The SSA was not only a powerful mechanism of financial control; it would be open to political manipulation to ensure that the electoral effects of the annual expenditure round were as beneficial as possible.

If every authority were to spend at its SSA in 1990/91, each would levy a community charge of around £278. This figure was widely seen as unrealistic, being derived from SSAs that bore an insufficient relation to actual local needs or priorities. And with any system designed to place the cost of marginal increases in expenditure on local charge-payers, the gearing effect was considerable, a 5 per cent overspend leading to a 15 per cent charge increase. In table 8.2 is shown the sensitivity of the actual charge level to two local factors: first, a decision to spend at 5 per cent above SSA; and, secondly, a further 5 per cent shortfall in collection of the charge.

The essential point of the example is to show the way in which the mechanics of the combined grant/charge system were to work. For the individual local authority, all depended on the assumptions brought to bear on the SSA calculation, and the extent of the correspondence between its outcome and the intended pattern of expenditure. Conservative 'flagship'

Table 8.2 Revenue Support Grant and poll tax levels

	£ billion	£ per adult
Government provision for local government spending (net of specific grants)	29.8	835.0
Less Revenue Support Grant	9.5	265.6
Less NNDR	10.4	292.5
= Poll tax level for spend at SSA	9.9	277.9
+ 5% for spend above SSA	11.4	319.2
+ 5% for collection write-offs	12.0	336.0

Source: Gibson, *Politics and Economics of the Poll Tax*, pp. 227–8.

authorities in Westminster and Wandsworth benefited from generous assessments, declared very low community charge levels, and profited from increased votes for the majority party. By the same token, the overall grant regime was distorted by the strains and political considerations involved in coping with the introduction of the poll tax. The SSAs declared for 1990/91 varied greatly from the GREs of the previous year, with the South-East and Greater London gaining massively at the expense of the North of England and the East Midlands in particular.

Michael Heseltine's return to the Department of the Environment following John Major's victory in the Conservative leadership election marked a new phase of even more rigorous control of local expenditure. Whether or not it met the criteria of fairness and accountability set down in *A New Tax for Local Government*, the council tax and its associated adjustments reflected the new government's preoccupation with restraining high-spending, generally Labour, local authorities. 'Restraint' was the fifth of the five criteria for an acceptable tax which Michael Heseltine set out in March 1991. Clearly, the steeper the gearing, the more marked the restraint. Following the introduction of the council tax, the gearing ratio averaged 7 : 1 nationally; that is to say, a 10 per cent increase in local expenditure would require on average a 70 per cent increase in council tax to fund.

The most important new departure in central control was the extension of 'capping'. The council tax level itself was now open to being effectively set by ministers through the powers of universal capping taken in April 1992. When the provisional SSAs were declared around December each year, the Secretary of State announced the criteria that he would use to decide whether or not a particular authority's budget was 'excessive'. Authorities were then expected to regulate themselves by working within these limits. To do otherwise would be to risk having the minister's figure substituted for their own.

Introduced by Michael Heseltine and further refined by his successors, Michael Howard and John Gummer, these new arrangements represented a tighter control on local authority expenditure than existed previously. For example, for 1994/95 the local authority associations argued for a total standard spending settlement of £46.2 billion. Treasury pressure pushed the DoE down to an even lower figure than hoped for, £42.7 billion, a figure substantially less in cash terms (once the earmarked community care funds were subtracted) than the 1993/94 budget totals. The result was to bring most authorities close to the risk of council tax capping and thus induce widespread budget cuts. Finally, control over borrowing for capital expenditure was further tightened, with 'basic credit approvals' forced down dramatically between 1992/93 and 1993/94, and with the option to fund capital projects out of local revenues effectively precluded by the council tax capping arrangements. From the point of view of the Treasury (and Major's own term of office there was a formative influence upon him), the Major government had put in place the mechanisms of local expenditure control that Chief Secretaries since Henry Brooke had yearned for.

In Search of Market Discipline

Of all the changes brought about in the past 20 years of British local government, the most important has probably been the subjection of local authority services to the disciplines of the marketplace. The first Thatcher government's espousal of contracting was aimed initially at Labour local authorities' direct labour departments, to tackle feather-bedding and break the power of the blue collar unions. It also sought managerial benefits from separating out client and contractor functions and introducing commercial disciplines into public services. Managers would be liberated from the constraints of the democratic and bureaucratic controls, while councillors could revert to setting objectives and determining service standards, leaving service delivery to be determined by the tendering and contract processes. By 1987, CCT had acquired doctrinal trappings, with Nicholas Ridley's claim that a new 'enabling' role had been defined by the adoption of competition and contracting out.[47]

Labour local authorities fiercely opposed this new regime. As a result, they were often slow to adapt to the new requirements, their very reluctance making it less likely that their in-house services would survive. Enforced competition brought about the unwelcome depression of pay and conditions. Without it, and without the slimming down of operations, and the adoption of new management practices, an authority was likely to lose the provision of the service to a private contractor.

Introducing competition

The origins of the CCT regime go a long way back, and are to be found in an expectation that local authorities should put a proportion of contracts out to tender before awarding a job to direct labour. In August 1959 the Macmillan government announced that one in every three local authority contracts should be subjected to competition, although this requirement had no statutory force. In 1965 Minister of Housing and Local Government Richard Crossman issued Circular 50/65, abolishing the one-in-three rule. He advised that local authorities should keep their own check on costs, and should submit schemes to competition only 'if they feel any doubt whether their direct labour costs are satisfactory'. The Ministry retained the right to ask for competitive tendering to be instituted if schemes appear to be expensive in relation to the general level of costs locally. In the face of strong criticism by contractors, Crossman announced that the government wished to increase the proportion of local authority housing built by direct labour and rejected the one-in-three rule as detrimental to the continuity of the work of direct labour departments. For Conservatives, this was tantamount to a declaration that the Labour government was in thrall to the public-sector trade unions.

In 1967 a Conservative party study group was appointed by Edward Heath to investigate the building and construction industries. Chaired by Robin Chichester-Clark MP, the group included Paul Channon, MP, A. B. Costain MP, chairman of Richard Costain, and M. J. Grafton of the National Federation of Building Trades Employers. Going beyond its initial remit, the group decided to make a separate report on local authorities' direct labour departments. It assessed the costs and benefits of direct labour organizations, and came out decisively in favour on placing local authorities under a competitive tendering regime, with 85 per cent of new construction and all 'major and recurring maintenance' being put out to tender.[48]

Neither the Heath nor the Wilson/Callaghan governments were disposed to venture into such dangerous waters, but on the Conservatives' return in 1979, there was a strong expectation within the party of government action to promote competition. The advocates of competitive tendering pointed to the inefficiencies of public-sector 'in-house' monopolies, with their restrictive labour practices and low productivity. Regular re-contracting would allow for a review of both the quality and cost of the service on offer, leading to better value for money and greater accountability for public spending. Both Mrs Thatcher and her succession of environment secretaries were drawn to competition as an alternative means of securing public-sector service delivery, and applied it progressively within local and central government and the National Health Service.[49] As a strategy for winning value for money and better service, CCT first appeared in the Local Government, Planning and Land Act 1980. The Act introduced limited CCT in local authority building construction and maintenance and highways maintenance work. It required these services to be subject to competitive tender. Local authorities were permitted to carry out the work themselves, through their Direct Labour Organisations (DLOs), only if they won the right to do so through successful competition against private tenderers. Subsequent regulations lowered the thresholds at which items of work had to be exposed to competition.[50]

If ministers expected much from this initial foray into the world of competition, they were to be disappointed. By 1987 only 350 contracts had been awarded to the private sector, while the Act did little to encourage the voluntary exposure of other core services to the tendering process.[51] On the other hand, the tendering of services during the early 1980s had significantly reduced costs. In 1984 the Audit Commission undertook a comprehensive examination of the refuse collection industry. The Commission's findings, published in *Securing Further Improvements in Refuse Collection*, estimated potential savings of £30 million per annum in England and Wales through contracting out. The report claimed that contractors performed better than the average DSO, and that councils that contracted out refuse collection activities provided the most cost-effective service,[52] although later Audit Commission studies suggested that supposed savings were not always realized in practice.[53] Other studies purported to show that, where a service had been subject to the tendering procedure, it resulted in a significant improvement in the efficiency with which the service was provided.[54] The introduction of competition, rather than the award of contracts to private firms, appeared to be the critical factor in achieving lower costs.[55]

Such evidence encouraged Conservatives, but did nothing to convince beleaguered Labour councils. When, in 1984, the government announced its intention to secure more competition in local services, the local authorities scarcely reacted. Labour councils in particular were cautious, judging that CCT would not be around after the next election, when a Labour government would have swept it away. Their reluctance to respond to competition, and their ingenuity in evading the CCT requirements, led to progressive tightening of government regulation of the competitive process, culminating in the Local Government Act 1988. This milestone legislation extended the competition requirement to such services as the cleaning of buildings, grounds maintenance, schools and welfare catering, street cleaning, vehicle maintenance and refuse collection. The Act also permitted the Secretary of State to add to the list of defined activities, and in 1989 sport and leisure management was included.

By compelling local authorities to put services out to CCT, the 1988 Act required authorities to define their objectives and adopt appropriate organizational arrangements. These frequently took the form of Direct Labour/Service Organisations (DLOs/DSOs), operating on a trading basis. Some councils were to develop radical and imaginative approaches to service delivery, management style and internal organization, while others sought to cushion the impact of the legislation, or evade it altogether. The more favourable responses generally came from Conservative controlled authorities, many of whom seized the opportunity to behave more commercially and to tackle their unions in ways which were not open to them in the past. A few went further, exceeding or anticipating the statutory requirements.

Labour councils generally adopted a policy of supporting in-house service provision, and retaining jobs in their own DLOs. One possible escape route involved the prior transfer of the entire service-providing capability to a consortium of former service managers by a management buy-out, and a very small number of authorities succeeded in selling their services off in this way.[56] Another option – externalization – required the local authority to transfer their staff and their associated work to a host company which then contracted to manage and deliver services to a specified level and standard, using the transferred staff. Both schemes represented pre-emptive strikes to remove a service from the scope of CCT before the appointed day when the 1988 Act provisions came into force.

The tactics of avoidance and the calculus of possible benefits of contracting out were, however, transformed during 1993 by rulings that European law applied to CCT transfers. The Transfer of Undertakings (Protection of Employment) Regulations (TUPE) were enacted by the UK government in 1981 in order to implement the European Commission's Acquired Rights Directive of 1977. The purpose of the Directive was to protect in law the rights of employees when the organization for which they worked was transferred from one employer to another. Where there was held to be a transfer for the purposes of the regulations, the main consequences were that the new employer had to take over the contracts of employment of the employees on the existing terms and conditions. Employees gained the benefit of continuity of employment, any dismissal connected with the transfer of being automatically unfair, unless the employer could show an economic, technical or organizational reason entailing changes to the workforce. Collective agreements with recognized trade unions were transferred to the new employer, and a duty to inform and consult with recognized trade unions prior to any transfer was imposed.

The 1981 UK regulations did not adequately implement the 1977 Directive. They restricted the application of the regulations to undertakings 'in the nature of a commercial venture'. The European Commission, however, decided that the Acquired Rights Directive would be revised to cover transfers by contract, and UK government guidance was issued to cover its possible application to competitive tendering by local authorities. The turning point came with a ruling by the Employment Appeals Tribunal in 1993 that all the circumstances had to be taken into account in determining where there was 'a recognisable economic entity, a going concern' which, having been run by the local authority, was to be continued by a contractor. The substance, not the form, was important; what mattered was whether or not the transfer of an economic function – and hence an undertaking – had taken place. This meant that a successful private contractor might have to take on board more than just the business when winning a contract against a local authority tender.

Competition extended

The replacement of Mrs Thatcher by John Major produced no let-up in the pressures to subject local authorities to this new market accountability. Quite the reverse: the new Prime Minister had earlier gone on record with his belief that those who work in the public services should become

> full participants in the more competitive and demanding economy which now surrounds them. They will have less insulation from economic risk and

uncertainty. But to the greatest extent possible in services with a strong monopoly element, they will have the same opportunities and incentives and the same responsibilities for efficiency and success as elsewhere in the economy.[37]

In November 1991, the government published the consultation paper *Competing for Quality in the Provision of Local Services* proposing the extension of CCT beyond manual work into professional and technical activities. *Competing for Quality* estimated the market for these activities to be worth £5–6 billion. The proposals were substantially enacted by the Local Government Act 1992, which not only extended CCT to finance, computing, personnel and architectural, library and construction services, but in addition required local councils to publish information about the standards of performance of their services.

The 1992 Act required all authorities to provide full statements of the gross costs of their operations in a *Statement of Support Services Costs* so as to enhance the transparency of central service provision. In November 1993 the government announced proposals defining the activities to be exposed to competition, the timetable for implementation and the sizes of contracts. The separate timetable for authorities affected by the Local Government Review was announced soon afterwards. Draft statutory instruments and guidance on the avoidance of anti-competitive behaviour were issued in January 1994. The guidance stressed that authorities should describe the service to be delivered, not the process by which it was to be delivered, so as to allow scope for contractors to propose better ways of delivering services. Each service identified by the government was to be described as a defined activity, and (except in the case of small authorities) the total cost of that activity within an authority would be the base on which a proportionate requirement to expose to competition was imposed.

Some councils already operated internal trading accounts for central services, having been prompted to do so by an 1988 Audit Commission report. In doing so, they anticipated the requirements of the 1992 Act, which required the corporate services of local authorities such as legal, financial and personnel services to introduce a consistent internal accounting regime as a preliminary stage before competitive tendering. The introduction of internal trading accounts, leading in some cases to the creation of a full internal market, fundamentally changed the relationship between service departments and central services within local authorities.

The New Accountabilities 261

By the summer of 1992, housing management was also in the frame with the publication of *Competing for Quality in Housing*, the government's consultation paper on the introduction of CCT into the management of council housing, on which modified proposals were incorporated in the 1992 Act. The Major government continued to view contracting out as an integral part of the new management of local government. Indeed, it pushed the competition regime forward, far beyond the limits seriously envisaged in Mrs Thatcher's time.

That regime introduced a new dynamic into local authority management and service provision. The impact of local authorities' exposure to competition was conditioned by their initial competitiveness in terms of service costs, their labour practices (in turn a reflection, to some extent, of political factors) and their management capability; and by the intensity of private companies' competition for contracts. Local government manning levels were more generous, while private contractors were able to operate flexibly, engaging and releasing workers on a seasonal basis as the demands of the work dictated. Adaptation was painful. Job losses, lower rates of pay, reduced benefits and a general drop in conditions of employment were required in order to sharpen competitiveness. To the extent that local authorities took these steps, they competed with success. To the extent that they did not, they lost contracts, and incurred redundancies. The limiting factor was, however, so often the universality of nationally agreed conditions. Councils found it difficult to be competitive, locked as they were into national agreements on pay and allowances, under which their terms and conditions were more expensive to maintain than those of the private sector.

Compulsory Competitive Tendering was among the most controversial of all the Thatcher/Major governments' local government measures. It cannot be doubted that the changes wrought by exposure to competition would not have come about without compulsion. A few Conservative authorities might have continued to experiment with new models of organization, but the great sea change would most certainly not have come about had local authorities not been compelled by law to submit a widening range of defined services to compulsory competition under conditions in which, year after year, the loopholes were inexorably closed. The boundaries betweeen public and private provision were transformed by the competition regime. So too, it seemed, was the ethos of 'the public' itself, and, in consequence, the motivating spirit of post-war local government. In this respect, exposing local authorities to market disciplines was perhaps the most significant un-making of the post-war settlement.

Notes

1. HLG 68/111.
2. J. Maud and S. E. Finer, *Local Government in England and Wales* (Oxford University Press, London, 1953), pp. 167–9.
3. H. Finer, *English Local Government*, 4th edn (Methuen, London, 1950), pp. 430–31.
4. N. Hepworth, *The Finance of Local Government*, 7th edn (George Allen & Unwin, London, 1984), p. 98.
5. *Report of the Committee of Inquiry into the Impact of Rates on Households*, Cmnd. 2582 (HMSO, London, 1966).
6. G. Rhodes, 'Local government finance, 1918–1966', in Department of the Environment, *Local Government Finance: Appendix 6 to the report of the Committee of Inquiry under the chairmanship of Sir Frank Layfield, QC: the relationship between central and local government: evidence and commissioned work* (HMSO, London, 1976), p. 141.
7. Rhodes, 'Local Government Finance', p. 143.
8. Rhodes, 'Local Government Finance', p. 144.
9. *Final Report of the Royal Commission on Local Taxation, 1901*, Cd. 638 (HMSO, London, 1901), ch. 5; *Final Report of the Departmental Committee on Local Taxation*, Cd. 7315 (HMSO, London, 1914).
10. Ministry of Housing and Local Government, *Local Government Finance*, Cmnd 209 (HMSO, London, 1957), p. 3.
11. *Report of the Royal Commission on Local Government in England, 1966–69: Volume 1*, Cmnd. 4040 (HMSO, London, 1969), para. 527.
12. Department of the Environment, *The Future Shape of Local Government Finance*, Cmnd. 4741 (HMSO, London, 1971).
13. *Report of the Committee of Inquiry into Local Government Finance*, Cmnd. 6453 (HMSO, London, 1976).
14. Department of the Environment, *Local Government Finance*, Cmnd. 6813 (HMSO, London, 1977), para. 2.8.
15. HLG 68/111.
16. Hepworth, *Finance of Local Government*, pp. 70–72.
17. M. Thatcher, *The Downing Street Years* (HarperCollins, London, 1993), p. 644.
18. Department of the Environment, *Alternatives to Domestic Rates*, Cmnd. 8449 (HMSO, London, 1981).

19 House of Commons Environment Committee, *Enquiry into Methods of Financing Local Government in the Context of the Government Green Paper (Cmnd. 8449)*, i–iii, House of Commons Papers 217, 1982.
20 The following account draws on D. Butler, A. Adonis and T. Travers, *Failure in British Government: the politics of the poll tax* (Oxford University Press, Oxford, 1994), ch. 2.
21 Department of the Environment, *Rates*, Cmnd. 9008 (HMSO, London, 1983), para. 14.
22 A. Crick and A. van Klaveren, 'Poll tax: Mrs Thatcher's greatest blunder', *Contemporary Record*, 5(3) (1991), p. 401.
23 Thatcher, *Downing Street Years*, p. 646.
24 See pp. 248–55 for an explanation of the grant system as it operated in the mid-1980s. Authorities could contest their selection by applying for a re-determination of their imposed expenditure level, a right that carried considerable possibilities of legal challenge to the DoE decisions.
25 Butler et al., *Failure in British Government*, ch. 3.
26 Adam Smith Institute, *The Omega File* (The Institute, London, 1985).
27 Michael Forsyth, *The Case for a Poll Tax* (Conservative Political Centre, London, 1985).
28 K. Baker, *The Turbulent Years: my life in politics* (Faber, London, 1993), p. 122.
29 Thatcher, *Downing Street Years*, p. 649.
30 Baker, *Turbulent Years*, p. 123.
31 A. Watkins, *A Conservative Coup: the fall of Margaret Thatcher*, 2nd edn (Duckworth, London, 1992).
32 N. Lawson, *The View from Number 11* (Corgi, London, 1993), p. 572.
33 Lawson, *The View from Number 11*, p. 573.
34 Department of the Environment, *Paying for Local Government*, Cmnd. 9714 (HMSO, London, 1986).
35 J. Gibson, *The Politics and Economics of the Poll Tax: Mrs Thatcher's downfall* (EMAS, Warley, 1990), pp. 49–95.
36 Quoted in Watkins, *A Conservative Coup*, pp. 91–2.
37 Financial details drawn from the *Council Tax Guide* (1994) and the periodic *Council Tax Facts* published by the Local Government Information Unit.
38 K. Walsh, 'Local government', in *Contemporary Britain: an annual review, 1992*, ed. P. Catterall (Blackwell, Oxford, 1992), p. 56.
39 R. J. Bennett, *Central Grants to Local Government: the political and economic impact of the Rate Support Grant in England* (Cambridge University Press, Cambridge, 1982), p. 127.
40 M. Loughlin, *Local Government in the Modern State* (Sweet and Maxwell, London, 1986), p. 42.

41 For a discussion of these cases, see Loughlin, *Local Government in the Modern State*, pp. 36–8, 43–5.
42 Department of the Environment, *Paying for Local Government*, para. 1.24.
43 Audit Commission, *The Impact on Local Authorities' Economy, Efficiency and Effectiveness of the Block Grant Distribution System* (HMSO, London, 1984).
44 Department of the Environment, *Paying for Local Government*, p. vii.
45 Department of the Environment, *Paying for Local Government*, para. 4.27.
46 Department of the Environment, *Paying for Local Government*, para. 1.41.
47 N. Ridley, *The Local Right: enabling not providing* (Centre for Policy Studies, London, 1988).
48 CPA, LCC 67, *Second Report of the Working Party on the Building and Contracting Industries*, January 1968.
49 K. Hartley and M. Huby, 'Contracting out policy: theory and evidence', in *Contracting Out Policy: theory and evidence in privatisation and regulation – the UK experience*, ed. J. Kay, C. Mayer and D. Thompson (Oxford, Oxford University Press, 1986); K. Ascher, *The Politics of Privatisation: contracting out public services* (Macmillan, Basingstoke, 1987).
50 N. Flynn, 'Direct labour organisations', in *Between Centre and Locality: the politics of public policy*, ed. S. Ranson, G. Jones and K. Walsh (George Allen & Unwin, London, 1985), pp. 119–34.
51 B. Wood, 'Privatisation: local government and the health service', in *Waiving the Rules: the constitution under Thatcherism*, ed. C. Graham and T. Prosser (Oxford University Press, Oxford, 1988), p. 124.
52 Audit Commission, *Securing Further Improvements in Refuse Collection: a review by the Audit Commission* (HMSO, London, 1984). See also S. Szymanski and T. Jones, *The Cost Savings from CCT of Refuse Collection Services* (London Business School, London, 1993).
53 Audit Commission, *Realising the Benefits of Competition* (HMSO, London, 1993).
54 Institute of Public Finance, *Competitive Tendering and Efficiency: the case of refuse collection* (IPF, London, 1986).
55 S. Domberger, S. Meadowcroft and D. Thompson, 'Competitive tendering and efficiency: the case of refuse collection', *Fiscal Studies*, 7(4) (1986), pp. 69–87.
56 M. Paddon, 'Management buy-outs and compulsory competition in local government', *Local Government Studies*, 17(3) (1991), pp. 27–52.
57 HM Treasury, *Public Service Management: the revolution in progress* (HMSO, London, 1989).

9 Into the Twilight, 1979–1995

The election of the Conservatives in 1979 marked the beginning of a period of radical change in the internal workings of local authorities, in their role as service providers, and in their relationship with central government. For the first time since 1945, the assumptions of the post-war settlement were decisively repudiated. Policy came now to be driven by different assumptions. The new government rejected the idea that worthwhile social ends could be achieved by a wide and increasing role for government, and asserted – with greater confidence than in 1970 – the primacy of the market. Margaret Thatcher and her mentor, Sir Keith Joseph, articulated this difference in terms drawn directly from Friedrich von Hayek. Markets and bureaucracies are in fundamental opposition. Markets operate with a plurality of players, and in a free market a multitude of individual decisions are made by people judging how best to provide for themselves and their families; they are the precondition of a free society. Bureaucracies, in contrast, provide for decisions to be taken by the few, on behalf of the many; their tendency is to extinguish freedom.

Mrs Thatcher's aim was to move decisively away from bureaucratic decision-making and allocation towards a freer market and thus (as she saw it) a freer society. This inescapably involved a shift of power outwards, opening up markets by bringing in competition to challenge the hitherto monopolistic position of public agencies, and downwards, to enfranchise or empower the individual consumer of public services. The problem was that these shifts of power required strong central intervention to achieve them, leading to a period of relentless centralization. This gave Mrs Thatcher no pause. Unusually for a Conservative, she harboured a strong distaste for local government, and was unabashed by the prospect of central intervention to liberate people from their local authorities.

John Major, who replaced Margaret Thatcher as Prime Minister in November 1990, had little of this animus. Unlike her, he had cut his political teeth in local government. And if he adopted some of Mrs Thatcher's rhetoric, he failed to carry the same conviction. Whereas his predecessor had sought to rewrite the history of social policy in Britain, Major's government was characterized by more limited aspirations, even if some of the earlier themes – choice, competition and empowerment – were to be carried forward after Major's 1992 general election victory. Housing and education would remain the key battlegrounds after 1990. A new and wholly different spirit had animated government policy towards these areas since 1979, and that spirit showed no sign of flagging.

Housing Policies and Programmes

Until 1979, local authorities had played a central role in the provision of social housing in Britain. Their role and their relationship with central government was to be changed dramatically by the 1979 election. As Baroness Thatcher (as she was to become) recalled in her memoirs:

> Of the three major social services – education, the health service and housing – it was, in my view, over the last of these that the most significant question mark hung. By the mid-1980s everything in housing pointed to the need to roll back the existing activities of government.[1]

The underlying aims of government policy after 1979 were to curtail the role of local authorities, to increase the contribution of housing associations and to revive the private rented sector, while continuing to encourage the expansion of owner-occupation. These changes could only be made at the expense of local government, where they would be directed to breaking the grip of the Labour party upon the political allegiances of council tenants. For political and other reasons, it was imperative 'to get local authorities out of managing and owning housing'.[2]

In time, this strategy would be encapsulated in a new vision of local government, based on a shift from 'providing' to 'enabling'.[3] In the case of housing, 'local authorities should increasingly see themselves as enablers who ensure that everyone in their area is adequately housed; but not necessarily by them'. Their function as providers of housing was to be substantially reduced, as 'there will no longer be the same presumption that the local authority itself should take direct action to meet new and increasing demands'.[4] Their role remained a strategic one, identifying housing needs and demands, and ensuring that they were met. Nicholas Ridley, the main exponent of the new approach, emphasized their regulatory role, for regulation, 'protecting the public interest in services provided by others, and seeing fair play', was 'the true function of government, both national and local'.[5]

In reality, however widely adopted the provisions of this strategy might have been, a major statutory role in housing for local authorities would still have remained in respect of housing the homeless. The general thrust of the housing reforms introduced during the Thatcher years conflicted with this requirement by drastically reducing the capacity of local housing authorities to respond to the problem. The government would not go so far as to repeal the Housing and Homeless Persons Act 1977; indeed, a later government review of the homelessness legislation would confirm local authorities as the main agents responsible for co-ordinating a response to homelessness. But none of the planks in the Conservatives' post-1979 platform – deregulation of the private rented sector, and disposal of council houses to tenants, housing associations or other landlords – were designed to meet raw housing needs. Their underlying aim was simpler: to restructure the tenure patterns of British housing to the disadvantage of the local authority role, so breaking the 'incestuous' relationship between councils and their tenants.[6]

Promoting home ownership

The most immediate step that could be taken to promote home ownership was to restore to local authorities' their ability to dispose of their houses and flats to sitting tenants. The lesson had been learned from 1970–74, and the new government was keen to avoid leaving the success of the policy to the responses of often hostile local authorities. The last months of the Heath government had seen an acceptance of the concept of a tenant's 'Right to Buy' – independent of any decision on the part of the local authority – and the new Prime Minister spoke glowingly in the debate on the Queen's Speech of 'making a giant stride towards making a reality of

Anthony Eden's dream of a property owning democracy' through council house sales. Michael Heseltine, incoming Environment Secretary, acted swiftly to implement that promise with the Housing Act 1980. Council tenants could now purchase their homes more easily, and against any opposition on the part of their municipal landlord.

The Housing and Planning Act 1986 gave a further impetus to sales by increasing the discounts offered on a basis of length of residence. As a result of this legislation, well over a million local authority and New Town tenants bought their homes during the 1980s. Annual sales rose rapidly as soon as the Conservatives came to power, doubling during their first year in office. They peaked at 226,000 in 1982, but fell to less than half this level in 1985 and 1986. Between 1986 and 1989 sales increased in each year before falling again in 1990 when only 140,000 dwellings were sold.[7]

For their part, Labour local authorities did their best to limit council house sales. Their efforts had the initial effect of reducing both the uptake and the speed with which sales progressed. One city council sought to frustrate the government's policies by refusing to appoint staff to give council sales priority over other housing policies and duties, instead appointing an officer to provide financial 'counselling' to prospective buyers, leading the Department of the Environment to intervene directly to stamp out this resistance.[8] Thereafter, sales to council tenants increased rapidly nationwide.[9]

It was not, however, on the more run-down estates that tenants exercised their right to buy; they were generally too poor to do so, and their homes were unattractive, unsaleable propositions.[10] Generally, sales had been highest in the more favoured areas – the South-East (outside Greater London), the East Midlands, the North and the South-West.[11] This marginal increase in owner-occupation was of course gained at the expense of a substantial decrease in the rented stock, as homes sold were removed from the rental sector. The standard Conservative response to this was to argue that the loss was apparent, not real, as the tenants would have otherwise have remained in place. Their case was weakened as the practice spread of new buyers selling on at a considerable capital gain, removing houses and their occupants permanently from the public sector. Labour had agonized over ways of squaring the aspirations of an increasing number of council tenants with the need to avoid such a depletion of the public resource of housing. Conservative policy had tacitly encouraged this development, both by increasing the discounts on sale prices and by softening the prohibition on early re-sale without penalty. Those incentives were required to drive the movement towards greater sales. To the extent that the Right to Buy enabled a million and a half tenants to buy their homes by 1992, the Conservatives could count the policy as a conspicuous success. Partly as a result of this initiative, the Thatcher years brought about major shifts in the scale and character of the British housing system. Council housing declined from its peak in 1979, when it accounted for 32 per cent of the UK housing stock, to 26 per cent in 1987.[12] Over the same period, its quality deteriorated, making council tenure increasingly undesirable.[13] There was also a consequential decline in social mix, and an increasing social polarization between the two main sectors of owner-occupation and municipal renting.[14] The decline of public housing was accompanied by continuing demands from local authorities and independent sources for more investment for new construction and renewal of the social housing stock. However, the Thatcher government was preoccupied with containing public expenditure, and the Treasury had a special interest in retaining the proceeds of council house sales, rather than seeing them ploughed back – as the local authorities wanted – into the housing programme. As a result, investment in housing fell heavily in real terms. This decline was vividly reflected in the number of housing starts. Public-sector starts fell from a peak of 173,800 in 1975, to 80,100 in 1979 and further still, to about 33,000, in 1986. The 1989 public expenditure white paper projected that local authority house building programmes would decline from 15,000 in 1988/89 to 12,000 in 1990/91 and 6,000 by the following year. In actuality, the fall-off was more rapid still, with just 4,100 starts made in 1991/92.[15] The housing development role of local authorities was disappearing.

Promoting choice and diversity

Arguably, it was only in the promotion of home ownership that the first two Thatcher governments achieved much success. The 1979–83 government largely restricted itself to implementing prior policy commitments; the 1983–7 government was preoccupied with other matters. The third term was distinguished by the introduction of much more far-reaching measures. The proposals for public housing included in the 1987 general election manifesto were largely based on policy papers that Nicholas Ridley had already drawn up. Mrs Thatcher planned 'a major shift away from the ossified system which had grown up under Socialism', and it fell to Nicholas Ridley, as Secretary of State for the Environment, to carry this programme forward.[16]

The first strand of the policy was to place renewed emphasis on the role of private renting. The private rented sector at that time accounted for less than 8 per cent of homes in Britain. The intention of the Housing Act 1988 was to reverse the long-term decline in private renting, to regenerate the sector through deregulation, and to stimulate its growth by removing rent controls and introducing new-style assured tenancies. Assured tenancies enabled landlords and tenants to devise their own rent levels through negotiation, with new tenancies no longer protected by the Rent Act by removing the rent controls that had brought it about. The sector could only be revived if letting property again became an economic proposition. This was a long-term aim. It was evident that, even if private renting was made profitable in the short term, because of the past history of rent controls, private investors were unlikely to risk future investment on any scale in housing for rent. They would avoid it in favour of more secure forms of investment.[17] Even so, an assessment of the short-term effects of these provisions showed about a 10 per cent increase in the number of tenancies to have occurred as a result of the Act by as early as 1990, with average rents rising by 43 per cent in the same period.

The second strand was to bring about a major shift in the housing association sector. The objective was to move housing associations away from quasi-public housing role into which they had developed since 1974 towards a more private-sector style 'independent' rental sector.[18] To this end, new housing association tenancies were deregulated to put them on much the same footing as those in the private rented sector. Housing association provision was to be expanded by drawing in private finance to create 'mixed funding' schemes. Part II of the Act further extended the activities of housing associations to enable them to operate in fields incidental to their main housing activity, including the creation or rehabilitation of commercial and industrial premises.

The third strand of the Ridley programme was tenants' choice. His 1987 white paper *Housing: the government's proposals*, while maintaining a strong commitment to owner-occupation, also set out the government's intention to give those council tenants who could not, or did not wish, to buy their home, the right to transfer to another landlord if they chose to do so:

The emphasis must be on greater consumer choice and more say for tenants. This can only be achieved by offering a variety of forms of ownership and management; this will help to break down the monolithic nature of large estates.[19]

There was a pressing need for 'more competition and choice in the housing market', as

> in the public sector too little attention has been paid to the wishes of tenants or to their views on how their requirements can best be met; tenants have generally not been allowed to express their choices clearly and have therefore not always found the kind of accommodation they want. In the worst cases this has led to understandable resentment and a consequential lack of commitment to their homes.[20]

Introduced in Part IV of the Housing Act 1988, tenants' choice was presented as a further development of the rights and choices already given to council tenants. These had developed steadily since 1980 through the statutory Tenants' Charter and the right to buy legislation in the Housing Act 1980. The new provisions enabled council tenants to choose to transfer their existing homes to another landlord. In this way it was hoped to 'open up the closed world of the local authority housing estates to competition and to the influence of the best housing management practices of other landlords'.[21]

The Housing Corporation was given the central role in servicing the tenants' choice arrangements. The Corporation was to provide objective information and advice to tenants to enable them to use their powers to choose. It also had a wider role in selecting and approving landlords ready to take over public housing, and in framing the guidelines on housing management practices to which all new landlords were required to subscribe. Tenants of houses were given the right to choose individually, but in blocks of flats or maisonettes they could decide to transfer only collectively. New independent landlords who had obtained prior approval as appropriate social landlords, under the conditions laid down by the Housing Corporation, had the right to take over council housing stock if a vote of the existing tenants decided on this. The approval criteria required applicants to show viability and competence, to commit themselves to the long-term provision of housing for rent and to subscribe to the 'tenants' guarantee' laid down by the Housing Corporation.

The aim of tenants' choice was to give more choice to those tenants who could not, or did not wish to, exercise their right to buy. Even where tenants voted against transfer to another landlord, they were still expected to benefit, the government's argument being that exposing councils to healthy competition would contribute to a better general standard of service. Despite these enticements, tenants showed very little interest in such transfers. A number of surveys carried out in the late 1980s found large majorities of tenants expressing a desire to remain with their councils.[22] Councils were apparently making efforts to meet the needs of their tenants, seeking their tenants' views and improving services, so as to forestall any moves to opt out of local authority tenancy. As a result, the Act failed to bring about a change in the pattern of municipal landlordism, although it may have done something to create a more responsive housing management regime. In the course of the next eight years, only 981 council tenants out of a possible six million opted to transfer control of their estates from their local authorities, and in only two cases did these moves involve estates of more than ten homes. Faced with so stark a disparity between the results of the scheme and its high administrative costs, tenants' choice was killed off in 1996.

The tenants' choice initiative had fallen far short of the expectations placed upon it by the third Thatcher government, partly because the government had failed to judge accurately the reactions of tenants and the adaptability of local housing authorities. The Major government was less preoccupied with grand schemes for public housing estates, and turned its attention instead towards the rental markets, which it could claim to understand better. In mid-1995, the white paper *Our Future Homes* announced the government's intention to bring forward measures to encourage new forms of landlordism. More choice would be provided through the encouragement of new types of landlord. Local housing companies could be formed to take on the transfers of housing from local authorities, and themselves to provide new cheap rented housing.[23] Determined to 'sustain the revival of the private rented sector that deregulation has achieved', *Our Future Homes* proposed housing investment trusts to encourage the financial institutions to invest in housing for rent. Further deregulation of the private rented sector was promised to make it easier to let property on assured shorthold tenancies and to speed up the time in which a landlord could recover possession.

Voluntary transfers

While the abortive tenants' choice scheme had been directed to the tenants themselves, the voluntary transfer arrangements sought to bring about a similar shift in the ownership of social housing on a larger scale by persuading local authorities to off-load whole estates, or even their entire stock, to housing associations. The Housing Act 1988 set out the ways in which councils could dispose of some or all of their housing stock to housing associations. Subsequent guidance notes issued by the Department of the Environment and the Housing Corporation set out the conditions for transfers. The interests of existing tenants were to be protected, and authorities were obliged to ensure that they were fully informed about the proposal and its implications for them, should it succeed. The authorities had also to ensure that they remained able to discharge their statutory functions post-transfer. The new landlords were to be viable, responsible and independent bodies. Guidance was also given as to the likely maximum size of the stock which could be transferred. Finally, three-quarters of any capital receipts realized as a result of a transfer were to be set aside for debt repayment.[24]

Local authorities proposing the voluntary transfer of their stock needed to demonstrate to the Secretary of State that their proposals had the support of the tenants. The way in which evidence of support was adduced, however, was not clearly specified, and in the absence of early guidance a number of authorities used the balloting arrangements laid down for tenants' choice. The difference between the two systems was fundamental. If a majority of eligible tenants voted 'no' under the tenants' choice system, then the application for transfer to another landlord failed. The procedure for voluntary transfer was not, however, one of simple majority, in that an abstention was counted in effect as a 'yes' vote.[25] Even so, surveys of tenants showed many of them to be wary of the uncertainties involved in such transfers. Some local groups campaigned on the grounds that the policy undermined the rights of tenants, concern also being expressed that where polls were held, 'tenants have been railroaded into a ballot before they can take in all the issues'.[26]

The reductions in housing investment allocations, and the further restriction of local authority borrowing, ensured that local authorities would find it increasingly difficult to provide new housing and repair their existing stock. The threat of Compulsory Competitive Tendering (CCT) and further financial restrictions held out little prospect of a future for them as local housing authorities. The fear of tenants' choice applications by 'predatory' landlords provided an incentive for local authorities to confront stark choices. In these circumstances, some were moved to consider voluntarily transferring their stock to alternative landlords.

The best publicized case of a authority trying this form of ballot was Torbay Borough Council. With 787 tenants voting in favour of transfer, 2,210 against and 2,209 abstentions, the council declared that a majority of tenants – 2,996 (787 plus 2,209) against 2,210 – were in favour, and it decided to go ahead with the transfer. However, following protests from tenants' groups, the Secretary of State refused permission for a voluntary transfer and the council was not able to proceed. This difficulty over the balloting system made the initial implementation of the policy difficult for many authorities which took the initial steps towards transfers, or were considering doing so.

Several other authorities subsequently failed to transfer their housing, when clear votes were cast against such transfers. In Rochford, Salisbury, Gloucester and Arun, tenants voted against the proposals to transfer and the councils had to retreat in the face of tenant opposition. On the other hand, strong votes in favour of opting out in Chiltern, Sevenoaks and Newbury enabled those councils to transfer their housing stock to newly created housing associations. Three years later, the number of transferring authorities had risen to eighteen, with 94,000 tenancies transferred and speculation that up to a hundred further authorities were preparing schemes.[27]

Yet, by the end of 1992, it had become clear that voluntary transfers were making less headway than had been hoped. Ministers did not conceal their disappointment. While they claimed that large-scale voluntary transfers 'have made a valuable contribution to the government's objective of diversification of tenure of rented housing' they had to concede that 'they have not brought about the break-up of social housing ownership into the smaller units that ministers had hoped to see'.[28] The way forward was to encourage other forms of transfers, and to limit the proportion of municipal housing stock transferred to any single recipient. A new emphasis on greater diversity and the avoidance of local monopolies was proposed.[29] But, early in 1996, this scheme too was abandoned.[30]

Into the Twilight 275

Renewing run-down estates

The third of the radical proposals made in the 1987 white paper was aimed at the wholesale rehabilitation of Britain's most run-down council estates, using private investment and a post-completion transfer out of local authority ownership. The problem which the new scheme of Housing Action Trusts (HATs) aimed to solve was the legacy of long-term, large-scale, municipal development:

> There are still too many estates where the quality of life is less than satis factory. It is not what tenants want, and it is not what the original designers of the estates had in mind. Tenants live there not from choice, but because they have nowhere else to live. Many tenants feel that standards of maintenance are inadequate and that management is too remote.[31]

HATs, established under the 1988 Act, were intended to improve the most run-down council estates and, ultimately, to give tenants of these estates a choice over whether the estates should be run by local authorities, housing associations or private companies.

Modelled on the Urban Development Corporations (UDCs), HATs were to have the job of drawing up and putting into effect comprehensive programmes of improvement. HATs were expected to seek the maximum possible support from the private sector, and to involve private-sector resources in the work of refurbishing stock and taking over landlord responsibilities. In designating the HATs, the government concentrated on those areas in which there was a predominance of the worst local authority housing. But questions about future rents, security of tenure and the ability of the local authority involved to deal with homelessness immediately arose. As a result, the HAT proposals were not well received by the tenants' associations. Energetic lobbying of Parliament was organized by tenant groups on the estates earmarked for HAT treatment. They contended that the introduction of HATs was not in tune with the feelings of tenants, most of whom feared being taken over by a private landlord. While many tenants blamed their local authorities, at least up to a point, for the deteriorating conditions on estates, councils nonetheless appeared to be the safer bet as landlords.

Tenants' opposition was so fierce that the chances of implementing so coercive and confrontational a policy were slim. Accordingly, the Department of the Environment made substantial changes to the terms on which HATs were to be designated. Tenants were given the opportunity to vote for a return of the ownership and management of their estates to the local authority when the HAT concluded its work. Most significantly, while the government had resisted tenant ballots on the initial establishment of a HAT, this right was conceded following the government's defeat on a House of Lords amendment in July 1988.[32]

HATs were to evolve still further. Granting a ballot did nothing to make the policy more acceptable, as it simply legitimized the tenants' opposition. It then became necessary to co-opt the local authorities themselves into HATs programme by offering such greatly improved packages that they themselves would have an incentive to lead tenant opinion. Thus the policy moved from one of coercion, through negotiation, to one of incentive. The effect was to increase the budget for the first six HATs from £125 million over three years (or around £20 million per area), to £160 in Waltham Forest, and £190 million in Liverpool alone. None of the local authority housing estates initially earmarked by the DoE for HAT status got off the ground in the face of tenant opposition. Although two HATs were subsequently negotiated, they were a significant departure from the original model, and involved compromise between central government and local authorities.

Financing public housing

Underlying all of these changes were new provisions for housing finance, embodied in the Local Government and Housing Act 1989. The capital and revenue regimes that it introduced set a new agenda for local authority housing. The government claimed the legislation to have three main purposes: to increase the efficiency of local authorities, to increase the efficiency of resource allocation and to 'influence the level of rents to a market-like level'. The Act introduced a new system for the regulation of local authority capital finance foreshadowed in the DoE/Welsh Office consultation paper *Capital Expenditure and Finance*. It also established the new financial regime for local authority housing which had been proposed in an earlier consultation paper.[33]

The government's starting point was that the system of capital controls introduced in the Local Government, Planning and Land Act 1980 had proved deficient. It argued that the system had not been able to deal effectively with high levels of capital receipts from council house sales and had not prevented local authorities from exploiting the loopholes. In addition, the system failed to bring local authorities' net capital expenditure into line with the government's public expenditure plans. The government's objectives for a new system of capital controls were to control the overall levels of local authority capital expenditure and borrowing; to bring about a distribution of capital expenditure which better reflected national and local needs; to reduce the size of the public sector by encouraging asset sales; and to provide local authorities with a more secure basis for planning their capital programmes.

As one of its measures to control borrowing, the government gave authorities credit approvals which took into account the authority's available capital receipts from asset sales. This new system enabled central government to direct borrowing ability towards those areas of housing need with severely limited resources, such as Inner London authorities. Authorities with under-average capital receipts but high General Needs Index (GNI) scores could expect higher allocation levels than in the past. The reverse was true for a number of authorities, particularly in the South East, which had amassed their capital receipts through vigorous sales.

Secondly, in order to pay off debt or meet known future borrowing commitments, local authorities were required to set aside 75 per cent of the proceeds from council house sales, and 50 per cent from other asset sales. Under the former system, central government had only restricted the use of capital receipts to 20 per cent in the year in which they were generated, permitting a carry forward of the unspent 80 per cent for re-use in the following years. By this means, councils had been able eventually to spend the whole value of their receipts.

The local authority associations, particularly the Association of Metropolitan Authorities and the Association of London Authorities, the members of which represented the urban areas of greatest housing need, criticized the new restriction on the use of capital receipts, arguing that the proposals would discourage new building, and that capital expenditure would have to be significantly reduced. The AMA and the ALA were concerned that their member authorities would be severely restricted in their ability to meet housing needs. The proposals implied a worsening housing repair service, deterioration in the maintenance of other council assets and an inability to make substantial new investments to, for example, house the homeless or meet other urgent needs. The Institute of Housing similarly predicted that the new capital control system would lead to a significant reduction in investment in major repairs and improvements. Few new dwellings would be built in the public sector, which would imply a poorer service for tenants. According to the Institute, this prospect had led many local authorities to consider voluntary transfer of their stock, as was indeed the logic of the housing reform package.

The 1988 Act also introduced major changes in the revenue funding of council housing. The 1987 white paper set out the government's intention to introduce a new financial regime to 'reinforce the present statutory distinction between the provision of housing and other local authority functions and replace the existing housing revenue accounts by arrangements which are more in accord with modern accounting practice'.[34] This was reiterated in the consultation paper of July 1988, which proposed a more tightly defined Housing Revenue Account (HRA) to 'reinforce the distinction between the provision of housing and other local authority functions'.

The changes dealing with the Housing Revenue Account and its constituent parts lay at the heart of the Conservatives' housing reforms. The HRA provided for day-to-day expenditure and income for the local authority housing stock. The main items of expenditure were loan charges for council house building, management and maintenance costs and surpluses transferred to the general rate fund. The chief sources of income at that time were rents (net of rebate) from council tenants, rent rebate subsidy, income from investments of capital receipts, rate fund contributions and housing subsidy. In addition, rents were henceforth to bear a close relationship to what properties were worth, and not to historic costs. Under the earlier system, nearly 50 per cent of the funding of the HRA was in respect of the historical costs of providing, modernizing and improving the council stock.

The new system of revenue finance introduced a single housing subsidy, which replaced housing subsidy, rate fund contributions (supported by rate support grant) and the rent rebate element of housing benefit subsidy. In the new HRA, the principal sources of income would be gross rents and HRA subsidy; and the main outgoings would be loan charges, management and maintenance spending, revenue contributions to capital expenditure on HRA dwellings (as provided for in the new capital system), surpluses transferred to other accounts of the general fund, and other charges including standard community charge (later council tax) on vacant dwellings. One of the most potent aspects of the new system was the 'ring fencing' of the HRA, whereby discretionary transfers in either direction were not permitted. Authorities continued to have to budget to avoid a deficit on the HRA. The Conservatives' claim was that by limiting the HRA in this way, council landlords would be more accountable to their customers, the tenants. Conservative governments had long sought to tackle subsidies from the rate fund, claiming that they had in the past allowed authorities to cushion their tenants against the effects of local authority inefficiency, and kept rents artificially low for political reasons. The Act removed local authority discretion over subsidization by combining existing schemes into a single subsidy controlled by central government. Prior to the introduction of this new system, only between seventy and eighty local authorities had received housing subsidy. Henceforth, virtually all authorities were brought into subsidy.[35]

Local authorities continued to retain local discretion in running their housing operations, balancing the rents that they set against the standards of management that they provided. The government's intention was, once again, to sharpen and clarify choice:

> Well run housing departments will be able to provide a good standard of service at a modest rent; on the other hand, inefficient landlords will be unable to conceal their poor standards or their extravagant costs. Tenants will thus be given clear signals about the performance of their council's housing operation. They will be able to take better informed decisions about the alternatives the government's housing policy is placing before them, and to decide whether to exercise the options that government is giving them through the right to buy and tenants' choice.[36]

Such a fundamental change in policy was to have important consequences for local authorities. In the first place, central government gained greater control over rent levels and the management and maintenance expenditure of councils. Under the previous system, only a quarter of all councils actually received subsidy; the new system meant that all authorities were brought into central government subsidy entitlement, thereby falling under central control. Central guidelines over rent levels were to have a major impact. Where authorities' HRAs were in surplus without any housing revenue subsidy, councils were required to transfer a specified surplus to the general fund, so that no financial cushion could remain on the HRA to protect tenants from future rent rises. Central government was thereby able to influence future rent levels even in those councils which required no further subsidy.

The exclusion of rate fund contributions reduced the ability of councils to hold rents down by switching money from ratepayers to the HRA. However, in the first year of the scheme from April 1990 there were no major average increases in rents, as the initial HRA subsidy was based on the average of previous subsidies including rate fund contributions. The switch to rents based on a return on the current values of the housing stock implied that council tenants were likely to be the losers. The new changes were intended to encourage tenants to move into the private housing market, despite the claim that 'rents should not exceed levels within the reach of people in low-paid-employment and in practice will be below market levels'.

The inclusion of rent rebate subsidy within the HRA marked a fundamental change in the financing of housing benefit. It meant that local authorities with surpluses on their HRA would receive a proportionately reduced government contribution to the rebates given to their tenants in the form of housing benefit. As a result of this, council tenants not in receipt of housing benefit would be helping to meet the costs of financial help to poorer tenants via housing benefit. This was seen by critics to represent a 'shift of welfare responsibilities not just from central government to local government but from central government to particular council tenants in areas where the housing revenue account is in surplus'.[37] For the Conservative government, it was but the latest episode in the long post-war history of attempts to find a politically acceptable basis for local authority rents.

Education in Schools

For the first twenty years following the end of the war, local authorities and schools had worked within the framework defined by the 1944 Education Act. A broad consensus about the distribution of power and responsibilities in education had prevailed. It was customary to refer to the *partnership* between central government, LEAs and teachers, a partnership in which power over the organization and content of education was diffused among these different elements, none of which could dominate the others.[38] Within this consensual structure of educational policy-making, firm leadership from the centre did not invalidate the concurrent assumption of strong local government, for these roles were distinct and complementary.[39]

Circular 10/65 changed all that. From that point, the consensus began to crumble, and the education system came under increasing criticism. Education was attacked for failing to make a sufficient contribution to national objectives, and the diffused responsibilities created by the 1944 Act were now seen to have protected education interests from change, and impeded, rather than facilitated, progress. Now new voices would be heard, and new issues raised. The general discontent voiced by employer representatives and given authoritative expression by Labour Prime Minister James Callaghan converged with a trenchant indictment of modern education made by conservative educationalists. During the latter half of the 1970s, these criticisms crystallized in a distinctive policy position which won favour within the Conservative party.[40] Having seized the agenda, they provided the impetus for a programme of legislative reform once the party came to power under Margaret Thatcher in 1979.[41] The LEAs were bound to be the losers.

The common ground that emerged from this new critique was the need to bring about a more responsive and more accountable education service. The newly powerful critics argued that market forces were the most effective way of determining a school's curriculum and of raising standards. Central government intervention was necessary only as an initial step to undermine the power of the vested interests that threatened educational standards and traditional values.[42] They laid the blame for education's failings at the door of the existing education 'establishment': the LEAs, the teachers' organizations, the teacher training institutions and various other groups associated with shaping the education system, who had ignored the demands of the consumers of the service – the parents and children. They had responded instead to the requirements of the producers: the LEAs, teacher training colleges, the teachers themselves and other professionals.[43] The problems facing education, in common with other public services, were those of 'producer capture'.[44]

The thrust of the criticism accordingly focused on poor and inadequate standards, irrelevant curricula, and the need to reconstruct the power relations within the education system to conform to the principles of consumer choice and accountability. Parents should be given the free choice of schools to which to send their children and a strong voice in their management. To make that possible, the control of schools should be removed from the hands of local authorities, and management devolved to the schools themselves. 'If the system itself were changed to one of self-governing, self-managing, budget centres, which were obliged, for their survival, to respond to the "market"', wrote Conservative education activist Stuart Sexton, 'then there would be an in-built mechanism to raise standards and change forms and types of education in accordance with the market demand'.[45] Making the education service more accountable and responsive to the choices of individuals was thus the key to improving standards. Such were the ideas which shaped the Conservatives' legislative programme, instigating what Sir Keith Joseph, Mrs Thatcher's first Education Secretary, promised would be a new era of 'choice and excellence'.

The Conservatives' 'new era'

In education, as in housing, Mrs Thatcher's ministers moved first to honour old promises before hastening to usher in the new era. And the firmest of these promises was the removal of the requirement that LEAs should go comprehensive. The Thatcher government's first Education Act was passed immediately in 1979, a limited measure designed to repeal the statutory obligation on LEAs to submit comprehensive schemes. Thereafter, the 1980 Education Act marked a true new beginning.

The first step was to enhance parental power, and under the 1980 Act at least two from among the parents of registered pupils were to be included among the governors appointed by the local authority. Such provisions were further enhanced in the Education (No. 2) Act 1986, which advanced the representation and power of parent governors on governing bodies.[46] Represented as a radical move towards empowerment, the government's actions could be equally said to reflect the emerging educational orthodoxy. Back in 1967, the Plowden report inquiry into primary schools had stressed the advantages, in terms of improving the quality of education, of involving parents and public. These latest measures were solidly supported by a succession of reports from Her Majesty's Inspectorate

(HMI) and the Department of Education and Science, but upset even Conservative educationalists, who foresaw running conflicts between governors and headteachers. Subsequently, the Education (Schools) Act 1992, pushed further the attempt to create an education market by requiring the publication of information on school performance. This requirement would remain a source of controversy, and the interpretation of the information thus gleaned was fiercely disputed.

The 1980 Act also re-established the Assisted Places Scheme, whereby academically able children whose parents had limited financial means could secure high-quality education at independent schools. Turning to the content of education, the government strengthened its own influence over the curriculum in 1984 by abolishing the teacher-dominated Schools Council, and establishing the new Secondary Examinations Council and the School Curriculum Development Committee, the members of which were nominated by the DES.

After 1981, Sir Keith Joseph began to take a more interventionist role, conceiving his mission as being to root out opposition to the enterprise culture where it was most deeply embedded, in the schools and teacher training colleges. The latter he addressed in his white paper *Teaching Quality* in 1983, and in the following year he introduced a system of specific grants to be paid to local education authorities in respect of expenditure incurred on certain training programmes initiated by the Secretary of State.[47] The Department also introduced criteria for in-service training, and LEAs had to meet these criteria before they could receive grant. In the years that followed, the centre assumed further powers. The Education Act 1986 gave the Secretary of State power to make regulations for the appraisal of teachers in schools and colleges, and for the approval of teacher training courses.

Sir Keith Joseph's next white paper, *Better Schools*, set out his alternative vision for education in terms that have been described as a modern 'Black Paper'.[48] Here the strategy of reversing post-war trends was expounded, the object being to restore 'a common-sense approach to education in place of Labour's dogma'.[49] However, this rhetoric was not followed up by much action. Not until Kenneth Baker replaced Sir Keith Joseph in 1986 was there any attempt to push the counter-revolution beyond the relatively limited achievements of the first two Thatcher governments. Baker was to recall in his memoirs that

284 *Into the Twilight*

> No one had yet grasped the nettle of major legislative overhaul. While Keith Joseph had planted many of the seeds . . . I realised that the scale of the problem could only be tackled by a coherent national programme, and time was not on our side. I knew what I wanted in the package . . . [50]

Baker's contribution was an Education Reform Act which did indeed reverse the post-war trends. The Baker Act was 'the most important and far-reaching piece of educational law-making in England and Wales since the Education Act of 1944'.[51] It restored to central government powers over the curriculum which had been effectively surrendered between the wars, and set up formal machinery for exercising power at the centre. It introduced limits on the functions of LEAs while giving greater autonomy to schools and governing bodies. Thereafter, education policy expressed a new and radical view of education management, the essence of which was to dismantle the old power structures and tip the balance of power firmly away from producers towards the consumers of education.

Curriculum reform and testing

The 1988 Act set out a framework for the school curriculum in England and Wales. It introduced a national curriculum which included three core subjects and seven foundation subjects, designed to raise standards by ensuring that all pupils studied a broad and balanced range of subjects throughout the compulsory schooling period. The idea was that all children were entitled to a common set of educational experiences, premised on the belief that there could be a new national consensus on the general aims and objectives of compulsory education. The national curriculum was also expected to facilitate the geographical mobility of families, thus removing a source of inflexibility in the labour market as well as increasing the accountability of schools.

The curriculum embodied a clear definition of the objectives and standards to be expected from state education. The DES – later to become the Department for Education (DfE) – would now direct the curriculum by specifying the subject areas to be covered and programmes of study for those subjects, and by setting up standards of assessment to match them. It laid down the duty for the governing bodies, headteachers and local education authorities to ensure that the curriculum is implemented. These new powers of the Secretary of State to define and amend programmes of study represented a sharp break with recent practice and presented another challenge to the teaching profession. Headteachers and staff lost a considerable degree of their former freedom.

Under the Act, two new bodies – the National Curriculum Council (NCC) and the Secondary Examinations Assessment Council (SEAC) – were set up under the control of central government. They were responsible for keeping all aspects of the schools' curriculum and assessment under review and for advising the Secretary of State on such matters concerned with curriculum and assessment as he might refer to them, or as they saw fit. The main thrust of the NCC was to assist the introduction of national curriculum. The SEAC took over the functions of the former Secondary Examinations Council, with responsibility for developing the assessment system. These two new bodies were, however, fated to be short-lived. In 1991, Secretary of State for Education Kenneth Clarke rejected their joint advice on curriculum and dismissed the chairmen of both. With the teaching unions launching a successful boycott of assessment of national curriculum, a new body, the School Curriculum and Assessment Authority (SCAA) replaced them. Sir Ron Dearing, chairman-designate of the new body, was first appointed to chair both the SEAC and the NCC in an attempt to find an agreeable formula for assessment.

The national curriculum was soon to run into difficulties. Margaret Thatcher had wanted a basic syllabus for English, mathematics and science, and not the complex framework that Baker had negotiated. Baker's successor, John MacGregor, sought to slim down the system that he had inherited, while his successor, Kenneth Clarke, was to move still further away from the Baker plans. In simplifying the system, Clarke brought the national curriculum proposals into closer alignment with the former Prime Minister's views and with the instincts of the Conservative party, although, ironically, the former Black Paper advocates of 'excellence' were to round on the government for their betrayal of the original aims of the project.

Meanwhile, the new regime was making few friends within the education service. A report in 1990 by HMI, on the implementation of the national curriculum in primary schools, found that in most schools resources were inadequate, that teachers were having problems with assessing and keeping achievement records, that there were insufficient teachers with the right kind of expertise and experience, and that schools were facing problems of recruiting experienced staff. Having to rely on temporary teachers was 'having damaging effects on the early stages of implementation'. Testing was to prove the most controversial of all the proposals and the most difficult to implement, dependent as it was on the co-operation of the teaching profession. Baker's preference for a broad entitlement curriculum had led him to agree a complex and comprehensive testing scheme. MacGregor attempted to simplify it, and Clarke was to condemn the forms of tests adopted as 'elaborate nonsense'. It fell to John Patten to try to make assessment of the national curriculum work, but by June 1993 the hostility of the teachers to the tests themselves, and to the administrative load that they imposed, threatened to derail this component of the education reform programme. For the remaining years of the Major government, implementing testing would continue to be a source of conflict and controversy.

Delegating to schools

Mrs Thatcher's governments had an easier ride in the third main plank of their programme, to devolve power from the LEAs down to the schools themselves. The Local Management of Schools (LMS) was a key aspect of their policies for improving teaching and learning in schools through the promotion of choice and competition.[52] At the same time, it reflected a much more general move to locate decision-making at the school level, enabling schools to use resources more effectively to carry out education activities according to their characteristics and needs. Despite appearances to the contrary, the government were flowing with the tide of education reform, for school systems in countries as diverse as Australia, Hong Kong, Holland and the USA were experiencing similar moves school-based management practices.[53]

In Britain, a number of Conservative local authorities, led by Solihull and Cambridgeshire, had experimented with forms of local management, although this had involved only financial devolution. Solihull had introduced financial delegation in 1981, when three of the authority's schools were given control over 90 per cent of their budgets under the scheme of 'local financial autonomy'. Influenced in large part by these experiments, the Education Reform Act compelled all LEAs to accept local management as a new form of partnership with their schools. In devolving management responsibilities to the school level, LEAs had to recognize that their main role in the future lay in providing overall leadership, and in enabling schools and colleges to implement the changes.

Local Management of Schools (LMS) was intended to enable heads and governors to manage schools efficiently by providing the information and support that they needed to make management decisions, while giving them the freedom to determine the use of resources to meet the needs and priorities they have identified.[54] By delegating the management of cash resources, personnel and premises to the local level, LMS aimed to improve the quality of education and learning for pupils and achieve better financial management. Some critics, however, thought that the overall financial arguments of the government's plans had not been adequately demonstrated.[55]

The Act required each authority to draw up its own scheme delegating to schools a budget which they might use at their discretion. In brief, the budget was arrived at by deciding which functions and activities should be retained by the local authority and dividing the total cost of the remaining functions and activities on a formula basis between the schools themselves. All local education authorities were required to submit schemes providing for such financial delegation to the Secretary of the State for his approval by September 1989. The Act required each authority to consult with the governing bodies and heads of each of its schools in preparing the scheme. By 1 February 1990, eighty-four authorities had either received formal approval for their schemes or were being consulted on modifications prior to approval. Fears that the new system would produce uniformity proved unwarranted; an analysis of the first ninety submissions by LEAs showed considerable differences of approach.[56]

Four years later, Circular 2/94 went much further to draw together the scheme of delegation and the curricular duties of the schools, governing bodies and LEAs:

> Within this statutory framework, governing bodies are free to allocate resources to their own curricular priorities from delegated budgets. Schemes should not include conditions or requirements which cut across the discretion and duties that governing bodies are given in that framework. LEAs should, however, provide in their schemes that governing bodies should spend their delegated budgets in a manner which is consistent with the implementation of the National Curriculum; with the statutory

requirements relating to the curriculum as a whole, including religious education and worship; and, for county and controlled schools, and special needs, with the LEA's curriculum policy as modified by the governing body . . . [57]

The local determination of formulae enabled LEAs to take different approaches, to retain different proportions of total budget for central services within the broad requirement, and to adopt a variety of methods for resource allocation.[58] Despite these variations in local arrangements for distribution, the formula was to be applied to all schools, and not restricted to those that became eligible for financial delegation. It was intended to be based on 'actual needs' rather than historic spending patterns. The funding of all the schools in a local authority area on the basis of a common formula prevented a local authority from intervening in favour of one school rather than another. Inevitably, though, as a result of the introduction of this new funding scheme, some schools were to gain and others lose, for as the resource allocation formula was heavily weighted by pupil numbers, the more pupils a school could attract, the greater were the resources that were allocated to it.[59]

The Act emphasized the need for each authority to consult with the governing bodies and heads of schools in preparing the scheme. In taking responsibility for spending the school's budget, governors were bound by their duty to ensure that the national curriculum was taught, and taught in accordance with the scheme. Delegation could be suspended by the local authority if it believed that the governors had been guilty of a persistent failure to do their job, although this power was constrained by a right of appeal by the governors to the Secretary of State.

Enhancing parental choice

The Education Reform Act set out important measures to extend parental choice. Open enrolment was designed to give parents a greater say in the schools that their children attended by eliminating school catchment areas. Under the Act, all maintained schools were required to accept a full complement of pupils up to the limit of their physical capacity. This was defined in terms of a 'standard' number of places set for each school. The Act spelt out the ways in which that standard number might be varied: the

LEA responsible for that school was required to publish proposals if it wished to increase or reduce a school's standard number, and to consider any objections made by local electors, or the governing body of any school affected by the proposals, or by any local education authority concerned.

Other measures which were presented as enhancing parental choice, while being primarily designed to achieve other ends, included the creation of city technology colleges and grant maintained schools. City technology colleges, set up by the Secretary of State, were to be independent of the local education authority, and substantially funded by industry. They were to provide a broad curriculum for eleven to eigtheen year olds and to recruit pupils representing a cross-section of the population in terms of ability. Their curriculum was to have a strong emphasis on science and technology, and they were to 'seek to develop the qualities of enterprise, self-reliance and responsibility and secure the highest possible standards of achievement'. By January 1994, just fifteen such schools had been established.

'Opting out' enabled governors and parents of all maintained secondary and primary schools to apply to the Secretary of State for Grant Maintained Status (GMS), under which a school escaped from LEA control and was directly funded by the DES (later the Department for Education; DfE). It was to provide a new form of the 'direct grant' school beloved of Conservatives. Originally, only those schools with more than 300 pupils could apply for GMS, but a policy change to remove this minimum size threshold was announced in October 1990. The Act made provision for the balloting of parents on whether to apply for Grant Maintained Status. The Act specified in detail the rules governing the transition of a local authority maintained school to GMS, but made no provision for grant maintained schools to opt back into the control of their local education authorities.

Some schools were quick to put forward the view that by opting out they could be more responsive to the community. They argued that they would be able to employ more appropriate staff and that in general they would be better run independently of LEA control. On the negative side, their reasons for applying included the wish to avert a threat of closure or amalgamation with other schools, and fear of political interference by the local authority. By 1995, over 1,000 schools nationally had achieved GMS.

The implicit aim of open enrolment and opting out was to provide a pincer movement so as to encourage competition for pupils between schools. The assumption was that schools which were responsive to choices made by parents in the market were more likely to produce high levels of achievement. Advocates of the market philosophy argued that the exercise of parental choice would ensure that bad schools would close, and good schools flourish.[60] The evidence in mid-1993, however, was that the reality of parental choice, as measured by success in getting children into the school of first choice, was more elusive than expected due to the intensification of competition.[61]

Opponents predicted that the government would ensure that grant maintained schools would be better-funded than their LEA-maintained counterparts, so as to ensure their success. The DES circular on opting out stated that grant maintained schools should not change the financial position either of the school or of the local ratepayers; and that a 'grant maintained school be funded on the basis of the same resource allocation formula as would apply to it had it remained within the local authority'. Nevertheless, the Act provided for some additional funding of GMS schools.[62] They were entitled to capital grants within the government's overall limits for capital spending, and to special-purpose grants, some of which were intended to compensate for the loss of LEA training grants, while the LEA lost revenue support grant and control over the property attached to schools. Because GMS schools received an allocation to meet the costs of the support and administrative services hitherto provided by the LEA, authorities feared that their ability to provide a comprehensive service to locally maintained schools would be constrained by widespread opting out.

Because the Major government was concerned about the slow uptake of opting out, the process was further streamlined and the LEA role reduced further. The Education (Schools) Act 1992 contained provisions to make it easier for schools to opt out, while a special funding regime for this new education sector was introduced in the Education Act 1993. That Act created two new Funding Agencies for Schools - one for England and one for Wales, through which grant maintained schools would in future receive their funding. The objective of the English Agency was defined by its chief executive as

> to preserve the new environment which allows the self-governing schools to become autonomous, to be creative, to flourish and have the freedom to meet parents and pupils needs more effectively and be more accountable to them

while assisting the Secretary of State to fulfil his or her accountability to Parliament.[63]

The Agency was 'an integral part' of the grant-maintained movement, and 'the fulcrum of this balancing out between freedom and national accountability'. All of these measures struck directly at the LEAs, one-time partners in a seemingly impregnable relationship between central and local government. Some Conservatives expected LMS and the other provisions of the ERA steadily to erode the LEA role, by empowering and making more demanding the parent body, so leading to the progressive exercise of the parental right to opt out. However, far from LMS leading inexorably to opting-out ballots, the response to the new opportunity to escape from LEA control was muted, at least in comparison with the wilder aspirations. By February 1994, 928 schools had achieved GMS, with another 115 in the pipeline. The frequency of ballots on opting out, although still running at a high level, appeared to be falling relative to the previous year, while a slightly smaller proportion had voted in favour of opting out in 1994 than in the corresponding period twelve months before. In the six months to the end of May 1993, 385 schools held ballots on GMS, with parents voting in favour of opting out at 302 of them. The corresponding figures for 1994 were 176 and 104.[64] For some observers, GMS was already a 'flagship on the rocks'.[65]

In their own terms, though, grant maintained schools have been something of a success. A number of studies have demonstrated benefits, even for small primary schools, of freedom from LEA control.[66] Separate Ofsted and National Audit Office investigations into the running of the GMS schools were similarly positive.[67] Conservative ministers, then, could feel justified in their upbeat verdict on the grant maintained schools:

> With self-governing schools we are seeing an increase in morale, a greater sense of achievement, greater value for money and, above all, more popularity with parents, as will be seen [next] September when in the main those schools are again overfull.[68]

Yet if the object of opting out was to free schools in general from LEA control and enable them to achieve Grant Maintained (or self-governing) Status, the Conservative government fell a long way short of its aim. By 1996 the LEA sector remained predominant, despite continuing

292 *Into the Twilight*

government effort to find new incentives to opting out, and a longer-term commitment to permit the establishment of new privately sponsored grammar schools.

Beyond 'partnership'

The overall effect of the post-1979 Conservative governments was to bring about a fundamental shift in the balance of power between the several participants in the educational process. The LEAs were marginalized by LMS, GMS and the other components of the 1988 and 1992 Acts. Power had flowed away to governors, parents and headteachers, as well as to the Secretary of State. With parents securing places on the governing bodies of their children's schools, the change in patterns of influence was considerable.

For much of the post-war period, the role of governors had been largely ceremonial.[69] Governing bodies had, for example, little influence on what was taught in schools. They could not impose their views on a school without the support of the local authority. Although Joseph's Education Act 1980 significantly extended the powers of governing bodies, in practice they were rarely seen to have had an important role. This was changed by the Education (No. 2) Act 1986 and the Education Reform Act 1988, which together enhanced their powers, duties and responsibilities. The first of these two statutes gave governors responsibility for an element of the school budget which they could spend as they thought appropriate. It further changed the balance of governing bodies by reducing the numbers of local authority governors and increasing those of parent governors.

Under the Conservative reforms, governing bodies gained virtual control of every aspect of their schools, within the framework of the policies of the local education authority and national legislation. The 1988 Act gave governing bodies the control of the budget, and the powers to direct the spending according to their needs and priorities. Most importantly, governors gained the responsibility for the oversight of the curriculum, and could examine any curriculum draft put before them. They were also given the right to obtain an explanation from the teaching staff on any matter that they might wish to pursue. They were given powers over the appointment and dismissal of both teaching and non-teaching staff.

In parallel with their new powers, the governors were also made more accountable to parents. They were to produce and keep up to date a curriculum policy document for parents, to show how they proposed to meet the requirements of the national curriculum. They were required to present annual reports to parents, discuss with them the progress of the school, and provide explanations on matters such as sex education policy, and the ways in which the budget had been spent. As well as giving the details to parents, the governors were also required to report to the LEA about the way in which its curriculum policy was being interpreted and the delegated money used.

The 1944 Education Act required LEAs to educate children in accordance with the wishes of parents. The idea of parents as partners, however, was largely ignored for much of the post-war period. The Education Reform Act brought parents centre-stage in an attempt to 'empower' them. Parents were to be seen as consumers who would judge the performance of the school on the basis of its results, and make informed choices. Schools were required to furnish information to parents on the performance of pupils by way of assessments and by publicizing results. Parents could demand explanations if the school failed to implement any policy, and could make their approval or disapproval known to governing bodies and teachers. They could thus force schools to deliver the national curriculum and, if unsatisfied, could appeal to the Secretary of State. Parents were given a notional right to demand a place for their child in a different school. Finally, they could, if they met the ballot requirements, vote to remove a school from the control of its local authority by achieving GMS.

These developments were in addition to some of the privileges parents already enjoyed under previous legislation. For example, the 1980 Education Act required governing bodies for the first time to include parent representatives. The government argued that parents, as clients, would be better able than others to monitor standards and quality. By the very fact of their representation on the governing body, the school would become more accountable to the community. It was claimed that by including parents on governing bodies, schools would be less subject to the inefficiencies of local education authorities, and governors would be more able than the education officers to make judgements about the real needs of schools. The Education Act 1986 increased parental representation on governing bodies. Taking these together with the Education Reform Act 1988, parents were placed in the forefront of the school education system.

The Education Reform Act dispensed with many of the traditional controls of the local education authority and created, in its place, the mechanisms for new controls; on the one hand, those imposed by the formal, legal and administrative machinery, and on the other those exercised by parents and governors. The aim was to inject pluralism and diversity into the existing system, by exposing education to the free play of market forces and consumer sovereignty.

Yet there was also the steering hand of the central government, for power had flowed upwards from the LEAs as well as downwards to schools and governing bodies. There is of course a tension between more central control and more autonomy at the school level. In terms of curriculum control, the 1988 Act placed additional restrictions on schools which otherwise were left to operate in a free market. Prime Minister Margaret Thatcher and her ministers argued that it was possible to take the risks inherent in setting schools free from local authorities only if there were to be a clearly defined national curriculum and an established framework within which schools could exercise their independence. Centralization and decentralization were both required.

By 1992, local authorities had conceded a greater influence to users in the running and management of local education services. The changes enforced by the Education Reform Act were unwelcome, but were recognized as irreversible. Yet adapting to them was another matter. Apart from the rhetoric of Conservative ministers, there was no guidance on how to make sense of the new power relations in education. In 1989, the Audit Commission attempted to provide that lead in a important paper *Losing an Empire, Finding a Role: the LEA of the future*.[70] The report warned of the need to rethink the future 'against the background of a clear understanding of the new power relationships'. It emphasized the shift from monopoly provision and manager status to a pluralistic system in which the distribution of power had moved downward to schools, outward to parent groups, and upward to the Secretary of State for Education.

At the very least, these developments sidelined the local education authorities, since they looked likely to lose any meaningful role in the education service of the future. John Patten clearly identified himself with this projection. His white paper, *Choice and Diversity: a new framework for schools*, and the subsequent Education Act 1993 signalled the intention to consolidate and extend the reforms of the Thatcher period.[71] For Patten, all schools should become free of LEA control and attain the status of grant maintained schools (or, in the new terminology, *self-governing* schools) and to this end, the Act facilitated opting out and speeded up the process.[72] Other protagonists on the Conservative Right felt that the 1988 and 1993 Acts did not go far enough; for them, the abolition of the Inner London Education Authority should have been taken as a dummy run for the abolition of all LEAs.[73] So drastic a step was unnecessary; the LEA of Attlee's time was not that of Major's. The local government of education had come a long way since 1945, when the local education authorities had a near monopoly of school and college provision, and when education was the most important of all local services. Now, grant maintained schools and local education authority maintained schools, as well as independent and public schools, were to compete for custom. Local government was no longer a partner, but now a mere player. Its future survival as a meaningful player in local education would depend upon the LEAs' ability to grasp and fulfil that new role.

Notes

1 M. Thatcher, *The Downing Street Years* (HarperCollins, London, 1993), p. 599.
2 Thatcher, *Downing Street Years*, p. 606.
3 P. Malpass, 'Housing policy and the disabling of local authorities', in *Housing Policy in the 1990s*, ed. J. Birchall (Routledge, London, 1992), pp. 10–28.
4 Department of the Environment, *Housing: the government's proposals*, Cm. 214 (HMSO, London, 1987), para. 5.1.
5 'Local government bill: last major legislation', *Municipal Review*, April 1989, p. 9.
6 N. Ridley, *'My Style of Government': the Thatcher years* (Hutchinson, London, 1991), pp. 86–92.
7 *Social Trends*, 22 (1992), p. 147.
8 A. Murie and R. Forrest, *An Unreasonable Act?* (University of Bristol School for Advanced Urban Studies, Bristol, 1985); A. Murie and P. Malpass, *Housing Policy: theory and practice* (Macmillan, London, 1987), pp. 233–4
9 J. Doling, 'British housing policy: 1984–1993', *Regional Studies*, 27(6) (1993), p. 583.
10 N. J. Williams and F. E. Twine, 'Increasing access or widening choice: the role of re-sold public sector dwellings in the housing market', *Environment and Planning*, 24(11) (1992), pp. 1585–98.
11 S. Cooper, *Public Housing and Private Property, 1970–1984* (Gower, Aldershot, 1985), p. 137.

12   See P. Willmott and A. Murie, *Polarisation and Social Housing* (Policy Studies Institute, London, 1988).
13   Audit Commission, *Managing the Crisis in Council Housing* (HMSO, London, 1986).
14   T. Brindley and G. Stoker, 'Housing renewal policy in the 1980s: the scope and limitations of privatisation', *Local Government Studies*, 14(3) (1988), p. 53.
15   Doling, 'British housing policy', p. 585.
16   Thatcher, *Downing Street Years*, p. 600.
17   C. M. E. Whitehead and M. P. Kleinman, *Private Rented Housing in the 1980s and 1990s* (Granta Editions for the University of Cambridge, Department of Land Economy, Cambridge, 1986); Willmott and Murie, *Polarisation and Social Housing*, pp. 84–5; I. Rauta and A. Pickering, *Private Renting in England 1990* (HMSO, London, 1992).
18   B. Randolph, 'The re-privatisation of housing associations', in *Implementing Housing Policy*, ed. P. Malpass and R. Means (Open University Press, Buckingham, 1993), pp. 39–58.
19   *Housing: the government's proposals*, para. 1.4.
20   *Housing: the government's proposals*, para. 1.3.
21   *Housing: the government's proposals*, para. 1.16.
22   London Research Centre, *Housing in Kensington and Chelsea: living in the Royal Borough* (LRC, London, 1988); London Research Centre, *London Housing Survey 1986–87: full report of results* (LRC, London, 1989).
23   Department of the Environment and Welsh Office, *Our Future Homes* (HMSO, London, 1995), p. 30.
24   See also S. Randall, F. Birch and R. Pugh, *Large Scale Voluntary Transfer of Housing: key legal and practical issues* (Lawrence Graham, London, 1992).
25   D. Mullins, P. Niner and M. Riseborough, *Evaluating Large Scale Voluntary Transfers of Local Authority Housing: an interim report* (HMSO, London, 1992).
26   'Tenants pushed into transfers, says TPAS', *Housing Associations Weekly*, 5 May 1989, p. 3.
27   D. Mullins, P. Niner and M. Riseborough, 'Large-scale voluntary transfers', in Malpass and Means, *Implementing Housing Policy*, p. 169.
28   Department of the Environment, *Local Authority Housing in England: voluntary transfers consultation paper* (HMSO, London, 1992), para. 3.
29   Department of the Environment, *Voluntary Transfers*, para. 13.
30   The Housing Act 1996 repealed the 1988 Tenants' Choice reforms.
31   Department of the Environment, *Housing: the government's proposals*, para. 5.3.
32   V. Karn, 'Remodelling a HAT', in Malpass and Means, *Implementing Housing*

Policy, pp. 74–90.
33 Department of the Environment/Welsh Office, *A New Financial Regime for Local Authority Housing in England and Wales: a consultation paper*, Welsh Office, 27 July 1988.
34 *Housing: the government's proposals*, para. 5.7.
35 'Paying for council housing', *Inside Housing*, 10(1) (1993), pp. 10–11.
36 Department of the Environment, *New Financial Regime*, p. 7.
37 'Making tenants foot the bill', *Roof*, September/October, 1988.
38 V. Bogdanor, 'Power and participation', *Oxford Review of Education*, 5(2) (1979), pp. 157–68.
39 S. Maclure, 'Forty years on', *British Journal of Education Studies*, 33(2) (1985), pp. 117–34.
40 S. Maclure, 'The endless agenda: matters arising', *Oxford Review of Education*, 5(2) (1979), pp. 111–27; L. Bash and D. Coulby, *The Education Reform Act: competition and control* (Cassell, London, 1989).
41 D. Lawton, *The Tory Mind on Education, 1979–94* (Falmer Press, Lewes, 1994), pp. 33–50; C. Knight, *The Making of Tory Education Policy in Britain, 1950–86* (Falmer Press, Lewes, 1990).
42 Hillgate Group, *Whose Schools? A Radical Manifesto* (The Hillgate Group, London, 1986); S. Sexton, *Our Schools – a Radical Policy* (Institute of Economic Affairs Education Unit, London, 1987).
43 R. Morris, '1944 to 1988', in *Central and Local Control of Education After the Education Reform Act, 1988*, ed. R. Morris (Longman, Harlow, 1990), pp. 9–14.
44 Adam Smith Institute, *The Omega File on Education* (The Institute, London, 1984).
45 S. Sexton, *Our Schools*, pp. 8–9.
46 See HM Inspectorate, *Good Teachers – Education Observed* (DES, London, 1985), p. 13; Department of Education and Science, *Parental Influence at Schools* (HMSO, London, 1984); Department of Education and Science, *Better Schools* (HMSO, London, 1985).
47 Department of Education and Science, *Teaching Quality* (HMSO, London, 1983); Education (Grants and Awards) Act 1984.
48 Knight, *The Making of Tory Education Policy*.
49 A phrase used in a Conservative Research Department briefing paper quoted in Lawton, *The Tory Mind on Education*, p. 91.
50 K. Baker, *The Turbulent Years: my life in politics* (Faber, London, 1993), p. 164.
51 S. Maclure, *Education Re-formed: a guide to the Education Reform Act 1988* (Hodder and Stoughton, London, 1988).
52 B. Davies and L. Ellison, 'Delegated school finance in the English education

system: an era of radical change', *Journal of Educational Administration*, 30(1) (1992), pp. 70–80.
53 L. E. Sackney and D. J. Dibski, 'School-based management: a critical perspective', *Educational Management and Administration*, 22(2) (1994), pp. 104–12; Y. C. Cheng, 'The theory and characteristics of school-based management', *International Journal of Educational Management*, 7(6) (1993), pp. 6–17; P. Sleegers and A. Wesselingh, 'Decentralisation in education: a Dutch study', *International Studies in the Sociology of Education*, 3(1) (1993), pp. 49–67; P. C. Cline and P. T. Graham, 'School-based management: an emerging approach to the administration of America's schools', *Local Government Studies*, 17(4) (1991), pp. 43–50.
54 K. Maychell, *Counting the Cost: the impact of LMS on schools' patterns of spending* (NFER, Slough, 1994).
55 R. Dixon, 'Local management of schools', *Public Money and Management*, 11(3) (1991), pp. 47–52.
56 G. Thomas, 'Setting up LMS', *Educational Management and Administration*, 19(2) (1991), pp. 84–8; R. Dixon, 'Repercussions of LMS', *Educational Management and Administration*, 19(1) (1991), pp. 52–61.
57 Department for Education, *Local Management of Schools*, Circular 2/94, para. 226.
58 T. Lee, *Carving Out the Cash for Schools: LMS and the new era of education*, Social Policy Paper No. 17 (University of Bath, Centre for the Analysis of Social Policy, Bath, November 1990).
59 H. Thomas and A. Bullock, 'School size and local management funding formulae', *Educational Management and Administration*, 20(1) (1992), pp. 30–8; R. Levacic, 'Local management of schools: aims, scope and impact', *Educational Management and Administration*, 20(1) (1992), pp. 16–29.
60 Others argued that that the very principle of opting out fatally undermined local authorities' ability to manage the local school system. See D. Halpin, J. Fitz and S. Power, *The Early Impact and Long-term Implications of the Grant-maintained School Policy* (University of Warwick, Department of Education, Coventry, March 1992); 'Local education authorities and the grant-maintained schools policy', *Educational Management and Administration*, 19(4) (1991), pp. 233–42.
61 R. Morris, *Choice of School: a survey, 1992–93* (Association of Metropolitan Authorities, London, 1993).
62 D. Halpin, S. Power and J. Fitz, 'Opting into state control? Headteachers and the paradoxes of grant-maintained status', *International Studies in the Sociology of Education*, 3(1) (1993), pp. 3–23.
63 H. Johnson and K. Riley, 'The impact of quangos and new government agencies on education', in *The Quango Debate*, ed. F. F. Ridley and D. Wilson

(Oxford University Press, Oxford, 1995), pp. 106–18.
64 House of Commons, *Debates*, Vol. 244, Col. 506.
65 M. Rogers, 'Opting out: a flagship on the rocks?', *Local Government Policy Making*, 19(5) (1993), pp. 35–9.
66 T. Bush, M. Coleman and D. Glover, 'Managing grant maintained primary schools', *Educational Management and Administration*, 21(2) (1993), pp. 69–78; T. Bush, M. Coleman and D. Glover, *Managing Autonomous Schools: the grant-maintained experience* (Paul Chapman, London, 1993).
67 Office for Standards in Education, *Grant Maintained Schools, 1989–92* (HMSO, London, 1993); National Audit Office, *Value for Money at Grant-Maintained Schools. a review of performance* (HMSO, London, 1994).
68 Department for Education Minister Robin Squire, MP, House of Commons *Debates*, 14 June 1994, Col. 506.
69 M. Kogan, D. Johnson, T. Packwood and T. Whitaker, *School Governing Bodies* (Heinemann, London, 1984).
70 Audit Commission, *Losing an Empire, Finding a Role: the LEA of the future*, Occasional Paper No. 10 (The Commission, London, December 1989).
71 R. Morris, E. Reid and J. Fowler, *The Education Act, 1993: a critical guide* (Association of Metropolitan Authorities, London, 1993).
72 P. Meredith, 'The Education Act, 1993: further development of the grant maintained schools system', *Education and the Law*, 6(3) (1994), pp. 125-31.
73 S. Lawlor, *Away with LEAs: ILEA abolition as a pilot* (Centre for Policy Studies, London, 1988).

10 Conclusion

Local government in 1995 was in a profoundly different condition to that which it had enjoyed fifty years earlier. The chapters of this book trace its transformation, from the status of respected partner to that of tolerated agent, on perpetual probation. In the past fifteen years or so, local government has at times been seen as no more than a residual and scarcely tolerated encumbrance to the political constitution. We have sought to show how, when and why this transformation came about. It is, at root, a story of changing expectations of what local government was there for, of what it could do. The record is one of shifting judgements about its fitness for whatever purpose it was supposed to serve. And the later years see the common ground shrinking, and a new polarization of views emerging.

Consensus and After

The wartime coalition's lasting achievement was the making of the postwar consensus. That consensus outlasted its architects and provided a secure foundation for local government growth during the next two decades. With reconstruction the overriding priority for all parties, the problem of local government was to ensure that it was able to deliver sustained growth in service provision. On the test of fitness for purpose – something proposed by the 1945 white paper – local authorities were judged adequate to these new tasks in most areas.

At the time, this was a remarkable affirmation of local government's role. Power had been centralized as never before during the period of total war. It would have been easy enough, on the face of it, to have by-passed the local authorities when re-making the post-war world. What is remarkable is that so few voices were raised in favour of doing so. The alternative, of perpetuating a regional structure of central government supervision, was ruled out of court, not just because of the hostility of the local authorities. With a long war against authoritarianism won at last, at so great a cost, this was no time to adopt the measures of the dictators.

So the future seemed secure. True, the New Towns were to be built by special-purpose agencies, direct prototypes of the urban development corporations that would displace local authorities from urban renewal in the 1980s. Most of the health service would be nationalized, taking local hospitals into state, and out of local, control (although even here some Conservatives fought a vigorous rearguard action in favour of the local authorities). Gas and electricity were foreseeable casualties of the new spirit of national efficiency. Overall, the balance sheet was positive. Important new responsibilities in town and country planning gave the local authorities a truly strategic role for the first time. The fire service was returned to local government, so honouring a wartime promise. The creation of a childrens' service foreshadowed that distinctive post-war development, the development of professionalized social welfare services for family support. The Education Act of 1944 widened the duties of LEAs and made them responsible for developing new patterns of secondary education. Local government, it seemed, was a fit partner of the centre in this new era of growth.

Yet the spirit of partnership came under increasing strain in the second half of our period. Increasingly, ministers became instrumental in their approach to local authorities. In 1964 the Wilson government made a sharp break from the past with its commitment to comprehensive schools, and the Heath government subsequently made another with its reforms of housing finance. The so-called 'ratchet effect' of central control began to appear. Powers seized by one government were exploited by the next.

The re-election of the Conservatives in 1979 began a new phase, one of radical change in the role of local authorities as service providers, and in their relationship with central government. Yet it would be a mistake to imagine that the post-war history of local government in Britain can be divided into two contrasting periods: before and after the advent of Mrs Thatcher. Rather, the half-century was one of episodic change – at times faster, at times slower – bearing yesterday upon one aspect of local government, bearing today upon another. This kaleidoscope of power can be seen in a brief recapitulation of the four organizing themes in this book: structure, finance, housing and education.

Structure

Was local government in fact 'fit for purpose' in 1945? Despite their rejection of regional direction, coalition ministers drew back from the wholesale reorganization of local government only because they feared it would disrupt and delay the reconstruction drive. The establishment of the Local Government Boundary Commission in 1945 signalled acceptance of the need for some further adjustment. But within two years the case for radical change was back on the table, although neither the short-lived Commission nor the squabbling Labour Cabinet would succeed in bringing it about.

The Conservatives inherited the enduring conflict between counties and county boroughs, edging the local authority associations towards accepting change. Their Local Government Commission appeared after a long gestation period, only to disappoint. The climate had already changed, and with 'modernism' gathering force, cumbersome procedures already looked dated. Labour quickly got rid of it, appointing instead the Royal Commission which many had advocated during the war itself. The Redcliffe-Maud report, and the further thoughts of the Heath government, were intended to finally bury 'the county borough problem'. But the free-standing towns were reluctant to lose their identity and, from the late 1970s to the mid-1990s, governments of both parties resurrected them. Labour flirted with the unitary principle – the Conservatives pursued it piecemeal. Comprehensive reform was again out of fashion. If there were any conclusions to be drawn from this fifty-year saga, they passed unnoticed, for by 1995 few believed that local government structure mattered very much.

Finance

The condition of local government developing as the single most important instrument of the Welfare State was the acceptance of an elaborate system of financial incentives and controls. These shifted the balance of expenditure on local services towards central grant, and enhanced the powers of Whitehall. Gradually, central government came to regard all local activities of financial significance as its concern. The expenditure, taxation and borrowing of local authorities came to be seen as matters for ministers, who increasingly sought to control them in the national economic interest.

Not that party political interest was an insignificant factor. Rates were increasingly unpopular. As local authority expenditure climbed steadily in the 1950s and 1960s, governments sought to cushion their impact upon households. But protection for the electorally volatile householder was achieved at the expense of industry and the national taxpayer. After 1974, both major parties became increasingly uneasy about paying for growth. Some began to see that shifting the burden from the ratepayer to the taxpayer actually exacerbated the underlying problem, weakening the link between those (locally) who advocated spending, and those (nationally) who would increasingly foot the bill.

Paradoxically, each attempt to control local expenditure drew central government still deeper into local finance, and weakened still further that fragile link of financial accountability to the local electorate. The ill-fated poll tax was intended to re-establish a direct link between voting for, and paying for, local services. Rashly introduced in a single bound, abandoned in a failure of nerve, it was the most contentious, and the shortest-lived, of all the post-war reforms in local government. The political and financial costs of restoring stability after 1992 were heavy.

Housing

Wartime bomb damage and dislocation had placed housing at the top of the post-war agenda. In the short term at least, local authorities would deliver the housing programme, with central subsidies as the principal means of encouraging them to build. For the first time, the major parties competed nationally on the basis of how many homes they could inveigle the local authorities into building.

It did not last. Before long, Conservatives started to reckon private house completions, and not just those achieved by local authorities, in the total housing achievement. In boom times, and without licensing restrictions, the market could deliver more, and faster, than the local authorities themselves. By the late 1950s, Conservatives were beginning to see the extent of the local authorities' role as an obstacle to meeting Britain's housing needs. Labour increasingly became the party of large-scale public building and low-rent municipal landlordism; and the Conservatives the party of the 'property owning democracy'. So foundered the initial consensus on post-war housing. Pursuing these competing visions, successive governments tightened the grip of Whitehall upon the local housing authorities.

Events favoured the Conservatives. Although Labour came to power in 1964 with a commitment to build 500,000 houses a year by 1970, they abandoned their target in the aftershock of devaluation. The Conservatives filled the vacuum, their attack on municipal housing bringing a new bitterness to central–local government relations. Despite the Labour interregnum of 1974–9, the steam had gone out of local authority housing, and councils were not to regain their role as large-scale providers. After 1979 it became clear that there would be no turning back. The private rented sector was progressively deregulated, and council homes disposed of to tenants, housing associations and other landlords. In terms of who provided the people's homes, Britain in 1995 was not the same country as 50 years before. Local authorities, initially so central to making the new Britain, had all but passed away as housing providers.

Education

If the main changes in housing concerned the shifting balance between the sectors, there was little reflection of this in education policy. Not until the late 1980s was the role of the local authorities in education seriously questioned. Until then, the education argument between central and local government pivoted on what type of education should be provided, and under what conditions – not by whom. Initially, even this argument was muted. The tripartite system expressed a pre-war expert orthodoxy. It soon became the post-war popular consensus. That consensus gradually dissolved. The system of grammar, technical and modern schools was founded on selection and, as Britain's middle class grew, selection became a subject of bitter disputes.

Disputes about policy inescapably became disputes between central and local government. The 1944 Act gave new and, for the time, sweeping powers to the Minister of Education to compel recalcitrant local authorities to fall into line. Within twenty years that power and influence were put to the test. Most LEAs developed their school systems on tripartite lines, recognizing that government policy and educational opinion at the time favoured selection, and accepted separate schools. Circular 10/65 changed all that.

Comprehensive education was at first resisted by many local authorities. Although their approaches did begin to change, the Conservatives were soon back in power, and could only marginally slow the growing momentum of the comprehensive movement. Thus, in one way or another, central government found itself locked in conflict with a minority of LEAs over a period of fifteen years. By the time the dust settled, a new and more fundamental critique had gained ground. The comprehensive struggle had taken place within a shared assumption that the great majority of education would be provided in schools controlled by LEAs. The emerging debate on educational standards challenged the continuance of the LEAs' role. Power would be devolved to schools themselves and – notionally at least – to parents. Schools were encouraged to break free of LEA control altogether. By the final year of the 1992–7 Parliament, the Major government had scheduled local education authorities to wither away.

The Future

Writing at the beginning of a new Parliament, and perhaps of an era, it is tempting to speculate about the future of local government. The readers of this book will see the value of caution. Several post-war British governments harboured ambitions for local government, but the outcomes of their intervention rarely matched up to the rhetoric. Even today, commentators – and they are many – like to forecast a coming renaissance of local democracy. We would be unwise to believe them. Local government in Britain has been treated throughout the post-war period as an instrument of central purposes. Councillors and officers were happy to go along with this, as implementing national policy meant growing budgets, staff and prestige. When expansion ended, the cutbacks that followed hurt badly. Redefining the place of local government in the political constitution was all the more painful.

The contrast between the history of local government in Britain and that elsewhere in Europe, North America and Australasia often attracts unfavourable comment. Paradoxically, though, British local authorities appear in some ways stronger than their foreign counterparts. They are generally much larger, in terms of population size and expenditure. But that apparent strength is at the same time a manifestation of weakness. The growing importance of their role as local deliverers of national services obscured the consequence, that they thereby became less the partners than the agents of the centre. Mergers and restructuring into fewer larger units also had to be accepted as the price of that functional growth. Looking upwards to Whitehall, rather than downwards to the people, local authorities lost their popular base. Research evidence suggests that today's local authorities are less widely trusted, respected, or thought important than was the case thirty years ago. The extent to which their areas reflect a sense of local attachment was diminished by the same restructuring that created the larger, notionally 'stronger' units of administration.

However weakened by these post-war developments, local government remains a fixture in the political landscape. 'A poor thing but mine own' was Harold Macmillan's wry judgement in 1954. His comment is the more apt today. Local government in the twenty-first century will continue to change and adapt, but the limits are more sharply drawn than before. True, it never did enjoy a golden age. But 1945 had been a time of hope and expectation. Therein lies the most telling contrast.

Bibliography

Abrams, P., 'The failure of social reform, 1918–1920', *Past and Present*, April 1963, pp. 43–64.

Adam Smith Institute, *The Omega File* (The Institute, London, 1985).

Addison, P., *Now the War is Over* (Jonathan Cape, London, 1985).

Addison, P., *The Road to 1945* (Jonathan Cape, London, 1975).

Alexander, A., *Local Government in Britain Since Re-organisation* (George Allen & Unwin, London, 1982).

Alexander, A., *The Politics of Local Government in the United Kingdom* (Longman, London, 1982).

Annan, N., *Our Age: portrait of a generation* (Weidenfeld and Nicolson, London, 1990).

Ascher, K., *The Politics of Privatisation: contracting out public services* (Macmillan, Basingstoke, 1987).

Association of District Councils, *Closer to the People: a policy for future local government structure, functions and finance* (The Association, London, 1987).

Audit Commission, *Losing an Empire, Finding a Role: the LEA of the future*, Occasional Paper No. 10 (The Commission, London, December 1989).

Audit Commission, *Managing the Crisis in Council Housing* (HMSO, London, 1986).

Audit Commission, *Realising the Benefits of Competition* (HMSO, London, 1993).

Audit Commission, *Securing Further Improvements in Refuse Collection: a review by the Audit Commission* (HMSO, London, 1984).

Audit Commission, *The Impact on Local Authorities' Economy, Efficiency and Effectiveness of the Block Grant Distribution System* (HMSO, London, 1984).

Audit Commission, 'We can't go on meeting like this: the changing role of local authority members', Management Papers, No. 8, September 1990.

Baker, K., *The Turbulent Years: my life in politics* (Faber, London, 1993).

Barker, R., *Education and Politics, 1900–1951: a study of the Labour party* (Oxford University Press, Oxford, 1972).

Barnett, C., *The Audit of War* (Macmillan, London, 1986).
Barnett, C., *The Lost Victory: British dreams, British realities, 1945–50* (Macmillan, London, 1995).
Bash, L. and Coulby, D., *The Education Reform Act: competition and control* (Cassell, London, 1989).
Benn, C., *Comprehensive or Coexistence – We Must Choose Which We Want* (National Union of Teachers, London, 1976).
Benn, C. and Simon, B., *Half-way There: the British comprehensive school reform* (McGraw-Hill, London, 1970).
Bennett, R. J., *Central Grants to Local Government: the political and economic impact of the Rate Support Grant in England* (Cambridge University Press, Cambridge, 1982).
Block, G., *Rating Revaluation*, Local Government Series No. 8 (Conservative Political Centre, London, 1963).
BMRB Ltd, *CCT: the private sector view* (Department of the Environment, London, 1995).
Board of Education, *Educational Reconstruction*, Cmd. 6458 (HMSO, London, 1943).
Board of Education, *Report of the Committee of the Secondary Schools Examination Council, Curriculum and Examinations in Secondary Schools* (HMSO, London, 1943).
Bogdanor, V., 'Power and participation', *Oxford Review of Education*, 5(2) (1979), pp. 157–68.
Boyson, R., *Case for Comprehensive Schooling: 'Not Proven'* (National Education Association, Barnet, Herts, 1970).
Brindley, T. and Stoker, G., 'Housing renewal policy in the 1980s: the scope and limitations of privatisation', *Local Government Studies*, 14(3) (1988), pp. 45–67.
Bush, T., Coleman, M. and Glover, D., *Managing Autonomous Schools: the grant-maintained experience* (Paul Chapman, London, 1993).
Bush, T., Coleman, M. and Glover, D., 'Managing grant maintained primary schools', *Educational Management and Administration*, 21(2) (1993), pp. 69–78.
Butler, D., Adonis, A. and Travers, T., *Failure in British Government: the politics of the poll tax* (Oxford University Press, Oxford, 1994).
Calder, A., *The People's War: Britain 1939–1945* (Jonathan Cape, London, 1969).
Campbell, J., *Aneurin Bevan and the Mirage of British Socialism* (Weidenfeld and Nicolson, London, 1987).
Cheng, Y. C., 'The theory and characteristics of school-based management', *International Journal of Educational Management*, 7(6) (1993), pp. 6–17.
Chester, D. N., *Central and Local Government: financial and administrative relations* (Macmillan, London, 1951).

Chester, D. N., 'Local democracy and the internal organisation of local authorities', *Public Administration*, 46(2) (1968), pp. 287–98.
Cline, P. C. and Graham, P. T., 'School-based management: an emerging approach to the administration of America's schools', *Local Government Studies*, 17(4) (1991), pp. 43–50.
Committee of Inquiry into the Conduct of Local Authority Business, *Report of the Committee* (HMSO, London, 1986).
Cooper, S., *Public Housing and Private Property, 1970–1984* (Gower, Aldershot, 1985).
Cox, C. R. and Dyson, A. E., *The Black Papers on Education* (DavisPoynter, London, 1971).
Crick, A. and van Klaveren, A., 'Poll tax: Mrs Thatcher's greatest blunder', *Contemporary Record*, 5(3) (1991), pp. 397–416.
Crosland, A., *The Future of Socialism* (Jonathan Cape, London, 1956).
Crossman, R., *The Diaries of a Cabinet Minister* (Hamish Hamilton/Jonathan Cape, London, 1975), vol. I: *Minister of Housing and Local Government*.
Cullingworth, J. B., *Essays on Housing Policy* (George Allen & Unwin, London, 1979).
Cullingworth, J. B., *Housing Needs and Planning Policy* (Routledge and Kegan Paul, London, 1960).
Cullingworth, J. B., *Reconstruction and Land-use Planning, 1939–47* (HMSO, London, 1975).
Curtis, S. J., *History of Education in Great Britain*, 6th edn (University Tutorial Press, London, 1965).
Davies, B. and Ellison, L., 'Delegated school finance in the English education system: an era of radical change', *Journal of Educational Administration*, 30(1) (1992), pp. 70–80.
Department of Education and Science, *Better Schools* (HMSO, London, 1985).
Department of Education and Science, *Parental Influence at Schools* (HMSO, London, 1984).
Department of Education and Science, *Teaching Quality* (HMSO, London, 1983).
Department of Local Government and Regional Planning, *Reform of Local Government in England*, Cmnd. 4276 (HMSO, London, 1970).
Department of the Environment, *A Fair Deal for Housing*, Cmnd. 4728 (HMSO, London, 1971).
Department of the Environment, *Alternatives to Domestic Rates*, Cmnd. 8449 (HMSO, London, 1981).
Department of the Environment, *Housing: the government's proposals*, Cm. 214 (HMSO, London, 1987).
Department of the Environment, *Local Authority Housing in England: voluntary transfers consultation paper* (HMSO, London, 1992).

Department of the Environment, *Local Government Finance*, Cmnd. 6813 (HMSO, London, 1977).
Department of the Environment, *Local Government in England: government proposals for reorganisation*, Cmnd. 4584 (HMSO, London, 1971).
Department of the Environment, *Local Government Review: the structure of local government in England: a consultation paper* (DoE, London, 1991).
Department of the Environment, *Organic Change in Local Government*, Cmnd. 7457 (HMSO, London, 1979).
Department of the Environment, *Paying for Local Government*, Cmnd. 9714 (HMSO, London, 1986).
Department of the Environment, *Rates*, Cmnd. 9008 (HMSO, London, 1983).
Department of the Environment, *The Future Shape of Local Government Finance*, Cmnd. 4741 (HMSO, London, 1971).
Department of the Environment and Welsh Office, *A New Financial Regime for Local Authority Housing in England and Wales: a consultation paper*, Welsh Office, 27 July 1988.
Department of the Environment and Welsh Office, *Our Future Homes* (HMSO, London, 1995).
Dixon, R., 'Local management of schools', *Public Money and Management*, 11(3) (1991), pp. 47–52.
Dixon, R., 'Repercussions of LMS', *Educational Management and Administration*, 19(1) (1991), pp. 52–61.
Doling, J., 'British housing policy: 1984–1993', *Regional Studies*, 27(6) (1993), p. 583.
Domberger, S., Meadowcroft, S. and Thompson, D., 'Competitive tendering and efficiency: the case of refuse collection', *Fiscal Studies*, 7(4) (1986), pp. 69–87.
Ernst and Young, *Analysis of Local Authority CCT Markets* (Department of the Environment, London, 1995).
Fenwick, I. G. K., *The Comprehensive School, 1944–1970: the politics of secondary school reorganisation* (Methuen, London, 1976).
Final Report of the Departmental Committee on Local Taxation, Cd. 7315 (HMSO, London, 1914).
Final Report of the Expert Committee on Compensation and Betterment, Cmd. 6383 (HMSO, London, 1942), para. 9.
Final Report of the Royal Commission on Local Taxation, 1901, Cd. 638 (HMSO, London, 1901).
Finer, H., *English Local Government*, 4th edn (Methuen, London, 1950).
First Report of the Local Government Manpower Committee, Cmnd. 7870 (HMSO, London, 1950).
Flynn, N., 'Direct labour organisations', in *Between Centre and Locality: the poli-*

tics of public policy, ed. S. Ranson, G. Jones and K. Walsh (George Allen & Unwin, London, 1985), pp. 119–34.

Flynn, N., Leach, S. and Vielba, C., *Abolition or Reform? The GLC and the Metropolitan County Councils* (George Allen & Unwin, London, 1985).

Forrest, R. and Murie, A., *Selling the Welfare State: the privatisation of public housing* (Routledge, London, 1988).

Forsyth, M., *The Case for a Poll Tax* (Conservative Political Centre, London, 1985).

Freeman, R., 'The Marshall plan for London government: a strategic role or regional solution?', *London Journal*, 5(?) (1979), pp. 160–75.

Game, C., 'Widdicombe: some considered responses', *Local Government Policy Making*, 14(3) (1987), pp. 3–28.

Game, C. and Leach, S., 'The county councillor: 1889 and 1989', in K. Young (ed.) *New Directions in County Government* (Association of County Councils, London, 1989), pp. 22–62.

Gibson, J., *The Politics and Economics of the Poll Tax: Mrs Thatcher's downfall* (EMAS, Warley, 1990).

Goodson-Wickes, C., *The New Corruption* (Centre for Policy Studies, London, 1984).

Gosden, P. H. J. H., *Education in the Second World War: a study in policy and administration* (Methuen, London, 1976).

Gyford, J., 'Local politics in the 1980s', *Politics*, 9(1) (1989), p. 26.

Halpin, D., Fitz, J. and Power, S., 'Local education authorities and the grant-maintained schools policy', *Educational Management and Administration*, 19(4) (1991), pp. 233–42.

Halpin, D., Fitz, J. and Power, S., *The Early Impact and Long-term Implications of the Grant-maintained School Policy* (University of Warwick, Department of Education, Coventry, March 1992).

Halpin, D., S. Power and J. Fitz, 'Opting into state control? Headteachers and the paradoxes of grant-maintained status', *International Studies in the Sociology of Education*, 3(1) (1993), pp. 3–23.

Hartley, K. and Huby, M., 'Contracting out policy: theory and evidence', in *Contracting Out Policy: theory and evidence in privatisation and regulation – the UK experience*, ed. J. Kay, C. Mayer and D. Thompson (Oxford, Oxford University Press, 1986).

Hawksworth, J. M., 'Some developments in local government, 1944–1948', *Public Administration*, 26(4), pp. 262–8.

Headey, B., *Housing Policy in the Developed Economy* (Croom Helm, London, 1978).

Hepworth, N. P., *The Finance of Local Government*, 7th edn (George Allen & Unwin, London, 1984).

Bibliography

Hillgate Group, *Whose Schools? A Radical Manifesto* (The Hillgate Group, London, 1986)

HM Inspectorate, *Good Teachers – Education Observed* (Department of Education and Science, London, 1985).

HM Treasury, *Public Service Management: the revolution in progress* (HMSO, London, 1989).

House of Commons Environment Committee, *Enquiry into Methods of Financing Local Government in the Context of the Government Green Paper (Cmnd. 8449)*, i–iii, House of Commons Papers 217, 1982.

Howard, A. *RAB: the life of R. A. Butler* (Jonathan Cape, London, 1987).

Institute of Public Finance, *Competitive Tendering and Efficiency: the case of refuse collection* (IPF, London, 1986).

Jackson, B. and Marsden, D., *Education and the Working Class* (Routledge and Kegan Paul, London, 1961).

James, P. H., *The Re-organisation of Secondary Education* (NFER, Windsor, 1980).

Jeffreys, K. (ed.), *Labour and the Wartime Coalition: from the diaries of James Chuter Ede, 1941–1945* (The Historians' Press, London, 1987).

Johnson, H. and Riley, K., 'The impact of quangos and new government agencies on education', in *The Quango Debate*, ed. F. F. Ridley and D. Wilson (Oxford University Press, Oxford, 1995), pp. 106–18.

Johnson, P. B., *Land Fit for Heroes: the planning of British reconstruction, 1916–1919* (University of Chicago Press, Chicago, 1968).

Jones, G. W., 'The Local Government Act 1972 and the Redcliffe-Maud Commission', *Political Quarterly*, 44(2) (1973), pp. 154–66.

Jones, G. W., 'The Local Government Commission and county borough extensions', *Public Administration*, 41(2) (1963), pp. 173–87.

Judge, H., 'After the comprehensive revolution: What sort of secondary schools?', *Oxford Review of Education*, 5(2) (1979), pp. 137–45.

Karn, V., 'Remodelling a HAT', in *Implementing Housing Policy*, ed. P. Malpass and R. Means (Open University Press, Buckingham, 1993), pp. 74–90.

Keith-Lucas, B., *Mayor, Aldermen and Councillors*, Unservile State Papers, No. 3 (Liberal Publications Department, London, 1961).

Keith-Lucas, B., 'Three white papers on local government', *Political Quarterly*, 28(4) (1957), p. 333.

Keith-Lucas, B. and Richards, P. G., *A History of Local Government in the Twentieth Century* (George Allen & Unwin, London, 1978).

Knight, C., *The Making of Tory Education Policy in Britain, 1950–86* (Falmer Press, Lewes, 1990).

Kogan, M., *Educational Policy-making* (George Allen & Unwin, London, 1975).

Kogan, M., Johnson, D., Packwood, T. and Whitaker, T., *School Governing Bodies* (Heinemann, London, 1984).

Labour Party Regional and Local Government Advisory Committee, 'Local government reform in England and the white paper', March 1970.
Land, A., Lowe, R. and Whiteside, N., *The Development of the Welfare State, 1939–1951* (HMSO, London, 1992).
Lansley, S., Goss, S. and Wolmar, C., *Councils in Conflict: the rise and fall of the municipal Left* (Macmillan, Basingstoke, 1989).
Lapping, B., *The Labour Government, 1964–70* (Penguin, Harmondsworth, 1970).
Lawlor, S., *Away with LEAs: ILEA abolition as a pilot* (Centre for Policy Studies, London, 1988).
Lawson, N., *The View from Number 11* (Corgi, London, 1993).
Lawton, D., *The Tory Mind on Education, 1979–94* (Falmer Press, Lewes, 1994).
Leach, S., 'Strengthening local democracy? The government's response to Widdicombe', in J. Stewart and G. Stoker (eds), *The Future of Local Government* (Macmillan, Basingstoke, 1989), pp. 101–22.
Leach, S., 'The local government review: a critical appraisal', *Public Money and Management*, January–March 1994, pp. 11–16.
Lee, J. M., *The Churchill Coalition, 1940–1945* (Archon Books, Hamden, Connecticut, 1980).
Lee, T., *Carving Out the Cash for Schools: LMS and the new era of education*, Social Policy Paper No. 17 (University of Bath, Centre for the Analysis of Social Policy, Bath, November 1990).
Lees, D. S. et al., *Local Expenditure and Exchequer Grants* (Institute of Municipal Treasurers and Accountants, London, 1956).
Letwin, S. R., *The Anatomy of Thatcherism* (Fontana, London, 1992).
Levacic, R., 'Local management of schools: aims, scope and impact', *Educational Management and Administration*, 20(1) (1992), pp. 16–29.
Lipman, V. D., *Local Government Areas, 1837–1945* (Blackwell, Oxford, 1949).
Lipman, V. D., 'The development of areas and boundary changes, 1888–1939', in *Essays on Local Government*, ed. C. H. Wilson (Blackwell, Oxford, 1945), pp. 25–66.
Local Government Boundary Commission, *Report for the Year 1948* (HMSO, London, 1949).
Local Government Commission for England, *Final Recommendations on the Future Local Government of: Basildon and Thurrock; Blackburn and Blackpool; Broxtowe, Gedling and Rushcliffe; Dartford, and Gravesham, Gillingham and Rochester upon Medway; Exeter; Gloucester; Halton and Warrington; Huntingdonshire and Peterborough; Northampton; Norwich; Spelthorne; The Wrekin* (HMSO, London, December 1995).
Lofts, D., 'The future pattern of local government in England and Wales', *Public Administration*, 37(3) (1959), pp. 275–92.

London Research Centre, *Housing in Kensington and Chelsea: living in the Royal Borough* (LRC, London, 1988).
London Research Centre, *London Housing Survey 1986–87: full report of results* (LRC, London, 1989).
Loughlin, M., *Local Government in the Modern State* (Sweet and Maxwell, London, 1986).
Lowe, R., *The Welfare State in Britain since 1945* (Macmillan, Basingstoke, 1993).
Lythgoe, Sir J., *Local Government Reform: a Warburton Lecture delivered in the University of Manchester on 24th April 1952*.
Macey, J. P., 'Housing policy and its implications, with particular reference to economic rents', paper to the Public Works and Municipal Services Congress, 16 November 1966.
Maclure, S., *Education Re-formed: a guide to the Education Reform Act 1988* (Hodder and Stoughton, London, 1988).
Maclure, S., 'Forty years on', *British Journal of Education Studies*, 33(2) (1985), pp. 117–34.
Maclure, S., 'The endless agenda: matters arising', *Oxford Review of Education*, 5(2) (1979), pp. 111–27.
Macmillan, H., *The Tides of Fortune* (Macmillan, London, 1968).
Maddick, H., 'Local government: reorganisation or reform?', *Political Quarterly*, 25(3) (1954), pp. 246–57.
Malpass, P., 'Housing policy and the disabling of local authorities', in *Housing Policy in the 1990s*, ed. J. Birchall (Routledge, London, 1992), pp. 10–28.
Marshall, Sir F., *The Marshall Inquiry on Greater London: report to the Greater London Council, Sir Frank Marshall, MA, LLB* (GLC, London, 1988).
Maud, J. and Finer, S. E., *Local Government in England and Wales* (Oxford University Press, Oxford, 1953).
Maychell, K., *Counting the Cost: the impact of LMS on schools' patterns of spending* (NFER, Slough, 1994).
McAllister, G. and E. G., *Homes, Towns and Countryside: a practical plan for Britain* (Batsford, London, 1945).
McIntosh, M., 'The report of the Royal Commission on Local Government in Greater London', *British Journal of Sociology*, 12 (1961), pp. 236–48.
Meredith, P., 'The Education Act, 1993: further development of the grant maintained schools system', *Education and the Law*, 6(3) (1994), pp. 125–31.
Midwinter, A. and Mair, C., *Rates Reform: issues, arguments and evidence* (Mainstream Publishing, Edinburgh, 1987).
Ministry of Health, *Local Government in England and Wales During the Period of Reconstruction*, Cmd. 6579 (HMSO, London, 1945).
Ministry of Housing and Local Government, *Local Government: areas and status of local authorities in England and Wales*, Cmd. 9831 (HMSO, London, 1956).

Ministry of Housing and Local Government, *Local Government Finance (England and Wales)*, Cmnd. 209 (HMSO, London, 1957).

Ministry of Housing and Local Government, *Local Government: functions of county councils and county district councils in England and Wales*, Cmnd. 161 (HMSO, London, 1957).

Ministry of Housing and Local Government, *The Housing Programme, 1965-70*, Cmnd. 2838 (HMSO, London, 1965).

Ministry of Town and Country Planning, *The Control of Land Use*, Cmd. 6537 (HMSO, London, 1944).

Minogue, M., *Documents in Contemporary British Government*, vol. 2 (Cambridge University Press, Cambridge, 1977).

Morgan, K. O., *Labour in Power, 1945-51* (Oxford University Press, Oxford, 1984).

Morris, J. H., *Local Government Areas* (Shaw and Sons, London, 1960).

Morris, R. (ed.), *Central and Local Control of Education After the Education Reform Act, 1988* (Longman, Harlow, 1990).

Morris, R., *Choice of School: a survey, 1992-93* (Association of Metropolitan Authorities, London, 1993).

Morris, R., Reid, E. and Fowler, J., *The Education Act, 1993: a critical guide* (Association of Metropolitan Authorities, London, 1993).

Mullins, D., Niner, P. and Riseborough, M., *Evaluating Large Scale Voluntary Transfers of Local Authority Housing: an interim report* (HMSO, London, 1992).

Mullins, D., Niner, P. and Riseborough, M., 'Large-scale voluntary transfers', in *Implementing Housing Policy*, ed. P. Malpass and R. Means (Open University Press, Buckingham, 1993), pp. 169-84.

Murie, A. and Forrest, R., *An Unreasonable Act?* (University of Bristol School for Advanced Urban Studies, Bristol, 1985).

Murie, A. and Malpass, P., *Housing Policy: theory and practice* (Macmillan, London, 1987).

National Audit Office, *Value for Money at Grant-maintained Schools: a review of performance* (HMSO, London, 1994).

Nettl, P., 'Consensus or elite domination: the case of business', *Political Studies*, 13(1) (1965), pp. 22-44.

Office for Standards in Education, *Grant Maintained Schools, 1989-92* (HMSO, London, 1993).

Paddon, M., 'Management buy-outs and compulsory competition in local government', *Local Government Studies*, 17(3) (1991), pp. 27-52.

Page, Sir H., *Local Authority Borrowing: past, present and future* (George Allen & Unwin, London, 1985).

Pimlott, B., *Hugh Dalton* (HarperCollins, London, 1985).

Pink, M. A., *Social Reconstruction* (Nelson, London, 1943).

Price Waterhouse, *Management and Employee Buy-outs in Local Government: a brief introduction* (Price Waterhouse, London, n.d.).
Randall, S., Birch, F. and Pugh, R., *Large Scale Voluntary Transfer of Housing: key legal and practical issues* (Lawrence Graham, London, 1992).
Randolph, B., 'The re-privatisation of housing associations', in *Implementing Housing Policy*, ed. P. Malpass and R. Means (Open University Press, Buckingham, 1993), pp. 39–58.
Rao, N., *The Making and Un-making of Local Self-government* (Dartmouth, Aldershot, 1994).
Rauta, I. and Pickering, A., *Private Renting in England 1990* (HMSO, London, 1992).
Report of the Committee of Inquiry into Local Government Finance, Cmnd. 6453 (HMSO, London, 1976).
Report of the Committee of Inquiry into the Impact of Rates on Households, Cmnd. 2582 (HMSO, London, 1966).
Report of the Committee on the Working of the Monetary System, Cmnd. 827 (HMSO, London, 1959).
Report of the Royal Commission on Local Government in England, 1966-69#@#, Cmnd. 4040 (HMSO, London, 1969).
Report of the Royal Commission on Local Government in England, Volume II: memorandum of dissent by Mr Derek Senior, Cmnd. 4040-1 (HMSO, London, 1969).
Report of the Royal Commission on Local Government in Greater London, 1957–1960, Cmnd. 1164 (HMSO, London, 1960).
Report of the Royal Commission on Local Government in Scotland, Cmnd 4150 (HMSO, Edinburgh, 1969).
Report of the Royal Commission on the Distribution of the Industrial Population, Cmd. 6153 (HMSO, London, 1940).
Report of the Working Party on the Internal Management of Local Authorities in England, Community Leadership and Representation: unlocking the potential (HMSO, London, 1993).
Rhodes, G., 'Local government finance, 1918–1966', in Department of the Environment, *Local Government Finance: Appendix 6 to the report of the Committee of Inquiry under the chairmanship of Sir Frank Layfield, QC: the relationship between central and local government: evidence and commissioned work* (HMSO, London, 1976), pp. 102–73.
Rhodes, G., *The Government of London: the struggle for reform* (Weidenfeld and Nicolson, London, 1972).
Rhodes, R. A. W., *The National World of Local Government* (George Allen & Unwin, London, 1986).
Richards, P. G., *The Reformed Local Government System*, 2nd edn (George Allen & Unwin, London, 1975).

Ridley, N., *'My Style of Government': the Thatcher years* (Hutchinson, London, 1991).

Ridley, N., *The Local Right: enabling not providing* (Centre for Policy Studies, London, 1988).

Robson, W. A., *Local Government in Crisis* (George Allen & Unwin, London, 1966).

Rogers, M., 'Opting out: a flagship on the rocks?', *Local Government Policy Making*, 19(5) (1993), pp. 35–9.

Sackney, L. E. and Dibski, D. J., 'School-based management: a critical perspective', *Educational Management and Administration*, 22(2) (1994), pp. 104–12.

Saran, R., *Policy-Making in Secondary Education: a case study* (Clarendon Press, Oxford, 1973).

Schultz, M., 'The control of local authority borrowing by the central government', in *Essays on Local Government*, ed. C. H. Wilson (Blackwell, Oxford, 1945), pp. 161–203.

Schultz, M., 'The development of the grant system', in *Essays on Local Government*, ed. C. H. Wilson (Blackwell, Oxford, 1945), pp. 113–60.

Seldon, A., *Churchill's Indian Summer: the Conservative government, 1951-55* (Hodder and Stoughton, London, 1981).

Sexton, S., *Our Schools – a Radical Policy* (Institute of Economic Affairs Education Unit, London, 1987).

Sharp, Dame E., 'The future of local government', *Public Administration*, 40(winter) (1962), pp. 375–86.

Sharpe, L. J., 'Elected representatives in local government', *British Journal of Sociology*, 13 (1962), pp. 189–208.

Sharpe, L. J., '"Reforming" the grass roots: an alternative analysis', in D. Butler and A. Halsey, eds *Policy and Politics: essays in honour of Norman Chester* (Macmillan, London, 1978), pp. 82–110.

Shaw, B., *Comprehensive Schooling: the impossible dream?* (Blackwell, Oxford, 1983).

Short, J. R., *Housing in Britain: the post-war experience* (Methuen, London, 1982).

Simon, B., *Education and the Social Order 1940–1990* (Lawrence and Wishart, London, 1991).

Sklair, L., 'The struggle against the Housing Finance Act', *Socialist Register* (1975), pp. 250–92.

Sleegers, P. and Wesselingh, A., 'Decentralisation in education: a Dutch study', *International Studies in the Sociology of Education*, 3(1) (1993), pp. 49–67.

Smith, B. C. and Stanyer, J., 'Administrative developments in 1967: a survey', *Public Administration*, 46(3) (1968), pp. 239–79.

Smith, G. (ed.), *Redcliffe-Maud's Brave New England* (Charles Knight, London, 1969).

Stanyer, J., 'The local government commissions' in *Local Government in England:*

1958–69, ed. H. V. Wiseman (Routledge and Kegan Paul, London, 1970), pp. 15–35.

Stanyer, J., 'The Maud report', *Social and Economic Administration*, 1(4) (1967), pp. 3–19.

Steer, W. S. and Lofts, D., 'The Mallaby Committee', in H. V. Wiseman (ed.), *Local Government in England* (Routledge and Kegan Paul, London, 1970), pp. 71–95.

Stewart, J. D., Leach, S. and Skelcher, C., *Organic Change: a report on constitutional, management and financial problems* (Institute of Local Government Studies, Birmingham, 1978).

Szymanski, S. and Jones, T., *The Cost Savings from CCT of Refuse Collection Services* (London Business School, London, 1993).

Taylor, A. J. P., '1932–1945', in *Coalitions in British Politics*, ed. D. Butler (Macmillan, London, 1978).

Taylor, A. J. P., *The Origins of the Second World War* (Penguin, London, 1964).

Thatcher, M., *The Downing Street Years* (HarperCollins, London, 1993).

Thatcher, M., *The Path to Power* (HarperCollins, London, 1995).

Thomas, G., 'Setting up LMS', *Educational Management and Administration*, 19(2) (1991), pp. 84–8.

Thomas, H. and Bullock, A., 'School size and local management funding formulae', *Educational Management and Administration*, 20(1) (1992), pp. 30–8.

Thornhill, W. (ed.), *The Growth and Reform of English Local Government* (Weidenfeld and Nicolson, London, 1971).

Timmins, N., *The Five Giants: a biography of the welfare state* (HarperCollins, London, 1995).

Walsh, K., 'Local government', in *Contemporary Britain: an annual review, 1992*, ed. P. Catterall (Blackwell, Oxford, 1992).

Watkins, A., *A Conservative Coup: the fall of Margaret Thatcher*, 2nd edn (Duckworth, London, 1992).

Weeks, A., *Comprehensive Schools: past, present and future* (Methuen, London, 1986).

Weir, S., 'Quangos: questions of democratic accountability', in *The Quango Debate*, ed. F. F. Ridley and D. Wilson (Oxford University Press, Oxford, 1995), pp. 128–44.

Wheare, Sir K. C., *Government by Committee: an essay on the British constitution* (Clarendon Press, Oxford, 1955).

Wheatley, Sir A., in Committee on the Management of Local Government, *Report of the Committee, Volume 1*, Section A.

Whitehead, C. M. E. and Kleinman, M. P., *Private Rented Housing in the 1980s and 1990s* (Granta Editions for the University of Cambridge, Department of Land Economy, Cambridge, 1986).

Williams, A., 'Local authorities and the national economy', in *Local Government Today . . . and Tomorrow*, ed. D. Lofts, reprinted from *Municipal Journal*, (1962), pp. 38–9.

Williams, N. J. and Twine, F. E., 'Increasing access or widening choice: the role of re-sold public sector dwellings in the housing market', *Environment and Planning*, 24(11) (1992), pp. 1585–98.

Willmott, P. and Murie, A., *Polarisation and Social Housing* (Policy Studies Institute, London, 1988).

Wilson C. H. (ed.), *Essays on Local Government* (Blackwell, Oxford, 1945); see Appendix A, 'Digest of proposals made by local authority associations and others for the reform of local government published 1941–45', pp. 232–48.

Wood, B., 'Privatisation: local government and the health service', in *Waiving the Rules: the constitution under Thatcherism*, ed. C. Graham and T. Prosser (Oxford University Press, Oxford, 1988).

Wood, B., *The Process of Local Government Reform, 1966–74* (George Allen & Unwin, London, 1976).

Yates, A. and Pidgeon, D. A., *Admission to Grammar Schools: third interim report on the allocation of primary school leavers to courses of secondary education* (NFER, Slough, 1957).

Young, K., 'Orpington and the Liberal "revival"', in *By-elections in British Politics*, ed. C. Cook and J. Ramsden (UCL Press, London, forthcoming).

Young, K., 'The party and the English local government', in *Conservative Century, the Conservative Party Since 1900*, ed. A. Seldon and S. Ball (Oxford University Press, Oxford, 1994), pp. 403–43.

Young K. and Garside, P. L., *Metropolitan London: politics and urban change, 1831–1981* (Edward Arnold, London, 1982).

Young, K. and Kramer, J., *Strategy and Conflict in Metropolitan Housing* (Heinemann, London, 1978).

Young, K. and Rao, N., 'Faith in local democracy', in *British Social Attitudes, the Twelfth Report*, ed. J. Curtice, R. Jowell, L. Brooke and A. Park (Dartmouth, Aldershot, 1995).

Index

Acquired Rights Directive, 1977 (EC) 258–9
Adam Smith Institute 243
Allen committee 235, 236, 239
Allen, R. G. D. 143
Amery, Julian 165
Anderson, Sir John 10, 29
Assisted Places Scheme 172, 180, 187, 283
Association of County Councils 217
Association of Directors and Secretaries 44
Association of District Councils (ADC) 209, 213
Association of Education Committees (AEC) 44, 127
Association of London Authorities (ALA) 277
Association of Metropolitan Authorities (AMA) 277
Association of Municipal Corporations (AMC) 25, 29, 31, 102, 104, 239
Astor, David 97
Astor, Lord 18–20, 97

Attlee, Clement 2, 10, 19–20, 29, 33, 76, 90, 94, 95, 295
Audit Commission 225, 227, 257, 260, 294
Avon 205, 213, 215, 216

Bacon, Alice 178
Bains, Laurence 222
Baker Act *see* Education Reform Act 1988
Baker, Kenneth 224, 242–4, 283–6
Banham Commission 215
Banham, Sir John 215, 216
Barber, Anthony 203
Barlow Commission on the Distribution of the Industrial Population 20, 34–5, 38
Bevan, Aneurin 5, 33, 55–9, 64, 66, 87–8, 90–101
Birch, Nigel 133
Birmingham 18, 37, 162
Black Country 108, 109
'Black Paper' 188, 189, 283, 285
Blackpool 140
blitz 4, 16–20, 34–5, 58
block grant system 248–52

Index 321

Board of Education 30, 40–2, 45, 46, 70, 71
Boards of Guardians 51
Bootle 94
boundary changes 13–14, 88–101, 105–9, 196, 205–6
Bournemouth 140
Boyd-Carpenter, John 135, 144
Boyle, Sir Edward 81, 83, 180–1
Boyson, Sir Rhodes 183, 188, 245
Bristol 209
British Psychological Society 168
Brittan, Leon 241
Brooke, Henry 67–8, 105, 108, 110, 124–6, 133–5, 139, 140, 141, 237, 255
Brown, Ernest 30–2
Burt, Sir Cyril 168
Burton-on-Trent 107
Butler Act *see* Education Act 1944
Butler, R. A. 30–1, 40, 41, 44, 45, 60, 61, 70, 72, 78, 97, 125, 137, 179–80
'Butskellism' 6

Callaghan, James 149, 151, 152, 281
   Ruskin College speech 189
Cambridgeshire 108, 286
Cardiff 198
caretaker government 53, 88
Central Housing Advisory Committee 36
Central Land Board 95
Central Valuation Committee 119
centralism 130–1
Centre for Policy Studies 223

Chamberlain, Neville 14, 102
Channon, Paul 256
Chester, D. N. 205, 221
Chichester-Clark, Robin 256
Children Act 1948 52
Christian Socialism 169
Chrystal, Sir George 23
Churchill coalition *see* coalition government
Churchill, Winston 9, 10, 32, 34, 36, 41, 44, 61, 70, 101
Circular 10/65 (DES) 173–7, 179, 180, 184, 186, 281, 305
Circular 50/65 (MHLG) 256
Circular 10/66 (DES) 176, 184
Circular 12/68 (DES) 178
Circular 10/70 (DES) 184–5
Circular 54/70 (DoE) 164
Circular 56/72 (DoE) 191
Circular 4/74 (DES) 186
Circular 70/74 (DoE) 165–6
Circular 2/94 (DfE) 287
City Action Teams 227
city technology colleges 289
civil defence 21–2
Clarke, Kenneth 285, 286
Clay Cross District Council 161–2
Cleveland 205, 213, 215, 216
coalition government 3, 4, 5, 9, 53, 87, 88, 218, 300
Cole, G. D. H. 28, 96–7
Committee on Prefabricated Houses 36
Committee on Reconstruction Problems 9–11, 28, 30
community charge *see* poll tax

322 *Index*

comprehensive education 76–83, 168–88, 305
Comprehensive Schools Committee 177–8
Compulsory Competitive Tendering (CCT) 7, 234, 255–61, 273–4
Confederation of British Industry 212, 245
consensus, post-war 2, 9, 300–302
Conservative and Unionist Teachers' Association 77
Costain, A. B. 256
council houses, sale of 6, 8, 37, 65, 157–8, 164–7, 268, 269
council tax 7, 235, 246–8, 254, 279
'Council for Greater London' *see* Greater London Council
councillors, personal qualities of 218–20, 226
county boroughs 13–16, 25, 89, 92, 101, 103, 207–8
County Boroughs Association 90
County Councils Association (CCA) 25, 27, 31, 96
Coventry 17–18, 35, 52, 76
Cripps, Sir Stafford 57, 59
Crosland, Anthony 149, 156, 162, 167, 169, 173, 176, 177, 182, 208, 238
Crossman, Richard 101, 150–53, 196–8, 236, 256
Crowther report 171
curriculum reform *see* national curriculum
Curry, David 216

Cutler, Sir Horace 157, 211

Dalton, Hugh 59, 100, 101
Dartford 217
Dearing, Sir Ron 285
decision-making in local authorities 218, 220–22, 226, 227
Dent, H. C. 43
Derbyshire 216
devolution 202, 208, 209
Direct Labour Organisation (DLO) 257, 258
Direct Service Organisation (DSO) 258
Douglas, Sir William 95
Douglas-Home, Sir Alec 112, 144, 148, 233
Durham 216

Eccles, Sir David 80–83, 132, 134
Ede, J. Chuter 33, 44, 70, 99
Eden, Anthony 268
Education Act 1944 5, 41, 45, 46, 52, 70–73, 76, 80, 125, 176, 178–9, 186, 190, 280, 284, 293, 301, 304
Education Act 1976 187
Education Act 1979 282
Education Act 1980 282, 283, 292, 293
Education Act 1986 293
Education (No. 2) Act 1986 282, 292
Education Act 1993 290, 294, 295
education provision politics of 74–5

structure of 72–4
Education Reform Act 1988 (ERA) 284–9, 292–5
Education (Schools) Act 1982 283
Education (Schools) Act 1992 290, 292
Elliot, Walter 97
Ely, Isle of 108
Employment Appeals Tribunal 259
ERA *see* Education Reform Act 1988
European Commission 258
Eve *see* Trustram Eve
Exchequer Equalisation Grant (EEG) 122, 126, 128
expenditure 52, 117–45
  on education 133–5
  local 131–6
Expiring Laws Continuance Acts 1950 and 1951 122

finance 233–55
  borrowing, control of 122–4
Finsberg, Geoffrey 211, 212
Forsyth, Michael 243
Foster, Christopher 242
Funding Agency for Schools 290–1

garden cities 38
Gas Board 137
General Exchequer Contribution 121
General Improvement Area (GIA) 154
General Needs Index (GNI) 277

Glasgow 18
Gloucester 274
Gloucestershire 216
Goodson-Wickes, Charles 223–4
Gow, Ian 212
Grafton, M. J. 256
Grammar Schools Association 43
Grant Maintained Status (GMS) 289–93
Grant-Related Expenditure (GRE) 248–51, 254
grant system 120–22
grants in aid 4, 6
Gravesham 217
'Great Debate' 189
Greater London Council (GLC) 112, 149, 157, 159, 163, 164, 195, 205
  abolition of 210–13
Greater London Plan 39
Greater Manchester *see* Manchester, Greater
'Green Book' 42, 43, 45
Greenwood, Anthony 164
Greenwood, Arthur 10, 18, 22–5, 28, 34
Griffin, Frank 157
Gummer, John 216, 254

Hadow committee 41, 45
Hailsham, Viscount 127
Hancock Commission *see* Local Government Commission
Hancock, Sir Henry 105
Harrow 72–3

324 *Index*

Heath, Edward   149, 150, 155, 157, 165, 179, 180–2, 202, 211, 245, 256
Her Majesty's Inspectorate (HMI)   282–3, 285
Herbert Commission   219–20
Herbert, Sir Edwin   111, 112
Heseltine, Michael   212, 214–16, 226, 240, 241, 246, 247–9, 254, 268
Holmes, Sir Maurice   30, 42–3
home ownership   *see* owner-occupation
homelessness   275, 278
Hornby, Richard   182
Horsbrugh, Florence   78–80
house building programme   269, 278
  1960s   150–55
  post-war   34–40, 52–70, 303–4
housing
  associations   158, 266–7, 270, 273–4
  expenditure on   133–5
  standards   55
  subsidies   155–7, 278–80
Housing Act 1952   61, 65
Housing Act 1957   165
Housing Act 1969   154
Housing Act 1974   165
Housing Act 1980   271
Housing Act 1988   270–3, 275, 278, 279
Housing Action Trusts (HATs)   275–6
Housing and Homeless Persons Act 1977   267

Housing and Planning Act 1986   268
Housing and Town Planning Act 1919   51
Housing Commissioners   161–2
Housing Corporation   271, 273
Housing Finance Act 1972   156, 160–1, 166, 167
Housing Finance (Special Provisions) Act 1975   163
Housing (Financial Provisions) Act 1946   56
Housing Rents and Subsidies Act 1975   157, 166, 167
Housing Revenue Account (HRA)   67, 155, 159, 278–80
Housing Subsidies Act 1956   66
Housing Subsidies Act 1967   153
Housing (Temporary Accommodation) Act 1944   36
Howard, Michael   244, 254
Hull   *see* Kingston upon Hull
Humberside   205, 213–16
Huntingdonshire   108
Hurd, Douglas   246
'hybridity'   217

Ilford   97, 103
Inland Revenue, Board of   136, 137
Inland Revenue Department   120
Inner City Task Forces   227
Inner London Education Authority (ILEA)   112, 252
Institute of Directors   212
Institute of Fiscal Studies   247

Institute of Housing 278
Institute of Municipal Treasurers and Accountants 237
internal market in services 260
Investment Programmes Committee 58
Isle of Wight 215

Jenkin, Patrick 224, 242
Jennings, Sir Ivor 90
Joseph, Sir Keith 68, 69, 108–9, 135, 142–4, 149, 157, 158, 161, 223, 235, 265, 282, 283, 292
Jowitt enquiry 22–9, 93
Jowitt, Sir William 22–33, 91, 94

Kilbrandon report (on the constitution) 204
King, Tom 212, 240–42, 245
Kingston upon Hull 94
Kingston upon Thames 186–7
Korean War 59

Lancashire 32, 108
Lawson, Nigel 243
Layfield committee 248
Layfield, Sir Frank 238
Leicestershire 107, 108
Lewis, J. Parry 158
Liverpool 94, 137, 276
Livingstone, Ken 212
Lloyd, Geoffrey 81
Lloyd, Selwyn 133–4, 135
Local Authorities (Education) Act 1931 72

Local Authorities Loans Act 1945 122–3
Local Government Act 1888 12–14
Local Government Act 1929 15, 120, 121
Local Government Act 1948 120, 122, 128, 136
Local Government Act 1958 105–7, 111, 126, 194, 198
Local Government Act 1966 236
Local Government Act 1972 194, 204–7, 213–14, 217, 222, 233
Local Government Act 1974 248
Local Government Act 1985 213
Local Government Act 1988 258
Local Government Act 1992 260
Local Government and Housing Act 1989 225, 276
Local Government and Miscellaneous Financial Provisions (Scotland) Act 1958 126
Local Government Board 13, 14, 32
Local Government Boundary Commission, 1945–9 5, 87, 88–9, 90–96, 107, 110, 197
Local Government Boundary Commission, 1972–92 206, 214, 302
Local Government (Boundary Commission) Act 1945 88
Local Government Commission 88, 105, 107–8, 110, 111, 194–7, 302

Local Government Commission (Dissolution) Act 1949 96
Local Government Commission for Wales 198
Local Government (County Boroughs and Adjustments) Act 1926 14
Local Government Finance Act 1982 250
Local Government Management Board 227
Local Government, Planning and Land Act 1980 248, 257, 276
local government reform 88–101
Local Government (Scotland) Act 1973 199
Local Management of Schools (LMS) 286–7, 291, 292
London 13, 14, 16–18, 39, 52, 69, 103, 108, 110, 111, 172, 173, 176, 178, 277
London Boroughs' Association 212
London County Council 12, 17, 76, 110, 111, 125
London Municipal Society 110
Luton 97, 102, 103, 107, 109
Lythgoe, Sir James 129

MacGregor, John 285, 286
Machinery of Government Committee 33
Macleod, Ian 102
Macmillan, Harold 5, 54, 60–65, 81, 88, 102, 103, 132, 139, 142, 144, 306

Major, John 2, 7, 190, 195, 216, 246, 254, 255, 259, 266, 295
Mallaby, Sir George 221
Manchester, Greater 109, 187, 199, 205
Manningham-Buller, Reginald 137–8
Manpower Committee, 1950 129
market accountability 255–62, 265, 282, 294
Marshall, Sir Frank 211
Mason, Douglas 243
Maud Committee 221–2
Maud, Sir John 79, 194, 197, 204, 207, 221
Maude, Sir John 25, 30, 90, 94
Maudling, Reginald 135, 136, 144
Mellish, Bob 153
Merseyside 108, 109, 199, 205
Middlesex 111
Middlesex County Council 76, 77
Morrison, Herbert 17, 93
Mulley, Fred 187, 189
Municipal Corporations Act 1835 226

National Advisory Committee on Local Government (Conservative party) 98
National Association of Head Teachers 185
National Association of Labour Teachers 74
National Association of Local Government Officers (NALGO) 31, 162

National Association of
 Schoolmasters 43
National Audit Office 291
national curriculum 284–6, 293
National Curriculum Council
 (NCC) 285
National Federation of Building
 Trades Employers 256
National Foundation for Economic
 Research (NFER) 168
National Health Service 59, 257
National Non-Domestic Rate
 (NNDR) 252
National Union of Teachers 43,
 127, 178
New Town Development
 Corporations 227
New Towns Act 1946 39
Newbury 274
Newport 198
Newsom Committee 171
Northampton 217
Northamptonshire 107
Norwich 217
Norwood Committee 45, 74, 76
Norwood, Cyril 45
Nottingham 107

Ofsted 291
Onslow Commission 107
Onslow, Lord 14
'Operation round-up' 103
'organic change' 208–10, 217
Orpington by-election 142
owner-occupation 54, 61, 62,
 64–6, 152, 158–9, 165,
 267–70, 304

parental choice 288–92
partnership 117–18, 127–31
 in education 292–5
Patten, Chris 202, 252
Patten, John 286, 294
Peterborough 72, 108
Plowden Committee (on schools)
 133, 135
Plowden report (on public
 expenditure) 282
Plymouth 17–19, 35, 52, 94
Police Act 1946 52
political management of local
 authorities 195
poll tax 7, 141, 234, 238, 240–8,
 253, 279, 303
Poole 103
Portsmouth 201
post-war consensus see consensus,
 post-war
post-war reconstruction see
 reconstruction, post-war
Powell, Enoch 110, 133, 183, 185
prefab 36
Prentice, Reg 174, 186, 187
Public Schools Commission 182,
 183
Public Works Loan Board 56, 63,
 123, 124

'quangos' 228

Rachman, Peter 69
Rachmanism 69, 150
Radcliffe report (on the monetary
 system) 123
Ramsbotham, Hereward 42

Rate Deficiency Grant (RDG) 126
Rate Support Grant (RSG) 236, 248, 253, 278
rate-capping 242
Rates Act 1984 242
rating system 4, 6, 118–20, 125, 126, 128, 131–2, 136–45, 235–55, 303
Rating Act 1966 236
Rating and Valuation Act 1925 119
Rating and Valuation Bill 1955 137
Rating (Interim Relief) Bill 1963 144
Reading, Lord 110
reconstruction, post-war 3, 9–11, 20–34, 37–8, 302
Redcliffe-Maud Commission *see* Royal Commission on Local Government in England
Redcliffe-Maud, Lord *see* Maud, Sir John
regional commissioners 4, 21–4
Regional Commissioners Act 1939 21
Reith, Sir John 11
Rent Act 1957 69, 154
Rent Assessment Panel 160
Rent Scrutiny Board 160, 166
rented property, private-sector 150, 153–4, 159–61, 165, 270, 272, 275
Rents Act 1968 159, 160
Rents and Mortgage (Restrictions) Act 1939 35

Revenue Support Grant 252–3
Ridley, Nicholas 214, 244, 252, 255, 267, 269, 270
'Right to Buy' 267, 269
Rippon, Geoffrey 162, 202
Rochford 274
Ronan Point disaster 154
Rossi, Hugh 157
Royal Commission on Local Government in England, 1966–9 194, 197–205, 222, 236, 237, 302
Royal Commission on Local Government in Greater London 111, 219
Royal Commission on Mental Health 132
Royal Institute of Public Administration 237
Rutland 107–9

Salisbury 274
Sandys, Duncan 60, 66, 88, 103–5, 110, 137
school building programme 79–81, 171
school leaving age 40–42, 44
school systems 76–8
School Boards 51
School Curriculum and Assessment Authority (SCAA) 285
School Curriculum Development Committee 283
schools
  church 40–41
  dual system 41

Index

grammar 43, 76–8, 80, 170–1, 174, 175, 178, 180–7, 304
grant maintained 289
public 43
secondary modern 81, 169–70, 178, 304
self-governing 294–5
testing in 284–6
tripartite system 43, 45, 70, 80, 168, 169, 171, 304
Schools Council 189, 283
Scotland 3, 198
Scott Committee on the Utilization of Land in Rural Areas 38
Secondary Examinations Assessment Council (SEAC) 285
Secondary Examinations Council 283, 285
Secondary Schools Examinations Council 45
Senior, Derek 200
Sevenoaks 274
Sexton, Stuart 187, 282
Sharp, Dame Evelyn 99, 100, 101, 197, 198, 219, 220
Sheffield 137
Shore, Peter 166, 194, 208–10, 238
Silkin, Lewis 99
Simon, Sir Ernest 22
slum clearance 51, 53, 63, 64, 66–70
'Social Contract' 166–7
Solihull 107, 109, 286
Somerset 216

South Yorkshire 205
Southampton 17, 19, 94, 201
Special Review Area (SRA) 106, 108
Speed, Keith 238
Spens committee 45
Spens, Sir Will 41, 90
St John Stevas, Norman 187
Standard Spending Assessment (SSA) 253, 254
Stewart, Michael 169, 173, 174
Straw, Jack 208
Swansea 198

Taylor report (on the management of schools) 190
Temple, J. M. 141
Tenants' Charter 271
tenants' choice 270–3
Thatcher, Margaret 7, 149, 157, 178, 183, 184, 186, 190, 195, 211–14, 223–4, 233–4, 239, 240–46, 257, 259, 265, 266, 270, 281, 285, 294, 301
Thorneycroft, Peter 133, 139
Tiverton 72
Tomlinson, George 75, 77, 78, 99
Torbay 107, 274
Town and Country Planning Act 1943 39
Town and Country Planning Act 1944 39
Town and Country Planning Act 1947 39, 52
Town and Country Planning Association 154

330   *Index*

Training and Enterprise Councils (TECs) 227
Transfer of Undertakings (Protection of Employment) Regulations (TUPE) 258
Trustram Eve Commission *see* Local Government Boundary Commission, 1945–9
Trustram Eve, Sir Malcolm 90, 92, 94, 95, 97–8, 101
Tyneside 108, 205

unitary grant 248
unitary principle 98, 195, 199, 200, 201, 203, 205, 209, 213–17, 302
urban renewal 275–6
Urban Development Corporation (UDC) 227, 275
Urban District Councils Association (UDCA) 26
Uthwatt Committee on Compensation and Betterment 37, 38

Value Added Tax 246
von Hayek, Friedrich 265

Waldegrave, William 242, 243
Wales 3
Walker, Peter 155, 165, 166, 182, 202–5, 220
Waltham Forest 276
Wandsworth 254
War Damage Commission 90, 95

War Works Commission 90
war-time coalition *see* coalition government
Welfare State 2, 4, 51, 89, 117, 302
West Midlands 108, 109, 199, 205
West Riding of Yorkshire 76
West Yorkshire 32, 108, 201, 205
Westminster 254
Wheatley Royal Commission on Scottish local government 198
Wheatley, Sir Andrew 221
Wheeler, John 212
Whitelaw, William 241, 244
Widdicombe Committee 224–7
Widdicombe, David 224
Wilkinson, Ellen 74, 75
Williams, Shirley 189, 190
Willink, Henry 32–3, 89, 90
Wilson, C. H. 28
Wilson, Harold 5, 69, 83, 149, 151, 169, 170, 171, 233
Wood, R. S. 42, 45
Wood, Sir Kingsley 29, 44
Woolton, Lord 62
Worcester 107
Workers' Educational Association 23

'Yellow Book' 189
Yorkshire *see* South Yorkshire, West Riding of Yorkshire, West Yorkshire